PROPERTY AND THE HUMAN RIGHTS ACT 1998

By giving further effect to the European Convention on Human Rights, the Human Rights Act 1998 has had a significant effect on property law. Article 1 of the First Protocol to the Convention is particularly important, as it protects against the interference with the enjoyment of possessions. Compulsory acquisition, insolvency, planning, taxation, environmental regulation, and landlord and tenant laws are just some of the fields where the British and European courts have already had to assess the impact of the Protocol on private property. The Human Rights Act 1998 also restricts the scope of property rights, as some Convention rights conflict with rights of private property. For example, the Article 8 right to respect for the home has been used to protect against environmental harm, in some cases at the expense of property and economic rights.

This book seeks to provide a structured approach to the extensive case law of the European Court of Human Rights and the UK courts on these issues, and to provide guidance on the direction the law is likely to take in future. Chapters cover the history and drafting of the relevant Convention rights, the scope and structure of the rights (especially Article 1 of the First Protocol), and how, through the Human Rights Act 1998, the Convention rights have already affected and are likely to affect developments in selected areas of English law.

Volume 7 in the series Human Rights Law in Perspective

Human Rights Law in Perspective

General Editor: Colin Harvey

The language of human rights figures prominently in legal and political debates at the national, regional and international levels. In the UK the Human Rights Act 1998 has generated considerable interest in the law of human rights. It will continue to provoke much debate in the legal community and the search for original insights and new materials will intensify.

The aim of this series is to provide a forum for scholarly reflection on all aspects of the law of human rights. The series will encourage work which engages with the theoretical, comparative and international dimensions of human rights law. The primary aim is to publish over time books which offer an insight into human rights law in its contextual setting. The objective is to promote an understanding of the nature and impact of human rights law. The series is inclusive, in the sense that all perspectives in legal scholarship are welcome. It will incorporate the work of new and established scholars.

Human Rights Law in Perspective is not confined to consideration of the UK. It will strive to reflect comparative, regional and international perspectives. Work which focuses on human rights law in other states will therefore be included in this series. The intention is to offer an inclusive intellectual home for significant scholarly contributions to human rights law.

Property and
The Human Rights Act 1998

TOM ALLEN
Professor of Law
University of Durham

·HART·
PUBLISHING
OXFORD – PORTLAND OREGON
2005

Hart Publishing
Oxford and Portland, Oregon

Published in North America (US and Canada) by
Hart Publishing c/o
International Specialized Book Services
5804 NE Hassalo Street
Portland, Oregon
97213-3644
USA

Hart Publishing is a specialist legal publisher based in Oxford, England.
To order further copies of this book or to request a list of other
publications please write to:

Hart Publishing, Salter's Boatyard, Folly Bridge,
Abingdon Road, Oxford OX1 4LB
Telephone: +44 (0)1865 245533 or Fax: +44 (0)1865 794882
e-mail: mail@hartpub.co.uk
WEBSITE: http//www.hartpub.co.uk

British Library Cataloguing in Publication Data
Data Available
ISBN 1–84113–203–9 (hardback)

Typeset by Hope Services (Abingdon) Ltd
Printed and bound in Great Britain by
MPG Books, Bodmin, Cornwall

To Helen, Isaac and Kate

Series Editor's Preface

The concept of a right to property has generated much debate in the law and politics of human rights. This study offers a comprehensive analysis of this right as defined in Article 1 of the First Protocol to the European Convention on Human Rights (other Convention rights are also examined). The book explores the jurisprudence of the European Court of Human Rights and developments in the UK following the enactment of the Human Rights Act 1998. It is a significant contribution to the existing literature and will be an invaluable source of reference for those working in this area.

Colin Harvey
Belfast
August 2005

Acknowledgements

I would like to thank Janet Ulph, André van der Walt and Colin Warbrick for reading draft chapters, and Edward Hetherington for his help in researching material. All remaining errors are mine, of course.

Contents

Table of Cases

Introduction

*Every natural or legal person is entitled to the peaceful enjoyment of his possessions.
No one shall be deprived of his possessions except in the public interest and subject to
the conditions provided for by law and by the general principles of international law.
The preceding provisions shall not, however, in any way impair the right of a State to
enforce such laws as it deems necessary to control the use of property in accordance with
the general interest or to secure the payment of taxes or other contributions or penalties.*
Article 1 of the First Protocol to the European Convention on Human Rights

WHETHER THE RIGHT to property should be a human right is a
controversial question. It seems less worthy of protection than, for
example, the right to life, the right not to be enslaved, or even the
right to respect for the home and private life. It is not a right that governments
are generally content to acknowledge, except when they feel that it can be
confined to relatively narrow circumstances. Indeed, while the member States of
the Council of Europe agreed that the European Convention on Human Rights
should have a right to property, it proved remarkably difficult to reach agreement
on its precise content. Delays were partly caused by the desire of some governments
to leave the right to property as hollow as could be managed. In the
United Kingdom, in particular, the idea that an international tribunal might
have sweeping powers of review over social and economic legislation was
anathema to Government ministers and advisers. To some extent, they were
successful in restricting its power. The text of the right to property, as contained
in Article 1 of the First Protocol ('P1(1)'), seems to leave the sovereign power
over property quite unrestricted. However, despite the best efforts of the British
government (and others), subsequent events have shown that the right to property
has a wide reach. In the last ten years, for example, the European Court of
Human Rights has decided several thousand cases on the right to property, with
violations being found in many of them.

Many of these cases have concerned the kind of issues that one might expect
any right to property to address. For example, valuation of land that has been
expropriated is a recurring issue, as are delays in the actual payment of compensation.
The regulation of land use comes up frequently, although in practice
the courts are reluctant to find that human rights are violated in such cases. On
a more dramatic scale, the unlawful destruction of property by Turkish security
forces has come before the Court in a number of cases.[1] There are, however,

---

[1] See eg *Akdivar and Others v Turkey*, Reports 1996-IV 1192 (1997) 23 EHRR 143.

many cases where violations have been found in circumstances that most lawyers in 1950 would not have expected to raise even a serious case. To give just a few examples, in recent years the European Court of Human Rights has found violations in respect of:

— the refusal to recognise a void 'contract'[2]
— the failure to protect a minority shareholder from oppression by the majority[3]
— the refusal to renew a lease of a tenant who had no contractual or statutory right to renewal[4]
— the Greek Government's refusal to return royal estates to the former King of Greece[5]
— the failure to prevent or warn of the risk of a landslide that destroyed an illegally-occupied dwelling[6]
— the execution of court orders issued in a private dispute between joint owners of land[7]
— the refusal to increase the amount of compensation paid for land, to reflect an increase in the value of land *after* it was expropriated (with full compensation)[8]
— the failure to honour a promise made in 1944 to provide land to those displaced from the old Soviet Union to Poland immediately after World War II.[9]

Since 2 October 2000, when the main provisions of the Human Rights Act 1998 came into force, the courts in the United Kingdom have been equally willing to give the right to property a wide scope. The first declaration of incompatibility to be issued under the 1998 Act concerned the right to property,[10] and for a period in 2002–03, one might have thought that the right to property would result in wholesale changes to English law. In separate cases, the Court of Appeal found incompatibilities in respect of the Water Industry Act 1991,[11] the Consumer Credit Act 1974,[12] the Immigration and Asylum Act 1999,[13] guidelines issued under the Customs and Excise Management Act 1979[14] and the

---

[2]   *Beyeler v Italy*, Reports 2000-I (2001) 33 EHRR 52.
[3]   *Sovtransavto Holding v Ukraine*, Reports 2002-VII 133 (2004) 38 EHRR 44.
[4]   *Stretch v United Kingdom*, (2004) 38 EHRR 12.
[5]   *Former King of Greece v Greece*, Reports 2000-XII 119 (2001) 33 EHRR 21 (merits) (2003) 36 EHRR CD43 (just satisfaction).
[6]   *Öneryıldız v Turkey*, Appl No 48939/99, 18 June 2002.
[7]   *Allard v Sweden*, (2004) 39 EHRR 14.
[8]   *Motais de Narbonne v France*, Appl No 48161/99, 2 July 2002.
[9]   *Broniowski v Poland*, Appl No 31443/96, 22 June 2004.
[10]   *Wilson v First County Trust Ltd (No 2)*, [2002] QB 74 (reversed by [2004] 1 AC 816 (sub nom *Wilson and others v Secretary of State for Trade and Industry*)).
[11]   *Marcic v Thames Water Utilities Ltd*, [2002] QB 929.
[12]   *Wilson* (n 10).
[13]   *International Transport Roth GmbH v Secretary of State for the Home Department*, [2003] QB 728.
[14]   *Lindsay v Customs and Excise Comrs*, [2002] 1 WLR 1766.

common law obligations regarding rectorial land.[15] Most of these cases were subsequently overturned by the House of Lords,[16] but plainly the right to property has not had a purely marginal influence on legal disputes. Moreover, the judicial conservativism of the House of Lords has not stopped litigants from raising the right to property in just about every conceivable instance; and in the light of the European jurisprudence, there are indeed many such instances. In any case, judgments on other Convention rights confirm that the law of property will not remain immune from human rights challenges. In *Ghaidan v Godin-Mendoza*,[17] for example, the House of Lords held that provisions of the Rent Act 1977 were incompatible with the right to respect for the home (Article 8), because members of a same-sex couple were treated differently than other couples in relation to the right to succeed to a statutory tenancy. The Rent Act 1977 had to be re-interpreted, with the result that the property rights of the landlord (a private person) were restricted.

This book attempts to impose some order on the ever-increasing body of case law. Chapter 1 gives the historical background to Article 1 of the First Protocol ('P1(1)'). This is particularly valuable because it demonstrates just how narrow the right to property was expected to be, but also just how poorly drafted the final text is. There are gaps in the final version that appear solely because no agreement could be reached on fundamental points and it seemed unlikely that agreement would ever be reached on these points. But there are also gaps that arose due to a failure to appreciate that a right to property would produce as many issues as it has. For example, the final text appears to distinguish between 'possessions' and 'property', between the 'public interest' and the 'general interest', and between the enforcement of taxes (and other liabilities) and their imposition. Moreover, these terms are not used in a manner that is consistent across the two official versions (French and English).

Chapters 2–5 set out the general principles that govern the right to property. In all cases, the court must first decide if there has been an interference with the protected interest. If so, the Convention right is applicable or, as it is sometimes put, the State's responsibility has been engaged. In relation to P1(1), the court must decide whether the claimant has suffered an interference with the 'peaceful enjoyment of his possessions'. This issue is covered in chapter 2.

If P1(1) is applicable to the facts, the Court must then consider whether the State can justify the interference. In this respect, P1(1) is similar to a number of other Convention rights, as the right is not absolute. It differs from, for example, the right not to be enslaved: the State cannot justify slavery under any

---

[15] *Aston Cantlow and Wilmcote with Billesley Parochial Church Council v Wallbank* [2002] Ch 51 reversed by [2004] 1 AC 546

[16] See: *Wilson and others v Secretary of State for Trade and Industry*, [2004] 1 AC 816, reversing *Wilson* (n 10)); *Marcic v Thames Water Utilities Ltd* [2004] 2 AC 42, reversing *Marcic* (n 11); and *Aston Cantlow and Wilmcote with Billesley Parochial Church Council v Wallbank*, [2004] 1 AC 546 reversing *Aston Cantlow, ibid.*

[17] [2004] 3 WLR 113.

circumstances.[18] It also differs from rights to property in the constitutional law of many States. For example, the Fifth Amendment to the Constitution of the US states that private property may not be taken for public use without compensation. Hence, if property *is* taken for public use, it can be justified only if compensation is paid. In effect, finding that the takings clause is applicable to the facts necessarily leads to the conclusion that compensation must be paid; the State cannot argue that no compensation is required because the specific circumstances are exceptional in some way. However, this is not the case under P1(1). Finding that the right to property is applicable merely puts the State to the burden of justification.

Chapters 3–5 therefore consider the burden in more detail. Chapter 3 deals with the legality condition, by which States must show that the interference was legal. In the vast majority of cases, this condition is satisfied fairly easily. Chapter 4 considers the structure of P1(1): the first sentence contains the right to property, and the second and third sentences describe specific types of interference. This is important because the European Court of Human Rights suggests that the burden of justification depends on the type of interference. In practice, however, it is not clear that justification does depend on the type of interference. As the chapter shows, the courts in the United Kingdom often ignore the structural aspects of P1(1).

Chapter 5 then considers one element of the justification in much more detail, as it examines the 'fair balance' test. This is, in essence, the property version of the proportionality test that applies to other Convention rights; indeed, in some cases, the courts seem to regard proportionality and the fair balance as equivalent concepts. However, as Chapter 5 explains, the standard of the fair balance is not as strict as the proportionality test, and in principle it should be easier for the State to justify an interference with P1(1) than it would be with other Convention rights.

Chapters 6–9 then examine several specific areas in more detail. Chapter 6 focuses on expropriation, with particular attention to the valuation of property. Unlike most constitutional rights to property, P1(1) does not contain an explicit guarantee of compensation on expropriation. However, the Commission and the Court in Strasbourg have read principles into P1(1) by which compensation is normally required in the case of the typical expropriation. This, of course, leaves it open to argue that the circumstances are exceptional, and this possibility is examined closely in this chapter.

Controls on the use of land are examined in the next chapter. It covers the idea of 'regulatory takings', as American lawyers would put it, as well as issues relating to the effectiveness of private law remedies for controlling the acts of third parties that affect the use of land. It also considers the use of the Convention as a means for establishing a right of access to land.

---

[18] Art 4(1) provides that "No one shall be held in slavery or servitude."

Chapter 8 then turns to the potential impact of the Convention on the private law of property. The horizontal effect of the Convention has already received a great deal of attention from commentators in this country, although not specifically in relation to property rights. There are, nonetheless, signs that human rights may have a significant effect on private law and property. *Ghaidan v Godin-Mendoza* is mentioned above; at the very least, it suggests that the British courts will consider using section 3 of the Human Rights Act 1998 to re-interpret statutory rules that modify private law relationships concerning property.

Chapter 9 moves the discussion from private law to public law, as it examines the confiscation and forfeiture of property following a criminal conviction and the imposition of civil liability as a response to wrongdoing. Modern law enforcement placing great emphasis on seizing property as a cost-effective response to wrongdoing (particularly when it can be done outside the criminal trial process). The most recent measures, in the Proceeds of Crime Act 2002, were enacted despite strong criticism from the Joint Committee on Human Rights, and already the Customs and Excise Commissioners have had to mod-ify forfeiture guidelines as a result of cases finding that their practices were incompatible with P1(1). The chapter therefore examines the human rights framework in which confiscation and forfeiture operate.

The final chapter considers the purpose of the right to property, as revealed by the case law of the European Court of Human Rights and the British courts. It argues that the primary purpose has been, and remains, a fundamentally conservative one. In most cases, P1(1) operates an instrument for ensuring the stability of entitlements, where the foundation for those entitlements is not questioned. There are some cases where the focus shifts to other values, such as the protection of autonomy and dignity, or fairness and equality, or even values relating to good governance. However, the focus in most cases remains remark-ably limited.

Since the book is concerned with property, the primary focus is on the right to property contained in the First Protocol. However, other Convention articles also raise issues relevant to property. Hence, there is some discussion of the procedural rights under Article 6,[19] the rights under Article 8 to respect for the home, the family, private life and correspondence,[20] and the Article 14 right to freedom from discrimination.[21] In addition, since any imposition of a financial

---

[19] Article 6 provides that "In the determination of his civil rights and obligations or of any criminal charge against him, everyone is entitled to a fair and public hearing within a reasonable time by an independent and impartial tribunal established by law." Property rights are a type of civil right, and hence procedural issues may arise under both Article 6 and P1(1).

[20] Article 8 protects the right of everyone "to respect for his private and family life, his home and his correspondence." The protection of the Article 8 interest in the home often overlaps with the protection of the proprietary interest protected under P1(1), but the 'home' under Article 8 need not be held as the property of the individual.

[21] Article 14 provides that "The enjoyment of the rights and freedoms set forth in this Convention shall be secured without discrimination on any ground such as sex, race, colour, language, religion, political or other opinion, national or social origin, association with a national minority, property, birth or other status."

liability is treated as an interference with property under P1(1), the use of any Convention right to create or extend an existing cause of action also raises issues under P1(1). Accordingly, there is some discussion of these other Convention rights, but there is no attempt to cover the history of their drafting or their doctrinal structure and development in any detail.

In addition, the focus is on the substantive elements of the P1(1). While procedural issues are covered, it is the substantive law that receives more attention. While the Court has said that that P1(1) includes procedural safeguards, the primary question for this book is whether the right to property requires or supports changes in the domestic law of property, both public and private. Consequently, the emphasis is on the substantive aspects of P1(1). In addition, the case law of the European Court of Human Rights receives more attention than that of the courts of the United Kingdom, for two reasons. The first is simply that there is more of it, and it covers many different fields: while the courts in the United Kingdom have dealt with P1(1) on many occasions since the Human Rights Act 1998 came into force, there are many areas where there has yet to be any consideration of the impact of the right to property. The second follows from section 2 of the 1998 Act, which requires the courts to take the Strasbourg jurisprudence into account "in determining a question which has arisen in connection with a Convention right". While the jurisprudence is not binding, and there may be some room for the British courts to adopt their own position on some points, it is clear that the Strasbourg cases determine the general content of the right to property. Hence, it is appropriate to determine what that content is.

1

The History of Article 1 of the First Protocol

⟫⟶◆⟵⟪

T HE IDEA THAT the sovereign power over property is a limited power has a long history in Western legal thought. The extent to which these limits could be enforced by individuals has varied from one country to the next and from one historical period to another, but it is clear that most lawyers recognised the twin ideas that the sovereign has the power to take or regulate private property and that the individual should have some protection from the excessive use of this power. It is against this background that the right to property that is the subject of this book has developed.

While constitutional and international versions of the right to property developed in different directions, the implementation of the European Convention on Human Rights in the member States of the Council of Europe has brought them together. In the United Kingdom itself, the possibility that Parliament would enact a constitutional bill of rights distinct from the European Convention was considered but ultimately rejected by the Government. Instead, we are left with the partial implementation of the European Convention through the machinery of the Human Rights 1998. The 1998 Act was enacted 'to give further effect to rights and freedoms guaranteed under the European Convention on Human Rights.'[1] A number of Convention rights can be employed to protect property interests, but it is Article 1 of the First Protocol that contains the right to property and hence is most important for this book.

It was originally hoped that the wording of P1(1) would discourage any expectation that it might provide fertile ground for judicial review; however, the database of the European Court of Human Rights indicates that this is exactly what happened, as it has been raised in thousands of judgments and decisions of the Court and Commission.[2] In the United Kingdom, it has already been the focus of a number of important appellate judgments. Moreover, this underestimates the extent to which human rights law is used in cases involving property, as Articles 6, 8 and 14 also have an important role to play in protecting property interests.

---

[1] Preamble, HRA 1998.
[2] <http://cmiskp.echr.coe.int/tkp197/search.asp?skin=hudoc–en>, also available through the Court's web site at <http://www.echr.coe.int/>.

Nevertheless, while these other Convention rights raise issues that are discussed in this book, it is P1(1) that provides the basis for most of the discussion.

This chapter therefore seeks to identify how the present wording of P1(1) was determined. Even a cursory glance reveals that it was not drafted with care: why, for example, do the first two sentences refer to 'possessions' and the third to 'property'? The French version does not clarify matters: it uses the terms '*biens*' for the first and third sentences and '*propriété*' in the second. The first objective is therefore to trace through the drafting process in the hope of shedding light on how some of the most obvious gaps and inconsistencies in P1(1) came into being.

The second objective relates to effect of the implementation of P1(1) (and related rights) in United Kingdom law. The institution of private property would have continued to exist if neither the First Protocol nor the Human Rights Act 1998 had ever come into force. Even the doctrinal developments on the right to property developed in Strasbourg do not deviate dramatically from common law principles. In that sense, the real development is in the constitutional place of the right to property as a human right. Hence, a preliminary question asks whether the new constitutional role of a right to property represents a radical break from the common law constitutional principles. It is with these principles that we begin.

THE RIGHT TO PROPERTY IN THE COMMON LAW CONSTITUTION

In its simplest form, a constitutional right to property recognises that the State has only a limited power to take and regulate property. In the middle ages and later, most writers believed that a right to property formed part of the fundamental law of England.[3] Fundamental law bound Parliament and the Crown, although the courts had only a limited power to enforce it against either body. In this sense, the constitution (in the broadest sense) included a right to property, despite the lack of a written constitution or a judicial power of review over legislation. In more recent times, the strength and practical relevance of the fundamental law regarding property has declined considerably,[4] as shown by a brief review of its influence on decision-making by Parliament, the courts and the executive branch.

---

[3] See generally: JW Gough, *Fundamental Law in English Constitutional History* (Clarendon Press, Oxford, 1955) 54; FA Mann, 'Outlines of a History of Expropriation' (1959) 75 *Law Quarterly Review* 188; WB Stoebuck, 'A General Theory of Eminent Domain' (1972) 47 *Washington Law Review* 553; PJ Marshall, 'Parliament and Property Rights in the Late Eighteenth-Century British Empire' in J Brewer and S Staves (eds), *Early Modern Conceptions of Property* (Routledge, London, 1995); GA Rubin, *Private Property, Government Requisition and the Constitution, 1914–1927* (The Hambledon Press, London, 1994).

[4] Although the technique of judicial interpretation has not: see *R v Lord Chancellor ex p Witham* [1998] QB 575.

Parliament and the right to property

Expressions of constitutional principle by Parliament tend to be vague, at least in comparison with judicial statements. Nevertheless, it is possible to say that Parliament has regarded itself as bound by a number of principles regarding property. For example, the power to acquire property compulsorily is normally made subject to an obligation to compensate the property owner. Indeed, Blackstone asserted that Parliament never expropriated property without providing compensation.[5] In the nineteenth century, this practice was reflected in the standard clauses of the Land Clauses Consolidation Act of 1845, and by the early twentieth century, in *A-G v De Keyser's Royal Hotel Ltd*,[6] counsel reported that they could find no instance of Parliament authorising an expropriation without requiring compensation.

Similarly, Parliament normally does not interfere with proceedings before the courts or with rights that have already vested according to law. *National & Provincial Building Society and others v United Kingdom*[7] provides an example. It concerned the transitional arrangements for the assessment of certain taxes payable by building societies. The transitional arrangements, as originally enacted, were subsequently found not to have properly imposed the tax that was collected. Several buildings societies brought proceedings for restitution of the money paid, but as the availability of restitution was uncertain, only the Woolwich Equitable Building Society proceeded through to judgment.[8] The other building societies supported the Woolwich's claim, as they hoped that a successful judgment would establish their claims. However, instead of honouring their claims, Parliament enacted the Finance Act 1991 and the Finance (No. 2) Act 1992, which extinguished the claims and imposed the tax with retroactive effect. It is significant, however, that the legislation did not extinguish the Woolwich's judgment. The principle of non-interference meant that its judgment was permitted to stand, although its claims had been no stronger than those of the other building societies. (As discussed below, the European Court of Human Rights decided that there had been no breach of P1-1.[9])

Beyond these fundamental principles, the restrictions on Parliamentary power were unclear. While Parliament did not dismiss issues of fundamental law when they did arise, there was rarely any real effort to develop a scientific approach to the development of principle. Two prominent twentieth century examples illustrate this point.

---

[5] W Blackstone, *Commentaries on the Laws of England I* (Clarendon Press, Oxford, 1765; reprint: Dawsons of Pall Mall, London, 1966) 135.

[6] [1920] AC 508, 542 (Lord Atkinson).

[7] Reports 1997–VII 2325 (1998) 25 EHRR 127.

[8] *Woolwich Equitable Building Society v Inland Revenue Commissioners* [1993] AC 70.

[9] See below, at 11 and 49ff.

The first concerns the Church (Scotland) Act 1905, which reversed the outcome of *General Assembly of Free Church of Scotland and Others v Lord Overtoun; Macalister v Young*.[10] This case concerned a schism in the Free Church which followed a vote by substantial majority of its members in favour of forming a new church. The property of the Free Church would be transferred to the new church, when the minority claimed that the transfer was contrary to the terms of the trusts on which the property had been given. The House of Lords upheld their claim, with the result that the old Free Church retained control over the full set of assets, despite lacking sufficient numbers to manage the property. The decision caused great concern in Scotland, as church schools and other institutions of public benefit were threatened with closure. A Parliamentary commission was formed to examine the issues, and it recommended that the new Church should have control over property, subject to 'equitable' treatment of the Free Church.[11] This solution was adopted in the 1905 Act, but only after lengthy debates in both Houses of Parliament. It is clear that there was strong support for allowing the majority to take over the assets of the old Free Church, but the constitutionality of reversing a final decision of the courts raised real concerns, especially since it took away property rights recognised by the courts. The debates show the majority of Members believed that it was important that the minority was treated fairly, as a matter of principle rather than mere expediency.[12]

Similarly, the debates on the bill that eventually became the War Damage Act of 1965 also focused on the issues of compensation and the *sub judice* rule. The Act concerned *Burmah Oil v Lord Advocate*,[13] in which the House of Lords upheld Burmah Oil's claim for compensation for the destruction of its property by British forces in World War II. The legality of the destruction was clear: the House of Lords held that the Crown had lawfully exercised its 'right and duty to protect its realm and citizens in times of war and peril',[14] because the property was destroyed to prevent it from falling into the hands of the advancing Japanese army. Soon after, in February 1943, the Chancellor informed the House of Commons that the Treasury would provide funds for rehabilitation or reconstruction, which would fall short of full compensation.[15] Funds were provided on this basis, and although the companies continued to press for full compensation, successive governments felt that there was no compelling ethical

---

[10] [1904] AC 515.

[11] See the United Kingdom, Report of the Royal Commission on Churches (Scotland) (Cd 2494, 1905).

[12] Parl Debs (series 4) vol 148 col 1003–70 (4 July 1905) (HC); Parl Debs (series 4) vol 150 col 369–407 (26 July 1905) (HC), col 840–79 (31 July 1905) (HL); Parl Debs (series 4) vol 151 col 231–39 (4 August 1905) (HL); cf *Bahamas District of the Methodist Church in the Caribbean and the Americas v The Hon Vernon J Symonette MP (Bahamas)*, [2000] UKPC 31 [62]–[74].

[13] [1965] AC 75.

[14] Above, p 143 (Lord Pearce).

[15] *Hansard* HC Deb vol 386 col 1942 (18 February 1943).

reason to provide more.[16] In 1962, Burmah Oil commenced proceedings against the Crown, and soon after the Deputy Treasury Solicitor informed the company that, if its claims succeeded, the Government would introduce legislation to indemnify the Crown against their claims.[17] Nevertheless, Burmah Oil continued to pursue its claim, and in 1964, by a 3-2 majority, the House of Lords held that it was entitled to compensation. The amount of compensation was left for the lower courts to determine: while Lord Reid suggested that it would be modest (given the imminent threat of seizure by the Japanese), there was no certainty that this would be the case.[18]

The new Labour Government then introduced the Bill that would become the War Damage Act 1965. The constitutionality of the Bill was debated at length, both inside and outside Parliament. Both the denial of compensation and the interference with the judicial process raised serious concerns. The Labour Government (with the support of many Conservative Members) did not simply reject these concerns as irrelevant; instead, it put forward carefully framed arguments on the constitutionality of the Bill.[19] Indeed, some of its points would probably receive a sympathetic hearing in Strasbourg. In particular, the argument that breadth of losses from war mean that rehabilitation, rather than compensation, was a legitimate response is broadly consistent with the Strasbourg judgments that the furtherance of social justice may justify a departure from the ordinary principles of compensation.[20] The Government also argued that the judgment in *Burmah Oil v Lord Advocate* had been quite unexpected, and in any case, Burmah Oil had been given ample warning that funds would only be provided on the basis of rehabilitation. Subsequently, in *National & Provincial Building Society and others v United Kingdom*, the European Court accepted that States may legitimately reverse unexpected judicial decisions, especially where the applicants did not have any moral expectation of benefiting from such decisions.[21]

While these examples demonstrate that governments have believed it necessary to defend bills said to be contrary to fundamental law, it is not the case that these debates made a lasting contribution to the development of fundamental law. Indeed, these debates had little influence beyond the immediate disputes in

---

[16] See the statement of Mr Niall MerDermot, Financial Secretary to the Treasury, HC Deb vol 705 cols 1091–99 (3 February 1965) on the factual background (the payments between $1/4$ and $1/3$ of the full value of lost property).

[17] The Deputy Treasury Solicitor's letter is discussed in the Outer House at 1962 SLT 347, 357–58.

[18] *Burmah Oil* (n 14) 113.

[19] *Hansard* HC Deb vol 705 cols 1091–220 (3 February 1965) (see especially cols 1091–99 for the Government's position); *Hansard* HC Deb vol 707 cols 1226–92 (2 March 1965); *Hansard* HL Deb vol 264 cols 730–44, 748–820 (25 March 1965); *Hansard* HL Deb vol 265 cols 289–351 (13 April 1965); *Hansard* HC Deb vol 712 cols 524–610 (12 May 1965); *Hansard* HL Deb vol 266 cols 723–94 (25 May 1965).

[20] *James v United Kingdom*, Series A No 98 (1986) 8 EHRR 123; *Lithgow v United Kingdom*, Series A No 102 (1986) 8 EHRR 329; see pp 180–93 below.

[21] *National & Provincial* (n 7).

which they arose: the debates on the Church of Scotland Bill were not discussed in the debates on the War Damage Bill, although it would appear that the earlier discussion of equity and fairness would have been relevant. It is apparent that Parliament has regarded itself as bound to respect property rights, but extremely difficult to discern the limits of those bounds. Hence, the Protocol is not incompatible with the principles of fundamental law, but primarily because the principles were so ill-defined.

The courts and the right to property

Fundamental law was reflected in the principles of statutory interpretation developed by the courts. In *A-G v De Keyser's Royal Hotel Ltd*, the House of Lords stated that 'unless the words of the statute clearly so demand, a statute is not to be construed so as to take away the property of a subject without compensation'.[22] In addition, courts have also tended to construe powers of expropriation narrowly, especially when the powers are held by a private undertaker.[23] If no compensation is provided, the court may conclude that Parliament did not intend to authorise the taking of property; conversely, if the intention to authorise a taking is clear, the courts may find an implied obligation to compensate.[24] The strongest statement to this effect was made in *Burmah Oil v Lord Advocate*, where Lord Upjohn said that 'it is clearly settled that where the executive is authorised by a statute to take the property of a subject for public purposes the subject is entitled to be paid unless the statute has made the contrary intention quite clear'.[25]

The role of these presumptions has declined in recent years. With modern courts, the presumptions are merely a guide to determining Parliament's actual intention. In *A-G Canada v Hallet & Carey Ltd*, Lord Radcliffe stated that 'There are many so-called rules of construction that courts of law have resorted to in their interpretation of statutes, but the paramount rule remains that every statute is to be expounded according to its manifest or expressed intention.'[26] If

---

[22] *De Keyser's* (n 6) 542 (Lord Atkinson).

[23] *Galloway v London Corp* (1866) LR 1 HL 34; *Rolls v London School Board* (1884) 27 ChD 639; *Donaldson v South Shields Corp* (1899) 68 LJ Ch 162; 79 LT 685 (CA); *Municipal Council of Sydney v Campbell* [1925] AC 338 (PC); and see generally M Taggart, 'Expropriation, Public Purpose and the Constitution' in C Forsyth and I Hare, (eds), *The Golden Metwand and the Crooked Cord: Essays on Public Law in Honour of Sir William Wade QC* (Clarendon Press, Oxford, 1998).

[24] *Commissioner of Public Works v Logan* [1903] AC 355 (PC); *Consett Iron Co Ltd v Clavering Trustees* [1935] 2 KB 42.

[25] *Burmah Oil* (n 13) 167, referring to *London and North Western Railway Co v Evans* [1893] 1 Ch 16, 18 (Bowen LJ); see also Mann (n 3) p 199n. However, it is also clear that 'Compensation claims are statutory and depend on statutory provisions': *Sisters of Charity of Rockingham v The King* [1922] 2 AC 315, 322 (PC). See also *Burmah Oil* (n 13) 118 (Viscount Radcliffe) and Anon, 'The Burmah Oil Affair' (1966) 79 *Harvard Law Review* 614, 633: 'Whatever the common law might say about the right to compensation for takings, the right to collect that compensation from the public treasury historically arose not from the common law but from the action of Parliament.'

[26] [1952] AC 427 (PC) 449 (Lord Radcliffe).

it is clear that the legislature intended to authorise a deprivation of property without compensation, the courts should not frustrate that intention by requiring express language where the intention is clear.[27] Similarly, in *Secretary of State for Defence v Guardian Newspapers Ltd*, Lord Scarman stated that 'there certainly remains a place in the law for the principle of construction . . . that the courts must be slow to impute to Parliament an intention to override property rights in the absence of plain words to that effect. But the principle is not an overriding rule of law: it is an aid, amongst many others, developed by the judges in their never ending task of interpreting statutes in such a way as to give effect to their true purpose.'[28]

Other presumptions that have the effect of protecting property are also worth considering. Two well-known examples are the presumption that statutory provisions are not intended to have retrospective effect and the presumption that they are not intended to interfere with vested interests. Both presumptions were discussed at length in *Wilson and others v Secretary of State for Trade and Industry*,[29] which concerned the effect of section 3 of the Human Rights Act 1998 on the construction of the Consumer Credit Act 1974. Section 127(4) of the Consumer Credit Act 1974 prohibits the enforcement of certain consumer loan agreements where there has been a failure to comply with regulations on the disclosure of the cost of credit. The question for the courts was whether section 127(4) is compatible with P1(1), and if not, whether the Human Rights Act 1998 would apply in proceedings regarding a credit agreement commenced before the Act came into force. Counsel for the borrower and the Secretary of State argued that the presumptions against retroactive effect and against the interference with vested rights and pending proceedings should be applied to the 1998 Act, thereby rendering any incompatibility with P1(1) of no effect on the specific facts. Ultimately, the House of Lords concluded that section 127(4) was compatible with P1(1), and hence it was not strictly necessary to consider the presumptions of interpretation. Nevertheless, their Lordships did examine the presumptions in some depth. In essence, they concluded that the presumptions reflected a general principle that interpretation should be fair. For example, Lord Rodger stated that, although some courts have sought to provide formal distinctions between vested rights and other existing rights, the results turn more on the perception of the fairness of applying new laws to existing rights.[30] In that sense, the presumptions provide a check on legislative power, but it is an uncertain and ill-defined check.

[27] Above.
[28] [1985] AC 339, 363 (dissenting on another point).
[29] [2004] 1 AC 816.
[30] Above [196].

The executive and the right to property

In relation to the executive, the issue is whether administrative policies regarding private property reflect principles of fundamental law. In many cases, this is not a difficult question: for example, if a statute requires compensation for expropriation, the administrative branch has no option but to pay compensation where required. In such cases, the constitutional principles that constrain its power relate more to Parliamentary supremacy and the separation of powers rather than the specific principles relating to the protection of property. The issue arises where neither Parliament nor the courts would prevent a public authority from acting in a way which would interfere with private property in a manner contrary to fundamental law. In such cases, can we find evidence of conduct that the public authority still considers itself bound by fundamental law?

In fact, it is difficult to find examples of such conduct. The development of the Crichel Down Rules on compulsory acquisition are probably the closest example that could be cited. As explained in Chapter 7, the Rules apply when Government departments and their agencies determine that land that was compulsorily acquired is surplus to their requirements. In such cases, they are required give the former owner the first opportunity to re-purchase it (at current market value).[31] As the Rules reflect a sense of the proper restrictions on sovereign power, they have a constitutional aspect. Moreover, they also have a human rights aspect to them. A senior judge has remarked that the 'elementary fairness demands no less' than the Rules promise,[32] and the European Court of Human Rights has indicated that the proportionality of an expropriation may be affected if the former owner is not permitted to share in the capital appreciation of property that has been not used for the purpose for which it was taken.[33] Nevertheless, it would go too far to describe the Rules as a principle of constitutional law.[34] They are plainly not so regarded by Parliament, as they are not routinely incorporated in statutes that confer the power of compulsory acquisition.[35] Moreover, even as a matter of administrative practice, they are only binding on Government departments and agencies: they are only commended to local authorities and privatised bodies to which public sector land has been transferred. Even at this level, it appears that there is no consistency in their application, and the Rules are often applied in a mechanical way with no sense of the principle they serve.[36]

---

[31] Chapter 7, 175–77.

[32] *Blanchfield v Attorney General of Trinidad and Tobago*, [2002] UKPC 1 [21] (Lord Millett).

[33] *Motais de Narbonne v France*, Appl No 48161/99, 2 July 2002 (see Chapter 7, p 176ff).

[34] Blanchfield (n 20).

[35] Although an early version of the Rules appeared in the Land Clauses Consolidation Act 1845, ss 127–32; see R Gibbard, 'The Crichel Down Rules: Conduct or Misconduct in the Disposal of Public Lands' in E Cooke, (ed), *Modern Studies in Property Law, Vol 2* (Hart Publishing, Oxford, 2003) 329, 331.

[36] Gerald Eve Chartered Surveyors and the University of Reading, *The Operation of the Crichel Down Rules* (Office of the Deputy Prime Minister, London, 2000) 43–83.

Hence, it appears that, if the Rules had been established as binding principles of general application, they might have been described as constitutional principles relating to sovereign powers over property. However, they have not been established with any conviction. The Office of the Deputy Prime Minister recently reviewed the Rules,[37] and it is is clear that its new guidance seeks to achieve greater fairness for those against whom the sovereign powers over property are exercised; in a very loose sense, its actions are therefore consistent with the human rights objectives of a right to property. However, it has not suggested that this sense of fairness arises out of its interpretation of binding obligations of fundamental law.

The European Union

The Human Rights Act 1998 is not the first example of legislation that incorporates fundamental rights under international law. Although the Treaty of Rome does not expressly protect a right to property, the European Court of Justice has stated that 'respect for fundamental rights forms an integral part of the general principles of law protected by the Court of Justice.'[38] As evidence of these general principles, the European Court of Justice looks to the constitutional traditions common to member states and the international treaties on which the Member States have collaborated or of which they are signatories.[39] The European Convention on Human Rights is the most important example of such a treaty. These principles were first established by the case law of the European Court of Justice, but as the Court noted in *Booker Aquaculture Ltd (t/a Marine Harvest McConnell) v Scottish Ministers*:

> The principles established by that case-law have been reaffirmed in the preamble to the Single European Act and in Article F(2) of the Treaty on European Union . . . They are now set out in Article 6(2) EU pursuant to which the Union shall respect fundamental rights, as guaranteed by the European Convention for the Protection of Human Rights and Fundamental Freedoms . . . and as they result from the constitutional traditions common to the Member States, as general principles of Community law.[40]

In the light of the protection of property under both Article 1 of the First Protocol and under the constitutions of many member states, the Court has declared that

---

[37] Office of the Deputy Prime Minister, *Compulsory Purchase and the Crichel Down Rules*, ODPM Circular 06/2004, Part 2.

[38] *Internationale Handelsgesellschaft* [1970] ECR 1125, 1134.

[39] Above; *Hauer v Land Rheinland–Pfalz* [1979] ECR 3727 [15]; *Booker Aquaculture Ltd (t/a Marine Harvest McConnell) v Scottish Ministers Booker* (C20/00) [2003] ECR I–7411 [65].

[40] Above [66].

> The right to property is guaranteed in the Community legal order in accordance with the ideas common to the constitutions of the Member States, which are also reflected in the first Protocol to the European Convention for the Protection of Human Rights.[41]

Since the European Communities Act 1972 incorporates 'All such rights, powers, liabilities, obligations and restrictions from time to time created or arising by or under the [Community] Treaties',[42] it also incorporates a right to property in areas of British law that are within the scope of Community law. Although this appears to provide an effective means of enforcing a right to property in domestic law, in fact it has rarely been used. *Booker Aquaculture Ltd* itself is a rare example, although even so, it was ultimately decided that there had been no violation of the fundamental right to property. This case concerned the destruction of fish under domestic disease control regulations,[43] which in turn implemented an EC directive.[44] The petitioners claimed that they should have been compensated for their loss, but on a reference from the Scottish courts,[45] the European Court of Justice held that there was no general principle to this effect in European law or under P1(1). Nevertheless, it is clear that there may be cases where it is the European Communities Act 1972, rather than the Human Rights Act 1998, that provides the mechanism for enforcing a right to property.

Conclusion

While it is possible to say that there are constitutional principles for the protection of property against sovereign power, they were never given clear expression and, in any case, their importance has declined in recent years. Currently, if they still apply as binding principles, it is only in the most general sense that the State should treat its citizens fairly. In any case, even if there is a general binding principle of fairness in relation to property rights, it is so ill-defined that it is of little practical force. Nonetheless, the waning influence of fundamental law has not had a dramatic effect on property. The institution of private property is not under threat, and propertied groups have not been denied a voice in the ordinary political process. In addition, the United Kingdom's record in Strasbourg on the right to property does not suggest that property has been at risk: while the United Kingdom is the respondent in a number of the leading cases on P1(1), these cases have been resolved in its favour.

---

[41] *Hauer* (n 39) [17]; see also *Booker* above [67].

[42] European Communities Act 1972 s 2(1).

[43] Reg 7 of the Diseases of Fish (Control) Regulations 1994, SI 1994/1447.

[44] Dir 93/53/EEC.

[45] 2000 SC 9, [2000] UKHRR 1 (Inner House); [1999] 1 CMLR 35 (Outer House) (the Outer House held in favour of the petitioners). See A O'Neill, 'The Protection of Fundamental Rights in Scotland as a General Principle of Community Law—the Case of *Booker Aquaculture*' [2000] 1 *European Human Rights Law Review* 18.

Hence, P1(1) does not represent a radical departure from traditional principles. The body of case law under P1(1) is plainly far more detailed than the fundamental law ever was but, with some exceptions, it does not present a serious challenge the existing set of laws on property. This is not to say that there would not be specific points where existing laws might be open to challenge: indeed, the frequency with which P1(1) is considered in the drafting of legislation by Parliament, the formulation of policy by administrative bodies, and the judgments of the United Kingdom courts demonstrates that it is in the detail rather than the broad sweep of law that affects the law in the United Kingdom.

EUROPEAN CONVENTION ON HUMAN RIGHTS AND THE FIRST PROTOCOL[46]

The European Convention on Human Rights is a product of the Council of Europe, which was set up in 1949 to counter the communist threat posed by the Soviet Union. At the time, it was believed that a purely military alliance would not be enough to counter Soviet threat; an ideological alternative to the communism had to be presented as well. Hence, the Council of Europe was intended to achieve 'a greater unity between its members for the purpose of safeguarding and realising the ideals and principles which are their common heritage and facilitating their economic and social progress.'[47] The protection of human rights was central to this aim, for not only does the Statute of Europe reaffirm the founding States' 'devotion to the spiritual and moral values which are the common heritage of their peoples and the true source of individual freedom, political liberty and the rule of law, principles which form the basis of all genuine democracy', but Article 1(b) provides that the aim of greater unity would be pursued by 'the maintenance and further realisation of human rights and fundamental freedoms'. In addition, every member of the Council of Europe would be required to 'accept the principles of the rule of law and of the enjoyment by all persons within its jurisdiction of human rights and fundamental freedoms'.[48]

The Statute was signed 5 May 1949 and the United Kingdom joined on the same date. The Statute set out the basic institutional structure of the Council of Europe. It provided that its primary organs would the Committee of Ministers and the Consultative Assembly, where the Committee of Ministers would hold the power to make all important decisions and the Assembly would only have the power to discuss matters and make recommendations to the Committee of

---

[46] E Schwelb, 'The Protection of the Right to Property of Nationals under the First Protocol to the European Convention on Human Rights' (1964) 13 *American Journal of Comparative Law* 518, 533–41; W Peukert, 'Protection of Ownership under Article of the First Protocol to the European Convention on Human Rights' (1981) 2 *Human Rights Law Journal* 37; AWB Simpson, *Human Rights and the End of Empire: Britain and the Genesis of the European Convention* (OUP, Oxford, 2001) ch 15.

[47] Statute of the Council of Europe, European Treaty Series—Nos 1/6/7/8/11, Article 1.a.

[48] Above, Article 3.

Ministers. In addition, to ensure that Assembly would not provide a forum for communist groups, the appointment of Assembly members was left to the discretion of each State.[49]

Discussions on what would become the European Convention on Human Rights began in August 1949. This immediately raised one of the most contentious aspects of the Convention: control over the drafting process. On 9 August, the Committee of Ministers voted 7-4 not to include human rights on the Assembly agenda.[50] After pressure from the Assembly, the Ministers relented. Even so, they directed the Assembly to confine its discussions to defining the rights which should be protected, thereby leaving any discussion of the institutional arrangements for protecting those rights to the Ministers.[51] The United Kingdom, in particular, sought to limit the power of the Council to intervene with domestic matters and was wary of surrendering any of its sovereign powers to an international tribunal. Those countries which had been under Nazi occupation were not so confident that their governments would respect human rights and the rule of law; hence, they were more willing to transfer some of their sovereignty to international institutions.[52] In a sense, however, this gave them common ground with the United Kingdom, as they also believed that the institutional arrangements for protecting rights were too important to leave to the Assembly.

The discussion then moved to the Assembly, which then set up a Legal Affairs Committee to prepare a draft of the rights to be included in the proposed convention. The inclusion of a right to property was controversial almost immediately. A narrow majority recommended that there should be a right to property based on Article 17 of the Universal Declaration, which provides as follows

1. Everyone has the right to own property alone as well as in association with others.
2. No one shall be arbitrarily deprived of his property.

The drafting of Article 17 demonstrated how difficult it would be to reach agreement on a right to property.[53] Earlier drafts limited the right to personal property, or any type of property 'as meets the essential needs of decent living, that helps to maintain the dignity of the individual and of the home'.[54] An earlier proposal to protect against the deprivation of property without 'just compensation' was changed to the prohibition against being 'arbitrarily deprived' of property; a Soviet proposal to restrict it to 'unlawful' deprivation

---

[49] On the fear of communist infiltration, see Simpson (n 46) 619.

[50] Council of Europe, *Collected edition of the 'Travaux Préparatoires' of the European Convention on Human Rights: Recueil des Travaux Préparatoires de la Convention Européenne des Droits de l'Homme* (M Nijhoff, The Hague, 1975–85) vol 1, 10–13; Simpson, above 667.

[51] Council of Europe, above vol 1, 22–27; Simpson, above 670.

[52] Simpson, above 601–2, 680.

[53] C Krause and G Alfredsson, 'Article 17' in G Alredsson and A Eide, (eds), *The Universal Declaration of Human Rights: A Common Standard of Achievement* (M Nijhoff, The Hague, 1999).

[54] Above 362.

was rejected on the basis that this would be too narrow.[55] After lengthy debates, the General Assembly adopted Article 17 unanimously.

A substantial minority in the Legal Affairs Committee objected that a right to property would take the proposed convention beyond the protection of the core rights which underpinned social democracy. If the convention was going to go beyond political rights, why should it not include other social and economic rights as well? Others protested that property was essentially a matter for domestic institutions: an international body should not be 'responsible for evaluating the legitimacy of the charges and the restrictions of various kinds which, according to the economic or social conditions of a country, might be imposed on private property, on account of its social function or general utility.'[56] Despite these objections, the majority 'considered that having regard to the importance of the part played by the right to own property in the independence of the individual and of the family, it was desirable to include it in the list of guaranteed rights.'[57]

When the Committee's report was debated by the Assembly, the right to property became the subject of greater controversy. Lord Layton, the Liberal representative, raised points of concern that were common to many members of the Assembly.[58] First, he argued that the immediacy of the threat to democracy meant that 'the list of rights should be limited to the absolute minimum necessary to constitute the cardinal principles for the functioning of political democracy.'[59] Like many other members, he grouped the right to property with other social and economic rights and believed that the protection of these rights could wait until democracy was secured. It would it take years of careful work to establish a framework for the protection of social and economic rights; moreover, protecting one of those rights without the others would present a distorted image of the work of the Assembly, particularly where the right in question would be perceived to have been included for the benefit of only the wealthy classes.[60] Indeed, a British Labour representative said that a guarantee of private property would be seen as a reactionary attempt to defend a system in which a 'tiny handful of people own the means by which millions of others live'.[61] Other members repeated the objection made in the Committee that property rights were essentially a matter for domestic jurisdiction, particularly since political views on the extent of ownership rights varied from State to State, and from one

---

[55] Above 363.

[56] Council of Europe (n 50) vol 1, 198; Simpson (n 46) 762 states that the quotation is from 'the Labour Party lawyer, Ungoed–Thomas'.

[57] Council of Europe, above vol 1, 198–200; see also vol 1, 270–72 (Teitgen, France).

[58] In a later debate, Lord Layton stated that he had opposed the inclusion of a right to property on 'tactical grounds that it was hard to define these rights [property and education] and that to attempt to do so might divide the Assembly, in which case it might imperil the ratification of the Convention.' (Above vol 6, 150.)

[59] Above vol 2, 52.

[60] Above vol 2, 54 56 (Layton); 80 (Elmgren, Sweden).

[61] Above vol 2, 80 (Nally).

political party to another within each State.[62] Finally, some representatives voiced fears that any proposal based on Article 17 of the Universal Declaration of Human Rights would be too vague to be enforceable, due to differences between jurists from different countries on scope of a right to property.[63]

Although the right to property was opposed by many members, especially amongst the British contingent, it also received also strong support from many other members. One group rejected the view that the right to property was less important than other human rights. Some argued that property was natural right and that protecting property made it possible for individuals to enjoy their other rights and freedoms.[64] Others took the view that a right to property would help avoid confiscations of the type that occurred before and during War.[65] As Simpson observes, the British may not have been fully aware of how deeply the experience of occupation affected some of the continental members of the Assembly.[66] In Britain, the State did not represent the threat to the rights and liberties of ordinary citizens as it had on the Continent; indeed, it was regarded as the protector of rights and liberties against foreign powers. On the Continent, the existence of collaborationist governments demonstrated that oppression was not merely attributable to an occupying force. The confiscation of property was one instrument used by oppressive governments to enforce their will. A further group of supporters believed that the Universal Declaration should guide the Council; after all, if the Declaration was truly universal, it would not be appropriate for the Council to pick and choose the rights it wished to protect.[67] A final group seemed to believe that the objections were directed at the possibility that the right to property would be absolute or that it would prevent the kind of social legislation which was planned in many States. They argued that it would be sufficient to recognise that the States would remain competent to regulate the use of property; for example, De Valera remarked that:

> The difference between the ownership of something and the use of that is made of it is vital if we are to have any agreement on matters of this kind. Those of us who claim that the right to own property is fundamental, admit, and readily admit, that there are the demands of social justice which must be met, and that it is the right of the State to see that justice is done, and to regulate, in the interests of the common good, the way in which individuals who own property use that property.[68]

---

[62] Above vol 2, 60–62 (Ungoed–Thomas).

[63] Above vol 2, 86 (Edberg, Sweden) and 120 (Layton).

[64] Above vol 2, 104 (de Valera, Ireland): 'I believe that it is a fundamental right necessary for the full development of the human being that he should have the right to own property'. Philip (France) was of the same view, but would limit the human right to personal property only (vol 2, 72–74).

[65] Above vol 2, 92 (Reynaud, France).

[66] Simpson (n 46) 601–2.

[67] Council of Europe (n 50) vol 2, 88 (MacEntee, Ireland).

[68] Above vol 2, 104.

Other members of the Assembly were not so confident that a right to property which protected only against the 'arbitrary' confiscation of property, such as Article 17, would not restrict the general regulatory or taxing powers of the State; their impression was that it would only guard against illegal takings of property.[69] Ultimately, the majority in the Assembly supported the inclusion of a right to property, but it was recognised that there that there was no common ground on its scope. Accordingly, the Assembly decided that simply transplanting Article 17 of the UDHR to the proposed Convention would not be satisfactory. It referred the issue to its Legal Affairs Committee. None of the other proposed rights had proved as controversial: the rest of the Committee's original proposal was referred to the Committee of Ministers.

The fear that the right to property would restrict economic planning was particularly acute with the British, who would have been familiar with the American experience with the judicial interpretation of its Bill of Rights. During the late nineteenth and early twentieth centuries, the Supreme Court had interpreted constitutional rights intended to protect property, commercial trade and freedom of contract in a manner which restricted the powers of the state in economic matters.[70] The Supreme Court changed tack in 1937, when it took a more deferential position on economic issues;[71] nevertheless, it was clear that judicial review could easily extend into areas of economic policy. The risk of judicial activism was not solely an American concern, as a series of Privy Council cases from the 1930s and 40s on the Canadian legislature's powers demonstrated that British judges could take a similarly restrictive line on economic matters.[72] While the Privy Council's defenders claimed that it had merely read the Canadian constitution according to the accepted principles of interpretation,[73] some Canadian lawyers argued that the decisions were motivated by primarily by conservative political and economic policies.[74]

---

[69] Above 126–32 (see especially Teitgen).

[70] *Lochner v New York* 198 US 45 (1905); see also: *Hammer v Degenhart* 247 US 251 (1918); *Bailey v Drexel Furniture Co* 259 US 20 (1922); *Adkins v Children's Hospital* 261 US 525 (1923).

[71] The conflict came to a head after the Court's restrictive decisions in *Schecter Poultry Corp v United States* 295 US 495 (1935); *United States v Butler* 297 US 1 (1936); *Carter v Carter Coal Co* 298 US 238 (1936). The restrictive doctrine was abandoned in cases such as *West Coast Hotel Co v Parrish* 300 US 379 (1937) and *United States v Carolene Products* 304 US 144 (1938) (and *cf Eastern Enterprises v Apfel* 524 US 498 (1998)). See generally LH Tribe, *American Constitutional Law,* 3rd edn (Foundation Press, New York, 2000) ch 8; for a comparison of the *Lochner*-era jurisprudence with the European jurisprudence, see MR Antinori, 'Does Lochner Live in Luxembourg? An Analysis of the Property Rights Jurisprudence of the European Court of Justice' (1995) 18 *Fordham International Law Journal* 1778.

[72] See eg *A-G Canada v A-G Ontario (Employment and Social Insurance Act Reference)* [1937] AC 355 and *A-G British Columbia v A-G Canada (Natural Products Marketing Act Reference)* [1937] AC 377.

[73] See, in particular, WI Jennings, 'Constitutional Interpretation: The Experience of Canada' (1937) 51 *Harvard Law Review* 1 and Lord Normand, 'The Judicial Committee of the Privy Council—Retrospect and Prospect' (1950) 3 *Current Legal Problems* 1.

[74] For a general review, see: E McWhinney, *Judicial Review in the English-Speaking World*, 2nd edn (University of Toronto Press, Toronto, 1960) chs 3, 4; AC Cairns, 'The Judicial Committee and Its Critics' [1971] 4 *Canadian Journal of Political Science* 301.

It is also clear that the British were not confident that careful drafting would avoid these problems. Indeed, within the constitutional system of the British Empire, there had been attempts to draft rights to property for some colonies. Section 299 of the Government of India Act 1935 contains one well-known example. The drafting of section 299 was dominated by the fear that general right to property would have an undesirable and unpredictable impact on matters such as taxation and the execution of civil judgments.[75] Consequently, section 299 only protected property in land and commercial or industrial undertakings, rather than all forms of property, and it only required payment of such compensation as specified by the law authorising the expropriation. This was typical of the British approach in the colonies, where the protection of property from the legislature was left primarily to the executive, rather than the judiciary. Hence, it is not surprising that the British were concerned with the potential impact of a right to property in an international charter, particularly if it would be enforced by an international tribunal.

To return to the Convention, the Committee of Ministers set up a Committee of Experts, partly to pre-empt further discussion of the right to property in the Legal Affairs Committee of the Assembly. Although the Experts recommended the inclusion of a right to property to counteract the tendency of totalitarian regimes 'to interfere with the right to own property as a means of exercising illegitimate pressure on its nationals', they did not put forward a draft clause.[76] They felt that the content of a right to property was 'more in the nature of a political question not falling within its competence.'[77] It seemed that the right to property was being sidelined.

The Committee of Ministers referred the Committee of Experts' proposals to a Conference of Senior Officials, which met from 8–17 June, 1950. The Conference ultimately produced a single draft convention,[78] but since the Committee of Experts had not drafted a property clause, and none was added by the Ministers, the Conference draft did not include one. Nevertheless, there were some elements of the Conference draft which were quite significant for the right to property that was eventually produced. In particular, the Conference resolved one of the most difficult issues in the drafting of the Convention. There had been disagreement over the nature of written limitations to the rights contained in the draft: not only was there disagreement over whether limitations would be necessary, but even those who favoured express limitations could not agree whether there should be a single limitation clause of general application or whether each right should have specific limitations attached to it. Existing models of human rights instruments took different approaches. So, for example, the Fifth Amendment of the United States Constitution states that '. . . nor shall private property be taken for public use, without just compensation'. While this

---

[75] T Allen, *The Right to Property in Commonwealth Constitutions* (CUP, Cambridge, 2000) 44–46.
[76] Council of Europe (n 50) vol 4, 18.
[77] Above.
[78] Above vol 4, 204–43 (report and draft); vol 4, 242–95 (final).

right appears to be absolute, the courts have developed limitations through the interpretation of the terms 'taking' and 'private property', 'public use' and 'just compensation', and by finding that certain types of takings lie outside the Fifth Amendment altogether.[79] With the Universal Declaration, however, some rights were made subject to express limitations. With some clauses, limitations were implicit: Article 17 (2) for example, only has meaning if one assumes that a person may be deprived of property where it is not arbitrary. The Conference of Senior Officials elected to follow the UDHR approach, by adding specific limitations to specific rights. Nevertheless, there were common elements to the specific clauses. In particular, all of the specific clauses reflected the general principle that the limitations should go no further than what was necessary in a democratic society. As discussed in chapter 5, this provided the basis for the proportionality doctrine, which was eventually adopted (although in a weaker form) in the P1-1 jurisprudence.

The Conference draft went back to the Ministers which, after some further revisions were made, met again on 7 August. By this time, however, the Legal Affairs Committee of the Assembly, which was drafting its own proposal for a right to property, had seen the draft convention of the Conference of Senior Officials. Teitgen submitted a motion for adding the following draft of a right to property to the Conference proposal:

> Every natural or legal person is entitled to the peaceful enjoyment of his possessions. Such possessions cannot be subjected to arbitrary confiscation. The present measures shall not however be considered as infringing, in any way, the right of a State to pass necessary legislation to ensure that the said possessions are utilised in accordance with the general interest.[80]

This recommendation was accepted by the Legal Affairs Committee by a 15-4 vote, as draft Article 10A. In the Committee's Report, Teitgen, as Rapporteur, acknowledged that there were differences in the Committee over the drafting of the clause, and stated that 'It represents an attempt to define the right as requested by the Assembly in September 1949, and endeavours to make the distinction between arbitrary confiscation and the social conception of property which allows it to be used by regulation legislation for the public good.'[81] Nevertheless, it is worth noting that the proposal includes a reference to both natural and legal persons. There is no discussion of this point in the *travaux préparatoires* and it does not necessarily follow from the Universal Declaration, which only states that 'everyone' has the right to property.

The Consultative Assembly gave overwhelming support to the draft Article: it was supported by a 97-0 vote, with 11 members abstaining.[82] The extent of the

---

[79] See generally LH Tribe, *American Constitutional Law*, 2nd edn (Foundation Press, Mineola, NY, 1988) ch 9.

[80] Council of Europe (n 50) vol 6, 6–10; see also vol 6, 52ff, 130–40.

[81] Above vol 6, 48, 54 and 60.

[82] Above vol 6, 156; it was sent to the Committee of Ministers as Recommendation No 24 (vol 6, 194) and included in a draft proposal (vol 6, 248).

support was partly due to assurances given by members of the Legal Affairs Committee to the Assembly that the draft Article would not interfere with the existing powers of States to carry out their social policies, whether by national-isation, or by regulating the use of property, or by imposing taxes and other levies.[83] The debate concentrated on general issues, rather than the technical aspects of the draft, and the proposal then went forward to the Committee of Ministers, as Recommendation 24.

The Committee of Ministers did not follow the Recommendation.[84] There was strong opposition from some countries, particularly the United Kingdom.[85] At this point, it appeared that attempting to reach agreement on the right to property (as well as education and political rights) would lengthen the drafting process to an extent that would be politically unacceptable. Accordingly, the Committee of Ministers decided that the areas where substantial agreement had already been achieved would become the subject of the Convention itself, and the most contentious issues—the right to property, education rights and polit-ical rights—would be referred to the Committee of Experts for further consid-eration and the preparation of a separate protocol, to be ratified at a later date. As a result, the European Convention on Human Rights was approved on 7 August and signed on 4 November, but without a right to property. This would await agreement on the separate protocol.

The Protocol

Once the decision had been made to leave the right to property to a separate protocol, an increasing amount of attention was put on the technical issues of drafting. Although it was known that the United Kingdom had led the opposi-tion to Recommendation 24, it was also assumed in the Assembly that the real objection was not to the principle of a right to property, but rather to the lan-guage in which the draft clauses had been expressed.[86] Some countries (includ-ing the United Kingdom) favoured drafting all the rights in the most precise language possible, whereas others favoured to drafting in general language,

---

[83] See Sir Maxwell-Fyfe (Rapporteur) in reply to a question from Miss Alice Bacon (UK) (vol 6, 138) as to whether he could give the British Labour Party assurances 'that this Article safeguards the right of any State to undertake schemes of nationalisation and for the taxation of wealth necessary to carry out its social policy.' Maxwell-Fyfe's reply was that schemes intended to further social poli-cies in the general interest would be saved, although arbitrary confiscations would not (vol 6, 138–40).

[84] Above vol 7, 24.

[85] See eg Davies (UK) above vol 7, 28: 'The British Government would find it very difficult at this stage to accept the amendments of the Assembly, and he knew that certain of his colleagues shares this view.' Simpson (n 46) reports that the brief for the British delegates was to remove the right to property from the proposed Convention, or to agree to its inclusion in a separate protocol.

[86] Above vol 7, 126–28.

with a view to allowing the proposed court to develop the principles over time.[87] Ultimately, the Committee of Experts 'rejected the method of general statement, and adopted the system of precise definition to the greatest extent possible of the specific rights to be secured.'[88] This made it necessary 'to define as accurately as possible what is meant by the right of property, what is meant by "arbitrary confiscation" and what exceptions are to be permitted in the general interest to the individual rights of enjoyment of one' possessions.'[89] This would take account of national legislation on matters such as 'nationalisation, requisition in time of war, expropriation for public use, agrarian reform, confiscation in criminal law, death duties and reversion to the State on intestacy.'[90]

The Committee of Experts met to discuss the Protocol in February, 1951. Simpson's comprehensive study of the British position on the right to property shows that Cabinet ministers and senior civil servants had real difficulty reconciling two opposed concerns.[91] On the one hand, they wished to safeguard the State's right to impose taxes and nationalise property. On the other, they wished to protect British investments overseas, and to do this, they sought to ensure that the right to property would impose a real constraint on governments. After working through several different proposals to put before Committee of Experts, the Cabinet finally agreed that the following should go forward as its proposal for the Protocol:

> Every natural or legal person is entitled to the peaceful enjoyment of his possessions. This provision, however, shall not be considered as infringing in any way the right of a State to enforce such laws as it deems necessary either to serve the ends of justice or to secure the payment of monies due whether by way of taxes or otherwise, or to ensure the acquisition or use of property in accordance with the general interest.[92]

A comparison with Recommendation 24, which was not acceptable to the British, makes it clear that the Cabinet was more concerned with the threat to its social policies (and sovereign power generally) than it was with the precision with which Teitgen's draft clause had been written.

In addition to the clause proposed by the United Kingdom, the Committee of Experts was also asked to consider a clause proposed by Belgium:

---

[87] Above vol 4, 248 it is reported that, in the Committee of Minsters, merely enumerating rights was favoured by France, Ireland, Italy and Turkey whereas United Kingdom, Greece, Norway, and the Netherlands favoured defining the rights; Belgium and Luxembourg favoured enumeration if a court would be able to develop a jurisprudence, but definition if there was not to be a court; Denmark and Sweden reserved their positions. See Simpson (n 46) 370–71, 687–88, 692–93, 705–7, 713–17.

[88] Above vol 7, 126–28 (memorandum of the Secretariat-General), although n also that the final product was also seen as a compromise: vol 4, 248.

[89] Above vol 7, 126–28.

[90] Above vol 7, 128.

[91] Simpson (n 46) 771–80.

[92] Council of Europe (n 50) vol 7, 186 and 194.

> Every natural or legal person is entitled to the peaceful enjoyment of his possessions. No-one shall be deprived of his possessions except in the public interest, in such cases and by such procedure as may be established by law and subject to fair compensation which shall be fixed in advance. The penalty of total confiscation of property shall not be permitted.
>
> The present measures shall not however infringe in any way the right of a State to pass legislation to control the use of property in accordance with the general interest or to impose taxes or other contributions.[93]

The Belgian clause raised the issue of compensation, which was to prove particularly difficult to resolve; indeed, the States deliberately left the issue unresolved in the final Protocol. The delegation from the United Kingdom opposed the inclusion of any reference to compensation, because their Government 'did not think it possible to express this principle in terms which would be appropriate to all the various types of case which might arise, nor could it admit that decisions taken on this matter by the competent national authorities should be subject to revision by international organs.'[94] The French argued that compensation was already implied by second sentence proposed by Consultative Assembly; that is, that the prohibition against arbitrary confiscation necessarily included a prohibition against expropriation without compensation.[95] In the light of British doubts, the majority decided to make the position explicit by amending the Belgian proposal as follows:

> Every natural or legal person is entitled to the peaceful enjoyment of his possessions. Such possessions cannot be subjected to arbitrary confiscation. No-one shall be deprived of his possessions except in the public interest, in such cases and by such procedure as are established by law and subject to compensation.
>
> The present measures shall not however infringe, in any way, the right of a State to pass legislation to control the use of property in accordance with the general interest or to impose taxes or other contributions.[96]

This, of course, did not satisfy the British concerns. They proposed an amendment that the clause should provide that the entitlement to compensation should be 'subject, in the case of acquisition, to such compensation as shall be determined in accordance with the conditions provided for by law.'[97] Even this concerned the Lord Chancellor; before the next meeting of the Committee of Ministers, he made it clear that he opposed any concession in relation to compensation. He raised the issue of the expropriation of development value under the Town and Country Planning Act 1947.[98] Jowitt's views were not those of all Cabinet members or senior civil servants, as there was a real concern over the rights of British companies in the event of the expropriation of their overseas

[93] Above vol 7, 194.
[94] Above vol 7, 208.
[95] Above.
[96] Above vol 7, 206–8.
[97] Above vol 7, 222–24.
[98] Simpson (n 46) 784–85; see Chapter 6, 169–71.

property by foreign States. If the Protocol did nothing to protect property, it could be argued that the rules of customary international law which served to protect foreign investment might no longer apply. Customary international law allows States to extend diplomatic protection to its nationals in respect of their overseas property where a foreign State expropriated property without compensation. Plainly, the British did not wish to degrade the protection which their overseas assets already received. The deliberate exclusion of any guarantee of compensation in an instrument intended to reflect minimum standards in the Contracting States might suggest that the international law regarding the expropriation of alien property would no longer apply.[99]

The Committee of Ministers met in March 1951, where it was decided to reconvene the Committee of Experts. The Experts met again in April 1951. The Belgian proposal had been revised, and now read as follows:

> Every natural or legal person is entitled to the peaceful enjoyment of his possessions. No one shall be deprived of his possessions except in the public interest, in such cases and by such procedure as are established by law and subject to such compensation as shall be determined in accordance with the conditions provided for by law.
>
> The present measures shall not however infringe, in any way, the right of a State to pass legislation to control the use of property in accordance with the general interest or to impose taxes or other contributions.[100]

The reference to arbitrary confiscation had been removed. According to a later report from the Secretariat-General to the Assembly,

> This change was made principally because the phrase "arbitrary confiscation" was thought to be too unprecise in a legal text, as it is capable of very varying interpretations. The phrase "subject to the conditions provided for by law" was believed to be more precise and to cover adequately the object in mind.[101]

The compensation clause was weakened to say that deprivations of property should only require 'such compensation as shall be determined in accordance with the conditions provided for by law'. While this appeared to give national legislatures the freedom to set compensation at whatever level they desired, the French, Saar and UK delegations stated that they 'could not accept a definition of the right to property comprising in all cases the principle of compensation in the event of private property being acquired by the State.'[102] Consequently, the Committee was unable to reach agreement.

There was now growing pressure on governments to find some common ground on the remaining issues which seemed to block progress on the Protocol. The next meeting of Ministers would open on May 2 and, according to Simpson,

---

[99] HR Fabri, 'The Approach Taken by the European Court of Human Rights to the Assessment of Compensation for "Regulatory Expropriations" of the Property of Foreign Investors' (2002) 11 *New York University Environmental Law Journal* 148, 162–63.

[100] Council of Europe (n 50) vol 7, 230.

[101] Above vol 8, 8.

[102] Above vol 7, 250 (the Swedish and Turkish delegations abstained).

'There appears to have been a disposition to accept more or less any text upon which agreement could be reached.'[103] Nevertheless, it proved impossible for the Committee of Ministers to reach a final agreement, and they requested Committee of Experts to attempt to reach an agreement on Protocol.[104]

The Committee of Experts finally agreed on a final text in their meetings on June 5–6, 1951.[105] The revised version of the Belgian text provided the basis for the final proposal, but second sentence was changed to the following: 'No one shall be deprived of his possessions except in the public interest and subject to the conditions provided for by law and by the general principles of international law.' The controversial reference to compensation had been dropped. The *travaux préparatoires* do not contain any explanation for the inclusion of the reference to international law, although it is plain that it represented the only viable compromise on the compensation issue.[106] The crucial point, noted by several delegations, was that international law does not obligate States to compensate their own nationals: the obligation only applies to aliens.[107] It therefore appeared that the Protocol would merely continue the position which already obtained at international law.

There were also final amendments to the third sentence, as a British proposal to change it was accepted. It now read 'The preceding provisions shall not however in any way infringe the right of a State to enforce such laws as it deems necessary to control the use of property in accordance with the general interest or to secure payment of taxes or other contribution or of penalties imposed by courts.'[108] The Secretariat-General reported that the changes from the Assembly's original draft were merely for the sake of achieving greater clarity although, as discussed below, this may be doubted.

The Committee of Ministers adopted the draft Protocol, with the right to property, and then sent it to the Assembly for review.[109] Some members of the Assembly proposed still further amendments, but were persuaded that the draft should be left as it is.[110] It does not appear that there was any conviction that the draft represented an ideal right to property, but merely that it was the best compromise that could be achieved. It came into force on 18 May 1954.

The interpretation of the Protocol

As a very broad observation, the European Court of Human Rights' interpretation of the Convention and Protocol has extended the scope of all the rights,

[103] Simpson (n 46), 788–89.
[104] Council of Europe (n 50) vol 7, 258–60 (1985); Simpson above 791.
[105] Above vol 7, 300, 304.
[106] Above vol 7, 320.
[107] Above vol 7, 316–18; vol 8, 8, 10; see also Simpson (n 46) 797.
[108] Simpson above 798.
[109] Council of Europe (n 50) vol 7, 336, 342.
[110] Above vol 8, 76, 160–62, 166.

including P1(1). These developments are covered in more detail elsewhere in this book; at this point, we examine several specific issues arising from points left unresolved by the drafting process.

Internal inconsistencies

There were several internal inconsistencies in the language of P1(1) that had to be resolved. First, the nature of the interest protected by P1(1) is described in different ways. The English version refers to 'possessions' in the first two sentences and 'property' in the final sentence; by contrast, the French version refers to '*biens*' in the first sentence and '*propriété*' in the second and third sentences. For English lawyers, this is especially confusing because, as a British representative in the Consultative Assembly had pointed out, 'possessions' is not a term normally used in the common law.[111] In addition, the first and third sentences in the English version also refer to the 'enjoyment of possessions' and 'controls on the use' of possessions, which suggest that other forms of interference or controls lie outside P1(1). Plainly, there was the potential for considerable confusion over these issues.[112] However, the Court has decided that the scope of P1(1) should be read broadly, and so it has adopted a construction of the provision that is probably closer to the French version.[113] Accordingly, the first sentence covers all forms of interference with all types of property, while the second only covers the acquisition of an ownership interest, and the first part of the third sentence covers regulatory controls on rights of exclusion and disposition, as well as use.

A further inconsistency appears in the English version, as it refers to the 'public interest' in the second sentence and the 'general interest' in the the third. Neither one of these expressions can be said to have a fixed or even clear meaning in English law. In constitutional law in common law countries, the tendency has been to give similar expressions in rights to property the broadest possible construction. The difficulty with P1(1) arises with the French version, which is potentially narrower: the second sentence states that deprivations are permitted only '*pour cause d'utilité publique*', whereas the third refers to the enforcement of controls on the use of property '*conformément à l'intérêt général*'. While legal doctrine does not suggest that there is any real difference between the 'public interest' and the 'general interest', the French conception of expropriation for '*cause d'utilité publique*' has a more specific conception. In particular, it would be more difficult to construe the French version as permitting the use of the State power to authorise the compulsory transfer of private property from one private person to another, for the private use of the recipient.

---

[111] Above vol 6, 88 (Roberts).

[112] See Schwelb (n 21) 520; D Feldman, 'Proportionality and the Human Rights Act 1998' in E Ellis, (ed), *The Principle of Proportionality in the Laws of Europe* (Hart Publishing, Oxford, 1999) 117, 120, who observes that the Schedule to the 1998 Act only contains the English version.

[113] Chapter 2, cases cited n 3, 4.

However, in *James v United Kingdom*, the Court made it clear that there no real distinction between the public and the general interest: both should be given the broader reading that common lawyers would probably regard as unobjectionable.[114] Moreover, both allow the redistribution of property, provided some public benefit arises therefrom.[115]

Omissions: the compensation guarantee and the imposition of taxes and penalties

The uncertainty over compensation continued after 1950. In its decision in *Gudmundsson v Iceland*, the Commission stated that the second sentence of P1(1) did not guarantee nationals the same treatment as aliens.[116] However, in *Sporrong and Lönnroth v Sweden*, the Court held that the process of expropriation had dragged on for so long that it 'could have been rendered legitimate only if they [the applicant owners] had had the possibility of seeking a reduction of the time-limits or of claiming compensation.'[117] Subsequently, in *Lithgow v United Kingdom*, the Court stated that 'compensation terms are material to the assessment whether a fair balance has been struck between the various interests at stake and, notably, whether or not a disproportionate burden has been imposed on the person who has been deprived of his possessions.'[118] Accordingly, the Court concluded that the 'the taking of property without payment of an amount reasonably related to its value would normally constitute a disproportionate interference which could not be considered justifiable' under P1(1).[119] However, as explained in chapter 6, this only a general principle, and exceptions are recognised. Indeed, in *James v United Kingdom*, the Court also held that a departure from full compensation could be justified where legislation is intended to achieve greater social justice.[120] Similarly, in the *Former King of Greece v Greece*, the Court discussed *James* and stated that 'less than full compensation may be equally, if not a fortiori, called for where the taking of property is resorted to with a view to completing "such fundamental changes of a country's constitutional system as the transition from monarchy to republic" '.[121] Accordingly, the present position is close to what the British probably would have accepted in 1950, had it been spelled out explicitly at that time: that is, there is a general principle that compensation must be paid to nationals as well as aliens, but it is open to the State to justify a departure from the principle.

A second question is whether the imposition of a monetary liability is an interference with possessions. Plainly, an individual may find it necessary to

---

[114] *James v United Kingdom*, Series A No 98 (1986) 8 EHRR 123.
[115] See p 131 below.
[116] (1960) 3 *Yearbook of the European Convention on Human Rights* 394, 423–24.
[117] *Sporrong and Lönnroth v Sweden*, Series A No 52 (1983) 5 EHRR 35 [73].
[118] *Lithgow* (n 20) [120]; see also *James* (n 20) [54].
[119] *Lithgow*, above [121]; *James*, above.
[120] Reports 2000–XII (2001) 33 EHRR 21 (merits), (2003) 36 EHRR CD43 (just satisfaction).
[121] Above [78] (the reference is to para 87 of the judgment on the merits).

liquidate assets to satisfy a liability; indeed, it is often the case that assets may be seized and sold to satisfy a liability. While the seizure of the assets would be an interference with the enjoyment of possessions, the liability itself is distinct from those assets. Consequently, it could be argued that, although an imposition of a tax or other financial liability may result in an interference with possessions, the imposition itself is not an interference with those possessions.

The final version of P1(1) does not provide a clear answer. The second paragraph only refers to the enforcement of laws to 'secure' the payment of taxes, and not to the imposition of taxes or other penalties. While it was intended that a tax imposed simply to confiscate specific possessions would be treated as an interference with those possessions, the question of taxes or other liabilities in more general terms was not raised.

References to the enforcement and imposition of financial liabilities first appeared in the British draft submitted to the Committee of Experts. As it only referred to 'the right of a State to enforce such laws as it deems necessary . . . *to secure* the payment of monies due whether by way of taxes or otherwise',[122] it may have been intended to distinguish between the imposition of taxes and other liabilities and their enforcement. In any case, the draft clause was plainly intended to exclude the securing of payment from the scope of P1(1), and not to include it; hence, it was probably assumed that the imposition of taxes would also lie outside P1(1) (except possibly in the case of a tax intended to confiscate all the individual's possessions). This was the position under rights to property found in colonial constitutions, which were framed in terms of deprivations, takings or compulsory acquisitions of property.[123] Similarly, the seizure of property in execution of a civil judgment or a criminal penalty was thought to come within the strict interpretation of the constitutional rights to property, and hence drafters of constitutions often included specific exceptions to insulate them from constitutional review. However, exceptions were not made for the imposition of the liability itself, as this was assumed not to be a deprivation of property.[124]

Whether the British drafters assumed that such distinctions would apply under the Protocol is not clear. However, the Belgian proposal that followed shows that many delegates believed that both the imposition and the enforcement of tax laws against property would be treated as an interference with the enjoyment of possessions, as the third sentence of this proposal provided that the right to property 'shall not however infringe, in any way, the right of a State to pass legislation to control the use of property in accordance with the general interest *or to impose taxes or other contributions.*'[125]

As explained above, the wording of this proposal was initially agreed by the Committee of Experts,[126] but it later decided to adopt another British proposal.

[122] Quoted above, text to n 92 (emphasis added).
[123] Allen (n 75) 185, 228–31.
[124] Above 45–82 *passim* (although *cf* the cases cited above p 185).
[125] Quoted above, text to n 96 (emphasis added).
[126] Above vol 7, 300, 304.

It returned to the original British formula, which eventually became the text of the second paragraph of P1(1). No comment was made on the shift between enforcing and imposing financial liabilities, and the Secretariat-General's Commentary on the draft states merely that the last sentence was expanded for greater clarity.[127] Indeed, as long as the second paragraph was read solely as an exclusion of certain types of interference from the right to property, it would have made little difference: as stated above, it was probably thought that the imposition of liability lay outside P1(1) in any event, and so an express reference to it would have been redundant. However, with the *Sporrong* case, it became clear that the second paragraph should not be read purely as an exclusionary clause.[128] The principles of legality and proportionality apply to the paragraph, with the effect that a measure to 'secure the payment of taxes' may breach P1(1). This therefore makes the issue of the imposition of taxes problematic. Is it really the case that, as the British probably assumed, imposing taxes or other liabilities is not an interference with property?

This question has arisen in a few cases, and the position is now clear that an imposition of a tax or other monetary liability is an interference with possessions, although the point has never been examined closely. In *Gudmundsson*,[129] it was assumed that taxation fell under P1(1); in *X v The Netherlands*,[130] social security contributions also fell under P1(1); and, as explained in chapter 9, it has never really been doubted that the imposition of a criminal fine also comes under P1(1). In *Darby v Sweden*, a case involving Article 14 in combination with P1(1),[131] the Court stated that the imposition of a tax was an interference with the enjoyment of possessions. Its explanation was limited to the statement that the second paragraph of P1(1) 'establishes that the duty to pay tax falls within its field of application.'[132] Then, in *Gasus Dosier und Fordertechnik GmbH v Netherlands*, the Court distinguished between a 'procedural tax law' regulating the enforcement of taxation and a 'substantive tax law', which it described as a law laying down the circumstances under which tax is due and the amounts payable; it stated that procedural laws are within P1(1) but it left open the question of the treatment of a substantive tax law.[133] This is the closest that the Court has come to examining the question as a matter of principle, and subsequently, in *Špaček v The Czech Republic*,[134] the Court assumed implicitly

---

[127] Above vol 8, 10–11 (the English version seems incomplete; compare with the French: 'La dernière phrase du texte de l'Assemblée a été quelque peu développée de façon à préciser que cet article ne porte pas atteinte au driot de l'Etat de percevoir des impôts ou d'autres pénalités, telles que des amendes, même s'ils représentent la totalité des biens de la personne en question.')

[128] *Sporrong* (n 117); see Chapter 4, 102–7.

[129] Gudmundsson (n 116).

[130] (1971) 14 *Yearbook of the European Convention on Human Rights* 224.

[131] Series A No 187 (1991) 13 EHRR 774 (a Finnish citizen who worked in Sweden objected to a change in Swedish laws which required him to pay full church taxes without the exemptions that were available to Swedish residents).

[132] Above [30] (no further justification was offered).

[133] Series A No 306–B (1995) 20 EHRR 403 [60].

[134] (2000) 30 EHRR 1010.

that the assessment of tax under Czech laws could be examined under P1(1). In this case, the applicant claimed that certain tax regulations had not been issued in accordance with the appropriate lawmaking procedures in the Czech Republic; in effect, it argued that the principle of legality had been infringed and consequently that there had been an infringement of P1(1). It appears, therefore, that the desire to apply overarching principles relating to discrimination and legality that led the Court to conclude that it would review laws imposing taxes, despite the conceptual distinctions between liabilities and property rights.[135]

SUBSEQUENT DEVELOPMENTS IN THE UNITED KINGDOM

The optional clauses

Before the enactment of the Human Rights Act 1998, the most significant development in the implementation of the Convention in the United Kingdom was the adoption of the optional clauses providing for the right of individual petition[136] and the compulsory jurisdiction[137] of the European Court of Human Rights. On the insistence of several countries (including the United Kingdom), these clauses had been made optional, and the United Kingdom did not accept them immediately. However, in late 1965, Prime Minister Wilson announced that the Government had decided to accept the optional clauses. After long discussions amongst ministers and senior civil servants, the United Kingdom gave notice of its acceptance of the optional clauses.[138]

As Lord Lester has shown, the Government delayed the United Kingdom's acceptance for several reasons.[139] One of its chief concerns was the possibility that Burmah Oil might rely on the right of individual petition to challenge the War Damage Act 1965. It was uncertain how the European Court would judge such a case: the policy to provide rehabilitation rather than compensation

---

[135] In addition to the cases cited above, see *WASA Ömsesidigt, Försäkringsbolaget Valands Pensionsstiftelse v Sweden*, Appl 13013/87, 14 December 1988; *Langborger v Sweden*, Series A No 155 (1990) 12 EHRR 416 [41]; *Finkelberg v Latvia*, Appl No 55091/00, 18 October 2001; *Aston Cantlow and Wilmcote with Billesley Parochial Church Council v Wallbank*, [2002] Ch 51 (reversed by [2004] 1 AC 546); *Jokela v Finland*, Reports 2002–IV 1 (2003) 37 EHRR 26. But *cf Van der Mussele v Belgium*, Series A No 70 (1984) 6 EHRR 163 [49], where the Court seemed to regard the imposition of a duty that involved a financial outlay as entirely outside P1–1. In this case, Belgian law required pupil barristers (avocats) to provide pro bono services which could involve personal expenditure. The Court held that there had been no violation of P1–1, on the basis that 'In many cases, a duty prescribed by law involves a certain outlay for the person bound to perform it. To regard the imposition of such a duty as constituting in itself an interference with possessions for the purposes of Article 1 of Protocol No. 1 (P1–1) would be giving the Article a far-reaching interpretation going beyond its object and purpose.'

[136] Article 25.

[137] Article 46.

[138] (1966) 9 *Yearbook of the European Convention on Human Rights*, 8 and 14.

[139] See A Lester 'UK Acceptance of the Strasbourg Jurisdiction: What Really Went On in Whitehall in 1965' [1998] *Public Law* 237; see also Simpson (n 46) ch 20.

would probably survive a challenge, given the nature of the public interest at stake,[140] the scale of the claims being made[141] and the continuity of official policy on the issue.[142] However, the interference with ongoing litigation might have been more difficult to justify.[143] In any case, the final acceptance was effective after the Act came into force, and so the threat of an adverse decision was avoided.

Human Rights Act 1998

The right to property did not figure in the discussions on the Human Rights Act 1998 to the same extent that it did in 1949–50 or 1965–66: by the late 1990s, there was a sufficient body of case law on property to show that the Human Rights Act 1998 would not require wholesale changes in British law to accommodate P1(1).[144] This has largely proved correct, although a series of judgments delivered by the Court of Appeal in 2001–02, in *Wilson v First County Trust*,[145] *Aston Cantlow and Wilmcote with Billesley Parochial Church Council v Wallbank*,[146] *Marcic v Thames Water Utilities Ltd*,[147] *International Transport Roth GmbH v Secretary of State for the Home Department*[148] and *Lindsay v Commissioners of Customs and Excise*[149] suggested that the implementation of P1(1) under the Human Rights Act 1998 would have a more dramatic impact. However, the House of Lords heard appeals in *Wilson*,[150] *Marcic*[151]and *Aston Cantlow*,[152] and in all three cases it indicated that the courts should take a much more conservative line on P1(1).

The rest of the book examines the emerging property jurisprudence in detail, but before closing this chapter, it is worth returning to some points made at outset. In particular, to what extent have human rights principles taken the place of fundamental law in the unwritten constitution?[153] Plainly, the Human Rights

---

[140] See eg *Former King of Greece* (n 120); *James* (n 20).

[141] *Lithgow* (n 20).

[142] See *United States v Caltex (Phillipines)* 344 US 149 (1952), where the opposite position was taken.

[143] Although *cf National & Provincial* (n 7).

[144] A number of cases from the European Court of Justice confirm this position: see E Drewniak, 'Comment: The *Bosphorus* Case: The Balancing of Property Rights in the European Community and the Public Interest in Ending the War in Bosnia' (1997) 20 *Fordham International Law Journal* 1007.

[145] [2002] QB 74.

[146] [2002] Ch 51.

[147] [2002] QB 929.

[148] [2003] QB 728.

[149] [2002] 1 WLR 1766.

[150] [2004] 1 AC 816 (sub nom *Wilson v Secretary of State for Trade and Industry*).

[151] [2004] 2 AC 42.

[152] [2004] 1 AC 546 (although primarily on the public authority point).

[153] See generally D Nicol, 'The Human Rights Act and the Politicians' (2004) 24 *Legal Studies* 451 and D Nicol, 'Are Convention Rights a No-go Zone for Parliament?' [2002] *Public Law* 438.

Act 1998 strengthens the judicial power over the legislature and executive. Sections 3 and 6 of the Act are at least as effective in upholding human rights as the principles of statutory interpretation were in upholding fundamental law. Other provisions—especially sections 4, 7 and 8—provide the courts with powers that they did not previously have. However, as is well-known, the courts do not have full review powers. The 1998 Act preserves Parliamentary supremacy and, in relation to the executive, the judgments of the House of Lords in *Wilson*, *Marcic*, *Aston Cantlow* and *Alconbury*[154] indicate that the executive has a broad area of discretion in relation to the policy-making and the regulation of property rights. The effect is to leave a substantial area of Parliamentary and administrative decision-making outside the scope of judicial review. Within this area, do human rights principles still operate as effective constraints on State power?

It will be recalled that fundamental law had had some impact on Parliament, although imprecise and uncertain. The 1998 Act was intended to have human rights issues aired in the preparation of Bills for Parliament. Section 19 requires the Minister in charge of a Bill to make a statement either that the Bill's provisions are compatible with the Convention rights, or that he or she is unable to make a statement of compatibility but the government nevertheless wishes the House to proceed with the Bill. The Parliamentary Joint Committee on Human Rights also considers matters relating to human rights in the United Kingdom, and its remit includes the scrutiny of Bills for compatibility with the Convention rights. As discussed below, some of its reports have been very critical of clauses that are, in its opinion, incompatible with P1-1.

In this sense, the previously vague and uncertain methods of elucidating fundamental law have been replaced by a more rigorous approach, as Parliament and the government may now draw on the domestic and European case law on Convention rights. Nevertheless, it is significant that this content is ultimately determined by the courts: Parliament's role in developing the right to property through its own procedures has been virtually eliminated. The debates and analysis are limited to determining whether the courts would find statutory provisions incompatible with Convention rights.

The most interesting example of the scope of Parliamentary consideration of human rights and property occurred in the exchanges between the Joint Committee and the Home Office over the Proceeds of Crime Bill.[155] The details of the Proceeds of Crime Act 2002 are discussed in Chapter 9;[156] at this point, it is the way in which the Home Office gathered and assessed evidence pertinent to human rights issues that is relevant. The Bill was intended to allow confiscation and civil recovery orders to be executed against the family home, thereby creating a potential conflict with Article 8 (and with P1(1), if the innocent family member has a property interest in the home). In the Joint Committee's first

---

[154] [2003] 2 AC 295.
[155] See generally D Feldman, 'Parliamentary Scrutiny of Legislation and Human Rights' [2002] *Public Law* 323.
[156] Chapter 9, 275–80.

report on the Bill, it asked why special protection was not going to be available for the home in England and Wales and Northern Ireland, as it was going to be available in Scotland.[157] The Home Office agreed that the enforcement of a confiscation might require the sale of a family home, but asserted that 'The need to ensure that criminals do not retain the benefit of their offending outweighs the interests of innocent family members in staying in their home.'[158] It also referred to clauses that would provide family members with some protection, such as the opportunity to buy out the defendant's interest in the home. No other evidence was provided.

The Joint Committee responded to the Home Office's claims as follows:

> . . . the Government's assertion that 'the public interest in preventing and detecting crime outweighs the loss suffered by the family' is very generalized. There may be many cases in which the assertion would be correct, although the Government has not offered any examples or referred us to empirical studies to support their claim as a general sociological proposition. Under ECHR Article 8, more than an unsupported assertion of this kind is required to justify authorizing an interference with the family home. Besides serving a legitimate aim under Article 8(2), the public authority seeking to interfere must show that the interference is necessary in a democratic society for that purpose, that is that it is a proportionate response to a pressing social need for action. In our view, the Government has offered no relevant or compelling *evidence* to support their claim that the interference would be justified.[159]

The issue arose again in the Parliamentary debates, but without further elaboration from Ministers as to the reasoning that led to the position expressed in the Home Office's memorandum. In the House of Commons, the Parliamentary Under-Secretary of State for the Home Department (Mr Bob Ainsworth) discussed the Bill, but went no further than the Memorandum from the Home Office.[160] In the House of Lords, Lord Rooker (Minister of State, Home Office) stated that

> To show that an element of principle is involved in both approaches, I should add that we have examined all three parts from the point of view of the European Convention on Human Rights. We are satisfied that the approaches are consistent with that convention. While Article 8 of the convention protects a person's home, that right must be balanced by virtue of paragraph 2 of Article 8 against other factors; in this instance the public interest in ensuring that criminals do not retain the benefits from their crimes. Nor do we see an arguable case under Article 14 of the convention over that issue.[161]

[157] Third Report of the Joint Committee on Human Rights (HL Paper (2001–02) No 43, HC Paper (2001–02) No 405) [27]; now see Proceeds of Crime Act 2002, s 98, which only applies to Scotland.

[158] See the Memorandum from the Home Office, published in the Eleventh Report of the Joint Committee on Human Rights (HL Paper (2001–02) No 75, HC Paper (2001–02) No 475, Appendix) [20].

[159] Eleventh Report of the Joint Committee on Human Rights (HL Paper (2001–02) No 75, HC Paper (2001–02) No 475) [14].

[160] *Hansard* HC Deb vol 380 col 586–628 (26 February 2002).

[161] *Hansard* HL Deb vol 634 col 53 (22 April 2002).

There was no further detail on the reasoning behind this statement, with the end result that there is no reasoned explanation for the position reached by the Home Office. It had, apparently, considered the position under the Convention, but as its analysis appears to be based solely on the clauses of the Bill and the balance struck by those clauses, it did not rely on evidence that would not have been available to the courts, or indeed to any other decision-maker. Moreover, there is no sense that the Home Office looked to anything more than the judicial response to the clauses as an appropriate yardstick for measuring compliance with human rights standards. Neither can it be said that the analysis in Parliament was more detailed than a judicial analysis would be. While the Joint Committee called for better evidence, this point was not taken up by the Home Office Ministers or other Members of Parliament in the debates in either House. In that sense, the Convention has not entered the British constitutional system in the way that fundamental law did: that is, from this one example, there is no evidence that the Convention rights provide a principled constraint on either Parliament or the executive beyond the purely legal constraint imposed by the courts.[162] Hence, while the legal constraints have become stronger, the extra-legal, ethical constraints have declined.

CONCLUSIONS

This review of the background to P1(1) demonstrates just how poorly drafted it is. Some of the defects are due to sloppy work under constraints of time; others were the result of weak compromises to find some common ground for agreement. Even so, it appears that it was not always clear precisely what it was that was being left unclear. Nevertheless, it has been over fifty years since P1(1) came into force and over forty years since the first decision on P1(1) was given by the Commission. In that time, the multitude of decisions and judgments of the Commission and Court have ironed out many of these gaps and inconsistencies. Indeed, as the rest of this book shows, the case law has given P1(1) a scope and structure that is largely independent of original intentions of the parties to the Protocol. To some extent, it has been the presence of the technical problems that has justified the judicial reconstruction of the right to property.

In the United Kingdom, it seems that the legal implementation of P1(1) by the courts will probably not go significantly further than the Strasbourg jurisprudence. Arguably, the Court of Appeal was beginning to develop an independent jurisprudence on property rights in its 2002 judgments, but the response of the House of Lords indicates that judicial activism in this regard is not to be encouraged. These judicial developments are examined in greater detail elsewhere in

---

[162] See Nicol (2004), above, n 153, p 475–79 for a careful analysis of the current positions taken in Parliament by the different political parties.

the book, but it is interesting that the conservativism seems to be reflected in extent to which human rights have become a part of all decision-making by Parliament and the executive. As of yet, there is little indication that human rights will acquire an extra-legal dimension as a set of ethical principles guiding the exercise of sovereign power.

2

The Applicability of the Right to Property

WHERE AN APPLICANT claims that a Convention right has been breached, the court must first determine whether the right is applicable to the facts or, as it is often put, whether the right is engaged. Under Article 1 of Protocol No 1 (P1(1)), this means that the court must decide whether the applicant has suffered an interference with the 'enjoyment of its possessions'. This issue is the focus of this chapter, with the first section of this chapter examining the meaning of 'possessions', and the second examining the idea of an 'interference' with the enjoyment of possessions.

Before investigating the interpretation of an interference with the 'enjoyment of possessions', it is worth examining the function of the applicability doctrine within the overall structure of P1(1). The crucial observation is that applicability only operates as a filter to screen out cases where the State's actions require no justification. As such, the function of applicability under P1(1) differs sharply from its function under many constitutional laws. For example, under the takings clause of the Fifth Amendment to the Constitution of the United States,[1] a finding that there has been a taking of private property for public use necessarily leads to the conclusion that compensation must be paid. In that context, applicability leads to liability, and hence the interpretation of the terms that define the right to property ('taking', 'private property', 'public use') carries a significance that it does not have under P1(1). Under P1(1), a generous view of applicability does not necessarily extend the State's obligations or enhance the protection of property, except in the limited sense that it extends the circumstances in which the State can be called upon to justify its actions. In effect, it does not restrict the State's power over property, but it does restrict the extent of the State's unreviewable powers over property.

The European Court has been more inclined to require States to justify their actions than not, and hence it has tended to take an expansive view of the

---

[1] The Fifth Amendment provides that 'No person shall be . . . deprived of . . . property, without due process of law; nor shall private property be taken for public use, without just compensation.'

applicability of P1(1). This can be seen in the rejection of a formal or legalistic interpretation of an interference with the 'enjoyment of possessions'. For example, a strict interpretation of 'possessions' would probably restrict it to rights of property arising under the private law of the relevant member State. Similarly, there would be no 'interference' with the 'enjoyment' of those rights without a compulsory transfer, extinction or modification of those rights. However, the Court has developed the 'autonomous meaning' doctrine to apply P1(1) to interests that would not be classified as property under private law and, in any case, it has held that P1(1) may be applicable even where there is no direct impact on property rights. This shifts the focus in most cases to the principles of justification (especially proportionality). Nevertheless, the question of applicability is still important. The Court has decided cases solely on basis that the applicant's complaint does not relate to anything recognised as a possession by the Court, or that there was no interference with a recognised possession. Accordingly, this chapter will first examine the meaning of an 'enjoyment of possessions', including the development of the autonomous meaning doctrine, before considering the meaning of an 'interference' with the enjoyment of possessions.

THE 'ENJOYMENT OF POSSESSIONS'

It is clear that P1(1) was formulated with very little concern for precision. It refers to 'possessions' in its first and second sentences and to 'property' in the third sentence. In addition, the first sentence refers to the '*enjoyment* of possessions' as opposed to the '*use* of property' in the third sentence. The French version uses *biens* in the first sentence, *propriété* in the second, and then *biens* again in the third, unlike the English version, which uses the same term ('possessions') in the first and second sentences. Moreover, the term 'possessions' is not generally used in the common law; indeed, in most common law constitutions, it is 'property' that usually carries a comprehensive meaning.[2] However, it is clear that P1(1) uses 'possessions' as the general term for all types of proprietary interests,[3] and despite the references to the 'enjoyment' and 'use' of possessions and

---

[2] See T Allen, *The Right to Property in Commonwealth Constitutions* (CUP, Cambridge, 2000) ch 5; see also the comments of Mr Roberts, a UK member of the Consultative Assembly of the Council of Europe, on proposed drafts of P1–1: 'The word "possessions", used in the English text, is not a really satisfactory word . . .. It is a word that would not be found in a British Act of Parliament or any other legal document' (Council of Europe, *Collected edition of the 'Travaux Préparatoires' of the European Convention on Human Rights: Recueil des Travaux Préparatoires de la Convention Européenne des Droits de l'Homme* (M Nijhoff, The Hague, 1975–85), vol 6, p 88).

[3] *Gasus Dosier und Fordertechnik GmbH v The Netherlands*, Series A No 306–B (1995) 20 EHRR 403.

property, P1(1) applies to all rights of property, including the rights to acquire and dispose of property.[4]

In most cases, the Court has been content to accept the position under the relevant national law. That is, if national law classifies an interest as a property interest, the Court is unlikely to find that the applicant does not have P1(1) possessions.[5] Indeed, the Court's initial position on applicability was fairly restrictive, as shown by the 1979 case, *Marckx v Belgium*.[6] This case centred on Belgian rules which denied illegitimate children the right to share in a parent's estate to the same extent as a legitimate child. On behalf of an illegitimate child, it was argued that these rules breached Article 14, and since this was tied to P1(1), it was necessary to show to show that the child had 'possessions' under P1(1). However, the Court held that the child did not hold possessions as long as her mother was still alive because, under Belgian law, rights in a parent's estate do not vest until the parent dies. The Court stated that P1(1) 'does no more than enshrine the right of everyone to the peaceful enjoyment of "his" possessions,' and 'consequently it applies only to a person's existing possessions and . . . does not guarantee the right to acquire possessions whether on intestacy or through voluntary dispositions.'[7]

The formal approach of distinguishing between vested rights and the mere hope of acquiring a property right was confirmed in *Inze v Austria*,[8] which concerned a claim of an illegitimate child to the estate of a deceased parent. Under Austrian law, illegitimate children took a joint, vested share in the estate with the legitimate children, but in some circumstances a legitimate child would have a higher ranking claim to certain assets than an illegitimate child.[9] On these

---

[4] See *Inze v Austria*, Series A No 126 (1988) 10 EHRR 394 and *Marckx v Belgium*, Series A No 31 (1979) 2 EHRR 330 [63]: 'By recognising that everyone has the right to the peaceful enjoyment of his possessions, Article 1 (P1–1) is in substance guaranteeing the right of property' and 'the right to dispose of one's property constitutes a traditional and fundamental aspect of the right of property'; *cf* the dissenting opinion of Sir Gerald Fitzmaurice in *Marckx* (at n 8):

> The apparent interchangeability of the terms 'possessions', 'property', '*biens*' and '*propriété*' in different contexts and without evident reason is confusing. The French '*biens*' is best translated into English by 'assets' not 'possessions'. But the best French rendering of the English 'assets' is '*avoirs*'. In addition, there is no really satisfactory French equivalent of 'possessions' as such, and in the plural. These anomalies of translation add to the difficulties. But they also thereby reduce the value of the Court's interpretation.

[5] *Papastavrou v Greece*, Appl No 46372/99, 10 April 2003; *Katsoulis v Greece*, 66742/01, 8 July 2004; *Broniowski* v *Poland*, Appl No 31443/96, 22 June 2004 (Grand Chamber). This includes rights under European Community law: *Dangeville SA v France*, Reports 2002–III 71 (2004) 38 EHRR 32 (but see 58–61 below on claims for the restoration of property).

[6] Series A No 31 (1979–80) 2 EHRR 330.

[7] Above [50]; it appears, however, that the applicant daughter's case was not based on P1(1) (singly or in combination with Article 14). *Marckx* was applied in *Tamar v Turkey*, Appl No 15614/02, 13 May 2004 to a claim to share in deceased mother's estate, but with no comment as to the status of the claim in Turkish law.

[8] Series A No 126 (1988) 10 EHRR 394.

[9] However, rules intended to prevent the dissolution of farms provided that the eldest legitimate child had a prior right to inherit the farm, on the condition that he or she paid off the other heirs.

facts, the Court distinguished *Marckx*, on the basis that the illegitimate child did not have a possession in that case.[10] Hence, the priority given to legitimate children in *Inze* could be challenged under Article 14.

Marckx and *Inze* suggest that there can be no P1(1) possessions unless rights of property have vested under national law. However, in earlier cases on other Convention rights, the Court declared its willingness to adopt its own 'autonomous' meanings of certain terms used in the Convention. In 1968, it held that the meaning of 'criminal charge' in Article 6 was not determined solely by the national law of the State, but should be interpreted 'within the meaning of the Convention'.[11] In 1971, the Court extended the doctrine to the interpretation of 'civil rights and obligations' under Article 6.[12] However, it was not until 1995 that the Court applied the doctrine to the interpretation of 'possessions'. In *Gasus Dosier-Und Fördertechnik GmbH v Netherlands*,[13] the applicant claimed that the Dutch tax authorities had infringed P1(1) by seizing goods belonging to him. He had delivered the goods to a Dutch buyer under a contract which provided that property would not pass until payment. Before the buyer made the payment, the tax authorities seized the goods to satisfy the buyer's tax debts. The applicant argued that the seizure amounted to a deprivation of his possessions contrary to the second sentence of P1(1).[14] However, the Dutch government argued that the retention of title clause only gave the applicant a 'security right in rem' rather than 'true' ownership under Dutch law, as only the purchaser held 'true' or 'economic' ownership; hence, it claimed that there had been no deprivation of 'possessions'.[15]

The Court did not agree, as it stated that:

> "possessions" . . . has an autonomous meaning which is certainly not limited to ownership of physical goods: certain other rights and interests constituting assets can also be regarded as "property rights", and thus as "possessions", for the purposes of this provision P1(1).[16]

---

[10] *Inze* (n 10) [38].

[11] See *Neumeister v Austria (No 1)*, Series A No 8 (1968), (1979–80) 1 EHRR 91; see also *Wemhoff v Germany*, Series A No 7 (1968), (1979–80) 1 EHRR 55; *Engel v The Netherlands (No1)*, Series A No 22 (1979–80) 1 EHRR 647.

[12] *Ringeisen v Austria (No 1)*, Series A No 13 (1971), (1979–80) 1 EHRR 455.

[13] Above (n 3). Although *Gasus* is the first case to refer explicitly to the autonomous meaning doctrine in relation to possessions, in *James v The United Kingdom*, Series A No 98 (1986) 8 EHRR 123 [42], the Court stated that the meaning of 'in the public interest' in the second sentence of P1(1) has an autonomous meaning. In *Tre Traktörer Aktiebolag v Sweden*, Series A No 159 (1991) 13 EHRR 309 [53], the Court did not say that it was adopting an autonomous meaning of possessions, although it concluded that a licence to sell alcohol was a P1(1) possession, although it appears that it would not have been classified as a property interest under national (Swedish) law. See also *Van Marle v The Netherlands*, Series A No 101 (1986) 8 EHRR 483, where a prohibition on the use of the title 'accountant' was an interference with possessions, although under Dutch law it was doubtful that either the right to use the title, or the business goodwill to which it related, were P1(1) possessions.

[14] Ultimately, the Court found that the third sentence applied to this case, and concluded that no compensation was necessary to satisfy P1(1).

[15] *Gasus* (n 3) [52].

[16] Above [53].

It was therefore not conclusive that the rights held under the retention of title clause would not be classified as an ownership interest under Dutch law.[17]

Although *Gasus* opens the door to the development of an autonomous conception of property, the Court did not suggest that *Marckx* and *Inze* were incorrect. Indeed, as discussed below, the technical approach evident in *Marckx* and *Inze* is still seen in most cases.[18] In addition, the idea that P1(1) is not an instrument for conferring entitlements or redistributing wealth remains a concern of the Court. Even on its facts, the *Gasus* decision is actually more significant as an illustration of the procedural flexibility of the Court than it is as an illustration of the autonomous meaning doctrine. That is, the applicant argued its case on the basis that the interference was a deprivation of possessions under the second sentence (which would normally require compensation).[19] Accordingly, the Dutch government sought to rebut this argument by concentrating on the specific point that there had been no deprivation of possessions, thereby avoiding the more general point that there had been no interference with the enjoyment of possessions.[20] However, the Court classified the seizure as a taxation measure, under the third sentence of P1(1) (which is less restrictive of State power). Under some constitutional systems, a similar failure to argue a right to property case under the correct point would have resulted in a dismissal of the property holder's case.[21] However, the Court plainly believed that it could, and should, deal with the case under a different aspect of P1(1) without dismissing it outright. While this shows that the autonomous meaning doctrine actually had little importance in *Gasus*, the case is nevertheless significant as establishing that the doctrine would apply to P1(1), and more specifically, to the interpretation of 'possessions'.

This raises two broad questions. The first asks how far the autonomous meaning doctrine extends the applicability of P1(1). To be more precise, what counts as a 'possession' under P1(1)? From *Gasus*, it is clear that the Court will apply the applicability doctrine to the classification of rights already recognised under national law. In such cases, the autonomous meaning doctrine has a limited and specific application, as it does not purport to find vested rights where none exist under national law. It would allow the Court to say that, for example, a bundle of rights classified as a non-proprietary interest under national law amounts to a P1(1) possession, but it would not allow the Court to say that someone who holds no rights, personal or proprietary, has a P1(1) possession.[22] Arguably, *Gasus* only suggests that the doctrine allows the Court

---

[17] The Court held that, although there was an interference with the applicant's possessions, the interference could be justified: above [60]–[74].

[18] See below 61–64.

[19] See Chapter 7.

[20] *Gasus* (n 3), [56], [58] (although the Dutch Government also argued that there had been no possessions: see [52]).

[21] See eg *Tahoe–Sierra Preservation Council, Inc v Tahoe Regional Planning Agency* 535 US 302 (2002).

[22] See eg *Iatridis v Greece*, Reports 1999–II 75 (2000) 30 EHRR 97; *Van Marle* (n 13).

to determine whether existing rights have the character of 'possessions' under P1(1), but no more than that.

The second raises a more general question: what function does the doctrine serve in relation to P1(1)? While *Gasus* shows that the Court believes that the autonomous meaning doctrine is applicable to P1(1), it does not tell us why. In the Article 6 cases, it was clear that the Court was concerned that a State might seek to limit its obligations by exploiting the differences in the legal systems of member States. In *König v Germany*, the Court stated that 'civil rights' should be given an autonomous meaning because 'any other solution might lead to results incompatible with the object and purpose of the Convention'[23] and in *Öztürk v Germany*, the Court stated that, in relation 'criminal charges',

> if the Contracting States were able at their discretion, by classifying an offence as 'regulatory' instead of criminal, to exclude the operation of the fundamental clauses of Articles 6 and 7, the application of these provisions would be subordinated to their sovereign will. A latitude extending thus far might lead to results incompatible with the object and purpose of the Convention.[24]

Plainly, States cannot be permitted to circumvent their Convention obligations simply by re-labelling existing criminal processes, civil rights or private property so as to put them outside the Convention. There are no cases where a State has so openly tried to avoid its obligations under P1(1); however, the emphasis on avoiding results 'incompatible with the object and purpose of the Convention' suggests that the autonomous meaning doctrine may be invoked in other circumstances as well. For example, under Article 6, the Court has said that the meaning of 'criminal charge' under Article 6 should reflect the common standards of the Contracting States. Accordingly, the Court does not rely solely on an abstract conception of criminality or the criminal process to define 'criminal charge', but acts partly on its observations of the practices of other Contracting States.[25] When it does so, it is not passing judgement on the justifiability of the common practice, as it does not state that certain kinds of conduct should or should not be decriminalised. Instead, it merely observes whether the processes by which States deal with the case resemble the criminal process. As such, the interpretation of 'criminal charge' is intended to reflect the common standards of the member States.

This approach was taken by the European Commission in *Gasus*, as it looked to comparative law to determine the nature of the seller's interest under a retention of title clause. As such, the approach is consistent with one of the original purposes of the European Convention, being 'the achievement of greater unity between its members', in part by 'the maintenance and further realisation of human rights and fundamental freedoms'.[26] In practice, however, the compara-

---

[23] *König v Germany (No 1)*, Series A No 27 (1976), (1979–80) 2 EHRR 170 [88].
[24] *Öztürk v Germany*, Series A No 73 (1984) 6 EHRR 409 [49].
[25] Above [49]–[53].
[26] Preamble to the Convention.

tive approach is used more by accident than design. Judges rely on conceptions of property derived from their own legal experience, and where those conceptions happen to coincide, the Court as a whole is inclined to reject the domestic law contrary to those conceptions. This is evident in *Frascino v Italy*,[27] where Italy argued that, since its national law did not recognise the right to construct buildings as one of the rights held by an owner of land, planning restrictions did not engage P1(1). This was not accepted by the Court, but with virtually no analysis. It appears that it took the view that, under the laws of other member States, an owner of land is normally entitled to broader rights of use than Italian law appeared to allow. The source of this 'normal' entitlement was not discussed, but it is likely that the individual judges found the Italian argument at odds with the position in their own systems. In that sense, the result may be consistent with a comparative analysis, but it is not truly a comparative method of analysis.

In any case, the securing of common standards is only one of the Convention's objects. Indeed, purposive interpretation may focus on objects specific to P1(1). For example, in many cases, the Court seems to regard P1(1) as a general protection for wealth, as it comes very close to limiting its interpretation of interference with the 'enjoyment of possessions' to acts or omissions which affect the individual economically. In *Krivonogova v Russia*, for example, the Court suggested that P1(1) is not applicable in the absence of some form of economic loss.[28] Similarly, in *Gaygusuz v Austria*,[29] the pecuniary nature of social welfare benefits was a material factor in the conclusion that they were P1(1) possessions. However, it is also clear that P1(1) can play a role in protecting individual autonomy and identity: in *Chassagnou v France*,[30] for example, legislation which forced the applicants to allow hunting on their property was not shown to cause them any economic harm, but it did undermine their own ethical objections to hunting. On this basis, the Court decided that France had violated P1(1).

Alternatively, the autonomous meaning could also take into account the place of P1(1) and property within the Convention and Protocols as a whole. In some cases, it is clear that the Court has not extended P1(1) because it feels that the facts would fit more comfortably under another Convention right. Examples can be seen in *Anderson v United Kingdom*[31] and *Appleby v United Kingdom*,[32] in which it was stated that a right of access to quasi-public property was not regarded as a P1(1) possession. In doing so, the Commission in *Anderson* suggested that the denial of access might constitute an interference with the right to liberty of movement, as reflected in Article 2 of the Fourth Protocol, which the

---

[27] Appl No 35227/97, 11 December 2003.
[28] Appl No 74694/01, 1 April 2004.
[29] *Gaygusuz v Austria*, Reports 1996–IV 1129 (1997) 23 EHRR 364.
[30] Reports 1999–III 21 (2000) 29 EHRR 615.
[31] (1998) 25 EHRR CD172.
[32] (2003) 37 EHRR 38.

United Kingdom has not ratified. The suggestion was that P1(1) would not be extended to cases that the United Kingdom might have chosen not to cover by not ratifying the Protocol.[33]

Finally, the autonomous meaning doctrine may have a more instrumental aspect, in the sense that it reflects the Court's own perception of its capacity to keep States to Convention standards. So, for example, the effectiveness of the Convention may relate to the need to resolve disputes over national law in a timely fashion. Accordingly, although the Court does not act as a court of fourth instance in matters of national law, it has applied the autonomous meaning doctrine in cases where title disputes in national law have remained unresolved for many years.[34] If the Court adjourned the case until the matter was resolved by the national courts, the Convention could be rendered ineffective. Or, the Court may feel that its limitations as a judicial body make it inappropriate to review certain types of governmental decisions. In *Gayduk and others v Ukraine*, for example, it held that P1(1) does not allow the Court to review a State's policy on reducing the impact of inflation on individuals, even where it appears that the State has bound itself to do so with specific individuals.[35] In such cases, it could invoke the margin of appreciation, but it could also use the applicability doctrine as a filtering device, by finding that the applicant did not hold 'possessions' or that, in any case, there has been no interference with the enjoyment of possessions.

Given the short life of the doctrine, it cannot be said that the doctrine is clearly used for one purpose only and no others. Indeed, any judicial tribunal, international or national, is likely to wish to assert at least some flexibility in determining the applicability of human rights, for any one of the reasons given above. The remaining sections of this chapter therefore attempt to bring out these issues, by discussing specific types of interests where it has considered whether the autonomous meaning doctrine should apply. We begin with the treatment of causes of action under P1(1).

Claims and causes of action

Whether a cause of action constitutes a possession has arisen in a number of cases. It is clear that intangibles such as a debt,[36] a share in a company[37] and a contractual right over property[38] are all treated as P1(1) possessions. By

---

[33] *Anderson* (n 31). See also *Vikulov v Latvia*, Appl No 16870/03, 25 March 2004; *Gribenko v Latvia*, Appl No 76878/01, 15 May 2003; cf *Loizidou v Turkey*, Reports 1996–VI 2216 (1997) 23 EHRR 513.

[34] Eg *Iatridis* (n 22); *Matos e Silva, lda v Portugal*, Reports 1996–IV 1092 (1997) 24 EHRR 573.

[35] Reports 2002-VI 405; see also *Appolonov v Russia*, Appl No 47578/01, 29 August 2002 and the dissenting opinion of Judge Vilhjálmsson in *Akkuş v Turkey*, Reports 1997-IV 1300 (2000) 30 EHRR 365 .

[36] *Stran Greek Refineries v Greece*, Series A No 301–B (1995) 19 EHRR 293.

[37] *Lithgow v The United Kingdom*, Series A No 102 (1986) 8 EHRR 329.

[38] *Gasus* (n 3) and *Wilson v Secretary of State for Trade and Industry* [2004] 1 AC 816.

contrast, there are no possessions in respect of income that may be earned in the future: the applicant must have a present right to the income for possessions to exist.[39] However, the status of other claims is not so clear. There have been a significant number of cases involving the extinction of civil claims brought against public bodies in the national courts. There is no real doubt that the final judgment would be a P1(1) possession, and hence the annulment of a judgment is an interference with possessions. However, it is not clear whether the extinction of the claim *before* the final judgment is also an interference with possessions. There may be a violation of Article 6, but in many of these cases the applicants also argue that there has been a violation of P1(1). A narrow approach (following *Marckx* and *Inze*) would suggest that there are no P1(1) possessions unless the cause of action is recognised as property in the national legal system, or (following *Gasus*) unless the cause of action has vested under national law, even if the cause of action is not recognised as property. Alternatively, a broad view of the autonomous meaning doctrine could extend 'possessions' at least some situations where the cause of action has not vested or acquired the character of property under national law. If so, the Court would look to alternative criteria to determine whether a P1(1) possession exists (such as the nature of the interest protected by the cause of action or the likelihood of success before the national courts).

None of these possibilities has been rejected; indeed, all have appeared in the cases at some point or another. Initially, the Court asked whether the applicant had obtained a final judgment on the merits before the national courts. This occurred in *Stran Greek Refineries v Greece*,[40] where the issue was first examined in detail. Here, the applicants had brought proceedings against the Greek government in the Greek courts in respect of a contract which had been terminated. In 1979, the Athens Court of First Instance issued a preliminary decision holding that the case should proceed to a full trial, without making any determination on the merits. In fact, the Government then took the dispute to arbitration. The applicants protested, but, in any case, a substantial award was made in their favour. The courts then upheld the arbitration award, but before a final appeal in the Court of Cassation could be heard, the Greek legislature passed a law which effectively annulled the arbitration award. The applicants

---

[39] See *Xenodochiaki SA v Greece*, Appl No 49213/99, 15 November 2001: legislation terminated a sublease previously granted by an applicant to a public agency, but the applicant obtained the property under a lease from another public body. Subsequently, the applicant was unsuccessful in proceedings for the rent following the termination. The Court held that P1(1) was not applicable to the claims for rent, because those constituted future income; oddly, it seems that the Court did not consider whether P1(1) was applicable to the termination itself. See also *Saggio v Italy*, Appl No 41879/98, 25 October 2001; *Sved v Finland*, Appl No 47131/99, 21 May 2002; *Manios v Greece*, Appl No 70626/01, 17 October 2002 and *Nerva v The United Kingdom*, Reports 2002–VIII 1 (2003) 36 EHRR 4: customers' tips were considered by the employer as remuneration for purpose of satisfying minimum wage laws, but since it was neither the expectation of the customers nor the employees that tips would be excluded from remuneration were incorporated in their contracts with the employer, P1(1) could not be applied so as to create such a contractual right.

[40] *Stran Greek* (n 36).

then proceeded to Strasbourg, where they claimed that they had been deprived of their possessions, either in the form of the arbitration award or the preliminary decision of the Athens Court of First Instance.

In Strasbourg, the Court indicated that the applicant had to show that proceedings 'had given rise to a debt in their favour that was sufficiently established to be enforceable'.[41] Arbitration awards are immediately enforceable under Greek law and no appeal is permitted on the merits; accordingly, the Court found that the awards were 'sufficiently established' to be 'possessions' under P1(1).[42] While this aspect of the decision is not controversial, the Court also suggested that there would have been no possessions in the absence of the arbitration award. In particular, the decision of the Athens Court of First Instance left the existence and extent of any damage to be determined. Hence, 'the effect of such a decision was merely to furnish the applicants with the hope that they would secure recognition of the claim put forward.'[43] This, it seems, was not sufficient to bring a P1(1) possession into existence.

Within a year, in *Pressos Compania Naviera SA and Others v Belgium*,[44] the Court appeared to relax the views expressed in *Stran Greek*. In 1983, an unexpected ruling of the Belgian Court of Cassation extended the State's liability in tort for shipping casualties; the Court of Cassation confirmed its ruling in 1985. Subsequently, legislation passed in 1988 retrospectively extinguished all pending and potential tort claims. Only cases that had been finally resolved by the courts were unaffected. The applicants, whose claims were retrospectively extinguished, claimed that they had been deprived of possessions contrary to P1(1). Belgium responded that P1(1) did not apply because none of the tort claims 'had been recognised and determined by a judicial decision having final effect',[45] and that the pending claims were no more than rights *to* property, rather than rights *of* property.[46] Therefore, as in *Marckx*, they were neither property under Belgian law nor 'possessions' under the Convention. The Commission agreed; however, the Court held that the pending tort claims were possessions (and ultimately that the extinction of the claims violated P1(1)).

The Court's position on Belgian law was somewhat ambiguous. It did say that, to determine if there is a 'possession', 'the Court may have regard to the domestic law in force at the time of the alleged interference'.[47] In this sense, the meaning of 'possessions' depends on national law. The Court noted that, under Belgian law, a victim of a tort acquires a claim for compensation as soon as the damage occurs. Although Belgian law does not classify a pending action as property, and the damages were yet to be quantified, it was more important that

[41] Above [59].
[42] Above [61]–[62]. (There was a breach of P1(1) in respect of the arbitration awards.)
[43] Above [60].
[44] *Pressos Compania Naviera SA v Belgium*, Series A No 332 (1996) 21 EHRR 301.
[45] Above [29].
[46] Above.
[47] Above [31].

the claim 'constituted an asset'.[48] In addition, the Court of Cassation judgments gave the applicants a ' "legitimate expectation" that claims deriving from the accidents in question would be determined in accordance with the general law of tort'.[49]

The *Pressos* judgment is significant because it appears to sweep aside the distinctions made in *Stran Greek* between final decisions based on the merits and other preliminary or procedural decisions. In addition, it also appears to develop a conceptual framework for determining whether P1(1) possessions exist. First, by referring to the tort claims as 'assets', it returns to the statement in the *Gasus* judgment that rights and interests 'constituting assets' may be regarded as P1(1) possessions. However, in *Gasus*, it was not explained whether an 'asset' is any thing of potential value or whether it must comprise recognised legal rights. The *Pressos* judgment offers further no clarification.[50]

Secondly, the Court in *Pressos* brought the idea of 'legitimate expectations' into play. Again, this idea had appeared in other P1(1) cases, although only in relation to representations by public authorities relating to future decisions affecting existing property interests. This is discussed further below,[51] but where the idea has arisen, the conduct that creates legitimate expectations does not create possessions: it relates to the exercise of State power over existing possessions, but that is all. However, in *Pressos*, the idea of legitimate expectations related to the strength of the claims, in the sense that the legal merits of the claims were sufficiently established that the victims would have expected to succeed if the legislature had not intervened. If so, the vesting of a recognised cause of action is enough to create P1(1) possessions.

The idea of legitimate expectations appears again in the judgment in *National & Provincial Building Society and others v United Kingdom*.[52] This case concerned intervention in proceedings in which the applicants claimed restitution of payments of a tax which had not been lawfully imposed, due to technical defects in the legislation.[53] The proceedings in the national courts were complex: although the tax provisions affected a number of building societies, the issues were first taken up in test cases brought by the Woolwich Building Society (with the support of other building societies, including the applicants). In the

---

[48] Above.
[49] Above.
[50] *Gasus* was not cited in *Pressos*.
[51] See below 67–70.
[52] Reports 1997–VII 2325 (1998) 25 EHRR 127.
[53] This concerned the application of transitional provisions of the Finance Act 1985 and associated regulations to the taxation of interest earned in building society accounts. These provisions created a 'gap period' in which interest was not taxable. The Treasury had not intended to allow the gap period and, pending a decision from the courts, it collected the tax during that period. The Woolwich Building Society successfully obtained a declaration that the legislation did not require the tax to be paid during the gap period; subsequently, it was also successful in obtaining an order for restitution of the amounts that it had paid. Other building societies then commenced claims for restitution of the amounts they had paid, but Parliament then extinguished their claims by the Finance Act 1991 and the Finance (No 2) Act 1992.

first set of proceedings, the House of Lords determined that the tax had been imposed unlawfully;[54] in the second, it allowed the Woolwich's claim for restitution of the money already paid.[55] The applicants commenced their own proceedings after the decision of the House of Lords in the first case, but before its decision in the second. At that point, Parliament enacted legislation making the tax lawful, with retrospective effect, thereby removing the applicants' right to restitution of the amounts already paid.[56]

As in *Pressos*, the applicants claimed that there had been a breach of P1(1). The Court held that, even if there had been an interference with possessions, it did not upset the fair balance. However, while it did not reach a firm conclusion on the applicability issue, it did express doubts that the applicants' claims amounted to P1(1) possessions. It reverted to the language of *Stran Greek*, as it observed that the applicants had not received final and enforceable judgments against the State when the claims were extinguished. It also observed that the applicants' writs were issued when the law on restitution was in a state of flux. Moreover, Parliament had already stated its intention to amend laws to correct the technical defects in the legislation.[57] Hence, the Court stated that the applicants did not have 'a legitimate expectation that Government would not seek Parliament's consent to adopt retrospective legislation to validate impugned Treasury Orders'.[58] For this reason, the Court doubted that the restitution claims constituted possessions.

The Court did not discuss the *Pressos* case in *National & Provincial*,[59] although there were similarities on the facts. In particular, the claims in both cases were legally sound, and would have succeeded in the absence of legislative intervention. The doctrinal distinction seems to lie in the effect of the emerging doctrine of legitimate expectations. However, it is not entirely clear how the doctrine applies, and it is therefore possible to extract several different conceptions of legitimate expectations that the Court may have in mind in these two cases, as set out below:

(1) It may refer only to the legal merits of the claim. By this reasoning, there is no legitimate expectation of recovery if the claim is not recognised in national law; in such cases, there are no P1(1) possessions. Conversely, an applicant with a legally sound claim would have P1(1) possessions, on the basis that it would have a legitimate expectation that the claim would be permitted to proceed through to judgment and enforcement. In effect, 'legitimate expectations' are

---

[54] *R v Inland Revenue Commissioners ex p Woolwich Equitable Building Society*, [1990] 1 WLR 1400, [1991] 4 All ER 92 (HL).

[55] *Woolwich Building Society v Inland Revenue Commissioners* [1993] AC 70.

[56] The legislation only applied to proceedings commenced after the Woolwich cases.

[57] By enacting earlier (though ineffective) legislation to remedy the gap.

[58] *National & Provincial* (n 52) [62]–[70]. See also *MA and 34 Others v Finland*, Appl No 27793/95, 10 June 2003; *Ogis–Institut Stanislas, Ogec St Pie X and Blanche de Castille v France*, Appl Nos 42219/98, 54563/00, 27 May 2004.

[59] It was referred to briefly in the summary of the applicants' argument ((n 52) [62]) and in the later tax case, *MA and 34 Others*, above.

simply a measure of the likelihood of the claim's success before the national courts.

Subsequent cases reveal that there is considerable support for concentrating solely on the legal merits of claims in determining whether the applicant has a P1(1) possession. Often, the Court does not put this in terms of legitimate expectations, but the emphasis on the legal merits is consistent with this approach. For example, it is clear that, at the very least, both the facts and the legal basis for the claim must be clearly established to constitute P1(1) possessions.[60]

Recently, the Grand Chamber in *Kopecký v Slovakia*[61] emphasised the formal, unconditional vesting of a cause of action as the constitutive event. This case concerned a claim to restitution of coins confiscated in 1959 as a result of a criminal conviction. The conviction and confiscation were quashed in 1992 and the applicant then claimed restitution of the coins. In cases where confiscations were quashed, Slovakian legislation required public officials to return movable property in response to a written request identifying the location of the property. In this case, the applicant could not say where the coins were, and indeed the authorities themselves could not find them. Consequently, his claim in the national courts failed. Before the European Court, he argued that his rights under P1(1) had been breached, either because the statutory condition on recovery was an interference with possessions, or because the State authorities had made it impossible for him to obtain the evidence needed to substantiate his claim.[62]

The Grand Chamber decided that the applicant had not acquired a vested right to the restitution of the coins, because he could not fulfil the statutory condition requiring him to identify their location. Accordingly, he had no P1(1) possessions. This overturned the judgment of the Fourth Section, where it was held that the quashing of the confiscation had re-established a clear property right to the coins, and the legislation merely imposed a procedure for their recovery.[63]

---

[60] The legal elements must be clear: see eg *Mentis v Greece*, Appl No 61351/00, 20 September 2001, where P1(1) was not applicable because there had been no judgment on the claim and there was no legitimate expectation of a successful judgment, given a series of contrary decisions in the Greek courts; and *Czerwinska v Poland*, Appl No 33828/96, 30 September 2003, where P1(1) was not applicable to a failure to honour a vague, general promise to raise pensions. In addition, facts must be established: *Spentzouris v Greece*, Appl No 47891/99, 31 May 2001; *Belaousof v Greece*, Appl No 66296/01, 28 February 2002; *Karabouyiouklou v Greece*, Appl No 63824/00, 6 February 2003; *Popovici and Dumitrescu v Romania*, Appl No 31549/96, 4 March 2003; *Kehagia v Greece*, Appl No 67115/01, 3 April 2003; *Deli Hatzoglou v Greece*, Appl No 67754/01, 3 April 2003. But *cf Dangeville SA* (n 5): the French courts held that the applicant did not have a remedy under French law, and yet the European Court of Human Rights held that the denial of the claim violated P1(1). It seems that the Strasbourg court decided that the French courts had failed to apply European Community law properly, with the result that P1(1) possessions conferred by Community law were not protected adequately under French law.

[61] Appl No 44912/98, 28 September 2004.

[62] A claim under Article 6 was rejected, on the basis that the national courts had not acted arbitrarily or unfairly in applying the law to his case: see Appl No 44912/98, 1 February 2001 (admissibility).

[63] Appl No 44912/98, 7 January 2003 (Fourth Section).

As such, the Grand Chamber's judgment indicates that a claim is not a P1(1) possession unless it has unconditionally vested under national law. However, it did not explain why the quashing of a confiscation order did not re-vest the property rights in the coins; more generally, it did not explain how the distinction between a condition on vesting and a subsequent condition on divesting is to be made. On the basis of Grand Chamber's own explanation of the legislation in question, it would have been equally valid to say that the quashing of the confiscation order re-established property, and the legislation merely set up the procedure by which the claim had to be made. Hence, the judgment is bound to raise further questions on the relevance of technical rules of private law in determining the scope of a State's human rights responsibilities.

In any case, as the claim had not vested, the *Pressos* case could be distinguished; however, the Court continued by explaining the role of the legitimate expectations generally:

> The Court [in *Pressos*] did not expressly state that the "legitimate expectation" was a component of, or attached to, a property right. . . . It was however implicit that no such expectation could come into play in the absence of an "asset" falling within the ambit of Article 1 of Protocol No. 1, in this instance the claim in tort. The "legitimate expectation" identified in *Pressos Compañía Naviera SA and Others* was not in itself constitutive of a proprietary interest; it related to the way in which the claim qualifying as an "asset" would be treated under domestic law and in particular to reliance on the fact that the established case-law of the national courts would continue to be applied in respect of damage which had already occurred.[64]

This reasoning reinforces the argument that legitimate expectations have no role to play in constituting possessions. There must be some 'asset', and an 'asset' is a type of P1(1) possession. This is consistent with the use of the term 'asset' in Gasus. In this context, the existence of an 'asset' appears to be determined entirely by the merits of the claim under national law.

Although it is reasonably clear that the claim must have vested according to domestic law, it is not so clear whether the claim must have proceeded to final judgment. *Stran Greek* and *National & Provincial* suggest that a final judgment is required. In *Pressos*, there were no final judgments, and yet there were P1(1) possessions; similarly, the Grand Chamber in *Kopecký* did not suggest that the applicant would not have had possessions if he had been able to identify the location of the coins. At that point, the applicant would have satisfied the statutory condictions for bringing a claim. While the Court did not decide the issue, it seems likely that it would have said that the notice would have perfected the claim and brought a P1(1) possessions into being. However, in *Stran Greek* and *National & Provincial*, it seems that the lack of a final judgment prevented P1(1) possessions from coming into existence. Recent cases go either way:[65] *Stran*

---

[64] *Kopecký* (n 61) [48].
[65] See eg *Mentis* (n 60); *Fernandez–Molina Gonzalez v Spain*, Appl No 64359/01, 8 October 2002.

Greek is cited as authority more often *Pressos*, and yet the Grand Chamber in *Kopecký* did not suggest that *Pressos* was incorrect.

The Court may be moving to a position under which at least some vested claims are P1(1) possessions at a given stage in proceedings, and others at the same stage of the legal process are not. In *Smokovitis v Greece*,[66] for example, the Court held that Greece violated both Article 6(1) and P1(1) when it passed legislation that had the effect of quashing awards made by a first instance court before a final appeal could be heard. The Greek Government argued that the applicants did not have possessions because the final judgments had not been handed down. The Court did not find this conclusive. However, it did so by applying *Stran Greek*, as it said that it was necessary to determine whether the first instance decision 'had given rise to a debt in the applicants' favour that was sufficiently established to be enforceable'.[67] While citing *Stran Greek* would appear to weaken the applicants' position, the Court went on to say that the Greek case law demonstrated that the claims had had a strong likelihood of success. Then, applying *Pressos*, it stated that the case law also created a legitimate expectation that the claims would be resolved in their favour.[68] Hence, *Smokovitis* suggests that claims are possessions once all the facts have accrued and, if there is any doubt as to the likelihood of success, there is at least a strong prospect of a favourable result.[69] Accordingly, the applicants' claims were possessions under P1(1), and 'legitimate expectations' merely expresses the strength of the applicant's claim under national law.

In addition, *National & Provincial* suggests that the legal merits of the claim should be considered at the time the claim is lost. The Court observed that the restitution claims were extinguished before the House of Lords gave its judgment in the *Woolwich* proceedings for restitution. Prior to that, it was not clear that the applicants' claims had a sound legal basis. Arguably, this was also the case in *Stran Greek*: the ultimate resolution of the claim was not clear before the arbitration award was made, and hence the preliminary judgment allowing the claim to proceed could not be said to have established its prospects of success with any degree of certainty. By contrast, in *Smokovitis*, a body of prior cases showed that the applicants' claims were likely to be successful.

If this is the current position, it appears to contain a fundamental contradiction. Ordinarily, the State would not intervene in the civil process unless it formed the opinion that the claimants had a real chance of success, and yet the

---

[66] Appl No 46356/99, 11 April 2002.

[67] Above [32].

[68] Above.

[69] There are no P1(1) possessions in respect of a claim dismissed by the national courts, where there has been no interference with the procedure or retrospective amendment of the law: see eg *Sardin v Russia*, Appl No 69582/01, 12 February 2004 and *Hourmides v Greece*, Appl No 12767/02, 19 May 2004. The reversal of a judgment by an appellate tribunal is not an interference with possessions: *Moschopoulos v Greece*, Appl No 43858/02, 15 January 2004; *Kolybiri v Greece*, Appl No 43863/02, 18 March 2004; *Korre v Greece*, Appl No 37249/02, 18 March 2004. Cf *Albina v Romania*, Appl No 57808/00, 3 February 2004 (merely decided that the case was admissible).

State seeks to avoid responsibility under P1(1) by arguing that the claimant's chances were marginal at best.

In any case, the courts in the United Kingdom have not required claimants to proceed to final judgment. This is apparent from *Wilson and others v Secretary of State for Trade and Industry*,[70] in which a lender claimed that the Consumer Credit Act 1974 violated P1(1) and Article 6 because it provided that consumer loan contracts were unenforceable unless disclosure of credit details had been made as required by the Act and regulations made pursuant to it. The approach taken in *Kopecký* suggests that the European Court would say that credit disclosure was necessary to constitute enforceable contractual rights, and hence the failure to satisfy the disclosure conditions meant that consumer lender did not acquire P1(1) possessions. However, the House of Lords concluded that the loan contract did provide the lender with P1(1) possessions. While there was disagreement as to whether the 1974 Act interfered with those possessions, it seems to have been clear enough that the loan agreement did create possessions.

(2) Legitimate expectations may also refer to the risk of intervention. Arguably, the Court's conception of legitimate expectations refers to the likelihood of obtaining a remedy in civil proceedings, but by taking into account both the legal merits of the claim *and* the risk of intervention. Since most claims proceed without legislative intervention, the analysis is normally the same as (1). However, where the legislature has clearly indicated its intention to intervene, there can be no legitimate expectation that the dispute will proceed to judgment (or enforcement). The result is that P1(1) does not apply because there are no P1(1) possessions. In terms of the doctrinal analysis of the facts, the existence of a legitimate expectation may be treated as a distinct issue from that of the merits of the claim, although both are directed to the same factual issue of the likelihood of obtaining relief.

This would explain the emphasis on the statements of legislative intervention in *National & Provincial*. Parliament had clearly indicated its intention to validate the tax rules, with retrospective effect: accordingly, the applicants could not have a legitimate expectation of recovery. But if the Court meant that the restitution claims would have been P1(1) possessions in the absence of the warnings of intervention, it must be wrong for it to say that the United Kingdom could exclude its responsibility under P1(1) by the simple measure of declaring

---

[70] *Wilson* (n 38); but *cf Ram v Ram (No 1)*, [2004] EWCA Civ 1452 which concerned the status of an order in matrimonial proceedings made against a bankrupt spouse. Although it appears to have been clear that the claimant would have an award made in her favour in the matrimonial proceedings, the Court of Appeal Court indicated that, since 'future rights do not fall under article 1 [of the First Protocol]', the bankruptcy rules that had an adverse effect on the likelihood of recovery under the matrimonial rules did not engage P1(1) (see [32]). However, Article 14 would be engaged, as the Court was 'prepared to accept that the wife's contingent or future interest in the matrimonial property sufficiently falls within the ambit of the Convention's concern for property rights as to engage the jurisprudence of Article 14' (at [35]). With the exception of a (very brief) discussion of *Inze* and *Marckx*, none of the other relevant authorities were examined.

its intention to extinguish those claims. Such declarations may be relevant to the justification for its actions, but if so, P1(1) is applicable and the focus should shift to the legality and fair balance tests.

(3) Legitimate expectations reflect the moral strength of the underlying claims. On one reading, the real distinction between *Pressos* and *National & Provincial* may lie in the suggestion that the building societies were trying to take advantage of a technical defect in the law. If so, the idea of legitimate expectations focuses more on legitimacy rather than expectation. To be more precise, the focus is on the legitimacy of the underlying claim, rather than the likelihood of success in the courts or the indications given by public authorities concerning the future treatment of the claim.

There is some (limited) support for this position in the case law. *Dangeville SA v France*,[71] for example, is similar to *National & Provincial* in that it concerned the rejection of a claim arising from over-payment of a tax that was not satisfied; however, there was no suggestion that the applicants were attempting to take advantage of a technical defect in the law.[72] In this case, the Court concluded that the failure to honour the claims engaged the State's responsibility under P1(1) (and that P1(1) was violated by failure to return the over-payment).

An even stronger example is *Ryabykh v Russia*,[73] where a final, binding judgment was set aside in circumstances which violated Article 6(1), but relation to P1(1) the Court held that there had been no violation. The reasoning on P1(1) is very brief, and it may be the case that the Court concluded only that there had been an interference but it was justifiable. However, the Court did not appear to distinguish between the judgment itself and the claim which gave rise to the judgment. The original judgment from the Russian courts was given to enforce legislative provisions intended to alleviate the impact of inflation on money deposited in financial institutions. The Court held that the facts 'do not disclose any appearance of a violation' of P1(1) because the Protocol does not 'oblige the State to maintain the purchasing power of sums deposited with financial institutions'.[74] While saying that P1(1) does not oblige States to safeguard individuals against inflation is not so controversial, the real issue was whether the judgment was a P1(1) possession. It seems, therefore, that even though a final, binding judgment had been obtained, the Court decided that it was not the type of judgment that is protected by P1(1).

Ryabykh is surely an anomalous decision, as it suggests that the Court would look behind a final judgment and say that it is not a possession, for the sole

---

[71] *Dangeville SA* (n 5).

[72] The French courts dismissed the claim, which would suggest that there was no 'asset' nor legitimate expectation that could be protected under P1(1). However, the Strasbourg Court held that the claim arose under European Community law, and hence the resolution of the claim by the French courts was not conclusive as to the status of the claim under P1(1).

[73] Appl No 52854/99, 24 July 2003.

[74] Above [63].

reason that the claim which led to the judgment was not one that would have sounded in human rights law. Not even the *National & Provincial Building Society* judgment goes this far. It would have made more sense to say that there had been an interference with possessions, but that interference was justifiable.[75]

Hence, it can be said that there is some support for relating the existence of P1(1) possessions to the legitimacy of the claim itself, but the Court normally considers the facts concerning legitimacy in relation to the fair balance.[76] Indeed, even in *National & Provincial*, the Court stated that it had no concluded view on the existence of possessions, and it considered the facts relevant to the legitimacy of the restitution claims in relation to the fair balance. Similarly, in *Stran Greek*, Greece argued that the applicant's claims were tainted by its dealings with the military government: this was relevant to the fair balance (although given little weight), but not to the issue of applicability. *Smokovitis* provides another example of this point: P1(1) was applicable, although there were suggestions that the applicants were seeking to rely on ambiguities in ministerial statements, just as the applicants in *National & Provincial Building Society* sought to exploit a loophole in tax legislation.[77] Nevertheless, this did not affect the position on the applicability of P1(1).

In conclusion, the set of principles put forward by the Court on the determination whether claims are possessions cannot be described as either clear or coherent. Nevertheless, some specific points are reasonably clear. For example, a final judgment is a P1(1) possession, even if the moral foundations of the underlying claim are questionable. At the other extreme, there is no property unless the facts constituting the cause of action have occurred and the action has vested. However, beyond this, uncertainty begins to creep into the law. While the Grand Chamber in *Kopecký* was clear that there are no P1(1) possessions unless all conditions on vesting have been satisfied, there are bound to be cases where the nature of conditions become the centre of dispute. It seems, from *Kopecký*, that the Court will apply a formal approach to such issues, involving a close examination of technical provisions of national law. In this respect, the remarks of Judge Strážnická, dissenting, are worth noting, as she stated that 'As regards the primary role of the national authorities in resolving the problems of interpretation of national legislation, the Court has noted that a particularly formalistic and strict interpretation cannot be compatible with the principles of the Convention'.[78] It now seems that this is precisely what the Court is calling for.

---

[75] As in *James* (n 13).

[76] See Chapter 6, 184–187.

[77] *Smokovitis* (n 66) [13]; *National & Provincial* (n 52) [81]–[83]. See also *MA and 34 Others* (n 58) and *Jahn v Germany*, Appl Nos 46720/99, 72203/01, 72552/01, 22 January 2004: the argument that the applicants were taking advantage of administrative confusion arising from the reunification of Germany did not affect the status of their claims as P1(1) possessions (see below, text to n 168).

[78] *Kopecký* (n 61) (and see also the Fourth Section judgment (n 75)).

As a more general observation, the formal analysis does not leave the doctrine of legitimate expectations with a significant role to play. Deciding whether conditions on vesting have been satisfied does not depend on expectations arising from State representations or other conduct. As far as legitimate expectations have anything to do with the characterisation of causes of action, it is solely as an alternative way of saying that a claim had a strong chance of success. In particular, it adds nothing to the Court's description of an 'asset'. While there are cases where the Court differentiates between P1(1) possessions in the form of assets and possessions in the form of legitimate expectations, there is no difference in substance. The idea of legitimate expectations is still relevant in other contexts, but not in the sense of constituting claims as P1(1) possessions. Instead, legitimate expectations relate to the future conduct of State authorities in relation to existing claims and property. The failure to fulfil the expectations may constitute an interference with those possessions, and the nature of those expectations and the manner in which the State failed to fulfil them would also be relevant to the fair balance, but the possessions exist independently of any expectations.

Transitional justice and the restitution of property

With the ratification of the Convention and Protocol by many formerly communist countries, there have been a series of cases concerning claims to property taken under the old regimes.[79] Many of these countries enacted legislation for the restoration of property, or alternatively for compensation to be provided in money or substitute property to those affected. Some of the P1(1) cases concern individuals who still have a legal title to property but cannot obtain its return; others concern individuals who are excluded from compensation schemes or otherwise treated unfairly.[80] There are therefore two distinct issues concerning the applicability of P1(1). The first is whether the formal title to property is a P1(1) possession, even where the property was taken many years ago and has since changed hands many times. The second arises when the original title is lost or not recognised as a P1(1) possession. Here, the issues concern statutory schemes for compensation or restoration of property where applicants fail to satisfy conditions on entitlement.

---

[79] See generally S Djajic, 'The Right to Property and the *Vasilescu v Romania* Case' (2000) 27 *Syracuse Journal of International Law and Commerce* 363.

[80] Plainly, private individuals currently in occupation may have human rights claims should they be dispossessed in favour of former owners: see eg *Pincová v The Czech Republic*, Reports 2002–VIII.

The survival of property rights

In *Malhous v Czech Republic*, the Grand Chamber laid down guidelines for determining such cases.[81] Land belonging to the applicant's father had been expropriated by the Czechoslovakian government in 1949. The expropriation was lawful under 1948 legislation, although no compensation was paid. In 1957, the authorities transferred some of the land to natural persons under procedures provided for by law. In 1991, after the fall of the communist regime, new legislation provided that specified lands which had been taken without compensation could be returned to the original owners, but only if the land was still in the possession of the State or a legal person. If the land had been transferred to natural persons, the original owners only had a claim for financial compensation or equivalent land. Since the land in this case had been assigned to natural persons, the applicant had no claim under the 1991 law for its return. There were some exceptions to this rule, but in restitution proceedings before Czech tribunals, the applicant failed to establish that his case fell within those exceptions. Before the European Court of Human Rights, the applicant claimed that the conduct of the restitution proceedings violated P1(1).[82]

The Court began by saying that, in effect, the 1949 expropriation had extinguished the father's ownership in the land. Moreover, the taking of property is not a continuing event, so the State cannot be made with responsible for events occurring before it ratified the Convention.[83] The Court stated that:

> "possessions" can be "existing possessions" or assets, including claims, in respect
> of which the applicant can argue that he has at least a "legitimate expectation" of
> obtaining effective enjoyment of a property right. By way of contrast, the hope of

---

[81] Reports 2000–XII 533. See also *Prince Hans–Adam II of Liechtenstein v Germany*, Reports 2001–VIII 1; *Poenaru v Romania*, Appl No 51864/99, 13 November 2001; *Polacek v The Czech Republic*, Appl No 38645/97, 10 July 2002 (Grand Chamber); *Gratzinger v The Czech Republic*, Reports 2002–VII 399 (2002) 35 EHRR CD202 (Grand Chamber); *Breierova v The Czech Republic*, Appl No 57321/00, 8 October 2002; *Hartman v The Czech Republic*, Appl No 53341/99, 17 December 2002; *Lastuvkova v The Czech Republic*, Appl No 72059/01, 17 December 2002; *Houfova v The Czech Republic*, Appl No 58177/00, 1 July 2003; *Slivenko v Latvia*, (2004) 39 EHRR 24.

[82] There was a separate claim under Art 6(1), relating to the conduct of the proceedings.

[83] See, for example: *Kopecký* (n 61) [35]; *Szechenyi v Hungary*, 21344/93, 30 June 1993 (Comm); *Gasparetz v Slovak Republic*, Appl No 24506/94, 28 June 1995 (Comm); *Seidlová v Slovak Republic*, Appl No 25461/94, 6 September 1995 (Comm); *Atlas v Slovak Republic*, Appl No 31904/96, 11 September 1997 (Comm); *Multiplex v Croatia*, Appl No 58112/00, 26 September 2002; *Smoleanu v Romania*, Appl No 30324/96, 3 December 2002 [45]–[46] (referred to the Grand Chamber]; *Lindner and Hammermayer v Romania*, Appl No 35671/97, 3 December 2002 (referred to the Grand Chamber) [40]–[41]. But *cf Agrotexim v Greece*, Series A No 330–A (1996) 21 EHRR 250, [56]–[58]; *Loizidou v Turkey*, Reports 1996–VI 2216 (1997) 23 EHRR 513; *Almeida Garrett, Mascarenhas Falcão v Portugal*, Appl No 29813/96, 30229/96, 11 January 2000 [41]–[43]; *Sovtransavto Holding v Ukraine*, Reports 2002–VII 133 (2004) 38 EHRR 44 [58]–[59].

recognition of the survival of an old property right which it has long been impossible to exercise effectively cannot be considered as a "possession".[84]

In this case, the applicant's only 'hope of recognition' had been crystallised by the 1991 legislation, as it did provide a means of claiming restitution; however, the applicant had failed to satisfy the conditions for the restitution of the land itself. In that sense, the likelihood of success in any claim for return of the land was remote before the 1991 legislation, and it remained remote after its enactment. Accordingly, there were no P1(1) possessions.

In *Malhous*, the applicant's father's property rights had been formally taken many years before the change in government, and were never restored. However, the principle seems apply even where property rights have been formally restored, as *Kopecký* and *Polacek and Polackova v Czech Republic* demonstrate.[85] *Kopecký* is described above; *Polacek* is similar, as it also dealt with applicants who lost property as a result of criminal convictions and associated confiscations of property.[86] As in *Kopecký*, the convictions and confiscation were quashed, with retrospective effect. However, in *Polacek*, the property was land, and so it had not been physically lost. Instead, it had been sold by the State to a private individual, JH. When the applicants contacted JH to demand restitution of the property, he refused. They brought proceedings in the Czech courts for restitution but their case failed, as they failed to satisfy a statutory condition limiting restitution claims to Czech nationals. In *Polacek*, as in *Kopecký*, the applicants argued that the quashing of their convictions and the associated confiscations meant that they held possessions in respect of the land itself. However, as the European Court characterised their interests as 'an old property right which it has long been impossible to exercise effectively', they did not have P1(1) possessions.[87]

The converse is shown in *Broniowski v Poland*,[88] where the applicants held claims against the Polish State for land or compensation to be given to certain

---

[84] *Malhous* (n 81) 553. This is consistent with a long line of Commission decisions: see eg *HK v Germany*, Appl No 20931/92; 10 February 1993; *Luck v Germany*, Appl No 24928/94, 30 November 1994; *Weidlich and Fullbrecht, Hasenkamp, Golf, Klausser and Mayer v Germany* Appl No 9048/91, 19049/91, 19342/92, 19549/92, 18890/91, 4 March 1996; *Firma 'Brauerei Feldschlösschen Ferdinand Geidel Kg', Davies, Geidel, The Estate Of Louise Geidel and Landgraf v Germany*, Appl No 19918/92, 24 February 1997; *Krug Von Nidda und Von Falkenstein v Germany*, Appl No 25043/94, 24 February 1997; *Kremer–Viereck and Viereck v Germany* Appl No 34197/96, 21 May 1998; *Peltzer and Von Werder v Germany* 35223/97, 21 May 1998; *Heuer v Germany*, Appl No 37255/97, 21 May 1998 and *Von Rigal–Von Kriegsheim v Germany*, Appl No 37696/97, 21 May 1998.

[85] *Polacek* (n 81).

[86] In 1975, under the laws in force at the time, a Czechoslovakian court convicted the applicants of deserting the Republic and ordered the confiscation of all of their property. They had left Czechoslovakia in 1968, without the consent of the authorities. Later, they moved to the United States and became citizens, thereby losing their Czechoslovakian citizenship.

[87] *Polacek* (n 81) [62]; *Kopecký* (n 61) [35].

[88] *Broniowski* (n 5); see also *Vasilescu v Romania*, Reports 1998–III 1064 (1999) 28 EHRR 241 [44]–[54].

classes of persons who lost property as a result of displacement by the Soviet Union. These claims had not been fully satisfied, but they had been acknowledged by the Polish authorities throughout the communist era and thereafter. Indeed, the Polish courts had described the claims as a 'debt chargeable to the State Treasury' which had 'a pecuniary and inheritable character'.[89] Consequently, although it may have been practically impossible to obtain satisfaction, the fact that the claims had 'continuously had a legal basis in domestic legislation' was sufficient to constitute P1(1) possessions.[90]

The idea that property is lost when a right cannot be exercised effectively has been applied in several other cases,[91] although it is doubtful that it would apply all circumstances. Plainly, the State cannot be permitted to destroy a property right simply through inaction. In *Loizidou v Turkey*,[92] for example, Turkey was held responsible for a deprivation of property caused by the continual denial of the applicant's access to her land.[93]

The effect of the long-lost property doctrine is significant because applicability is merely a filter, and denying applicability denies that any human rights issue arises on these facts. It is therefore noteworthy that the Court has framed these judgments in terms of formal rules of general application, thereby giving the appearance of neutrality in relation to issues of restitution. We return to this point after discussing the second aspect of restoration claims, relating to statutory provisions for compensation.

---

[89]   Above [130]. The obligation was first accepted in 1946, and then re-affirmed in legislation passed in 1985 and 1987 and by different representations (although equivocal) in the 1990s, although in the applicant's case it had never been fully satisfied. In addition, the highest courts in Poland had affirmed that the claims had the status of vested rights under national law, rather than mere possibilities of making claims. These re-affirmations were sufficient to show that the right had continued to exist.

[90]   See also *Abrial v France*, Reports 2001–VI 339 and *De Dreux–Breze v France*, Appl No 57969/00, 15 May 2001, concerning compensation paid for securities cancelled by the USSR in 1918, under terms of agreements made in 1996: the 1996 agreements created P1(1) possessions, but the fact that compensation was only at 1% of the value of the securities was not disproportionate, given the length of time over which repayment on the securities had been unexpected.

[91]   See eg *Prince Hans–Adam II* (n 81); *Des Fours Walderode v The Czech Republic*, Appl No 40057/98, 4 March 2003; *Kosek v The Czech Republic*, Appl No 68376/01, 2 December 2003; *Koktava v The Czech Republic*, Appl No 45107/98, 2 December 2003.

[92]   Reports 1996–VI 2216 (1997) 23 EHRR 513; see also *Stran Greek* (n 36) and *Vasilescu* (n 88) [44]–[54].

[93]   The applicant, a resident of Greek Cyprus, fled northern Cyprus after the Turkish occupation. Her case was brought against Turkey, on the basis that it was responsible for the actions of the Turkish Cypriot authorities. *Loizidou* has been followed in *Cyprus v Turkey*, Appl No 25781/94, 10 May 2001, *Eugenia Michaelidou Developments Ltd v Turkey*, Appl No 16163/90, 31 July 2003; *Demades v Turkey*, Appl No 16219/90, 31 July 2003. In these cases, the Turkish Government argued that the applicant's title had been expropriated by a constitutional declaration of the Turkish Republic of Northern Cyprus (the 'TRNC') in 1985, by which all 'abandoned' property was deemed to belong to the new government. Since Turkey has accepted the jurisdiction of the Court only with respect to its acts from 1990, it argued that it could not be held responsible for any alleged breach of P1(1) arising from the expropriation. However, the Court refused to recognise the validity of the declaration at international law and therefore concluded that the applicant still held a P1(1) possession in 1990, although it was clear that the chances of recovering the property in 1990 were remote and had been for many years. Plainly, the likelihood that the applicant could have been successful before the relevant national courts was not decisive.

Statutory claims for restoration

In *Malhous*, the applicants also argued that the statutory condition that excluded them from claiming compensation or restitution infringed Article 14 taken in combination with P1(1). However, the Court found that their failure to satisfy the condition meant that the applicants had no possessions and hence no Article 14 claim for discrimination. As the Court put it in *Malhous*, P1(1) possessions do not include 'a conditional claim which lapses as a result of the non-fulfilment of the condition'.[94] As explained above, this principle was recently confirmed by the Grand Chamber in *Kopecký*.[95]

These cases suggest that the Court looks at statutory pre-conditions on the vesting of rights in a highly formal way. However, it has taken the opposite position where restitution is not at stake. *Gasgusuz v Austria*[96] is one clear example. It involved a Turkish resident of Austria who claimed emergency assistance under Austria's Unemployment Insurance Act. Although he had worked in Austria for ten years and made contributions to the insurance scheme required by the Act, the Austrian authorities refused his claim on the sole ground that he was not an Austrian citizen. Under the Act, only citizens qualified for emergency assistance. While the strict logic of *Marckx*, *Inze*, *Malhous* and *Polacek* suggest that the applicant had no possessions in respect of the assistance, the Court not only found that there were possessions but also held that Austria violated Article 14 in combination with P1(1). Moreover, *Gaygusuz* is not an anomalous decision: as explained below, it has been upheld and applied in a number of social welfare cases.[97]

Although *Gaygusuz* was not discussed in *Kopecký*, the Court would probably distinguish it on the basis that the applicant had at least some entitlement under Austrian unemployment law. As explained below, once the applicant can show that it has possessions, the Court is flexible about saying that the decisions regarding other associated benefits or rights is an interference with the existing possessions.[98] That is, the Court in *Gaygusuz* did not conclude that the applicant had possessions in respect of the emergency assistance taken alone, but that he had possessions under the welfare scheme generally, and those possessions included a right to be considered for emergency assistance. Consequently, Article 14 was applicable in respect of any decisions concerning emergency assistance. In *Kopecký*, the Fourth Section picked up on this idea, as it distinguished *Malhous*

---

[94] References omitted.

[95] See above; see also *Gratzinger* (n 81); *Des Fours Walderode* (n 91); *The Synod College of the Evangelical Reformed Church of Lithuania v Lithuania* (2003) 36 EHRR CD94; *Jasiūnienė v Lithuania*, Appl No 41510/98, 6 March 2003; *Harrach v The Czech Republic*, Appl No 77532/01, 27 May 2003 (confirmed 18 May 2004); *Uzkureliene v Lithuania*, Appl No 62988/00, 8 January 2004. This follows from earlier Commission decisions, cited above n 84, and *Z v Germany*, Appl No 36265/97, 21 May 1998; *Frank v Germany*, Appl No 29554/95, 21 May 1997.

[96] *Gaygusuz* (n 29).

[97] See below 71–75.

[98] Above.

and similar cases on the basis that 'the applicants were excluded from the very beginning from the possibility of having the property restored as it was obvious either that they failed to meet the relevant requirements or that their claim clearly fell outside the relevant law.'[99] In relation to the coins, it said that the retrospective quashing of the confiscation gave the applicant some kind of entitlement, and hence the claim was sufficiently within the scope of the law that he had established the existence of a possession under P1(1). To say that the applicant did not have a P1(1) possession would be 'too formalistic and would render the protection of the rights under the Convention and its protocols ineffective and illusory.'[100]

However, as explained above, the Grand Chamber reversed the Fourth Section's judgment in *Kopecký*. What this says about the effect of retrospective effect of quashing the confiscation of the coins is not at all clear. The property right may have been 'long lost' before the confiscation was quashed, but it does seem that it had been revived. More broadly, however, it shows that the Court has begun to get bogged down in technical questions regarding nature of conditions: plainly some conditions on claims put them outside P1(1), but others do not, and there is no sensible distinction between them as yet. The difficulty is that there is also no clear sense that this is being approached in a purposive sense, where the role of Convention or the Court itself is central. Indeed, as the Court noted in *Malhous*, its approach has made the protection under the Convention significantly weaker than it is under the International Covenant on Civil and Political Rights, as the United Nations Human Rights Committee had already held that provisions which rule out compensation or restitution to non-citizens violate Article 26 of the International Covenant on Civil and Political Rights.[101] In the Committee's view, limiting the rights to citizens makes an arbitrary and discriminatory distinction between individuals who were equal victims of prior State confiscations.[102] Plainly, the European Court is concerned with the potential cost and conflict of restitution, but even so, as a doctrinal matter, these are issues could be better addressed in relation to the justification stage of analysis rather than the applicability stage.[103]

---

[99] Appl No 44912/98, 7 January 2003 [27].

[100] Above [29].

[101] 'All persons are equal before the law and are entitled without any discrimination to the equal protection of the law. In this respect, the law shall prohibit any discrimination and guarantee to all persons equal and effective protection against discrimination on any ground such as race, colour, sex, language, religion, political or other opinion, national or social origin, property, birth or other status.'

[102] Compare *Des Fours Walderode* (n 91) with *Des Fours Walderode v The Czech Republic*, Communication No 747/1997, UN Doc CCPR/C/73/D/747/1997 (United Nations Human Rights Committee) [8.4], and see generally P Macklem, 'Rybná 9, Praha 1: Restitution and Memory in International Human Rights Law' (2005) 16 *European Journal of International Law*.

[103] See eg *Broniowski* (n 5); *Rissmann, Höller and Loth v Germany*, Appl No 72203/01 and 72552/01, 15 May 2003; *Wittek v Germany*, Reports 2002–X 43. On the question of justification for those whose property was confiscated on conviction for illegal departure, see *Simunek, Hastings, Tuzilova and Prochazka v The Czech Republic*, Communication No 516/1992, UN Doc

When considered with the long-lost property doctrine, it is apparent that the Court has managed to exclude a great many restitution disputes from its review. States are able to determine the scope of their obligations to those who now demand justice, and this determination does not appear to raise any human rights issues. One particularly interesting aspect of this body of cases is the reliance on formal rules of general applicability: for example, in *Kopecký*, the Court explained its conclusions in terms of formal rules of general application. This contrasts sharply with the way in which the Court justifies the margin of appreciation, where the specific factual context determines whether the margin should be wide or narrow. Of course, one might argue that applicability and the margin of appreciation serve entirely different purposes, and reflect different concerns. In terms of their effect, however, they are similar: by finding that P1(1) is not applicable, the Court relieves the State of the burden of justifying its actions; and by finding that an interference falls within a wide margin of appreciation, the Court lightens that burden. Yet the doctrinal structure of the Court's jurisprudence takes a highly formal aspect with respect to applicability, and not with the margin of appreciation.

There are several justifications for this position that might be offered. The first concentrates on the nature of P1(1) possessions as interests determined by national law. Plainly, the scope of the margin of appreciation is not determined by national law, and hence a more fact-oriented, contextual approach is appropriate. However, the Court does not always apply a formal approach in a coherent way: indeed, the 'long-lost property' doctrine contradicts it. In some cases, the initial loss of property was as little as eight years before the collapse of communism;[104] and in *Kopecký* and *Polacek*, the property had been formally restored by the quashing of the criminal convictions and confiscations. Moreover, the inconsistency with *Gaygusuz* is a real one.

The second justification lies in a belief that these restitution issues are political in nature, and as such they lie outside human rights law. That is, the Court may feel that a balance must be struck between corrective justice and reconstruction and rehabilition, and that this balance can only be struck by the States themselves. Human rights law is neutral on this balance, and the applicability doctrines are presented as formal doctrines because that gives them an appearance of neutrality. But if so, the Court uses the applicability doctrine as another means of expressing the principles lying behind the margin of appreciation. However, the message given to applicants differs: that is, the use of the

CCPR/C/54/D/516/1992 (1995) [11.6]: 'Taking into account that the State party itself is responsible for the departure of the authors, it would be incompatible with the Covenant to require them permanently to return to the country as a prerequisite for the restitution of their property or for the payment of appropriate compensation.'

[104] See eg *Ivanovic v Slovak Republic*, Appl No 37892/97, 4 March 1998: in November 1982, the applicant was convicted of departing from Czechoslovakia illegally and his property was confiscated as a result; in 1990, the conviction and confiscation were quashed. However, due to failure to satisfy residency requirements, he was not able to recover the property.

margin of appreciation would say to these applicants that their case does raise human rights issues, but those issues can only be resolved by their own legislatures and governments. The applicability doctrines says that their case does not even raise a human rights issue.

These cases may also reveal that the Court does believe that it is capable of striking the balance between corrective justice and reconstruction, and that the balance lies on the side of reconstruction. More generally, P1(1) protects entitlements, however obtained. The State may justify a redistribution in special circumstances, but P1(1) has no transformative or redistributive role in national systems. In effect, the only claim to human rights protection lies on the side of the present occupants of the land or other property. That is, the use of formal criteria to determine applicability obscures the real reasons for the decision, and it seems that this was deliberate. This seems to be the best explanation for the current position, when considered in the light of some of the cases on compensation where restitution is allowed under State schemes, as discussed in chapter 6.[105]

Claims arising from void or unenforceable transactions

The cases on causes of action and the restoration of property suggest that the European Court is likely to say that at least two types of interest should be treated as P1(1) possessions: (i) interests already classified as property under national law and (ii) interests in the form of claims to property which would have a good chance of success before the national courts. There are exceptions and qualifications: *Malhous, Polacek, National & Provincial Building Society* and *Kopecký* show that other factors enter consideration, and there are still issues to be resolved. However, the European Court has sometimes found P1(1) applicable to a third type of interest, where the applicant's claim to an asset derives from a void or otherwise unenforceable transaction. In these cases, the applicant does not have a recognised interest under national law, and yet the Court has sometimes found that P1(1) is applicable.

These cases fall into two categories: those in which a private law 'contract' is void by reason of some technical defect in formation, and those in which public officials acted beyond their powers in conferring property rights on the victim.

Contracts void under national law

The leading example of this category is the *Beyeler v Italy*,[106] which concerned the exercise of a right of pre-emption by the Italian Government over a Van Gogh painting which the applicant had agreed to buy. The applicant claimed

---

[105] Chapter 6, 184–190 *passim*.
[106] Reports 2000–I 57 (2001) 33 EHRR 52; BH Oxman and B Rudolf, 'Beyeler v Italy' (2000) 94 *American Journal of International Law* 736; see also *Synod College* (n 95).

that the pre-emption infringed his rights under P1(1). Under Italian law, sales involving certain works of art must be declared to the appropriate authorities, and the sale is automatically void if the declaration is not made. A full declaration should have been made for the sale of the painting, but it was not.[107] Accordingly, the Italian Government argued that the applicant never acquired a proprietary interest in the painting, and hence he did not have a 'possession' under P1(1).

The Grand Chamber made the point that 'possessions' has an autonomous meaning and concluded that, although the purchase was 'null and void' under Italian law,[108] the applicant had held 'a proprietary interest recognised under Italian law—even if it was revocable in certain circumstances—from the time the work was purchased until the right of pre-emption was exercised'.[109] From this, it seems that the Court rejected the interpretation of Italian statutes by Italian courts. However, the Court also observed that the Italian authorities had treated the applicant as the owner of the painting for at least some purposes.[110] Hence, the Court said it did not 'need to give an opinion on the Italian courts' view that under the relevant domestic provisions the 1977 sale should be considered as null and void.'[111] In effect, the Court held that, even if the initial sale was void, subsequent events demonstrated that the Italian authorities regarded the applicant as holding a proprietary interest in the painting.

In *Beyeler*, the Court did not make it clear whether it decided that the Italian laws did confer property interest, or whether the conduct of public officials created legitimate expectations that should be protected under P1(1).[112] This was not clarified in *Kötterl and Schittily v Austria*,[113] decided about three years later. In 1973, the applicants took a 100 year lease of an apartment from another private person. A sale of an apartment would have required certain declarations to be made; without the declarations, a sale would have been void. However, leases were not subject to the same rules. (One of the purposes of the law was to restrict sales to foreigners, such as the applicants.) In 1993, the Austrian courts declared that the 'lease' agreement was, in substance, an agreement to sale. Consequently, the 1973 transaction was void and the applicants lost their

---

[107] Neither the identity of the buyer nor the place of delivery were disclosed.

[108] Above [101]; the statute referred to is Law No 1089 of 1939.

[109] Above [105].

[110] Above [104]. In particular, between 1985 and 1987, officials of the Ministry of Cultural Heritage communicated with the applicant's lawyer and the applicant directly, to request information on the location of the painting, to give permission for it to be moved to the Guggenheim museum in Venice, to make arrangements to inspect the painting and to draw up minutes of the inspection, and to inform him that the State was interested in purchasing the painting.

[111] Above [106].

[112] Compare *Sroub v The Czech Republic*, Appl No 40048/98, 24 September 2002, where applicant paid tax: this was a factor in leading the Court to conclude that the applicant had legitimate expectations protected by P1(1); see also *Zwierzynski v Poland*, Appl No 34049/96, 19 June 2001 [64]–[65]: the fact that the public authorities treated applicant as owner for some purposes supported conclusion that it had legitimate expectations relating to the property.

[113] (2003) 37 EHRR CD205.

interest in the apartment. They were entitled to restitution of the price paid, but plainly by 1993 this was hardly a desirable outcome.

The applicants then brought their case to Strasbourg. In substance, it appears to be very similar to *Beyeler*: agreements were entered into and performed, although subsequently it became clear that the agreements had never had legal effect. Moreover, in both cases, possession changed hands. In *Kötterl*, it was material that the Court accepted the Austrian court's conclusion that the 'contract' was a deliberate sham, intended to avoid the law regarding sales to foreigners. While it did not go so far in *Beyeler*, it did accept that the applicant had not acted with complete honesty or openness. Despite these similarities, the Court in *Kötterl* stated that 'the findings of the Austrian courts according to which the 1973 agreement was void, must be the basis of its assessment of the relevant facts'[114] and hence the agreement did not confer any P1(1) possessions on the applicants. The claim was therefore inadmissible. This is plainly contrary to *Beyeler*, given the fact that the applicants in *Kötterl* had been in possession for twenty years.[115] Arguably, in *Beyeler,* the Court found it material that Italian officials acted on the basis that the applicant had property in the painting, whereas it made no such finding in *Kötterl*. However, in the twenty years that the applicants' title was unchallenged, it seems doubtful that the Austrian authorities did not act on the basis that the applicants had some kind of property interest in the land subject to the agreement. In any case, these points should have gone to the issue of proportionality. Indeed, the Court did observe that Austrian law allowed a claim for restitution of the price, and on that basis, it would appear that the enforcement of the rules on sales would have justified the measures taken.

Beyeler was cited in *Kötterl*, but not discussed. Subsequently, the Court has cited *Beyeler* in numerous cases on transactions of questionable validity and *Kötterl* seems to have been forgotten. While *Kötterl* is consistent with the approach in cases such as *Marckx*, *Inze*, *Malhous*, it seems that it does not represent the position on the type of case it deals with. In cases with transactions that are not recognised under national law, the Court seems to adopt a more practical approach, where neither the formal validity of the transaction nor the likelihood of success in domestic legal proceedings are conclusive. In these cases, the Court has placed more weight on the fact of possession. *Beyeler* itself is an example: the Court might not have found P1(1) applicable if the applicant had never obtained possession of the painting. Another example is *The Synod College of the Evangelical Reformed Church of Lithuania v Lithuania*,[116] where a 1993 decision awarding the applicant church the title to a building was

---

[114] Above CD208.

[115] *Cf Rieberger and Engleitner v Austria*, Appl No 8749/02, 7 October 2004: the applicant had no possessions in respect of an unregistered sales 'contract', as it could not take effect without registration. Unlike *Beyeler* and *Kötterl*, there was no extended period of undisturbed possession, nor any conduct suggesting that the agreement had effect.

[116] *Synod College* (n 95).

annulled as void in 1997. The Court held that the applicants had possessions, despite the subsequent annulment, because 'the fact remains, that from 27 December 1993 until at least 14 May 1998, the applicant church had exercised the control of the building on the basis of the decisions of 8 and 20 December 1993'.[117] Similarly, in *Öneryildiz v Turkey*,[118] the Court found that a squatter held P1(1) possessions in respect of a dwelling he had constructed, although it was clear that both the occupation of the land and the construction of the dwelling contravened Turkish law. However, it appeared that the authorities had taken no steps to evict the applicant or take down the dwelling. Indeed, the council taxes were levied and public services were supplied to the property, and it was against this background that the Court held that the applicant had P1(1) possessions in respect of the dwelling.[119] Only *Kötterl* suggests that the fact of possession is not important.[120]

While *Kötterl* appears to be an anomalous decision, at least in relation to void transactions, it would also have its attractions for national courts. *Beyeler* raises difficulties for national courts, even if we leave aside the matter of the conduct of public officials, for a finding that a void 'contract' creates a P1(1) possession might be taken as suggesting that it also has some effect in private law. This is not necessarily the case, however, as it means only that the State's obligations are engaged. The private law rights of the other party to the void 'contract' need not be affected, but the State may be under a duty to compensate the victim or otherwise ensure that the impact on them is not disproportionate. Indeed, in *The Synod College of the Evangelical Reformed Church of Lithuania v Lithuania*,[121] the 1997 annulment was found not to be disproportionate, in part because the applicant was entitled to compensation for the loss of its possessions.

Ultra vires representations by public authorities

The *Beyeler* case also casts some doubt on the common law rules regarding ultra vires representations by public authorities. As a matter of administrative law, representations made by public bodies may create legitimate expectations that decisions will be made in a particular way. To some extent, where those expectations relate to the exercise of rights of property, English administrative law already reflects principles of the European Court's P1(1) jurisprudence. That is, the withdrawal of a permission to use property in particular way would

---

[117] Above CD101. The applicant had, for example, arranged and paid for heating in that period.

[118] Appl No 48939/99, 30 November 2004 (Grand Chamber).

[119] Oddly, the Court also held that the applicant had no possessions in respect of the land. That is, if the dwelling was not a fixture (but more like an illegally parked car or caravan), then it seems clear that the dwelling would remain the applicant's property, irrespective of the authorities' conduct; conversely, if the dwelling was a fixture, then the fact that the authorities' conduct gives rise to possessions in respect of the dwelling would seem equally applicable to the land itself.

[120] Although note the dissenting opinions of Judges Türmen and Mularoni in *Öneryildiz* (n 118).

[121] *Synod College* (n 95).

normally be regarded as an interference with the enjoyment of those possessions under P1(1),[122] in addition to providing grounds at common law to apply for judicial review. However, under the common law, these principles have been subject to an important limitation: a promise or representation by a public authority to act beyond its statutory authority does not normally create legitimate expectations.[123] For example, in *Stretch v West Dorset District Council*,[124] the individual had no redress under common law principles of administrative law where he had made a contract with a public body that was beyond its statutory powers. The contract granted him a lease of 22 years with an option to renew for another 21 years, but his application for a renewal was refused when the district council discovered that its successor did not have the statutory power to grant the option to renew. This contrasts with the position in Strasbourg, where acts of public authorities may create legitimate expectations such that failing to honour those expectations constitutes an interference with the enjoyment of possessions. Indeed, in *Stretch v United Kingdom*,[125] the claimant in *Stretch v West Dorset District Council* succeeded in persuading the European Court of Human Rights that he was the victim of a violation of P1(1). Other cases confirm the Court's position. In *Pine Valley Developments v Ireland*,[126] for example, it held that the annulment of a grant of planning permission interfered with the applicant's possessions, even though the original grant of planning permission had been ultra vires the public authority.

These cases (particularly *Stretch v United Kingdom*) show that, under the Human Rights Act 1998, public authorities must now consider the effect that resiling from ultra vires representations would have on individuals, at least where those representations relate to P1(1) possessions. Of course, not all representations have this effect, and in any case the nature of the expectations created may not be as extensive as the applicant might have hoped. In *Stretch*, the Court referred to the fact that the applicant (and council) had honestly believed that the option would be effective, and for 22 years they worked on the basis that the entire agreement was valid.[127] It may be asked whether P1(1) would have been applicable if the council discovered the mistake in 1969, before the applicant had taken possession or paid any rent.[128] In this respect, it is also worth noting that in *Stretch* and *Pine Valley*, the representations related to assets that were indisputably P1(1) possessions: in *Stretch*, original 22 year

---

[122] See licence cases, below, 75–78.

[123] *See R (Bibi) v Newham LBC (No 1)* [2002] 1 WLR 237 (CA), [46] (Schiemann LJ), referred to by Peter Gibson LJ in *Rowland v Environment Agency* [2004] 3 WLR 249 (CA) [69].

[124] *Stretch v West Dorset District Council*, (1998) 96 LGR 637. The council had a power to let the property, but this was held not to include a power to grant an option to renew. See *also Hazell v Hammersmith and Fulham LBC* [1992] 2 AC 1.

[125] (2004) 38 EHRR 12.

[126] Series A No 222 (1992) 14 EHRR 319.

[127] *Stretch* (n 125) [33]–[35].

[128] See also *Contal v France*, Appl No 67603/01, 3 September 2002, where the failure to continue paying of an army pension at a higher level, due to a mistake, was not a violation of P1(1).

period and lease contract were possessions; and in *Pine Valley*, the land to which the planning consent related was plainly a possession. In that sense, the representations created legitimate expectations which enhanced the bundle of rights held by the applicant, but they did not create new possessions. Whether ultra vires representations can create possessions where previously there were none has yet to be considered.

It also appears that the representations need not be as direct as those in *Pine Valley* and *Stretch*. *Beyeler* suggests that such expectations can arise more indirectly, simply by a public authority acting on the basis that certain rights exist, even though it did not itself have any role in creating the putative rights. That is, the Court did not identify any positive representation by the Italian authorities regarding the future treatment of the applicant's interests. At the most, the the Italian authorities had treated the applicant as owner in some circumstances for some purposes:[129] at no time did any public officials make a statement of intention regarding the applicant's claim to ownership; arguably, the conduct only showed that the authorities had not been fully apprised of the legal situation at the time of the communications. Similarly, in *The Former King of Greece v Greece*,[130] the former King claimed to own certain assets in his private capacity whereas Greece argued that he held them in his public capacity. The Court held that the assets were held privately, and hence were P1(1) possessions, largely on the basis that Greek officials had allowed his family to deal with the assets in a private capacity.[131]

The recent case, *Rowland v Environment Agency*,[132] shows how P1(1) may be used to obtain relief in the English courts in respect of an indirect, ultra vires representation. In this case, the owner an estate on the banks of Hedsor Water (a bend in the River Thames) claimed that the Water was private water. To back her claim, she pointed out that navigation authorities had, for many years, mistakenly treated Hedsor Water as the private water of herself and her predecessors in title. While the Court of Appeal upheld the authorities' own determination that public rights of navigation over Hedsor Water had never been extinguished, and that the authorities had never had the power to extinguish them, it also said that their conduct created legitimate expectations that were protected under P1(1).

While *Pine Valley*, *Stretch* and *Rowland v Environment Agency* show that ultra vires representations do carry weight under P1(1), their effect should not be overestimated. To begin with, in each of these cases, the victims did have

---

[129] *Beyeler* (n 106) [104]. In particular, between 1985 and 1987, officials of the Ministry of Cultural Heritage communicated with the applicant's lawyer and the applicant, to request information on the painting's location and to give permission for it to be moved to the Guggenheim museum in Venice, and then to make arrangements to inspect the painting and to inform him that the State was interested in purchasing the painting.

[130] Reports 2000–XII (2001) 33 EHRR 21.

[131] See also *Matos e Silva lda v Portugal*, Reports 1996–IV 1092 (1997) 24 EHRR 573; *Iatridis* (n 22).

[132] *Rowland* (n 123).

some rights of private property: in *Pine Valley*, it was the land subject to the (void) grant of planning permission; in *Stretch*, it was the lease period of 22 years; and in *Rowland*, it was the estate. Hence, the Court did not suggest that the ultra vires acts of the public authorities created entirely new property interests: instead, they had made the existing property interests appear more extensive than they were. For example, in *Rowland*, these expectations were not expectations that Hedsor Water would become private water: in that sense, in private law terms, the expectations did not create a property right. Similarly, in *Stretch*, the Court made it clear that the applicant's expectations were only that it would have the opportunity to renew the lease. This is important because, by saying that the P1(1) possessions are limited, the Court makes it easier for the State to satisfy the fair balance test. The impact on the applicant is not as great as it would be for the taking or destruction of ordinary rights of private property. Indeed, other counter-balancing factors come into play. In particular, the impact on the victim must be weighed against the public interest in ensuring that public authorities do not exceed their statutory powers, and that the exercise of powers outside the statutory scheme does not prejudice third parties. In many cases, the public interest would be so compelling that any impact on the victim would not be considered disproportionate. For example, in *Rowland*, the applicant did not succeed in obtaining private rights over Hedsor Water; nor was it necessary for the Environment Agency to offer her monetary compensation. The Agency satisfied P1(1) by assuring the claimant that its exercise of the public rights of navigation would be done in a way which would minimise the interference with her personal enjoyment of her estate.[133] In *Stretch*, the Court did not say that the local council should have renewed the lease or offered equivalent financial compensation. While there was an award of damages, it was fairly modest.[134] Hence, it appears that the policy consideration lying behind the common law position are still present in the European jurisprudence, but they do not exclude the review of the conduct of the public authorities. The considerations come through in the justification stage of the analysis of the fair balance rather than the applicability stage.

Observations on void and ultra vires acts

The flexibility in the Court's methods in cases involving void or ultra vires acts makes a striking contrast with the formal methods seen in the restoration cases,

---

[133] See also *Bruncrona v Finland*, Appl No 41673/98, 16 November 2004 [84]–[86], on the manner in which the State terminated a lease of Crown land: the termination, although lawful and effective under Finnish law, still had to follow a procedure that respected the applicant's rights; for example, it had to specify the date of termination.

[134] *Stretch* (n 125) (see especially [42]–[51]: the assessment of damages did not proceed on the basis (as the applicant had argued) that it should receive compensation for the 'loss' of the 21 year extension to the lease (corresponding to a renewed lease) taken from it without compensation).

and indeed in many of the cases on causes of action. While it is easy to see that the ultra vires cases are motivated by a concern with the abuse of power in relations between the State and individuals, it is not clear why this concern carries so little weight in the restoration cases and particularly in the cause of action cases. The cases on causes of action may reflect a belief that it is unnecessary to use P1(1) where Article 6 already applies. Since the extension of P1(1) to cases involving ultra vires acts does not encroach on the fields covered by other rights, the Court may feel fewer constraints on interpretation that broadens the scope of P1(1). But this could also be said of the restoration cases: in the absence of Article 14 (with P1(1)), there is no other basis for a human rights claim. Perhaps there is a belief that these issues can only be addressed under the free-standing right to freedom from discrimination in Twelfth Protocol,[135] but this does not seem to be a concern with the social welfare cases. Consequently, the impression is one where the cases on specific areas may form a tolerably clear body of law, but no sense of any overarching principles governing the development of the jurisprudence

However, as stated above, the importance of finding that P(1) is applicable should not be over-estimated. The victims in these cases did hold private property: indeed, in *Pine Valley v Ireland*, *Stretch v United Kingdom* and *Rowland v Environment Agency*, they held interests in land. At the most, the public authorities conducted themselves in a way that made these existing property interests seem more extensive than they actually were. Hence, the courts were able to say that the conduct of the public authorities did not create new possessions, but that their conduct merely affected the enjoyment of existing possessions. It was the potential for an abuse of power in relation to existing possessions that was central, and from this the courts concluded that a broad view of applicability should be taken.

Social welfare benefits

Under P1(1), alone or in combination with Article 14, it may be possible raise both substantive and procedural issues regarding social welfare schemes. However, to the extent that P1(1) only guarantees existing property, it would not apply where the case is simply that social welfare benefits have not been provided. P1(1) does not guarantee a minimum level of subsistence or other social

---

135 The Twelfth Protocol provides that: '1 The enjoyment of any right set forth by law shall be secured without discrimination on any ground such as sex, race, colour, language, religion, political or other opinion, national or social origin, association with a national minority, property, birth or other status. 2 No one shall be discriminated against by any public authority on any ground such as those mentioned in para 1.' As it refers to the enjoyment of 'any right set forth by law', it might still be argued that it would not apply where an individual fails to satisfy the statutory conditions precedent on the vesting of a right.

benefits; nor does it apply to general promises to provide or enhance benefits.[136] However, if an existing benefit qualifies as a P1(1) possession, the withdrawal or modification of the benefit should also qualify as an interference with that possession. The first issue is therefore whether social welfare benefits are P1(1) possessions.

This question raises many of the same doctrinal points that arise in relation to causes of action and the restitution cases, as many of the social welfare cases concern the refusal of benefits to an applicant who has failed to satisfy a statutory condition for entitlement. The formality of the *Marckx/Inze/Malhous* line of cases suggests that benefits are not possessions until they have vested. However, in relation to social welfare, the approach has not been so strict. In several early decisions on Article 6, the Commission remarked that basic subsistence requires a minimum level of wealth and, if this wealth is not secured by property, life becomes too precarious for an autonomous existence. At the same time, it also suggested that P1(1) possessions arise only if there is a direct link between contributions made by the claimant and the specific claim to benefits.[137] These ideas were taken up by the Court, and in *Feldbrugge v Netherlands*, the Court observed that social insurance schemes have both public and private features; where the private features dominate, the claim is an Article 6 civil right.[138] In *Feldbrugge,* the private features dominated because (1) the right in question was 'a personal, economic and individual right'[139] and the interference with it affected the applicant's means of subsistence, (2) the right was a positive statutory right, and not merely a possibility of benefiting from the exercise of a discretionary power and (3) it was 'closely linked' with a private contract of employment because the applicant contributed directly to the statutory scheme by salary deductions.[140] These three factors are independent, in the

---

[136] See eg *Sardin v Russia*, Appl No 69582/01, 12 February 2004, regarding the denial of medical and other benefits: 'As to the applicant's complaint about an alleged deprivation of medical and other benefits, the Court recalls that Article 1 of Protocol No. 1 does not guarantee the right to acquire possessions . . . and therefore it could not be construed as guaranteeing a favourable outcome of the litigation over social benefits' (references omitted). See also: *Czerwinska v Poland*, Appl No 33828/96, 30 September 2003 (a failure to honour a general promise to raise pensions was not an interference with possessions); *Leinonen v Finland*, Appl No 33898/96, 7 June 2001, *Kanakis v Greece*, Appl No 59142/00, 20 September 2001; and *Blanco Callejas v Spain*, Appl No 64100/00, 18 June 2002 (there is no right to a State pension of a specific amount); and *Salvetti v Italy*, Appl No 42197/98, 9 July 2002: 'even if the applicant could be said to have a right to compensation [for injury suffered as a result of compulsory inoculation], it would not imply compensation of a specific level.' But this does not necessarily mean that there would be no other applicable Convention right: see *Larioshina v Russia*, Appl No 56869/00, 23 April 2002: 'the Court considers that a complaint about a wholly insufficient amount of pension and the other social benefits may, in principle, raise an issue under Article 3 of the Convention which prohibits inhuman or degrading treatment.'

[137] See: *X v The United Kingdom*, Appl No 4288/69 (1970) 13 *Yearbook of the European Convention on Human Rights* 892; *X v The Netherlands* (1971) 14 *Yearbook of the European Convention on Human Rights* 224.

[138] *Feldbrugge v The Netherlands,* Series A No 99 (1986) 8 EHRR 425 [36]–[40]; see also *Deumeland v Federal Republic of Germany*, Series A No 100 (1986) 8 EHRR 448 [70]–[74].

[139] *Feldbrugge*, above [37].

[140] Above [38] and [39].

sense that the first reflects a concern with subsistence and autonomy and hence it would not apply to forms of social welfare given to individuals not in need; the second seems to rely on objective, formal characteristics of the right irrespective of their social function; and finally the third looks to similarities with private law forms of property. In any case, in *Salesi v Italy*,[141] the Court held that a statutory right to social assistance for those unfit to work was a civil right under Article 6(1), even though there was no link with a private law contract and the applicant had not contributed to the statutory scheme. The crucial point was that the applicant 'suffered an interference with her means of subsistence and was claiming an individual, economic right flowing from specific rules laid down in a statute'.[142] It seems, therefore, that the first two criteria of *Feldbrugge* are more important, although their relative weight is uncertain.

Although *Feldbrugge* and *Salesi* deal with Article 6, the Court has taken a similar view on the characterisation of social security rights under P1(1). However, the *Marckx, Inze* and *Malhous* cases puts a greater emphasis on formal aspects of property and less on its social function. This is reflected in *Gaygusuz v Austria*, where it was sufficient to establish P1(1) possessions that a claim had the characteristics of a pecuniary right under the relevant statute, as opposed to a purely discretionary allowance. As explained above, *Gaygusuz* dealt with the claim of Turkish national who had met all the statutory conditions for entitlement to unemployment insurance except that of citizenship. While the Court observed that only those who had made contributions to the scheme were entitled to assistance under the statute, it also stated that a statutory right to emergency assistance was a 'pecuniary right for the purposes of Article 1 of Protocol No. 1 (P1(1)). That provision (P1(1)) is therefore applicable without it being necessary to rely solely on a link between entitlement to emergency assistance and an obligation to pay "taxes or other contributions".'[143] It therefore seems that the existence of a pecuniary right is sufficient to establish 'possessions', and the link to either the social function of benefits or the existence of contributions and similarities with private law rights is not important.

As such, the analysis in *Gaygusuz* is formal, but it is not the same as the analysis in *Marckx, Inze* and *Malhous*. Indeed, the differences are made clear by comparing *Gaygusuz* with *Polacek*,[144] where, as explained above, the Court held that the failure to satisfy a citizenship requirement for a statutory restitution scheme meant that the applicant had no P1(1) possessions, and hence Article 14 was not applicable. This suggests that the apparent formality of the analysis of

---

[141] *Salesi v Italy*, Series A No 257–E (1998) 26 EHRR 187.

[142] Above [19]. See also *Schuler–Zgraggen v Switzerland*, Series A No 263 (1993) 16 EHRR 405 [46] where the Court stated that 'the principle of equality of treatment warrant[s] taking the view that today the general is that Article 6(1) does apply in the field of social insurance, including even welfare assistance'.

[143] *Gaygusuz v Austria*, Reports 1996–IV 1129 (1997) 23 EHRR 364 [41].

[144] *Polacek* (n 81); see above, text to n 85.

Gaygusuz gives an incomplete picture of the basis for decision. Perhaps the Court was more sympathetic to the applicant because of the obvious link between emergency assistance and subsistence; perhaps the Court believed it unfair that someone whose nationality did not exempt him from making contributions to a scheme should be denied benefits solely on the basis of nationality.[145] Alternatively, *Gaygusuz* supports a broader view of 'interference with the enjoyment of possessions,' in the sense that the Court may be satisfied that there has been an interference if the applicant has *some* entitlement under the relevant scheme. In *Gaygusuz*, it was clear that the applicant had rights to other forms of assistance under the applicable legislation, and in that sense the Court may have felt that the only real issue under national law was the extent of the possessions rather than their existence.[146] Plainly, this would be consistent with the approach in the ultra vires cases, discussed above.

It therefore appears that the Court does not consider the formal tests regarding conditions of entitlement to be conclusive, despite the contrary reasoning in *Polacek* and the related restitution cases. In *Gaygusuz* and several admissibility decisions, the Court has indicated that an applicant who would have had a clear pecuniary right but for a discriminatory condition should be treated as having a P1(1) possession.[147] This is quite clear in *Willis v United Kingdom*[148] and *Koua Poirrez v France*,[149] where applicants complained that benefits had been denied solely on grounds of discrimination based on sex or nationality. In both cases, the Court held that the applicants did have possessions, despite the States' arguments that the applicants had not fulfilled all the statutory conditions for entitlement. There is plainly a sound basis for this approach, as it enables the Court to apply a human rights review to the discrimination issue, and it prevents States from avoiding review by framing the discriminatory element as a condition of entitlement.

Finally, recent cases confirm that it is not necessary to show that the applicant must have contributed to the social welfare scheme to qualify for benefits.[150] In

---

[145] For the contrary situation (ie where no contributions were made) see *Neill v The United Kingdom*, Appl No 56721/00, 29 January 2002, concerning a complaint by former members of the armed services that the pension their widows would receive was affected by discriminatory criteria: there was no suggestion that contributions had been made but the entitlement denied.

[146] Other cases consistent with this point are: *Wessels–Bergervoet v The Netherlands*, Reports 2002–IV 239 (2004) 38 EHRR 37; *LB v Austria*, Appl No 39802/98, 18 April 2002; *Duchez v France*, Appl No 44792/98, 26 September 2002; and *Koua Poirrez v France*, Appl No 40892/98, 30 September 2003.

[147] See *Wessels–Bergervoet*, above; *Koua Poirrez*, above; *Willis v The United Kingdom*, Reports 2002–IV 311 (2002) 35 EHRR 21; *cf Van Den Bouwhuijsen and Schuring v The Netherlands* (2004) 38 EHRR CD188.

[148] Above.

[149] *Koua Poirrez* (n 146); see also *Wessels–Bergervoet* (n 146) and *Darby v Sweden*, Series A No 187 (1991) 13 EHRR 774.

[150] Although a pension paid under a contributory scheme, and calculated by reference to the amount of contributions, is almost certain to qualify as a P1(1) possession: see eg *Kuna v Germany*, Reports 2001–V 545.

Wessels-Bergervoet,[151] for example, the Dutch government argued that the relevant scheme (for old age pensions) was based on 'solidarity', in the sense that benefits were not linked to contributions and hence the class of contributors to the pension fund was not the same as the class of beneficiaries; accordingly, the benefits should not be classified as possessions.[152] The Court simply observed that the dispute concerned a reduction in an old age pension, and since it was not disputed that the applicant was entitled to a pension of some amount, she had possessions under P1(1).[153] Arguably, the Court might decide differently if there was no entitlement at all; however, the absence of contributions would not be a material factor in any event.[154]

Licences granted by State

A further issue is whether rights which have their source in the exercise of public powers should be treated as possessions. As the discussion of the social welfare cases shows, the European Court of Human Rights is likely to treat a vested pecuniary right as a possession, despite its origin in the exercise of a public power. This leaves open the question of whether other, non-pecuniary rights would be treated as possessions. This would include, for example, licences or consents relating to specific property, such as planning permission or a vehicle licence, but there are many example of valuable licences that do not relate to specific property, such as a monopolies, franchises, and intellectual property rights.

The simplest cases are those where the licence is attached to specific property. In such cases, the Court has little difficulty in finding that the withdrawal or

---

[151] *Wessels–Bergervoet* (n 146); see also *Willis* (147), where at [35], the Court rejected the judgment in *Hooper v Secretary of State for the Department of Work and Pensions* [2002] EWHC 191 (Admin). The case concerned Widow's Payment and Widowed Mother's Allowance (to which the applicant, if a woman, would have become entitled immediately). The High Court decided that there were no possessions, because widower has no entitlement at all under domestic legislation arising from contributions of deceased wife. The UK took this line in *Willis*, but the European Court of Human Rights, stated that 'The Court does not consider it significant that the statutory condition requiring payment of contributions into the National Insurance Fund required the contributions to have been made, not by the applicant, but by his late wife.' The judgment in *Hooper* was overturned on appeal ([2003] 1 WLR 2623, [2003] 3 All ER 673), but on the basis that Article 14 in combination with Article 8 had been violated; there was no separate analysis of contributions and P1(1).

[152] See also *Meyne–Moskalczuk v The Netherlands*, Appl No 53002/99, 9 December 2003 (inadmissible on other grounds). Cf *Azinas v Cyprus*, Appl No 56679/00, 28 May 2004 (Grand Chamber), where, in a concurring opinion joined by Judges Rozakis and Mularoni, Judge Wildhaber stated that the pension in question could not be considered a P1(1) possession because it was 'non-contributory and contingent on the fulfilment of certain legal conditions' (the majority dismissed the case on other grounds).

[153] See also *Czerwinska* (n 136).

[154] This is not to say that link is irrelevant where proven; ie where there are contributions, it is likely that there are P1(1) possessions.

modification of the licence comprises an interference with possessions.[155] The *Pine Valley* case is one example, as the Court stated that the annulment of a grant of planning permission was an interference with the possessions of the landowner.[156] In such cases, the Court does not regard the licence as a distinct, 'free-standing' P1(1) possessions, but a withdrawal or modification of the licence is an interference with the enjoyment of the existing possession.[157] This can also be seen in *Tre Traktörer Aktiebolag v Sweden*,[158] where the applicant claimed that the withdrawal of an alcohol licence from his restaurant was an interference with his possessions. Sweden argued that the licence was not a possession and, since the withdrawal of the licence did not affect the applicant's title to the restaurant, there had been no interference with possessions of any form. However, the Court observed that the restaurant could not operate successfully without the licence, and hence it concluded that the withdrawal of the licence engaged P1(1).[159] In effect, as in *Pine Valley*, the argument that the licence was not a possession on its own missed the point, since the Court does not take the view that each right relating to a specific object is itself a distinct property interest. Removing the licence or right is an interference with possessions, but that does not necessarily mean that a licence or right unattached to a specific object is itself a possession.

Where the licence carries no value, except as a means of earning income, it appears that it is not a P1(1) possession taken on its own. However, the withdrawal of the licence may still constitute an interference with possessions, but only if it is necessary to the running of an existing business. In *Van Marle v The Netherlands*,[160] accountants complained when they lost their professional practices when they could not satisfy new regulations for the use of the title of accountant. While the Court rejected their claims, it was only on the basis that the regulations did not upset the fair balance. The Court recognised that the goodwill in the accountancy practice as a P1(1) possession, and hence the loss of the right to use the title of accountant was an interference with those possessions.

---

[155] Indeed, failure to grant a licence may be an interference: eg refusal of planning permission plainly limits the use of property. It does not necessarily follow, however, that there is any sort of substantive legitimate expectation to planning permission: see eg *Taveirne and Vancauwenberghe v Belgium*, Appl No 41290/98, 29 April 2003, where the claim that P1(1) was violated by the refusal of permission to increase capacity of a pig farm was inadmissible.

[156] See above, text accompanying n 126 and following.

[157] See *Belfast Corporation v OD Cars Ltd* [1960] AC 490, for the corresponding common law position.

[158] *Tre Traktörer* (n 13).

[159] Above [53]. See also *Crompton v Department of Transport North Western Traffic Area* [2003] EWCA Civ 64, [2003] RTR 34 [19]: the withdrawal of haulage licence made P1(1) applicable, simply on the basis that 'In *Traktorer Aktiebolag v Sweden* [1989] 13 EHRR 309 it was said by the European Court of Human Rights at para 59 that a licence such as this (in that case a restaurant liquor licence) can be revoked lawfully in pursuit of a legitimate aim, but the action must be proportionate.'

[160] Series A No 101 (1986) 8 EHRR 483; see also *Holder v Law Society* [2003] 1 WLR 1059 (CA) and *Re Solicitor (No.8 of 2004)*, [2004] EWCA Civ 1358 (the withdrawal or modification of licence to practice law is an interference with possessions), and *Endenburg v Germany*, Appl No 71630/01, 6 February 2003 (a legal practice may constitute P1(1) possessions).

It therefore disregarded Dutch law, which does not recognise goodwill as property. Nevertheless, the Court held that 'by dint of their own work, the applicants had built up a clientèle; this had in many respects the nature of a private right and constituted an asset and, hence, a possession within the meaning of the first sentence of Article 1 (P1(1)).'[161] By contrast, in *Baquel v France*, the Court stated that P1(1) is not applicable where a professional licence is refused to someone who has not built up a practice.[162] This could be explained by saying either that P1(1) only protects rights of property rather than rights to property, and hence a refusal of a licence to someone who has never had one lies outside P1(1), or by saying that a professional licence by itself is not protected by P1(1).

Van Marle and *Baquel* suggest that a licence to carry on a business is not property taken alone: there must also be some sort of investment in reliance on the licence, and that investment must have created something of value. Moreover, it is not the licence, but the business or other thing of value that is the P1(1) possession. As such, the emphasis remains on the investment and the value created as a result of that investment rather than the licence alone. It is important to note, however, that *Van Marle* and *Baquel* concern personal titles and qualifications, rather than transferable licences with a market value. Whether transferable rights of value are necessarily P1(1) possessions has not been considered by the Court in such plain terms. There are many examples where the Commission or Court has stated that such rights are possessions: for example, there is no doubt that shares in a company are P1(1) possessions.[163] However, the reasoning is based on national or comparative law: that is, if classified as property interest in the law of the respondent State, or by the law of most member States, then it should be a P1(1) possession.[164]

One important issue concerns intellectual property rights. In the United Kingdom, intellectual property rights are treated as another form of property. For this reason alone, it is likely that they would be protected as possessions under P1(1). In *Smith Kline and French Laboratories Ltd v The Netherlands*,[165] the

---

[161] Above [41]; see also *Izquierdo Galbis v Spain*, Appl No 59724/00, 20 May 2003; and *Gallego Zafra v Spain*, Appl No 58229/00, 14 January 2003.

[162] *Bauquel v France*, Appl No 71120/01, 3 February 2004; see also *Dimos v Greece*, Appl No 76710/01, 8 January 2004, where the emphasis was on the no 'right to property' protection, and *Martinie v France*, Appl No 58675/00, 13 January 2004, where the applicant was in a similar position as *Van Marle*, but failed to substantiate the claim with details of, *inter alia*, financial loss (and similar to *Martinie* is *Wendenburg v Germany*, Appl No 71630/01, 6 February 2003).

[163] Eg *Lithgow* (n 37), *Bramelid and Malmström v Sweden* (1983) 5 EHRR 249 Eur Comm HR at 255; *Cesnieks v Latvia*, Appl No 56400/00, 12 December 2002.

[164] See eg *Posti and Rahko v Finland*, Appl No 27824/95, 24 September 2002: the right to fish for salmon in specified waters was a P1(1) possession. There was virtually no discussion of the point in the case, but the right was granted in the form of a lease over the waters and was treated as property in domestic law.

[165] Appl No 12633/87, 4 October 1990; see also *Lenzing AG v The United Kingdom*, Appl No 38817/97, 9 September 1998. Cf *Aral, Tekin and Aral v Turkey*, Appl No 24563/94, 14 January 1998, in which the Commission asserts that copyright, as a form of intellectual property, is covered by P1(1), and cites in support its decision in *AD v The Netherlands*, Appl No 21962/93, 11 January 2004, although in that case it did not reach any conclusion on this point.

Commission held that a patent was a P1(1) possession, on the basis that patents are deemed to be transferable personal property under the relevant Dutch laws. At present, however, the European Court of Human Rights has not confirmed this position. In the *British-American Tobacco Company Ltd v The Netherlands*,[166] the applicant claimed that the process by which Dutch authorities had considered its patent application breached its rights under both Article 6(1) and P1(1). The Dutch Government accepted that the patent application involved a determination of civil rights under Article 6(1), but argued that the patent application was not a P1(1) possession. The Court found that the claim that there had been an interference with possessions was substantially the same as the claim that it had been denied access to the courts for the determination of its civil rights, and so it was not necessary to separately consider the status of the patent application under P1(1).[167] Nevertheless, while this appears to leave the issue of the intellectual property rights unsettled, it is likely that the *Smith Kline* decision would be followed and intellectual property rights would be treated as P1(1) possessions as long as they are a recognised form of property under national law.

Conclusions on the meaning of 'possessions'

The case law on the scope of P1(1) possessions is characterised by reasoning that is formal, and ostensibly neutral, in the sense that it relies almost exclusively on national law to determine the content of P1(1) possessions. As such, the cases reveal that P1(1) is essentially conservative in its function. To the extent that there is an ethical theory underpinning the jurisprudence, it is only that property must be protected because it is property. The ethical basis for entitlement is determined at the national level, and P1(1) simply provides further support for that determination. Indeed, one of the clearest indications for this is provided by *Jahn v Germany*,[168] where the Germany had argued that the applicants had obtained title to land by exploiting bureaucratic failings in the former German Democratic Republic. According to the German argument, the applicants held a purely formal title to land, at best. Accordingly, any interference with that title was minimal and could be justified easily. However, the Court dismissed this argument with little discussion: the idea of illegitimate ownership was 'an eminently political concept', which had little bearing under P1(1).[169] Indeed, even where the Court does take a more open view of P1(1) possessions (as in the cases on void and ultra vires acts) it reaffirms the value of stability of entitlement. Other values—such as autonomy, dignity, and equality—are only given weight in specific circumstances, and as such are not central to the purpose of P1(1).

---

[166] Series A No 331 (1996) 21 EHRR 409.
[167] Above [91]; see also *Aepi SA (Societe Hellenique pour la protection du droit d'auteur) v Greece*, Appl No 48679/99, 3 May 2001.
[168] *Jahn* (n 77).
[169] Above [90].

THE INTERFERENCE WITH THE ENJOYMENT
OF POSSESSIONS

Even where it is clear that the applicant does hold possessions, the Court may still find that there has been no interference with those possessions or that any interference lies outside the Protocol. Broadly speaking, there are three different ways that the Court could approach this issue, with varying degrees of formality. The first would limit P1(1) to direct interferences with formal rights of property: only a direct restriction, modification or extinction of a right of property would engage the State's responsibility under P1(1). The second approach would still require an interference with the enjoyment of rights of property, but would accept that an interference may occur indirectly, where the value derived from holding those rights is affected. The third would move furthest from the formal approach, as it would regard P1(1) as applicable whenever the interests that property is intended to protect are affected. A private law analogue would be with pure economic loss: there is no direct or indirect interference with any right of property, and yet there may be a basis for recovery.

While it is clear that a direct interference normally comes within P1(1),[170] the Court has stated that indirect or de facto restrictions may also come within P1(1). In some cases, it has done so to prevent States from circumventing P1(1) by adopting measures which do not formally restrict or extinguish rights of property but nonetheless do so in practice. However, it is also clear that the Court has applied P1(1) where there is no attempt at circumvention. In this sense, the autonomous meaning doctrine also applies to the conception of an interference with the enjoyment of possessions, although the Court rarely puts it in these terms.

This part opens by examining several important examples of indirect interferences. It then considers cases where there is no direct or indirect interference with rights of property. This raises issues relating to shareholders' interests in corporate property, as well as the State's positive obligations relating to property.

Indirect interferences

The leading case on de facto interferences with property is *Sporrong and Lönnroth v Sweden*,[171] which concerned the issue of permits authorising the City of Stockholm to expropriate the applicants' land. The permits were

---

[170] *Cf Krivonogova* (n 28) (discussed below): although primarily about positive obligations, the Court stated that there is no interference with possessions in the absence of an economic loss. As explained below, this is contradicted by *Chassagnou* (n 30).

[171] Series A No 52 (1983) 5 EHRR 35; see also *Matos e Silva, lda v Portugal*, Reports 1996–IV 1092 (1997) 24 EHRR 573 and *Terazzi srl v Italy*, Appl No 27265/95, 17 October 2002.

initially for periods of five to ten years and were extended several times. The applicants complained that the issue of the permits affected the value of their land by making it more difficult to sell or rent it. However, Sweden claimed that there had been no interference with applicants' enjoyment of their possessions because the permits did not formally restrict the rights of use or disposition. On this point, the Court sided with the applicants:

> Although the expropriation permits left intact in law the owners' right to use and dispose of their possessions, they nevertheless in practice significantly reduced the possibility of its exercise. They also affected the very substance of ownership in that they recognised before the event that any expropriation would be lawful and authorised the City of Stockholm to expropriate whenever it found it expedient to do so. The applicants' right of property thus became precarious and defeasible.[172]

While this passage suggests that it was enough that the permits reduced the value of the property, the Court also took into account the impact of restrictions on construction on applicant's land that plainly interfered with the use of the property. In that sense, the facts are not those of a purely indirect impact on property. Nevertheless, the case shows that the Court would be willing to apply P1(1) to such cases.[173]

The concern with indirect measures also arises where a public body and the individual both have rights in the same asset and the exercise of rights by the public body deprives the individual of value. For example, on liquidation, employees of the company have a preferential claim to the assets in respect of unpaid wages and other entitlements.[174] Indirectly, the employees may thereby deprive the holder of a floating charge of the value secured by the charge. However, the security rights of chargeholder are not directly affected, since the floating charge retains its priority over unsecured creditors.[175] The reasoning in *Gasus*[176] suggests that the exercise of the preferential rights would interfere with the security. As explained above, the applicant's possessions comprised a security interest in specific assets of a company that became insolvent. On liquidation, legislation gave the Belgian tax authorities priority to the assets. The assets were seized and sold, and the applicant's security was rendered valueless as a result, although the rights that constituted the security interest were not affected

---

[172] Above [60].

[173] A further issue concerned the classification of the interference as a deprivation of possessions under Rule 2, and whether indirect acts amount to a *de facto* deprivation: see above [62]–[63] and Chapter 4, 112–14.

[174] Insolvency Act 1986, Sch 6, Para 9–15.

[175] Another example arising on insolvency concerns 'restraint orders' issued under the Drug Trafficking Act 1994, the Criminal Justice Act 1993 and the Proceeds of Crime Act 2002 (Section 26(1) of DTA, s 77(1) of CJA, s 41 of PCA). A restraint order prohibits any person from dealing with 'realisable' property of the defendant. The statutes provide that, if the restraint order is made before the bankruptcy order, the property subject to the order does not become part of the bankrupt's estate. The Crown thereby gains priority over the other unsecured creditors. See P Alldridge, *Money Laundering Law* (Hart Publishing, Oxford, 2003) 163–64.

[176] *Gasus* (n 3).

directly. If there had been a surplus after the payment of the tax debts, the applicant would still have had priority to the surplus over the other creditors. Nevertheless, the Court assumed that the seizure of the assets by the authorities interfered with the applicant's possessions, because the seizure deprived the assets of their value.[177]

Gasus concerned rights over a tangible asset; arguably, where the competing claims concern intangible resources, as in the case of goodwill, any interference is too remote to make P1(1) applicable. For example, a State-owned or operated business may benefit from advantages or subsidies which make it impossible for private operators to compete with it. In such cases, the State may indirectly but effectively take over the market and destroy the value of the goodwill of the private business. To date, there have been no P1(1) cases on this point and, given the modern preference for privatisation, it may be unlikely that such cases would arise in the near future. However, older Commonwealth cases decided by British judges on the Privy Council suggest that there is no interference unless the property of the victim has been the direct object of the exercise of a coercive State power.[178] In the light of *Gasus*, this is probably too narrow a position in relation to P1(1).[179] Causation may be in doubt in many such cases, as it would not necessarily follow that the conferral of advantages on a public body would damage the value of the property of a private person.[180] However, where the link is clear, it would seem close to *Gasus*. Nevertheless, the cases concerned with corporate bodies and their shareholders shows that this cannot be assumed.

This raises a further question, as it is not clear whether P1(1) would apply as long as the applicant can take proceedings in the domestic courts to vindicate its rights. To date, the successful Strasbourg cases have also involved a denial of any effective means of recovering the property or damages through the national legal systems. However, there are several English cases which suggest that it is not strictly necessary to show that the applicant's normal remedies have been denied. For example, in *Marcic v Thames Water Utilities Ltd*,[181] a landowner brought claims in both nuisance and under the Human Rights Act 1998 in

---

[177] Above [53] (the interference was not disproportionate).

[178] *Société United Docks v Government of Mauritius; Marine Workers Union v Mauritius Marine Authority* [1985] 1 AC 585, 603–5 (PC).

[179] *Cf Gustafsson v Sweden*, Reports 1996–II 637 (1996) 22 EHRR 409.

[180] See *Pinnacle Meat Processors Company v The United Kingdom*, Appl No 33298/96, 21 October 1998; *Voggenreiter v Germany*, Appl No 7538/02, 28 November 2002 and the series of cases on the handgun controls: *Ian Edgar (Liverpool) Ltd v The United Kingdom*, Appl No 37683/97, 25 January 2000; *Andrews v The United Kingdom*, Appl No 37657/97, 26 September 2000; *Findlater v The United Kingdom*, Appl No 38881/97, 26 September 2000; *CEM Firearms Ltd v The United Kingdom*, Appl No 37674/97 and Appl No 37677/97, 26 September 2000; *London Armoury Ltd and AB Harvey & Son Ltd and 156 others, AG Wise and 5 others, Powderkeg Ltd and 2 others, Reepham Moore Rifle & Pistol Range, Warwick Rifle and Pistol club and 42 others v The United Kingdom*, Appl No 37666/97, 37671/97, 37972/97, 37977/97, 37981/97, 38909/97, 26 September 2000; *Denimark Ltd and 11 others v The United Kingdom*, Appl No 37660/97, 26 September 2000.

[181] [2004] 2 AC 42.

relation to the failure of the statutory sewerage undertaker to prevent flooding of his property. The human rights claim related to alleged breaches of Article 8 and P1(1). While there might have been an argument that an interference under P1(1) (and Article 8) does not occur unless there is no civil remedy, the courts at all levels seemed to assume that the human rights claim could go forward even if the ordinary tort claims were available.[182]

In any case, the European Court does consider whether an apparent remedy is effective. The *Holy Monasteries* case is a clear example: although Greek legislation deemed certain monasterial lands to belong to the State, Greece argued that it had not interfered with the monasteries' possessions because the deeming provisions merely created a rebuttable presumption for cases where title was uncertain. In effect, the legislation merely required the monasteries to provide proof of their title. However, the combined effect of other provisions meant that, unless the monasteries could locate their original title deeds, they could not discharge the burden of proof. Since it was known that many of the deeds would be impossible to locate, the Court concluded that the monasteries had been deprived of their property.[183]

No direct or indirect impact on rights of property

As explained in chapter 1, the imposition of a financial liability engages State responsibility under P1(1).[184] Plainly, there is no direct impact on rights of property in such cases; neither is there an indirect impact, except in the remote sense that the victim may be required to liquidate assets to discharge the liability. Arguably, these cases suggest that any State action that is likely to result in the loss of property is itself an interference with possessions, even where the interference cannot be identified with any specific possessions. When considered with *Gasus* and *Sporrong*, it moves the doctrine even further from the strict formal approach in favour of an approach that concentrates on economic loss as the criterion for applicability.

Before examining the cases on shareholder claims, it is worth mentioning that it is usually clear that the applicant has suffered some loss as a result of State actions or omissions. The issue is whether the connection between the State's acts or omissions and the applicant's loss is close enough to amount to a P1(1) interference, de jure or de facto. However, if there is no real loss, or only a trifling loss, the Court is likely to say that P1(1) is not applicable. For example, in *Pitkänen v Finland*,[185] the applicant complained of a court order granted to

---

[182]   The House of Lords dismissed the claims in nuisance and under the Human Rights Act 1998, and hence it did not consider the issue; however, the Court of Appeal allowed both claims (see [2002] QB 929). See also *Dennis v Ministry of Defence* [2003] EWHC 793 (QB).

[183]   *Holy Monasteries v Greece*, Series A No 301–A (1995) 20 EHRR 1 [56]–[66]; but *cf Kopecký* (n 61).

[184]   Chapter 1, 31–33.

[185]   *Pitkänen v Finland*, Appl No 30508/96, 4 March 2003.

his neighbour that required him to tear down a building on his land. It appeared, however, that circumstances had developed so that neither the neighbour nor the public authorities would take any steps to enforce the order. For that reason, the Court decided that the order did not actually affect his property, and hence P1(1) was not applicable.[186] Similarly, in *Kienast v Austria*,[187] the applicant complained about a modification in the land registry that recorded two separate but adjoining parcels of land as a single parcel instead of two. The applicant's rights over the land were unaffected. While he claimed that the single registration made it more difficult to dispose of the plots separately, the Strasbourg Court said that this was due to their geographical situation rather than their registration: one plot was contained entirely inside the other. Hence, there was no interference, direct or indirect, by reason of the changed registration.[188] However, it would go too far to say that it is always necessary to demonstrate an economic loss.[189] In *Chassagnou v France*, for example, the Court found a violation of P1(1) in respect of French laws allowing entry onto private land for the purpose of hunting, even though the applicants themselves did not frame their case in terms of economic loss.[190] They were deeply opposed to hunting on ethical grounds, and objected that forcing them to allow hunting on their land subjected them to a real impact. In most cases, however, the complaints do reflect an economic impact, and hence the Court is justified in dismissing the complaint where the economic loss is more imagined than real.

Corporate ownership and shareholders

The status of shareholders in relation to interference with company property is not entirely clear. P1(1) states that 'legal persons' are entitled to the protection of P1(1) in respect of property in its name, but the property of a shareholder is

---

[186] It was admissible in relation to other acts. See also *Allen v The United Kingdom*, Reports 2002–VIII 357 (2002) 35 EHRR CD289; *Ashworth v The United Kingdom*, Appl No 39561/98, 20 January 2004; *Haider v Austria*, Appl No 63413/00, 29 January 2004.

[187] *Kienast v Austria*, Appl No 23379/94, 23 January 2003; *Woonbron Volkshuisvestingsgroep v The Netherlands*, Appl No 47122/99, 18 June 2002: a change in State financing for non-profit social housing associations by reason of various offsets in association accounts was not a direct change in any property rights, although it possibly made it more difficult to raise money.

[188] See also *Langborger v Sweden*, Series A No 155 (1990) 12 EHRR 416 [41], where the requirement to pay a small monetary contribution to a tenants' union was not regarded as a breach under P1–1 because 'In the Court's view, the obligation to pay the small sums involved cannot be regarded as inconsistent with this Article (P1–1).' This suggests that large contributions would have come within P1–1. Cf *Van der Mussele v Belgium*, Series A No 70 (1984) 6 EHRR 163, [49].

[189] But cf *Krivonogova* (n 28). The applicant complained that the bailiff's release of a charge over property interfered with her possessions (in the form of a civil judgment); however, she had not shown that she would not suffer as a result, ie the judgment was still being pursued by the bailiff. Enforcement was only possible through the bailiff: 'Accordingly, to substantiate her property complaint the applicant would first have to demonstrate that she had lost her chance of receiving her award, or a certain part of it, and then that the loss could be ascribed, solely or largely, to the impugned act.'

[190] *Chassagnou* (n 30).

the share itself.[191] A restriction on the exercise of the rights attached to the share would be an interference with the shareholder's possessions,[192] but whether an interference with the company's possessions is also an interference with the shareholder's possessions is a different issue. In *Pine Valley*, the Court treated the sole shareholder and managing director of a company as a victim of an interference with land held by the company.[193] The reasoning was brief, as the Court said only that the shareholder had intended to use the company as a 'vehicle' for his development plans and hence it would be 'artificial' to distinguish between them in respect of their status as victims of a breach of P1(1) (and Article 14 in combination with P1(1)).[194] Several interpretations of the judgment are possible. Firstly, the Court may have meant that their possessions were distinct, but the reduction in the value of shares amounted to an interference in the enjoyment of shareholder's possessions.[195] This would support the argument that, as in the tax and liability cases, P1(1) can apply to indirect economic loss where it would be clear that the loss would have followed from the State action. Alternatively, the Court may have believed it appropriate to pierce the corporate veil on these specific facts: since the company only had one shareholder, who was also its managing director, any harm caused to the company was also caused to the shareholder. This is the narrower interpretation, as it would not apply to other forms of property holding and indeed, it would probably not apply to companies with more than one shareholder.

Subsequently, in *Agrotexim and Others v Greece*,[196] the Court seems to have followed the narrower interpretation. Here, the applicants were majority shareholders in a company which was put into liquidation in 1983. They claimed that liquidation followed from a series of breaches of P1(1) suffered by the company at the hands of local public authorities. The liquidator did not pursue human rights claims before the Council of Europe, but the leading shareholders did.

---

[191] See Chapter 1, n 81: the inclusion of a reference to legal persons was neither explained nor discussed.

[192] A share is property: see the cases cited above, n 163.

[193] *Pine Valley* (n 126). There were two companies, but as the first company had transferred the property to the second, it was only the second that was relevant to this issue.

[194] Above [42]. Several earlier Commission decisions ask whether the applicant was 'directly and personally affected' by the measures in question: see *S–S, I AB and BT v Sweden*, Appl No 11189/84, 11 December 1986; *Fridh and Cifond Aktiebolag v Sweden*, Appl No 14017/88, 2 July 1992, and *Yarrow* (1983) 30 D&R 155, 164–165 (confirmed by the Court in *Lithgow* (n 37) [102]), where the Commission held that the applicant shareholders, who did not hold a majority or controlling interest in the company in question, were not directly and personally affected by the nationalisation of a wholly owned subsidiary, even though it undoubtedly reduced the value of their shareholdings. Accordingly, they could not claim to be victims of an interference with their possessions. *Cf Kaplan v The United Kingdom* (1982) 4 EHRR 64, the Commission found that the applicant, the managing director and 82% shareholder of a company which held 99% of the shares of another company which owned the company in question was a victim under Article 25, but at least partly on the basis that the shareholder was personally implicated in the investigation in question.

[195] Finally, the Court could be taken as saying that there was no interference with any of Mr Healy's possessions, but he was nonetheless a victim of the State's breach of its obligations under P1–1.

[196] Series A No 330–A (1996) 21 EHRR 250.

The shareholders' argument was based on the broader interpretation of *Pine Valley*: that is, the interference with the company's possessions caused a depreciation in the value of their possessions. However, the Court rejected the applicants' claims, on the narrower basis that it would be inappropriate to pierce the corporate veil on these facts. It was concerned that allowing shareholders to make their own applications would cause 'difficulties in determining who is entitled to apply to the Strasbourg institutions'.[197] It would only pierce the veil in exceptional circumstances, 'in particular where it is clearly established that it is impossible for the company to apply to the Convention institutions through the organs set up under its articles of incorporation or—in the event of liquidation—through its liquidators.'[198]

The Court in *Agrotexim* did not refer to the *Pine Valley* case, although its reasoning left the scope of the earlier case in doubt, as the company could have applied to the Convention institutions for redress (in fact, it did, as it was one of the parties before the Court). The issue was addressed again in *Eugenia Michaelidou Developments Ltd and Michael Tymvios v Turkey*,[199] which involved an interference with property in the name of the first applicant, a company in which the second applicant was the director and principal, but not sole, shareholder. During the period of the violation, the second applicant held 1,960 and then 1,999 of the 2,000 outstanding shares of the company. His wife was the only other shareholder. The Court stated that 'both applicants are so closely identified with each other that it would be artificial to regard each as an applicant in its/his own right. In reality, the first applicant is the second applicant's company and the vehicle for his business projects.' On that basis, the Court considered the case from the standpoint of the second applicant alone.[200]

Where this leaves the ruling in the earlier cases is unclear. *Eugenia Michaelidou Developments* seems to return to the reasoning in *Pine Valley*: indeed, it extends it to cases where there is more than one shareholder, so long as the applicant shareholder is in control of the company. This, of course, is bound to raise difficult questions regarding the meaning of 'control'. In *Eugenia Michaelidou Developments*, the Court again described the company as a 'vehicle' for the shareholder's business projects without further explanation, but in both *Pine Valley* and *Eugenia Michaelidou Developments*, the applicant shareholder was the sole director of the company: would the company still be a 'vehicle' if there was only one shareholder, but more than one director? In any case, it is clear that the principle underlying *Pine Valley* and *Eugenia Michaelidou Developments* is diametrically opposed to that of *Agrotexim*. *Pine*

---

[197] Above [65].
[198] Above [66]; see also *Olczak v Poland*, Appl No 30417/96, 7 November 2002, [57]–[59]; and *Mihailescu v Romania*, Appl No 47748/99, 26 August 2003 (a claim regarding non–payment of debts owed to applicant by a private company, in which State was minority shareholder, was inadmissible as incompatible *ratione personae*).
[199] Appl No 16163/90, 31 July 2003.
[200] Above [21].

Valley and *Eugenia Michaelidou Developments* state that the separate personality of a company may be ignored if the shareholder controls the company (however 'control' may be defined), but *Agrotexim* states, in effect, that shareholders have standing only where they have lost control of the company.[201] [202] Moreover, the reason for invoking such a formal test to applicability is unclear. The practical concerns relating to multiple proceedings are plain enough, but if the causing of economic loss is an interference with possessions, it seems dangerous to rely entirely on the corporate form as the means of redressing those harms for the sole purpose of keeping the Court's docket under control.

The analysis in *Agrotexim* rules out the argument that the State's responsibility is engaged in every case where it acts in a way which is bound to reduce the value of property, even where that property is held by a known class. Specifically, it raises questions over the status of the beneficiaries of trusts and powers of appointment. *Agrotexim* suggests that the potential for conflicting claims should mean that only the trustees may bring claims to Strasbourg.[203] This is particularly compelling in the case of a pension fund with a large class of beneficiaries, as the potential for a multiplicity of claims is very high. However, there is no corporate veil, and since individual joint owners may apply to Strasbourg[204] and both trustees and beneficiaries with vested interests have property in the trust assets, both should have standing to apply to Strasbourg to protect their respective interests.[205] This means, of course, that they can only protect their own interests: a trustee, for example, has an interest in managing the trust according to its terms, and should not be able to apply to Strasbourg on the basis that an interference with the trust property affects him or her personally.[206] If, however, the beneficiary does not have a vested interest), then the Court is likely to say that there is no P1(1) possession.[207]

---

[201] In this respect, it is significant that the Court in *Agrotexim* referred to *Barcelona Traction Light & Power Co Case (Belgium v Spain)* (Second Phase), ICJ Reports 1970, in which the International Court of Justice held that Belgium did not have standing to recover reparation from Spain for acts against a Canadian company in which Belgian nationals held shares. See, in particular, *Barcelona Traction* [94], which suggests that the extent of one individual's holding should make no difference to existence of a State's right of diplomatic protection, which casts further doubt on *Pine Valley*.

[202] The liquidator had brought proceedings in the Greek courts, but having lost at first instance, did not appeal.

[203] And that they must act unanimously in doing so, following the general principle that trustees must act unanimously, unless the trust deed or statute law provides differently (or court order, in exercise of supervisory jurisdiction).

[204] *Allard v Sweden*, (2004) 39 EHRR 14.

[205] There is no doubt that trustees can bring claims: eg in *James* (n 13), the applicants were trustees acting under the Will of the Second Duke of Westminster.

[206] *Polvillo e Hijos SA v Spain*, Appl No Appl No 164/03, 3 February 2004 where the applicant held as an agent, but her complaint suggested that she held as a principal; the Court held that there had been no interference.

[207] If, for example, distribution is entirely discretionary, or the property is subject to a power to appoint rather than a trust.

The positive obligation to protect possessions

Obligations relating to acts of third parties

It is clear that the State is responsible under P1(1) if it confers a sovereign power over property on a private individual. In *James*,[208] for example, the Court had no doubt that the enactment of the Leasehold Reform Act 1967, as amended,[209] engaged the State's responsibility, although the Act only enabled tenants (rather than public authorities) to purchase the freehold from their landlords. Similarly, failing to take steps to ensure that private law rights are upheld may also constitute an interference with the enjoyment of possessions.[210] A long line of Italian cases on police assistance demonstrate this clearly.[211] In 1983, the Italian legislature passed laws that limited the security of tenure previously enjoyed by many residential tenants. Many landlords then proceeded to obtain court orders requiring tenants to vacate after their leases expired. However, under Italian law, a tenant who refused to vacate could not be evicted without police assistance. Police assistance was often not forthcoming: in some of these cases, landlords had to wait over ten years to before they could remove the tenant.[212] Many landlords brought cases before the European Court of Human Rights and, in almost all cases where the delay was greater than four years, the Court found violations of both Article 6(1) and P1(1).[213] While the Court stated that the immediate interference was caused by the tenant's continued and unlawful occupation, the failure to provide any effective remedy, with the consequent loss, was sufficient to engage the State's responsibility.

Conversely, where there is a private law remedy, the positive obligations are discharged and there is no P1(1) issue. In *Gustafsson v Sweden*,[214] the owner of a restaurant and youth hostel was put under a 'blockade' by a union for refusing to accept collective bargaining or a 'substitute agreement', with the result that, suppliers could not make ordinary deliveries to his business. The Swedish authorities refused to help, on the basis that the matter was private. The

---

[208] *James* (n 13); see also *Bramelid* (n 163).

[209] The legislation governing leasehold enfranchisement considered by the Court comprised the Leasehold Reform Act 1967 as amended by the Housing Act 1969, the Housing Act 1974, the Leasehold Reform Act 1979, the Housing Act 1980 and the Housing and Building Control Act 1984.

[210] *Novoseletskiy v Ukraine*, Appl No 47148/99, 11 March 2003: a P1(1) claim regarding the failure of the authorities to investigate theft of property was admissible.

[211] Cited in Chapter 5, n 176. See also *Sovtransavto Holding v Ukraine*, Reports 2002–VII 133 (2004) 38 EHRR 44; *Kurkchian and Kurkchian v Bulgaria*, Appl No 44626/98, 22 January 2004; *Prodan v Moldova*, Appl No 49806/99, 18 May 2004; *Fuchs v Poland*, Appl No 33870/96, 11 December 2001 (P1(1) was applicable to a complaint that the public authorities had not done enough to enforce an order requiring the applicant's neighbour to demolish a building).

[212] These delays were not due simply to administrative problems, as the Italian authorities had adopted a policy of staggering evictions in order to avoid the disruption that would have been caused by widespread evictions.

[213] See Chapter 5, 159.

[214] *Gustafsson* (n 121).

Strasbourg Court agreed: 'not only were the facts complained of not the product of an exercise of governmental authority, but they concerned exclusively relationships of a contractual nature between private individuals, namely the applicant and his suppliers or deliverers.'[215]

While such cases may raise issues under both Article 6(1) and P1(1), the Court has said that there is a distinction in the scope of each provision, even where complaints relate to the same acts or omissions.[216] In practice, however, there is little to distinguish the analysis under the two provisions, at least in cases where the applicant complains that a judicial order was not enforced within a reasonable time. In some of the cases where the Court has decided that there has been a violation of Article 6(1) it has said that there is no need to examine the P1(1) point arising from the same facts[217] and yet in others, it has decided that both provisions have been violated.[218] There seems to be no tactical advantage in obtaining a judgment that both rights have been violated as a result of the same defect in the proceedings. In the Italian cases, for example, the Court did not assess damages by treating the interests protected by each right as having been separately harmed: that is, the Court did not work out separate figures for the damage caused by the breach of Article 6(1) and P1(1). In this sense, there is a single breach, and hence a single assessment of damages which produces a figure no different than an assessment of a breach under one provision only.[219]

While the State's responsibility is engaged if it fails to provide a means for vindicating private law rights, it is unclear whether it is similarly engaged when it does provide an effective means. In other words, is P1(1) applicable where a court order or judgment upholds private law rights or where the court or police officials assist in the execution of an existing judgment? This raises the issue of horizontal effect, which is examined in more detail in Chapter 8, on private law. Briefly, the European Court has often found such claims inadmissible, and it has gone as far as saying that 'domestic court regulation of property disputes according to domestic law does not, by itself, raise any issues under Article 1 of

---

[215] Above 60; see also *MS v Bulgaria*, Appl No 40061/98, 17 May 2001 and *Josephides v Cyprus*, Appl No 2647/02, 24 September 2002; but *cf Kurkchian* (n 211): P1(1) was applicable to a complaint that the excessive length of the proceedings had allowed their neighbours to finish the construction which prevented the access of sunlight to their house.

[216] *Poiss v Austria*, Series A No 117 (1988) 10 EHRR 231; *Gavrielides v Cyprus*, Appl No 15940/02, 7 January 2003.

[217] *Koua Poirrez* (n 146); *Grela v Poland*, Appl No 73003/01, 13 January 2004; *Davenport v Portugal*, Appl No 57862/00, 29 January 2004 (inadmissible on another point); *Credit and Industrial Bank v The Czech Republic*, Appl No 29010/95; *Cvijetic v Croatia*, Appl No 71549/01, 26 February 2004.

[218] In addition to the Italian cases on repossession of rented property (cited Chapter 5, n 176), see *Karahalios v Greece*, Appl No 62503/00, 11 December 2003.

[219] An associated problem was with rent control: in many of the cases, the landlords did not wish to occupy the flats for their own use, and hence, the real harm was the loss of rent from being unable to put the flat on the market. However, in 1989, in *Mellacher v Austria*, Series A No 169 (1990) 12 EHRR 391, the European Court had found that fairly strict rent controls did not violate P1(1). This may have persuaded the applicants to frame their complaint in terms of the inability to enforce civil judgments.

Protocol No 1 to the Convention.'[220] Similarly, the Court has said that P1(1) is not applicable to the termination of a contract according to its terms.[221] There is some support for this in the domestic cases. In *Qazi v Harrow LBC*, Lord Scott stated that the enforcement of property rights could never breach Article 8,[222] and in *Aston Cantlow and Wilmcote with Billesley Parochial Church Council v Wallbank and another*, several members of the House of Lords believed that P1(1) could not apply to the ordinary enforcement of civil obligations.[223] However, it seems that the position in the United Kingdom is closer to saying that the enforcement of property rights is not normally disproportionate. That is, P1(1) may be applicable, but it would be very unusual to find that it has been breached.[224]

Obligations relating to other harm to possessions

It is well-accepted that the State's obligation to protect Convention rights may require it to take positive action. This principle was put forward in *Airey v Ireland*,[225] where the Court found that the denial of legal aid for separation proceedings interfered with the Article 8 rights relating to private and family life. Similarly, in *X and Y v The Netherlands*, the Court held that a failure to provide adequate criminal procedures for prosecuting the perpetrator of a sexual offence against a mentally handicapped person amounted to a breach of Article 8.[226] Then, in a line of cases beginning with *López Ostra v Spain*, the Court held that the failure to protect individuals from pollution may interfere with Article 8 rights to respect for the home and private and family life.[227] This was extended to P1(1) with the *Öneryildiz v Turkey* judgment.[228] In 1993, the applicants' homes were buried under a landslide caused by a methane explosion in a nearby tip. Thirty-nine people were killed and ten homes were destroyed. The tip was the responsibility of the local city council. An official report in 1991 had highlighted the risks to those living next to the tip, including the specific risk of a methane explosion, but nothing significant was done to reduce the risk. The applicants claimed that the failure of the authorities to take steps to protect their lives and dwellings violated both Article 2 and P1(1).

---

[220] The same passage appears in both *Eskelinen v Finland*, Appl No 7274/02, 3 February 2004; *Tormala v Finland*, Appl No 41258/98, 16 March 2004. See also *Sesztakov v Hungary*, Appl No 59094/00, 16 December 2003; but cf *Teuschler v Germany*, Appl No 47636/99, 4 October 2001: private civil claim for restitution regarded as a Rule 1 interference.

[221] See eg *Öztürk v Turkey*, Appl No 44126/02, 2 October 2003.

[222] [2004] 1 AC 983 [145].

[223] [2004] 1 AC 546.

[224] See Chapter 9, 231–41.

[225] Series A No 32 (1979–80) 2 EHRR 305.

[226] Series A No 91 (1986) 8 EHRR 235 (see especially [23] and [30]).

[227] *López Ostra v Spain*, Series A No 303–C (1995) 20 EHRR 277 [58]; *Guerra v Italy*, Reports 1998–I 210 (1998) 26 EHRR 357, [57].

[228] Appl No 48939/99, 30 November 2004 (Grand Chamber).

Since the complaint related to the inaction of the authorities, the claims were cast in terms of the State's positive obligations to protect Convention rights. In relation to P1(1), the Court stated that

> Genuine, effective exercise of the right protected by that provision does not depend merely on the State's duty not to interfere, but may require positive measures of protection, particularly where there is a direct link between the measures which an applicant may legitimately expect from the authorities and his effective enjoyment of his possessions.[229]

Here, the fact that the risks were known to the authorities was significant, and led to the conclusion that there had been an interference.

Nevertheless, the extension of *López Ostra* to P1(1) deserves closer examination than it received in *Öneryildiz*. In *Öneryildiz*, the risk to life and risk to the dwelling arose from the same omissions; having determined that the omission violated the right to life, and that it caused the destruction of possessions, it may have seemed obvious that it also violated P1(1). But what should the Court have concluded if the likelihood of an explosion had been the same but there had been no risk to life: if, for example, buildings that were destroyed in the landslide had never been occupied as dwellings? The positive obligations relating to Article 2 or 8 relate to interests of a different type than P1(1), and it is not obvious that they are co-extensive. That is, knowledge of a risk to possessions should not automatically lead to the conclusion that the failure to address that risk is an interference with the enjoyment of those possessions.[230] In terms of the Court's judgment, the identification of 'measures which an applicant may legitimately expect from the authorities' was not explored in detail, as it was already clear that the measures in respect of the methane risk should have been taken.

How far the awareness of risks gives rise to positive obligations in other cases is unclear. In *Öneryildiz*, the State's positive obligations arose as a result of a specific warnings regarding an identified risk to a small group of property owners; moreover, the risk was to both life and property. Where the risk or the affected group is not identified, it is less likely that P1(1) is engaged. Nevertheless, in *Marcic v Thames Water Utilities Ltd*,[231] P1(1) was applicable in respect of the failure of a statutory sewerage undertaker to prevent repeated and severe flooding of the claimant's home. Although the risk of flooding was identified, it applied to many landowners and hence the affected group was much broader than it was in *Öneryildiz*. In any case, both cases concerned risks

---

[229] Above [134].

[230] See the partly dissenting opinion of Judge Casadevall in the Fourth Section judgment (18 June 2002), joined by Judges Türmen and Maruste:

> It merely underscores, in my view, the point that the primacy of the obligations on States under Article 2 of the Convention bears no comparison to that accorded by the majority to the right enshrined in Article 1 of Protocol No 1 which it describes as being of 'key importance' before ultimately deciding, somewhat hastily, that the Contracting States will henceforth have to satisfy positive obligations in this regard (see paragraphs 144 and 145 of the judgment).

[231] [2004] 2 AC 42; see also *Lough v First Secretary of State*, [2004] EWCA Civ 905.

of physical damage to tangible property. Where the risks are purely economic, and affect a broad cross-section of public, it is unlikely that positive obligations would arise. For example, the Court has held that there is no interference with property arising purely from a loss in value caused by inflation, even where public authorities have undertaken to protect specific assets held by specific classes of individuals from the effects of inflation. In *Gayduk and others v Ukraine*,[232] the Ukrainian legislature had passed laws undertaking to 'maintain and update the real value of individual savers' deposits' in specified accounts and banking institutions, and had gone as far as setting up schemes to compensate those whose savings were affected by inflation. However, the legislation stated that individuals had no entitlement to payment of compensation until funds had been allocated to the scheme. Although the legislature appeared to provide some guarantee to individuals, possibly within the scope of the Court's notion of 'legitimate expectations', it held that P1(1) was not applicable.[233]

CONCLUSIONS

Some aspects of the applicability tests have been clarified by the case law. For example, it is clear that interests recognised as private property under national law are normally treated as P1(1) possessions. Similarly, direct restrictions or modifications of rights of property are interferences with possessions. There are also rules of a more specific nature which can be stated with some confidence: for example, a final judgment is a P1(1) possession, and a cause of action relating to the protection of a property interest is also a P1(1) possession. Social welfare benefits are P1(1) possessions if they are vested, pecuniary rights based on contributions; indeed, it is probably not necessary to demonstrate that they are fully vested or based on contributions. In addition, the imposition of a tax or other financial liability is an interference with the enjoyment of possessions, and the failure to provide an effective legal process for vindicating property rights also makes P1(1) applicable.

Nevertheless, it is fair to say that the development of general principles has not been central goal of the European Court, at least in relation to the applicability issue. For the most part, reasons for judgment respond to the specific facts of the case and do not set down general principles to be applied in subsequent cases or by national authorities. Moreover, judgments that do set down general principles are more likely to open lines of inquiry instead of closing them.

---

[232] Reports 2002–VI 405.

[233] See also *Rudzinska v Poland*, Reports 1999–VI 523; *L'Association et la Ligue pour la Protection des Acheteurs D'Automobiles, Abid et 646 others v Romania*, Appl No 34746/97, 10 July 2001; *Appolonov v Russia*, Appl No 47578/01, 29 August 2002. However, the effects of inflation may be taken into account in considering delays in satisfying other obligations: see eg *Akkuş v Turkey*, Reports 1997–IV 1300 (2000) 30 EHRR 365 and *Angelov v Bulgaria*, Appl No 44076/98, 22 April 2004.

Examples can be seen in the cases on the autonomous meaning doctrine and de facto interferences with property, where the tendency is to broaden the range of facts for consideration without providing clear rules for determining the relevance or weight of facts. Indeed, even where the Court seems to lay down clear rules, it leaves many issues open simply by making little or no reference to other, potentially inconsistent cases. The failure of the Court in *Agrotexim* to refer to its earlier holding in *Pine Valley* is one example; the inconsistency between *Polacek* and *Gaygusuz* is another. Hence, as a very general observation, we can say that the jurisprudence that is developing is not one that is directed toward providing doctrinal coherence. In many cases, the results may be predictable, but this is due to the accumulation of cases on similar facts rather than the way in which reasons are expressed in those cases.

There are some general aspects of the European Court's position which might explain the failure to develop a clear jurisprudence. To begin with, it lacks the control over its docket that most higher appellate or constitutional courts have; hence, it cannot select test cases on the basis that they would be particularly useful for resolving difficult or important points of interpretation. Moreover, it is not at all clear that all member States see any cases as 'test cases'. This is clearly illustrated in relation to P1(1), as there have been several series of cases where fundamentally similar issues are addressed by the Court again and again. For example, in 1995, the Court dealt with its first case on the failure of the Italian system to facilitate the repossession of flats by landlords. Since then, the same issue has come before the Court on well over 100 occasions. Plainly, the Court's own judgments carry little weight with the Italian authorities, except as a resolution of the dispute on the specific facts before it. In these circumstances, it is hardly surprising that the development of doctrine has not been as significant as might have been hoped.

This may change with the development of a body of cases by the Grand Chamber, but there are no signs at present that it will. To date, the only applicability cases decided by the Grand Chamber are the restoration cases.[234] In these cases, the Grand Chamber's approach is significant because, firstly, the reasoning is quite formal and, secondly, the view of P1(1)'s scope is quite narrow. If the Grand Chamber does indeed have an important role in developing a jurisprudence, we would expect to see one or both of these aspects of the restoration cases reflected in subsequent applicability cases. However, there are no signs that this is the case.

The lack of doctrinal development also reflects the tension between the issues of applicability and justification that first arose during the drafting of the Convention. The British Government believed that the substantive content of rights should be settled before the powers of the proposed court could be determined. By contrast, many other governments believed that the jurisdiction of the court could be settled independently of the content of the specific rights.

---

[234] See the cased cited above, n 81.

Indeed, many of those from the civilian tradition (especially the French) argued that the court should determine the scope of rights on a case-by-case basis, and hence there was no real need for the rights to be defined in advance.[235] At the drafting stage, the British view prevailed but to some extent the subsequent history of the Court has shown that the British objective was not achieved. That is, if British view carried through to interpretation and applicability, the Court would examine scope of rights carefully so as not to exceed its jurisdiction. However, if the civilian view dominated, then flexibility would be required in the interpretion of the Convention rights and the Court would show a preference for the general Convention principles, such as legality, proportionality, and the effectiveness of remedies, which in turn would be developed in the light of the general objectives mentioned in the Preamble.

The end result has been an uncomfortable mix of these two approaches. The civilian view is apparent the cases where the autonomous meaning doctrine and the idea of 'de facto' interferences led to a broad view of applicability, whereas the British approach is seen where the Court relies on more technical tests for determining applicability. In addition, the civilian view is apparent in the cases which make little distinction between Article 6 cases on the determination of civil rights and the P1(1) cases involving causes of action and judgments. By contrast, the British view is seen in the cases where the Court has limited the scope of P1(1) on the basis that, in its view, applicants have sought to extend it into territory covered by other rights. Nevertheless, the tendency has been to take a generous view of applicability, thereby concentrating the analysis on the issue of justification.

In the UK courts, it is perhaps too soon to identify trends in relation to the applicability test. Plainly, the appellate courts in the United Kingdom are in a much better position to set down principles in leading cases. There is evidence in some cases that the courts have attempted this. For example, in *Wilson*, some of their Lordships preferred the clarity that would result from holding that an unenforceable agreement cannot confer P1(1) possessions. However, it is doubtful that the majority view in *Wilson* can be accepted as a categorical rule, given the European Court's judgments in *Beyeler*, *Stretch* and *Pine Valley*. At the same time, the courts have also demonstrated a preference for applying justification rules, even where they have come to the conclusion that P1(1) is not applicable in any event. *Wilson* itself is an example, where even the judges who found P1(1) inapplicable made it clear that the relevant legislation could be justified in any event. The willingness to concentrate on justification, if it does come to characterise the UK jurisprudence, would probably be closer to the spirit of the Convention jurisprudence.

---

[235] Chapter 1, 24–25.

3

The Legality Condition

———————

THE SECOND AND third sentences of Article 1 of Protocol No 1
(P1(1)) refer to legality expressly, as second sentence states that a
deprivation of property must be 'subject to the conditions provided for
by law' and the third sentence permits the States to enforce 'such laws' as it
deems necessary for the purposes prescribed. There is no reference to legality
in the first sentence, but it applies to Rule 1 in any event. In *Iatridis v Greece*,
the Court pointed out that the rule of law is 'one of the fundamental principles
of a democratic society', 'inherent in all the Articles of the Convention'.[1]
Accordingly, 'the first and most important requirement of (P1(1)) is that any
interference by a public authority with the peaceful enjoyment of possessions
should be lawful'.[2]

The principle of legality can be regarded as a threshold issue, as the fair balance 'becomes relevant only once it has been established that the interference in
question satisfied the requirement of lawfulness and was not arbitrary.'[3] While
this suggests that it should be central to the outcome of many cases, cases are
rarely decided against the State on this basis. In the vast majority of disputes, it
is either applicability or the proportionality/fair balance test which is conclusive. This reflects the fact that States are generally careful to draft their laws
with sufficient breadth to ensure that an interference is lawful, and that most
national systems provide a remedy for unlawful action of public officials.

This chapter examines the two elements to the legality principle: first, the
State must comply with national law; secondly, even if the State does comply
with national law, it must also comply with the general principles regarding the
rule of law, as laid down by the Strasbourg institutions.

---

[1] Reports 1999–II 75 (2000) 30 EHRR 97 [58]. On the Convention idea of legality, see
H Mountfield, 'The Concept of an Unlawful Interference with Fundamental Rights' in J Jowell and
J Cooper, (eds), *Understanding Human Rights Principles* (Hart Publishing, Oxford, 2001).
[2] Above.
[3] Above.

LEGALITY AND COMPLIANCE WITH THE
CONDITIONS OF NATIONAL LAW

A failure of public authorities to comply with national law raises a strong case of unlawfulness under the Convention. Some of the most extreme cases under P1(1) involve the unlawful destruction of property by Turkish security forces;[4] other cases include: the eviction of a tenant from property without authority of law, and for the benefit of a public body;[5] the refusal of local authorities to comply with a judicial decision regarding planning control;[6] the re-opening and quashing of a final judgment contrary to the conditions under national law;[7] and generally the failure of public authorities to implement judgments of the courts that bind them directly.[8]

However, the European Court of Human Rights does not seek to settle disputed issues of national law. It does not invariably accept the State's own determination of its compliance with national law, but it is not likely to question a determination by a national court unless it has applied the law 'manifestly erroneously or so as to reach arbitrary conclusions'.[9] Nevertheless, in at least one case, the Court has suggested that it does not review compliance with national law at even this level of scrutiny. In *Špaček, sro v The Czech Republic*,[10] the applicant claimed that the publication of tax and accounting regulations did not comply with Czech law. The Court said, *inter alia*, that 'it is not for the Court to express a view on the appropriateness of the methods chosen by the legislature of a Contracting State, or to decide on whether the manner of publishing tax and accounting principles is compatible with the requirements of Czech law.'[11]

In some cases, the State argues that a delay in implementing a judgment can be justified. The Court has accepted that there may be cases where a legislative provision found to be unconstitutional may be permitted to continue in force, if its immediate repeal would itself create a high degree of certainty. Hence, the Court held that there is no violation of P1(1) where a national court declares tax legislation unconstitutional, but allows it to remain in force until new

---

[4] *Akdivar v Turkey*, Reports 1996–IV 1192 (1997) 23 EHRR 143.

[5] *Iatridis* (n 1).

[6] *Frascino v Italy*, Appl No 35227/97, 11 December 2003.

[7] *Valová, Slezák and Slezák v Slovakia*, Appl No 44925/98, 1 June 2004.

[8] *Brumărescu v Romania*, Reports 1999–VII 201 (2001) 33 EHRR 35 [79]; *Burdov v Russia*, Reports 2002–III 317 (2004) 38 EHRR 29; *Metaxas v Greece*, Appl No 8415/02, 27 May 2004; *Piven v Ukraine*, Appl No 56849/00, 29 June 2004; *Zhovner v Ukraine*, Appl No 56848/00, 29 June 2004; *Bocancea v Moldova*, Appl No 18872/02, 6 July 2004.

[9] *Beyeler v Italy*, Reports 2000–I 57 (2001) 33 EHRR 52 [108]; *Tre Traktörer Aktiebolag v Sweden*, Series A No 159 (1991) 13 EHRR 309 [58]; *Håkansson and Sturesson v Sweden*, Series A No 171 (1990) 13 EHRR 1 [47].

[10] (2000) 30 EHRR 1010.

[11] Above [57].

legislation is enacted[12] or corrects any defects only with prospective effect.[13] If the State can show that there was a risk that there would be a 'substantial legal lacuna' in the relevant field of law, the Court may accept the delay in implementation.[14]

It is odd that a failure to comply with the conditions laid down by a State's own law does not violate the Convention's legality principle. It seems, however, that the Court has decided not to determine legality by purely formal criteria. As explained below, it has developed the 'quality of law' principle, by which it may find a law that satisfies the State's formal requirements for legality is insufficiently accessible, precise or foreseeable to satisfy the Convention requirements. It also appears that the contrary is true: a law that does not satisfy the State's formal requirements may satisfy the Convention requirements, where denying effect to a formally invalid 'law' would itself threaten the objectives of accessibility, precision and foreseeability.

In any case, the Court's preference for deciding cases on the fair balance test has sometimes led it to gloss over the legality analysis. For example, in *Broniowski v Poland*, the failure of the Polish authorities to comply with judgments of the Polish courts had become so striking that some of the Polish courts described the situation as 'lawless'.[15] However, although these statements were noted by the European Court of Human Rights, it simply decided to consider the situation under the fair balance test.[16] However, it ultimately concluded that the fair balance had been upset, in part because 'it was incumbent on the Polish authorities to remove the existing incompatibility between the letter of the law and the State-operated practice which hindered the effective exercise of the applicant's right of property.'[17] The fact that judgments were ignored was relevant, but by considering it under the fair balance test, it was no longer conclusive.

LEGALITY AND THE QUALITY OF LAW

The principle of legality is not limited to compliance with national law. In *Carbonara and Ventura v Italy*, the Court stated that 'the requirement of

[12] *Roshka v Russia*, Appl No 63343/00, 6 November 2003; *Walden v Liechtenstein*, Appl No 33916/96, 16 March 2000.

[13] *Roshka* above; *Mika v Austria*, Appl No 26560/95, 26 June 1996 (Comm); see also *NAP Holdings UK Ltd v The United Kingdom*, (1996) 22 EHRR CD114, where it was held not disproportionate not to legislate retrospectively, where doing so would have brought law into step with expectations of both the Revenue and a taxpayer.

[14] *Roshka* above.

[15] Appl No 31443/96, 22 June 2004 (Grand Chamber); see also *Zwierzyński v Poland*, Reports 2001–VI 203 (2004) 38 EHRR 6.

[16] Above [154]

[17] Above [184]

lawfulness means that rules of domestic law must be sufficiently accessible, precise and foreseeable.'[18]

Accessibility of law

The Court views the question of accessibility in practical terms. The issue is whether the applicant could have reasonably been aware of the relevant laws. In *Špaček v The Czech Republic*,[19] the Czech Ministry of Finance issued various rules and regulations on the publication of tax legislation. The applicant argued that certain tax provisions should have been published in the Official Gazette, but had not; hence, they could not be applied without breached the legality requirement. The Court rejected this argument, but also considered whether the provisions were sufficiently accessible in any case. These specific provisions were distributed in the same outlets and to the same subscribers as the Official Gazette, and so it was safe to assume that they received the same publicity as the Gazette. In this case, it was sufficient that the applicant could have readily discovered the relevant provisions (if it was not already aware of them). In addition, it was relevant that the applicant was a company, rather than an individual, and as such it could be expected to contact specialists who would ascertain the relevant regulations on its behalf.[20]

Predictability

The question of predictability arose in a series of Italian cases on 'constructive expropriation'. Italian local authorities were finding that formal expropriation procedures had become so cumbersome that plans to construct public works and buildings were suffering from severe delays. The legislature therefore allowed the authorities to apply for permission to occupy land for two years, during which they could commence work, on the condition that they would subsequently expropriate the land formally. However, in a number of cases the authorities completed their work but then failed to complete the formal procedure. In such cases, the land should have been returned to the landowner, but the Court of Cassation developed a doctrine under which an owner dispossessed by the authorities automatically lost title when the works were completed. The

[18] Reports 2000–VI 91 [64]; see also *Beyeler* (n 9) [109]; *Hentrich v France*, Series A No 296–A (1994) 18 EHRR 440 [42]; *Lithgow v The United Kingdom*, Series A No 102 (1986) 8 EHRR 329 [110]; *cf* Judge Bonello, concurring, in *Belvedere Alberghiera srl v Italy*, Reports 2000–VI 135, on whether the 'quasi-law' on constructive expropriation satisfies minimum criteria of Convention, Judge Bonello remarked that 'The Court has, it seems to me, lost a priceless opportunity to extend the examination of the "quality of law" principle adopted in other cases, to the case of deprivation of property under Article 1 of Protocol 1. It is a pity.'

[19] *Špaček* (n 10).

[20] Above [60].

owners could bring a claim for damages against the authorities, subject to a five year limitation period running from the date of the work was completed and a statutory ceiling on damages. In *Carbonara and Ventura v Italy*,[21] the owners' claims were time-barred; in *Belvedere Alberghiera v Italy*,[22] no action for damages had been commenced. The Court concentrated on the unpredictability of the Court of Cassation's doctrine, since it was being applied inconsistently and resulted in unforeseeable or arbitrary outcomes.

It is not clear how the specific context in which the rules operate affects the standard of predictability. In the constructive expropriation cases, the Court also stated that it had 'reservations as to the compatibility with the requirement of lawfulness of a mechanism which, generally, enables the authorities to benefit from an unlawful situation in which the landowner is presented with a *fait accompli*.'[23] The use and acceptance of unlawful action as a means of achieving State objectives went too far, to the point that the Court felt that there was no need to consider the impact on the landowners (under the fair balance test). In an indirect way, however, the property owner's position is important. In the Italian cases, the landowners were entirely innocent of any kind of wrongdoing. By contrast, the fact that (for example) smugglers cannot predict when their contraband will be seized cannot mean that the confiscation laws fail the legality test. The predictability of enforcement may be relevant to the fair balance test, but it would be an exceptional case where it fell below the quality of law standard. Nevertheless, *Hentrich v France*[24] demonstrates that the Court has sometimes had considerable sympathy for property owners. It concerned French laws which gave tax authorities a right of pre-emption wherever it appeared that property had been transferred at an undervalue. The Court found that the pre-emption against the applicant's land breached P1(1), in part because the 'pre-emption operated arbitrarily and selectively and was scarcely foreseeable'.[25]

Hentrich is a difficult case, because the Court's approach to predictability is confusing. Plainly, the operation of the law is important, but precisely what it was that made the operation of the pre-emption law unlawful in this particular case was not made clear. The Court observed that transferees who were unaware of true value of land would innocently declare a lower value, and therefore not expect the authorities to pre-empt them. If so, foreseeability has a subjective element. The Court also observed that pre-emption occurred quite rarely. It did not explain why this was important, but it may have been suggesting that even the transferee who is aware that the declaration is below market value would not be able to foresee the exercise of the right of pre-emption. In either case, however, its finding on the specific facts is contradicted by its

---

[21] *Carbonara* (n 18).
[22] *Belvedere Alberghiera* (n 18).
[23] *Carbonara* (n 18) [66].
[24] *Hentrich* (n 18).
[25] Above [42].

decision in *Gasus Dosier und Fordertechnik GmbH v Netherlands*,[26] which also concerned tax enforcement. In *Gasus*, the Dutch authorities were authorised to seize any assets on the premises of a tax debtor, including those subject to a retention of title clause in favour of a seller. Sellers were in no position to ascertain the actual risk of seizure, because the purchaser's tax debts were confidential and would not be released by the authorities. The sellers were therefore at least as blameless as the transferees in *Hentrich*, and the seizure of property appears to have been just as unforeseeable as the pre-emption, and yet the Court in *Gasus* readily concluded that the seizure had been lawful.[27] The Court in *Gasus* took note of the fact that the seller had approached the transaction as a commercial venture, where it would have been aware of the risk that a buyer would get into financial trouble. Hence, it should have been aware of the laws empowering the tax authorities to seize the assets, and should be expected to take that risk into account before entering the transaction.

A variation on this issue also arose in *Håkansson and Sturesson v Sweden*.[28] The applicants in this case had purchased agricultural land at an auction. Before the auction, potential buyers were told that the Land Acquisition Act 1979 provided that they could be forced to resell within two years, unless the County Agricultural Board granted them a permit to retain the land. The applicants bought land at more than double its market value, having been told by a representative of the Board would grant them a permit. Subsequently, the Board decided that the land should be incorporated into existing farms, so it refused to grant the permit to the applicants and later forced them to resell the land at a substantial loss. The applicants argued that the legality of the Board's actions was affected by its decision to go back on the representative's statement that the relevant permits would be granted. The Court rejected this argument, on the basis that the applicants could not have reasonably considered the statement binding as a matter of Swedish law.[29]

The specific warnings at the time of the auction made *Håkansson* relatively clear, as it seems that there had been no suggestion that the representative had the authority to bind the Board in any way. It was not necessary to consider whether the absence of a specific warning on the effects of legislation would have made a difference. Moreover, there was no suggestion that the legislation itself was unclear or inaccessible. Hence, it is difficult to get any sense of the circumstances in which a representation by a public official on the future exercise of a legislative power by a public body would affect the legality of the exercise of that power. In any case, these issues are seen through the lens of the fair balance test, where the Court balances the need to maintain some flexibility in public decision-making with the individual's interest in legitimate expectations created by public conduct.

---

[26] Series A No 306–B (1995) 20 EHRR 403.
[27] And that there was no violation of P1–1.
[28] *Håkansson* (n 9).
[29] Above [48]; see also *NAP Holdings* (n 13).

To the extent that the value of accessibility and predictability depend on the context, the principle of legality and proportionality may become more difficult to distinguish. In *Špaček* and *Gasus*, the Court considered the impact of inaccessibility or unpredictability on the applicants. Since the proportionality also involves an assessment of the impact on the individual, it may appear that legality and proportionality necessarily overlap. Arguably, there is a real distinction: proportionality considers the impact of the interference with the individual's possessions, whereas legality considers the impact of inaccessibility and unpredictability. However, in practice the distinction is often difficult to see. For example, in *Hentrich*, the Court also considered that pre-emption was not attended by basic procedural safeguards. In particular, the principle of equality of arms should have been observed; on the facts, it was not, because the applicants were not given the opportunity to challenge tax authorities on the issue of the underestimation of the price or the tax consequences of their valuation. The Court therefore concluded that the interference with the applicant's possessions had not been lawful. This would appear to dispose of the case, since the legality principle should be distinct from the proportionality principle. However, the Court then considered whether the interference was disproportionate, where it stated that 'In order to assess the proportionality of the interference, the Court looks at the degree of protection from arbitrariness that is afforded by the proceedings in this case'.[30] On this point, it raised again the point that the pre-emption operated 'only rarely and scarcely foreseeably'.[31]

This shows that unpredictability which is not great enough to amount to unlawfulness may still be great enough to upset the fair balance. In *Beyeler*, for example, the Court found that an Italian pre-emption law for the protection of cultural works exhibited an element of uncertainty, but not enough to amount to unlawfulness; however, the Court also found that 'the element of uncertainty in the statute and the considerable latitude it affords the authorities are material considerations to be taken into account in determining whether the measure complained of struck a fair balance.'[32] The enquiry into legality is more narrowly focused, as it does not involve an explicit balancing between community and private interests. Where the Court believes that community interests is so compelling that it may justify laws for which there are issues regarding accessibility and predictability, it may treat the case as only raising issues of proportionality.

[30] *Hentrich* (n 18) [45].
[31] Above [47].
[32] *Beyeler* (n 9) [110].

4

The Structure of Article 1 of the First Protocol

N O CONSTITUTIONAL OR human rights instrument can guarantee a right to property that is both absolute and extensive. Either the right must be hemmed in by limitations and exceptions or it must be very narrowly drawn. As chapter 2 shows, Article 1 of Protocol No 1 (P1(1)) is not narrowly drawn: it can apply to void 'contracts', social welfare entitlements, indirect and de facto interferences, and it even extends to the positive obligation to protect property against others. Nevertheless, applicability has only a limited function in the Convention jurisprudence, as it is merely a filter: even if P1(1) is applicable, the State to justify its may actions. Hence, as one might expect, the focus of the dispute often falls on issues relating to justification.

Chapters 3–5 consider the general principles relating to justification, with this chapter examining the structure of the express limitations on the right to property, as set out in the second and third sentences of Article 1 of the First Protocol. The previous chapter considered the principles of legality and the next considers proportionality. These are not set out in a single provision of general application, but are derived from similar expressions found in the express limitations of a number of Convention rights.

Hence, the right to property in Council of Europe is subject to limitations at three levels: the first from the applicability doctrines; the second from the specific limits in the second and third sentences; and the third from the general limits arising from the doctrines of legality and proportionality. Taken singly, the limitations at each level raise issues of their own, but there are also fundamental issues concerning their relationship to each other. This point was not addressed during the drafting of P1(1), because the focus was almost entirely on a small set of specific issues. For example, with the second sentence, discussions centred on whether there should be a duty to compensate for the deprivation of possessions, and the meaning of a 'deprivation of possessions' was largely ignored. Similarly, in relation to the third sentence, the meaning of a 'control on the use of property' was not considered in any depth by the delegates. Consequently, there are situations where it seems fairly clear that there was no intention to make State action incompatible with P1(1), and yet the text of P1(1) seems to say nothing to indicate the doctrinal basis for this position. To take just one example, it is not stated that property may be seized or sold to satisfy the judgment debts of a private creditor. Plainly, P1(1) could not have been intended to prohibit civil execution against property, but there are several different ways in which this could be explained. The first would rely on applicability: arguably, P1(1) only applies to interferences by the State for public use, and not to a taking of property by a private person for a private use, even where that taking has the backing of a court order. Alternatively, the express limitations could be invoked. The taking of property to satisfy a civil debt might be regarded as sufficiently similar to a taking of property 'to secure the payment of taxes or other contributions or penalties' that it would be subject to the limitation in the third sentence of P1(1). Finally, the general limitations might be applied, by concluding that even if P1(1) is applicable, civil execution satisfies both the legality and proportionality principles.

To some extent, all three approaches are evident in the case law. This chapter therefore begins with the Court's seminal judgment in *Sporrong and Lönnroth v Sweden*,[1] in which it divided property cases into three categories, each covered by a different 'Rule'. This division into Rules provides the basis for determining how the limitations apply. It then describes, as far as it is possible to do so, the type of case falling into each category, and how the categorisation of a set of facts affects the outcome in the case.

THE SIGNIFICANCE OF *SPORRONG AND LÖNNROTH v SWEDEN*

The relationship between the different elements of P1(1) was clarified in *Sporrong and Lönnroth v Sweden*, where the Court stated that P1(1) sets out three rules regarding rights to property:

> The first rule, which is of general nature, enounces the principle of peaceful enjoyment of property; it is set out in the first sentence of the paragraph. The second rule covers deprivation of possessions and subjects it to certain conditions; it appears in the second sentence of the same paragraph. The third rule recognises the States are entitled, amongst other things, to control the use of property in accordance with the general interest, by enforcing such laws as they deem necessary to that purpose; it is contained in the second paragraph.[2]

In *James v United Kingdom*, the Court elaborated on this structure, as it said that the three Rules are not distinct: 'The second and third rules are concerned with particular instances of interference with the right to peaceful enjoyment of property and should therefore be construed in the light of the general principle enunciated in the first rule.'[3]

---

[1] Series A No 52 (1983) 5 EHRR 35.
[2] Above [61].
[3] Series A No 98 (1986) 8 EHRR 123 [37].

It is therefore necessary to identify the 'general principle' of Rule 1. In *Sporrong*, the Court stated that it reflects the principle that there must be a 'fair balance' between 'the demands of the general interest of the community and the requirements of the protection of the individual's fundamental rights.'[4] Since Rule 1 is general, and Rules 2 and 3 are merely specific types of interferences with possessions, it follows that the fair balance principle applies to them as well. But if the fair balance principle is reflected in all three Rules, it should make little difference whether a given set of facts is considered under the first, second or third Rule. That is, even if an interference is incorrectly classified under one Rule instead of another, the application of the fair balance principle to the specific facts should ultimately produce the same result. If so, the process of classification is not particularly important, because the fair balance test allows the Court to consider all the facts which might have been considered in tests for distinguishing between the Rules. That is, the elaboration of tests for distinguishing between different Rules would only be necessary where categorisation under a specific Rule affects the outcome.

This raises one further point on Rule 1. In *Sporrong*, the Court indicated that Rules 2 and 3 are not comprehensive: some cases do not fall under either Rule, but must be analysed under the general principle of Rule 1. It is not entirely clear why the Court did so. The case dealt with the issue of expropriation permits, which a substantial dissenting group felt that should have been evaluated under Rule 3. They did not comment on the application of the fair balance principle under Rule 1, but it seems that they regarded the second and third sentences as comprehensive expressions on the limitations on the right contained in the first sentence. The majority plainly thought that this was not the case, but offered no explanation for this. The Court has not explained its position subsequently, but it seems that there may have been (and still is) a desire to maintain some conceptual clarity in relation to Rules 2 and 3 and the right to compensation. As discussed below, under Rule 2, there is a general principle that compensation should be paid to ensure that the fair balance is maintained, whereas under Rule 3, compensation is generally not required.

Had the European Court concluded that all cases fell under either Rule 2 or Rule 3, it could have found itself drawn into difficult questions regarding the distinction between the types of cases that fall under each Rule. To some extent, the absence of a compensation guarantee under P1(1) avoids these issues, as a result-oriented court need not focus on formal distinctions between types of interference to reach an appropriate decision on compensation. In addition, the development of the Rule 1 category as an open or residual class into which some of the difficult cases can be located has also allowed the Court to treat Rule 2 and Rule 3 as comparatively specific categories.

The effect of this on judicial rulemaking can be appreciated by contrasting the Convention jurisprudence with the American jurisprudence on regulatory

---

[4] *Sporrong* (n 1) [69].

takings under the takings clause of the Fifth Amendment to the Constitution.[5] The Supreme Court has acknowledged that regulation is not normally a taking, except when it 'goes too far'.[6] Since a taking must be compensated, the Supreme Court has attempted to lay down clear rules to identify when regulation does go too far. In the absence of flexibility on compensation, the making of rules for distinguishing types of interference with property assumes much greater importance than it does under P1(1). Indeed, the Strasbourg Court has tended to put problematic cases into Rule 1, and has sought to develop Rule 2 and Rule 3 as conceptually distinct categories where reasonably clear consequences regarding compensation follow from the categorisation, but always subject to the flexibility of a fair balance test that allows it to make exceptions where it sees fit. Whether it has been successful in developing Rules 2 and 3 as distinct categories subject to clear rules is debateable, and dealt with in more detail below, but it demonstrates that the Court believes that the classification exercise is relevant. Indeed, in *Sporrong* and *James* the Court has stated that the legal analysis of a factual situation should begin by considering whether it fits within the second and third rules; the first rule should be considered only after it is determined that the second and third do not apply.[7] Moreover, the importance that is given to classification suggests that there is a real difference in the application of the fair balance test under each of the rules. Since it is very unusual for the Court to find that an interference which falls under the third sentence has breached the Convention, applicants often argue that the interference with their possessions is a Rule 1 or Rule 2 interference.

The foregoing suggests that the European Court regards the identification of the Rule applicable to a case as relevant but not conclusive of the outcome. However, despite the statements in *Sporrong* and *James*, it is not clear that the categorisation of cases under one Rule or another has any real impact on the outcome, as it does not seem to narrow the facts to be considered in the fair balance test or to dictate how the test should be applied to the facts. Even where the categorisation seems to affect the outcome, it is not clear how it has done so. For example, in *Gasus Dosier und Fordertechnik GmbH v Netherlands*, the Court treated the interference with the applicant's property as a Rule 3 interference, although the Commission had said that it was a Rule 2 interference; nevertheless, both the Court and the Commission concluded that there was no violation of P1(1).[8]

In this respect, it is worth noting that are many cases where courts have not found it necessary to identify the relevant Rule.[9] In the United Kingdom, the

---

[5] The Fifth Amendment provides that 'No person shall be . . . deprived of . . . property, without due process of law; nor shall private property be taken for public use, without just compensation.' See *Eastern Enterprises v Apfel* 524 US 498 (1998) for a discussion of the limitation of the right to compensation to takings of property and the distinction between the deprivations and takings.

[6] *Pennsylvania Coal Co v Mahon* 260 US 393, 415 (1922).

[7] *Sporrong* (n 1) [61]; *James* (n 3) [37].

[8] Series A No 306–B (1995) 20 EHRR 403 [57], [59].

[9] See eg *Stretch v The United Kingdom*, (2004) 38 EHRR 12; *Zvolský and Zvolská v The Czech Republic*, Reports 2002–IX 163; *Öneryıldız v Turkey*, Appl No 48939/99, 30 November 2004 [133].

House of Lords has yet to do so in any of its cases on P1(1). These cases dealt with interferences that should come within the third sentence: *Marcic v Thames Water Utilities Ltd* dealt with modifications of private law rights regarding flooding;[10] *Wilson and others v Secretary of State for Trade and Industry* with the regulation of consumer loan contracts;[11] and *Aston Cantlow and Wilmcote with Billesley Parochial Church Council v Wallbank and another* with the enforcement of (arguably) tax measures.[12] In all three cases, the House of Lords overturned Court of Appeal judgments and found no violation of P1(1), but in none of them did their Lordships feel it necessary to identify the specific Rule that applied to the facts.[13] The outcomes are consistent with the Strasbourg cases, and yet it seems that the categorisation of facts into a specific Rule would have contributed nothing useful to the analysis.

The pattern in Strasbourg is similar. To date, the Court has not set out any general principles on categorisation. Indeed, there are cases where the Commission and Court reached different conclusions on which Rule should apply, and yet ultimately the conclusion on the application of the fair balance test was the same. That is, while there are some types of cases that are usually classified under one Rule or another, no general theory of classification is being developed. For example, the Court might look to two types of criteria in classifying cases: those relating to the impact of the interference, and those relating to its purpose. The first looks at the applicant's loss: for example, a court might ask whether the interference was temporary or permanent, whether it was partial or complete, or whether it related to an ownership interest or something less. From this, it would identify the Rule applicable to the facts. The second looks at the purpose of the interference: distinctions may be made between, for example, the acquisition of property for use by a public body and the destruction of property for public safety, or between the redistribution of property rights between private persons and the taking of property rights to enhance the State's resources and wealth. However, neither the wording of P1(1) nor the jurisprudence of the Court offers any direction in this regard. In P1(1) itself, the first and second sentences seem to concentrate on the impact of the interference ('interference with the enjoyment of possessions' and 'deprivation of possessions'), whereas the third sentence refers to both the impact of the interference ('controls on use') and its purpose ('to secure payment of taxes . . .'). In the cases, there is almost

---

[10] [2004] 2 AC 42.

[11] [2004] 1 AC 816.

[12] [2004] 1 AC 546.

[13] In *Wilson* (n 11) [44], Lord Nicholls' reasoning suggests that the interference was a Rule 2 deprivation of possessions (although it should have been treated as a Rule 3 control on the use of property); Lord Hobhouse described the relevant statutory provisions as causing a deprivation of property, but it does not seem that he was referring to any specific Rule but merely that P1–1 was engaged (at [136]). In *Aston Cantlow* (n 12) [68], Lord Hobhouse criticised the Court of Appeal for failing to take into account the passage of *Sporrong* (n 2) that sets out the three Rules, but it seems that his criticism was concerned with the Court of Appeal's position on the applicability of P1–1, rather than the Rule it applied.

no discussion of the method of classification. For example, in *National &
Provincial Building Society and others v United Kingdom* and *Gasus*, the Court
applied Rule 3 because it was 'the most natural approach',[14] but without giving
any sense of what makes one approach natural and another unnatural. Both
cases concerned taxation: in *National & Provincial Building Society,* the cancellation of a restitution claim allowed State to retain funds to satisfy taxes that
were retrospectively imposed; in *Gasus*, the tax authorities' seizure of goods and
the proceeds of their sale facilitated the satisfaction of the tax debts of a third
party. This suggests that it is the purpose of the interference or ultimate use of
the property which is important. However, in *Hentrich v France*,[15] where
French tax authorities exercised a right of pre-emption as a means of enforcing
tax laws, the Court held that Rule 2 applied because the applicant had
been deprived of ownership. Here, it seems that the impact on the applicant's
interests is more important. Moreover, even where the Court does identify a
particular fact as relevant in different cases, it does not necessarily follow the
fact has similar significance. For example, both *Bramelid and Malmström v
Sweden*[16] and *James*[17] concerned legislation enabling private persons to compulsorily acquire the property of other private persons: in *Bramelid*, shareholders holding 90% of the voting power in a company were empowered to buy
out the minority; in *James*, tenants could buy the freehold from their landlords.
In both cases, the Court distinguished between such private takings and the
ordinary public expropriation, but in *Bramelid*, it was Rule 1 that applied and
in *James* it was Rule 2.[18]

In conclusion, the position on the internal structure of P1(1) is in a confused
state. The Strasbourg court seems to insist that the exercise of classifying cases
under a specific Rule is relevant to its analysis and final decision, and yet it is not
clear that there is indeed any impact on either the analysis or the decisions.
Nevertheless, the fact that the Court does seem to believe that classification is
important suggests that, at the very least, there may be some tactical advantage
to be gained by arguing that a specific Rule applies to a set of facts. Accordingly,
we now consider the factors relevant to classification as identified by the Court.

---

[14] *National & Provincial*, Reports 1997–VII 2325 (1998) 25 EHRR 127 [79]; *Gasus* (n 8) [59]; see
also *MA and 34 Others v Finland*, Appl No 27793/95, 10 June 2003; *Dangeville SA v France*, Reports
2002–III 71 (2004) 38 EHRR 32 [51].

[15] Series A No 296–A (1994) 18 EHRR 440 [35] (it appears that the French Government did not
contest the point).

[16] (1982) 5 EHRR 249 (Comm).

[17] *James* (n 3).

[18] In *Bramelid* (n 16) at 255, the European Commission stated that:

Even though the word 'expropriated' does not appear in the text, the terms of this provision, in
particular the words 'deprived of his possessions . . . in the public interest' as well as the reference to 'the general principles of international law' show clearly that it relates to expropriation,
whether formal or de facto, that is to say the act by which the state seizes—or gives another the
right to seize—a specific asset to be used for realisation of a goal in the public interest.

RULE 1—INTERFERENCE WITH THE ENJOYMENT OF POSSESSIONS

Function of Rule 1

While many types of interferences with possessions fall under Rule 2 or 3, there are some types which are covered only by Rule 1. In this sense, Rule 1 is a residual category, described negatively as those cases which do not fall under one of the other Rules. There are, arguably, definable categories of Rule 1 cases (considered below), such as interferences relating to the expropriation of property, the appropriation of intangibles and interests short of ownership, but at this point, there is no single conception of a Rule 1 case.

Actions related to expropriation

The first category includes cases where the interference is a preliminary step toward an expropriation of the property. Once the expropriation is completed, Rule 2 applies; but before completion, the Court often declares that Rule 1 applies.[19] This follows from the *Sporrong* judgment,[20] as the applicants argued that the issue of permits authorising the City of Stockholm to expropriate their land interfered with their possessions. There was an interference with possessions, as the permits rendered the applicants' right of property 'precarious and defeasible'; however, there was no Rule 2 deprivation of possessions, because the permits 'left intact in law the owners' right to use and dispose of their possessions'.[21] This left open the possibility that the permits might have been considered 'controls on the use of property' under Rule 3. In terms of their impact, they were similar to regulatory controls on the disposition of property, since they made it more difficult for the owners to sell or lease the property. However, the Court stated simply that, since the permits were 'an initial step in a procedure leading to deprivation of possessions', they did not fall under Rule 3.[22]

The Court did not elaborate on the distinction between Rules 1 and 3, but it came to similar conclusions in a series of cases concerning an Austrian land consolidation scheme.[23] The consolidation process involved interim 'provisional'

---

[19] Rule 1 has also been applied where the complaint does not relate to the amount of compensation, but delays in the actual payment of compensation: see eg *Tsirikakis v Greece*, Appl No 46355/99, 17 January 2002; *Nastou v Greece*, Appl No 51356/99, 16 January 2003.

[20] *Sporrong* (n 1); see also *Terazzi srl v Italy*, Appl No 27265/95, 17 October 2002; *Matos e Silva, lda v Portugal*, Reports 1996–IV 1092 (1997) 24 EHRR 573; *Pialopoulos v Greece* (2001) 33 EHRR 39 [56]. See M Redman, 'Compulsory Purchase, Compensation And Human Rights' [1999] *Journal of Planning & Environment Law* 315, 318–21.

[21] Above [60], [63].

[22] Above [65].

[23] *Erkner and Hofauer v Austria*, Series A No 117 (1987) 9 EHRR 464; *Poiss v Austria*, Series A No 117 (1988) 10 EHRR 231; *Prötsch v Austria*, Reports 1996–V 1812 (2001) 32 EHRR 12.

transfers before the scheme was finally settled. Compensation was available for those left worse off by consolidation, but no compensation was available for 'provisional' transfers because they could be revoked before the final scheme was settled. According to the Court, the possibility that the transfers could be reversed meant that they fell under Rule 1 rather than Rule 2. The Court also found that the provisional transfers did not fall under Rule 3, because they were not intended to control the use of the land. They were merely preliminary steps in a process which would ultimately culminate in a deprivation of the land.[24]

Finally, although restrictions on the development of property would ordinarily fall under the third sentence as a control on the use of property, there have been suggestions that they are covered by Rule 1 if they are intended to facilitate expropriation. In particular, development restrictions may be imposed so as to ensure that the amount of compensation is not affected by development before the date of valuation. Indeed, in *Sporrong*, prohibitions on building on the land were imposed at the same time as the issue of the permits (probably to preserve the state of the property pending the expropriation), but since these were related to the expropriation, the classification under Rule 1 was not affected.[25] Similarly, in *Phocas v France*,[26] the applicant had applied for planning permission in 1965 to convert a building into flats, but was refused permission on the basis that the local municipality was about to adopt a crossroads scheme which would have been jeopardised by the applicant's plans. The land was eventually expropriated in 1982, but the applicant sought compensation for prohibition on development in the intervening period. On the face of it, the denial of planning permission appears to be a control on use under the third sentence, but the Court applied Rule 1 because the applicant 'did not complain of a deprivation of his property within the meaning of the second sentence of the first paragraph (P1(1)) or of specific measures restricting the use of it within the meaning of the second paragraph (P1(1)), but of an infringement of his right of property resulting from the authorities' general conduct.'[27]

The appropriation of intangibles and interests short of ownership

One idea that emerges from some of the cases is that Rule 1 is concerned with the appropriation of resources for public use, where such appropriation is not in the form of a taking of a full ownership interest (to which Rule 2 would ordinarily apply). Accordingly, the Court has held, in a number of cases, that the

---

[24] *Erkner*, above [74]; *Poiss*, above [64]; *Prötsch*, above [42].

[25] Contrast *Jacobsson v Sweden*, Series A No 163 (1990) 12 EHRR 56, where it was argued that building prohibitions of similar effect to those in *Sporrong* should be examined under Rule 1: the Court held that Rule 3 applied, because no expropriation permits had been issued and there was no evidence that the authorities had ever formed a firm intention to expropriate property (at [54]).

[26] Reports 1996–II 519 (2001) 32 EHRR 11.

[27] Above [52].

extinction of a judgment debt is a Rule 1 interference.[28] The Court's reasoning has been very brief, as it said little more than the extinction of a debt is neither a deprivation nor a control on the use of property. Plainly, where the judgment is against a public body, the extinction benefits the State in a manner similar to an ordinary expropriation, despite the absence of any direct transfer of property rights. Indeed, in *Pressos Compania Naviera SA v Belgium*,[29] the Court went against its general line and treated the extinction of civil claims as a Rule 2 interference. There was no discussion of its decisions to the contrary, but it does demonstrate the close similarity between the extinction of debts or claims against the State and an ordinary expropriation. Moreover, the application of the fair balance test is very similar in both types of cases, as the Court has made it clear that compensation is normally required for the extinction of debts. It seems that they are classified differently solely to preserve some conceptual clarity for Rule 2.

A similar concern with conceptual clarity was shown in *Iatridis v Greece*,[30] where the Court suggested that Rule 2 applies only to the deprivation of a full ownership interest in property. The applicant complained that a leasehold interest in a cinema had been taken from him. Under common law constitutional rights to property, such action would probably be treated as an expropriation,[31] but the Court stated simply that since the applicant 'holds only a lease of his business premises, this interference neither amounts to an expropriation nor is an instance of controlling the use of property but comes under the first sentence of the first paragraph of Article 1.'[32] On the basis of these cases, it could be argued that cases involving State measures directed toward the enhancement of its resources fall under Rule 1, except where there is the transfer of the full set of property rights of an owner. So, for example, Rule 1 has not been applied to rent controls[33] or planning restrictions on the use and development of land.[34]

By this reasoning, measures which redistribute property amongst private persons should not fall under Rule 1. In fact, the Court has not always taken this line; indeed, there are number of important cases to the contrary. In particular, in *Bramelid*, the Court treated legislation which allowed majority shareholders to buy out a minority as an instance of a Rule 1 interference, because it felt that

---

[28] *Stran Greek Refineries v Greece*, Series A No 301–B (1995) 19 EHRR 293; *Brumărescu v Romania*, Reports 1999–VII 201 (2001) 33 EHRR 35; *Ambruosi v Italy* (2002) 35 EHRR 5; *Smokovitis v Greece*, Appl No 46356/99, 11 April 2002; but *cf National & Provincial* (n 14), where the extinction of the debt was treated as ancillary to the enforcement of a tax debt, and hence as falling under Rule 3.

[29] Series A No 332 (1996) 21 EHRR 301.

[30] Reports 1999–II 75 (2000) 30 EHRR 97.

[31] T Allen, *The Right to Property in Commonwealth Constitutions* (CUP, Cambridge, 2000) ch 6.

[32] *Iatridis* (n 30) [55]. See also *Wittek v Germany*, Reports 2002–X 43; *Boudouka and 57 others v Greece*, Appl No 58640/00, 16 May 2002; *Bruncrona v Finland*, Appl No 41673/98, 16 November 2004 [70]–[78].

[33] *Mellacher v Austria*, Series A No 169 (1990) 12 EHRR 391.

[34] *Pine Valley Developments v Ireland*, Series A No 222 (1992) 14 EHRR 319.

Rule 2 should apply only to acquisitions by a public body.[35] However, if Rule 1 is concerned with appropriations for public use, the Court should have classified *Bramelid* as a Rule 3 control on property. Similarly, the set of cases on provisional transfers pursuant to Austrian land consolidations have been treated as Rule 1 cases, although the State does not gain directly from the transfers.[36]

Rule 1 as a residual category

The desire to preserve conceptual clarity in respect of Rule 2 and Rule 3 is most evident in the series of cases where the Court applies Rule 1 simply because the facts do not fit easily within the confines of the other Rules. For example, in *Jokela v Finland*,[37] where an inheritance tax was imposed on land that was subsequently expropriated, the applicant complained that the valuation for tax purposes was about four times higher than the valuation on expropriation, with the result that the tax paid to inherit the land was about as much as the compensation received on its expropriation. The Court described the expropriation as a Rule 2 deprivation and the inheritance tax as a Rule 3 tax, but also said that the combined effect of the two could be seen as a separate Rule 1 interference. Ultimately, neither the inheritance nor the expropriation were, taken alone, disproportionate; however, in combination, the impact was excessive.

It also appears that Rule 1 may be applied where the State denies access to property. The leading example is *Loizidou v Turkey*,[38] which concerned claims by a Greek Cypriot to land which she had owned and occupied prior to the Turkish occupation of northern Cyprus. As the Turkish forces prevented her from obtaining access to her land, she had 'effectively lost all control over, as well as all possibilities to use and enjoy, her property'.[39] The Court held that the denial of access was neither a Rule 2 deprivation of possessions or a Rule 3 control on the use of property. Had a public authority occupied and used the land as a de facto owner, there may have been an argument for saying that a Rule 2 deprivation of possessions had occurred;[40] or if lawful regulations had limited

---

[35] *Bramelid* (n 16); *cf James* (n 3), where legislation allowing tenants to purchase the freehold was treated as a Rule 2 case.

[36] *Erkner* (n 23); *Poiss* (n 23); *Prötsch* (n 23); see also *Teuschler v Germany*, Appl No 47636/99, 4 October 2001.

[37] Reports 2002–IV 1 (2003) 37 EHRR 26.

[38] Reports 1996–VI 2216 (1997) 23 EHRR 513; confirmed in *Demades v Turkey*, Appl No 16219/90, 31 July 2003 and *Eugenia Michaelidou Developments Ltd v Turkey*, Appl No 16163/90, 31 July 2003. See also *Vikulov v Latvia*, Appl No 16870/03, 25 March 2004.

[39] Above [63].

[40] Temporal issues regarding Turkey's responsibility for events in northern Cyprus were also relevant. Since Turkey accepted jurisdiction of Court only with respect to acts after 22 January 1990, it could not be found in breach of P1–1 unless the interference with the applicants' possessions continued after the occupation. This required the Court to find that the applicants had not lost their possessions with the occupation, but this in turn meant that finding that the occupation had not amounted to a *de facto* deprivation; otherwise, any interference by the Turkish State would have been completed before its acceptance of the Court's jurisdiction was effective.

access to land, Rule 3 might have applied. However, in the 'exceptional circumstances' of the case, only Rule 1 was relevant.[41]

Rule 1 is also used where there is an interference with an interest that is not recognised as a property interest under national law.[42] For example, in *Beyeler v Italy*,[43] the applicant complained that the compulsory purhase of a painting violated P1(1), even though he did not have a property interest in the painting under Italian law because had acquired the painting under a void 'contract'. Nevertheless, the Court decided that P1(1) was applicable, and that the compulsory purchase should be examined under Rule 1 rather than Rule 2 because 'The complexity of the factual and legal situation position prevents its being classified in a precise category'.[44] Again, it seems that Rule 1 is used as a residual category, to avoid any uncertainty regarding the nature of a Rule 2 deprivation or a Rule 3 control on use. That is, the applicant plainly lost something, but since he did not have a property interest under Italian law, it is difficult to see this as a control on the use of property under Rule 3.[45] Moreover, the Court does not resolve issues of national law for the national courts and so it would not say that the applicant has an ownership interest under national law. As long as Rule 2 applies only to the deprivation of an ownership interest, it cannot apply to these types of cases. Accordingly, Rule 1 must apply.

One of the consequences of this approach is that it is difficult to identify any specific principles regarding proportionality which apply to all Rule 1 cases. This should be one of the benefits of classification: it should make it easier (for example) to determine whether the applicant should have been compensated for its loss. However, since Rule 1 is used as a residual class, this is not the effect. To be sure, there are guidelines for the sub-categories considered here: in the cases involving interim steps to a final expropriation, or an appropriation falling short of a full deprivation, the Court has indicated that payment of compensation *or* improvements in procedures would satisfy the fair balance. *Sporrong* itself is an example.[46] The applicants' position was exacerbated by the inflexibility of the permit system: permits were granted for five years and could be extended, and once in place there was no real opportunity to apply for their

---

[41] *Loizidou* (n 38) [63].

[42] That is, where the European Court has applied the autonomous meaning doctrine (see Chapter 2).

[43] Reports 2000–I 57 (2001) 33 EHRR 52.

[44] Above [106]; see also *The Synod College of the Evangelical Reformed Church of Lithuania v Lithuania* (2003) 36 EHRR CD94; *Broniowski v Poland*, Appl No 31443/96, 22 June 2004 (Grand Chamber) [136].

[45] See also *Matos e Silva* (n 20); *Former King of Greece v Greece*, Reports 2000–XII (2001) 33 EHRR 21; *Papastavrou v Greece*, Appl No 46372/99, 10 April 2003; *Katsoulis v Greece*, Appl No 66742/01, 8 July 2004. The position is similar in respect of the frustration of legitimate expectations due to administrative failures: see eg *Stretch* (n 9); *Frascino v Italy*, Appl No 35227/97, 11 December 2003, where the refusal of administrative officials to honour a court order to issue a planning permit was treated as Rule 1 interference rather than Rule 3, although ordinarily planning regulations would fall under Rule 3 (as in *Pine Valley* (n 34)).

[46] See also *Terazzi* (n 20).

withdrawal. The Court concluded that the applicants 'bore an individual and excessive burden which could have been tendered legitimate only if they had had the possibility of seeking a reduction of the time-limits *or* of claiming compensation.'[47] As such, compensation was not strictly necessary to maintain the fair balance and it would have been sufficient to make changes in procedure.[48] However, where Rule 1 is a residual category, no general principles can be derived from the jurisprudence.

RULE 2—DEPRIVATION OF POSSESSIONS

Nature of a deprivation

De jure and de facto deprivations

There may be some tactical advantage in persuading a court that a given interference is a Rule 2 deprivation of possessions. Although the Protocol does not expressly require compensation, the Court has said that a deprivation of possessions normally requires compensation in order to maintain the fair balance.[49] Moreover, the intensity of review is usually higher than it is under other Rules, with the result that the Court looks closely at the rules of national law regarding the valuation of property on expropriation. As explained above, even if one cannot be certain that the classification does make a real difference in a specific case, this is one area where the tactical possibilities should not be ignored.

The wording of the second sentence may be confusing to lawyers from common law systems, since most constitutions in the common law world use the expression 'deprivation of property' to refer to the regulation of property rather than compulsory purchase.[50] However, under the Convention, a 'deprivation of possessions' is closer to compulsory purchase. As the Court pointed out in *Handyside v United Kingdom*, the structure of P1(1) shows that the second sentence 'applies only to someone who is "deprived of ownership" ("privé de sa propriété")'.[51]

---

[47] *Sporrong* (n 1) [72] (emphasis added).

[48] See also *Phocas* (n 26) and *Poiss* (n 23).

[49] See Chapter 7.

[50] See eg the United States, as discussed above, text accompanying n 1, and *La Compagnie Sucriere de Bel Ombre Ltee v The Government of Mauritius* [1995] 3 LRC 494 (PC).

[51] Series A No 24 (1979–80) 1 EHRR 737 [62]. Also n that the French version uses *biens* in the first and third sentences, and *propriété* in the second: ie unlike the English version, which has the same term in the first two sentences and changes in the third. (On the differences between English and French versions of Convention rights, see E Schwelb, 'The Protection of the Right to Property of Nationals under the First Protocol to the European Convention on Human Rights' (1964) 13 *AJCL* 518, 520; D Feldman, 'Proportionality and the Human Rights Act 1998' in E Ellis (ed), *The Principle of Proportionality in the Laws of Europe* (Hart Publishing, Oxford, 1999) 117, 120, who observes that the Schedule to the 1998 Act only contains the English version.)

On this reading of P1(1), an acquisition of legal title without taking physical possession is a Rule 2 deprivation of possessions.[52] However, taking possession without acquiring title may also amount to a deprivation of possessions. The Court has said that 'it must look behind the appearances and investigate the realities of the situation complained of' and ascertain whether there was a 'de facto expropriation'.[53] For a de facto expropriation to have occurred, the owner must have been left permanently unable to exercise any of his or her rights of property. In *Papamichalopoulos v Greece*,[54] for example, the Greek Navy unlawfully occupied and constructed a naval base on land belonging to the applicant. The Court had little difficulty in finding that the occupation of the land amounted to a Rule 2 deprivation of possessions, particularly as the applicant had been unable to use or dispose of the land and the Navy acted as though it held the rights of an owner throughout the relevant period.[55]

The Court is unlikely to find that a de facto deprivation has occurred if the owner is not wholly deprived of the rights of ownership, even if the effects are very harsh.[56] In *Mellacher v Austria*, a landlord protested that rent control legislation stripped his property of most of its economic value, but the Court found that no deprivation had occurred because 'There was no transfer of the applicants' property nor were they deprived of their right to use, let or sell it.'[57] There was no doubt that the rent controls were harsh: as put by the dissenting judges, 'The applicants do not seem to be far wrong when they say that the reduced [monthly] rent now corresponds to the price of a simple meal for two persons in a cheap restaurant.'[58] Similarly, in *Sporrong*, the Court found that there had been no de facto deprivation of possessions, even though the issue of the expropriation permits reduced the value and marketability of the applicants' land dramatically.[59] As long as the applicants remained free to sell and use their land, no Rule 2 deprivation had occurred.

---

[52] See eg *Holy Monasteries v Greece*, Series A No 301–A (1995) 20 EHRR 1; see also *Vasilescu v Romania*, Reports 1998–III 1064 (1999) 28 EHRR 241 [44]–[54].

[53] *Sporrong* (n 1).

[54] Series A No 260–B (1993) 16 EHRR 440.

[55] Above [45]; see also *Karagiannis v Greece*, Appl No 51354/99, 16 January 2003 and *Vasilescu* (n 52).

[56] In addition to these cases, see the cases on the impact of the introduction of a handgun ban on UK gun dealers and related businesses: despite the complete loss of goodwill, was no Rule 2 deprivation: *Ian Edgar (Liverpool) Ltd v The United Kingdom* Appl No 37683/97, 25 January 2000; *Andrews v The United Kingdom*, Appl No 37657/97, 26 September 2000; *Findlater v The United Kingdom* Appl No 38881/97, 26 September 2000; *CEM Firearms Ltd and Bradford Shooting Centre and 11 others v The United Kingdom*, Appl No 37674/97 and Appl No 37677/97, 26 September 2000; *London Armoury Ltd and AB Harvey & Son Ltd and 156 others, AG Wise and 5 others, Powderkeg Ltd and 2 others, Reepham Moore Rifle & Pistol Range, Warwick Rifle and Pistol club and 42 others v The United Kingdom*, Appl No 37666/97, 37671/97, 37972/97, 37977/97, 37981/97, 38909/97, 26 September 2000; *Denimark Ltd and 11 others v The United Kingdom*, Appl No 37660/97, 26 September 2000.

[57] *Mellacher* (n 33) [44]; see also *Pine Valley* (n 34).

[58] Above 12 EHRR, 415.

[59] *Sporrong* (n 1) [60]; see also *Terazzi* (n 20).

The relevance of the purpose of State action

There are cases where the State deprives the applicant entirely of its property interest, without the deprivation falling under Rule 2. This is provided for explicitly in the third sentence, as it allows States 'to enforce such laws as it deems necessary to control the use of property in accordance with the general interest or to secure the payment of taxes or other contributions or penalties.' Enforcement may include a complete deprivation of possessions without being classified as a Rule 2 deprivation.[60] For example, in *Handyside*, the Court treated the forfeiture and destruction of 'items whose use has been lawfully adjudged illicit and dangerous to the general interest'[61] as falling under Rule 3; similarly, in *AGOSI v United Kingdom*[62] and *Air Canada v United Kingdom*,[63] the seizure of contraband and aircraft carrying contraband fell under Rule 3 'controls on the use of property', rather than Rule 2. In addition, regulatory controls on the use of property may have the effect of destroying a business, and yet the interference is still a Rule 3 interference.[64]

Comparing the language of the second and third sentences justifies this distinction, and it also makes sense as long as the Court takes the view that deprivations of possessions normally require compensation. Obviously, in cases such as *Handyside*, where the forfeiture of property is an aspect of a criminal penalty, it would defeat the purpose of the penalty to require compensation. Similarly, the seizure and sale of property to satisfy a tax liability should be excluded from Rule 2, since the purpose of satisfying the liability would be frustrated by requiring compensation. Hence, the purpose of the State action is relevant, even where there has been a complete loss of property.

This is plain enough in relation to criminal penalties and tax liabilities, but whether it can be taken further is more controversial. This is illustrated by considering the compulsory redistribution of property amongst private persons. Assuming that a redistribution satisfies the public interest test, it could be argued that it does not demand the same degree of judicial scrutiny as an acquisition by a public body, because the risk of an infringement of human rights is different. This follows from the observation that public bodies have the incentive to use their compulsory powers solely to avoid the open market and hence to obtain property at an advantageous price. The most obvious case

---

[60] A complete loss of property may be intended (as in forfeiture) or unintended (as in *Pinnacle Meat Processors Company and 8 others v The United Kingdom*, Appl No 33298/96, 21 October 1998). But *cf Allard v Sweden*, (2004) 39 EHRR 14: the demolition of a building was treated as a Rule 2 interference (the point seems to have been accepted by the parties).

[61] *Handyside* (n 51) [63].

[62] Series A No 108 (1987) 9 EHRR 1.

[63] Series A No 316 (1995) 20 EHRR 150.

[64] See eg *Pinnacle Meat Processors Company and 8 others v The United Kingdom*, Appl No 33298/96, 21 October 1998, *Marschner v France*, Appl No 51360/99, 13 May 2003 as well as the cases on the handgun ban, cited above n 56.

would arise if public authority used a power of compulsory purchase to acquire below the market rate, solely for resale on the market at a profit. As Joseph Sax has argued, a compensation guarantee serves as a check on self-interested acts of public authorities.[65] Plainly, it may be possible to prevent this by taking a strict view of the public interest requirements, or of the Crichel Down rules, but the incentive to engage in such acts can be reduced by requiring the authority to pay full compensation at market rates for the property. In any case, this risk of an abuse of power does not arise when public authorities act only to prevent harmful activity or to redistribute property. Arguably, the intensity of review should be greater where the risk of abuse is greater. In terms of the structure of P1(1), if Rule 2 is reserved for cases ordinarily requiring close scrutiny, then it would be justifiable to treat redistribution cases as either Rule 1 or Rule 3. The principle of the fair balance still applies, of course, and ordinarily compensation may be required; but the nature of the review would be different.

There is some support for this position in the case law. In particular, in *Bramelid*, the Commission applied Rule 1 to Swedish laws which empower the holders of 90% of the shares in a company to require the minority to sell them their shares.[66] The Court stated that the second sentence only applies to 'the act by which the State seizes—or gives another the right to seize—a specific asset to be used for the realisation of a goal in the public interest.'[67] While the reference to the State giving the right to seize assets to another person suggests that no distinction is made for redistributions, it seems that the Court was more concerned with parties that acquire property for public use, such as a public utility or rail company. It went on to say that:

> The Swedish legislation of which the applicants complain is of an altogether different kind. It is in fact the expression and the application of a general policy with regard to the regulation of commercial companies and concerns above all the relations of shareholders *inter se*. It goes without saying that, in enacting legislation of this type, the legislature is pursuing the general aim of reaching a system of regulation favourable to those interests which it regards as most worthy of protection, something which however has nothing to do with the notion of 'the public interest' as commonly understood in the field of expropriation.[68]

Other examples include the the readjustment of debts owed by one private person to another,[69] or the consolidation of agricultural land.[70]

Although such examples would be ordinarily be classified under Rule 1 or 3, there are also cases where Rule 2 has been applied to redistributions of property

---

[65] J Sax, 'Takings and the Police Power' (1964) 74 *Yale Law Journal* 36.
[66] *Bramelid* (n 16).
[67] Above 255.
[68] Above 256.
[69] *Bäck v Finland*, Appl No 37598/97, 20 July 2004.
[70] See cases cited above n 23.

without any direct public benefit, as in *James*.[71] While this contradicts the position taken by Sax, one might argue that P1(1) is not solely concerned with removing incentives for the abuse of power. In any case, in terms of P1(1) doctrine, the Court has not said that compensation is only required under Rule 2, nor that compensation is always required under Rule 2. Hence, even if redistributions did not normally require compensation, they could be treated as Rule 2 cases. Indeed, in *James*, the Court did acknowledge that redistributions present different issues, as it stated that flexibility in relation to compensation may be permitted where legislation is intended to achieve greater social justice.[72] However, it is that flexibility which means that redistributions need not be taken out of Rule 2. It also demonstrates, however, that the categorisation of the facts under Rule 2 does not provide an indication of the level of scrutiny to be applied to the case; neither does it provide guidance on the specific issue of compensation, in that no conclusion on compensation can be reached simply by the exercise of categorisation.

International law and the purpose of State action

The second sentence of P1(1) states that a deprivation of property must be subject to the conditions provided by international law. General principles of international law require States to provide compensation to aliens for the deprivation of their possessions. As such, the obligation is stronger than the fair balance test of P1(1). The international obligation is also broader, as shown by the *Metalclad* arbitration.[73] The issues in *Metalclad* related to Chapter 11 of the North American Free Trade Agreement, which requires compensation for measures 'tantamount to expropriation'.[74] Metalclad, an American waste-disposal company, acquired a hazardous waste and landfill operation in Mexico from a local company. The Mexican government assured Metalclad that it had all the permits and consents it needed to continue the operation, and so it spent a considerable amount on its development. However, the State and municipality

---

[71] *James* (n 3); see also *Tsironis v Greece*, Appl No 44584/98, 6 December 2001, where the forced sale of the applicant's property to satisfy a judgment debt was examined under Rule 2, without explanation; and *R (on the application of Clays Lane Housing Cooperative Ltd) v Housing Corp*, [2004] EWCA Civ 1658 [11], where it was common ground that a compulsory transfer of land from one non-profit social landlord to another fell was a deprivation of possessions (the transfer fell within the Housing Corporation's powers under the Housing Act 1996, sched 1).

[72] Above [54].

[73] *Metalclad Corp v United Mexican States*, ICSID Case No ARB(AF)/97/1, (2001) 16(1) *ICSID Review—Foreign Investment Law Journal*. On the agreement of the parties, the arbitration was referred to the British Columbia Supreme Court for judicial review: see *United Mexican States v Metalclad Corp* [2001] BCSC 664; [2001] BCSC 1529 (supplementary reasons for judgment).

[74] Art 1110 of NAFTA provides that 'No party shall directly or indirectly . . . expropriate an investment . . . or take a measure tantamount to . . . expropriation . . . except: (a) for a public purpose; (b) on a nondiscriminatory basis; (c) in accordance with due process of law and Art 1105(1); and (d) on payment of compensation . . ..' Art 201(1) defines a 'measure' as including 'any law, regulation, procedure, requirement or practice'.

had environmental and safety concerns about the landfill site and, after a series of local protests, the State governor issued an 'Ecological Decree', which prohibited further use of the site as a landfill operation. Metalclad claimed that the Decree was a measure tantamount to expropriation and claimed $90 million in compensation.

According to the Arbitration Panel, the purpose of the Decree was irrelevant: all that mattered was the impact on the property holder.[75] In customary international law, this point is not free from controversy: for example, the Iran-United States Claims Tribunal did not investigate issues regarding the intent of public authorities, but did accept that regulations in pursuance of the police power were not expropriations.[76] Under P1(1), it is clear from cases such as *Mellacher* and *Pine Valley v Ireland* that regulatory measures are examined under Rule 3, with a low level of scrutiny and no presumption that compensation should be paid.[77] However, in *Metalclad*, the environmental concerns of the Mexican public authorities carried little weight with the Panel, and it appears that this reflects the modern trend in international law.[78]

It is also worth noting that the breadth of the *Metalclad* conception of measures tantamount to expropriation is clearly greater than the Convention conception of a de facto expropriation, as the Ecological Decree did not vest any ownership rights in the State or put the State in the position to exercise or benefit from any such rights. In addition, the deprivation of property was not complete, as Metalclad still held valuable assets in its Mexican operation. Again, it appears that this is consistent with position taken by other international tribunals.[79]

Metalclad also raises a question regarding the scope of Rule 2 where the victim is an alien: does the analysis of measures 'tantamount to expropriation' mean that regulations which would be classified as Rule 1 or Rule 3 interferences now carry a stronger, international law right to compensation? Under P1(1), this seems to turn on the scope of the reference to international law in the second sentence. As worded, it seems to be limited *only* to deprivations of possessions as described under the Convention, rather than measures 'tantamount to expropriation' as described under international law. By this reasoning, there may be cases involving aliens for which general principles of international law

---

[75] *Metalclad* (n 73) [102]–[112], especially [111]. This ground was upheld on review by the British Columbia Supreme Court (n 73).

[76] GH Aldrich, 'What Constitutes a Compensable Taking of Property? The Decisions of the Iran–United States Claim Tribunal' (1994) 88 *American Journal of International Law* 585, 605–6; see M Brunetti, 'The Iran–United States Claims Tribunal, NAFTA Chapter 11, and the Doctrine of Indirect Expropriation' [2001] 2 *Chicago Journal of International Law* 203 on the sources of law used by the Iran–United States Claims Tribunal.

[77] *Mellacher* (n 33), *Pine Valley* (n 34).

[78] R Dolzer, 'Indirect Expropriations: New Developments?' (2002) 11 *New York University Environmental Law Journal* 64, 79–93.

[79] See Aldrich (n 76) and Dolzer, above.

would require compensation, and yet under the Convention the fair balance is not upset. *Metalclad* itself would be one example of this.[80]

As a final comment on Rule 2, it is worth noting that the importance of categorisation depends on its effects. For example, if compensation were guaranteed for a deprivation of possessions, categorisation under Rule 2 would be material. Indeed, it would be material even if there was a strong presumption that full compensation would be necessary for a deprivation and there was little or no margin of appreciation to regarding the valuation of property. Alternatively, even if Court did not apply a strong presumption, the categorisation would be important if the Court invariably refused to review Rule 1 or Rule 3 interferences on the basis of their economic impact. If any of these conditions applied, we would expect to see 'deprivation of possessions' to be interpreted with a view to effects. However, the absence of an express or implied compensation guarantee and the rise of the proportionality test has meant that this is not the case. Hence, it is doubtful that the delimitation of the boundaries of Rule 2 has had a significant effect on the outcomes of specific cases.

RULE 3—CONTROLS ON THE USE OF PROPERTY

The initial proposal for the third sentence referred to the State's right 'to pass necessary legislation to ensure that the said possessions are utilised in accordance with the general interest',[81] which was intended to 'make the distinction between arbitrary confiscation and the social conception of property which allows it to be used by regulation legislation for the public good.'[82] However, for the British government in particular, this proposal went too far, and it introduced the idea that the State should be entitled 'to enforce such laws *as it deems necessary*'.[83] This was much more generous to the State than similar clauses in other Convention rights: in particular, while Articles 8-11 allow for some limitations where 'necessary in a democratic society', it is not left to the State themselves to determine what is necessary. However, as there was a general belief that a right to property should not hamper the development of social democracy, this aspect of the British proposal was not controversial and won acceptance. Consequently, it must have appeared to lawyers at that time that regulatory measures were only required to be lawful and in the general interest, and that the tax measures only had to be lawful.

[80] See BH Oxman and B Rudolf, '*Beyeler v Italy*' (2000) 94 *American Journal of International Law* 736, 739–40, where it is pointed out that the effect of applying Rule 1 in *Beyeler* (n 43) was to deny the applicant his status as a foreign applicant, and hence the stronger guarantee afforded under Rule 2.

[81] Council of Europe, *Collected edition of the 'Travaux Préparatoires' of the European Convention on Human Rights: Recueil des Travaux Préparatoires de la Convention Européenne des Droits de l'Homme* (M Nijhoff, The Hague, 1975–85) vol 6, pp 6, 10 and 52.

[82] Above vol 6, p 48 (see also 54).

[83] Emphasis added.

This confidence would have been vindicated by the *Handyside* judgment, where the Court stated that, unlike Article 10(2), the third sentence of P1(1) 'sets the Contracting States up as sole judges of the "necessity" for an interference. Consequently, the Court must restrict itself to supervising the lawfulness and the purpose of the restriction in question.'[84] However, this was followed by *Sporrong* and *James*, where it was made it clear that the proportionality test applies to all three Rules. Nevertheless, the level of scrutiny has remained low, and it is unusual to see the Court find that a Rule 3 interference fails the proportionality test on the basis that the impact on the victim was too harsh.[85] The same is true in the United Kingdom: although the courts were initially fairly quick to find that regulatory laws violated P1(1), the House of Lords has taken a more conservative view in these types of cases.[86]

The judicial reconstruction of the third sentence is also reflected in the determination of its scope. For example, the sentence seems to distinguish between the enforcement and the imposition of controls on use and taxes, contributions and other penalties. Arguably, the imposition of such laws is not covered by Rule 3, but only by Rules 1 or 2. However, the Court has assumed that both the enforcement and imposition of such laws is covered by Rule 3. This certainly makes sense: it would be odd if the broad reservation of power in the third sentence applied only the enforcement of these laws.

A second aspect of the scope of Rule 3 concerns the distinction between controls on the use of property and other controls over property. Arguably, by referring only to the use of property, the third sentence excludes controls on rights of possession or disposition from its application. However, the Court has not applied the sentence in this way. In *Chassagnou v France*,[87] for example, the third sentence was applied to restrictions on the right of possession and in *Marckx v Belgium*[88] and *Mellacher*,[89] it was applied to restrictions on rights of disposition. The idea of 'controls on use' therefore seems to apply to any kind of control falling short of a deprivation of possessions.

Although Rule 3 extends to the enforcement and imposition of controls on use and other rights, the nature of the interference is not conclusive, as the Court has indicated that Rule 1 applies to controls on use that are intended to facilitate an eventual expropriation.[90] The purpose is also relevant in cases where the applicant has suffered a complete loss of its property interest. As explained above, some international tribunals have stated that the purpose of an interference with

---

[84] *Handyside* (n 51) [62]; see also *Marckx v Belgium*, Series A No 31 (1979) 2 EHRR 330 [64].

[85] For a rare example, see *Chassagnou v France*, Reports 1999–III 21 (2000) 29 EHRR 615.

[86] See eg *Aston Cantlow and Wilmcote with Billesley Parochial Church Council v Wallbank* [2002] Ch 51 reversed by [2004] 1 AC 546; *Wilson v First County Trust Ltd (No 2)* [2002] QB 74 reversed by [2004] 1 AC 816 (sub nom *Wilson v Secretary of State for Trade and Industry*); and *Marcic v Thames Water Utilities Ltd* [2002] QB 929, reversed by [2004] 2 AC 42.

[87] *Chassagnou* (n 85).

[88] *Marckx* (n 84).

[89] *Mellacher* (n 33).

[90] See above, text accompanying n 16ff.

property is not material when determining whether there have been measures 'tantamount to expropriation'. However, under P1(1), the third sentence states that it applies to the enforcement of certain laws; presumably, the purpose of enforcement was intended to distinguish Rule 3 cases from Rule 2 deprivations of possessions. Nevertheless, the Court's position has not been clear. In some cases, the State's purpose has been material. In particular, *Handyside* demonstrates that Rule 3 may apply to the confiscation of property, and similar rulings can be found in a number of other cases.[91] However, the Court has sometimes treated the destruction or confiscation of property as either a Rule 1 or Rule 2 interference. For example, in *Allard v Sweden*[92] a joint owner of land was ordered to destroy a house she had constructed without the consent of her fellow owners. It was clear that the order was made to enforce private law rules on joint ownership, and as such it should have fallen under Rule 3; however, the Court instead saw it as a Rule 2 case.[93] No explanation for this categorisation was offered. Similarly, in *Azinas v Cyprus*,[94] the applicant complained about the loss of entitlement to retirement benefits suffered as a consequence of his dismissal from the civil service for corrupt acts. The Cypriot government argued that the third sentence of P1(1) should apply, since the loss of rights was more like a penalty than a deprivation of property. However, the Court stated simply that 'The interference in question was neither an expropriation nor a measure to control the use of property; it therefore falls to be dealt with under the first sentence of the first paragraph of Article 1.'[95] Finally, measures taken to control tax evasion were treated as a deprivation of possessions in *Hentrich*,[96] although in other cases, the Court has regarded tax enforcement measures involving the seizure of property as falling under Rule 3.[97]

Even in cases on land use planning, where one would expect that restrictions on land use would be seen as Rule 3 controls on the use of property, there are inconsistent decisions. In *Katte Klitsche de la Grange v Italy*, the applicant complained that an official land use plan imposed a prohibition on construction over his land.[98] The Court treated this as an example of a Rule 1 interference, but without explaining why it was not a Rule 3 interference.[99] By contrast, in *Pine Valley*, the Court held that Rule 3 applied to planning restrictions because there had been neither a de jure or de facto expropriation, as the owner's 'powers to

---

[91] See also AGOSI (n 62) and *Air Canada* (n 63).

[92] *Allard* (n 60).

[93] See also *Owen v Ministry of Fisheries and Food* [2001] EHLR 18 (QBD), where it was assumed that destruction of a cow pursuant to BSE regulations was deprivation of possessions.

[94] Appl No 56679/00, 20 June 2002 (Third Section), 28 May 2004 (Grand Chamber).

[95] Above Third Section, [43] (the issue was not addressed by the Grand Chamber).

[96] *Hentrich* (n 15) [35].

[97] See *Gasus* (n 8); *National & Provincial* (n 14). Indeed, in *Gasus*, the seizure of goods in which the applicant held property rights fell under Rule 3 because it was sold to satisfy tax liabilities, even though the liabilities were in fact not those of the applicant.

[98] Series A No 293–B (1995) 19 EHRR 368.

[99] Above [40].

take decisions concerning the property were unaffected' and 'the land was not left without any meaningful alternative use, for it could have been farmed or leased'; accordingly, 'although the value of the site was substantially reduced, it was not rendered worthless, as is evidenced by the fact that it was subsequently sold in the open market'.[100]

Since the proportionality principle applies to all three rules, the classification is not conclusive as to the issue of compensation or proportionality generally. Nevertheless, it is worth noting that in *Allard*, *Azinas*, and *Hentrich*, the Court held that the States had violated P1(1) because the interference upset the fair balance. Whether the conclusions on proportionality would have been different if the Court had seen these as Rule 3 cases is uncertain. However, the brevity of reasoning on the structure of P1(1) makes it difficult to believe that the classification exercise made a material difference to the result. Indeed, the insignificance of classification is borne out by cases where the Court seems to ignore the distinctions between the rules completely, or at least apply them in ways that are contrary to the general principles.

CONCLUSIONS

A central question of this chapter is whether the three-rule structure of P1(1) is still relevant. While the Court has not said that the structure can be ignored, it is still not clear how the structure affects the judicial analysis in specific cases. If we consider the place of the three rules within the analysis of the typical P1(1) case, we see that there are a number of supposedly distinct steps that the tribunal should follow in determining whether there has been a violation. The first asks whether P1(1) is applicable, the second identifies the Rule applicable to the specific facts, and the third whether the interference can be justified. In this analysis, the function of the second step is to narrow the scope of inquiry in the third step. That is, even if the third step is a fairly open-ended analysis, the second step should at least indicate which facts can be eliminated from the analysis of legality and (especially) proportionality, as well as the weight and significance of the facts that must be considered. If the second step does not in some way perform this function, then it has no useful purpose in the analysis of cases.

While the House of Lords has not yet concerned itself with questions of classification, the European Court has not dropped the categorisation step from its analysis. Nevertheless, it is not clear how categorisation affects the outcomes. This uncertainty arises partly because the second and third sentences were not written with a precise conception of their function in determining the scope of the right to property. In broad terms, it is clear from the *travaux* that the drafters used the second sentence to deal with the issue of compensation and

---

[100] *Pine Valley* (n 34) [56]; see also *Chassagnou* (n 85) [74].

the third sentence to deal with other types of regulation and financial measures. However, no clear conclusion was ever reached on compensation, and the third sentence was written to achieve an almost complete exclusion of any review of regulatory or financial measures. If some agreed formula had been reached on a compensation standard, the distinction between deprivations and regulatory and financial measures would have been necessary. Similarly, if regulatory and financial measures were entirely insulated from review, then again a distinction would have been necessary. But, since all interferences are subject to the same test of proportionality, these distinctions no longer perform an important function.

5

Property and the Fair Balance

———➤●◄———

THE DOCTRINE OF proportionality plays a central role in the jurisprudence of the European Court of Human Rights. However, it is not obvious that it was intended to be relevant in the application of Article 1 of Protocol No 1 (P1(1)). The express limitations on the right to property that are found in the second and third sentences of P1(1) do not refer to actions that are 'necessary in a democratic society'. Since this phrase was seen as the textual source of the proportionality test under other Convention rights, it was not certain that the test would apply to P1(1). Indeed, it could be argued that the limitations set out in the second and third sentences of P1(1) embody a specific application of the idea of proportionality. That is, the member States may have believed that the right to property should reflect a balance between public and private interests, but that the balance had been achieved by the language of the second and third sentences and hence there was no need for the Court to develop further principles of balancing.

In any case, the Court incorporated the proportionality test in its analysis of P1(1) in *Sporrong and Lönnroth v Sweden*[1] and *James v The United Kingdom*.[2] In *Sporrong*, it stated that the first sentence of P1(1) sets out the right of property and, crucially, that it implicitly incorporates a 'fair balance' test:

> For the purposes of the latter provision [the first sentence of P1(1)], the Court must determine whether a fair balance was struck between the demands of the general interest of the community and the requirements of the protection of the individual's fundamental rights. The search for this balance is inherent in the whole of the Convention and is also reflected in the structure of Article 1 (P1(1)).[3]

While this statement is significant, it may have been intended to apply only to the first sentence of P1(1). If so, interferences under the second or third sentences would have still been governed solely by the specific conditions in those sentences, and there would have been no need to ask whether an interference that fell under one of those two sentences struck a 'fair balance' between 'the

---

[1] Series A No 52 [1982] EHRR 35.
[2] Series A No 98 (1986) 8 EHRR 123 [37].
[3] *Sporrong* (n 1) [69] (references omitted).

demands of the general interest of the community and the requirements of the protection of the individual's fundamental rights'. However, in *James*, the Court recalled that *Sporrong* sets out the three rules of P1(1), and went on to say that:

> The three rules are not, however, 'distinct' in the sense of being unconnected. The second and third rules are concerned with particular instances of interference with the right to peaceful enjoyment of property and should therefore be construed in the light of the general principle enunciated in the first rule.[4]

Two points follow from this. The first is that the fair balance test applies to all interferences with possessions.[5] The second and third sentences of P1(1) lay down criteria relevant to the fair balance, but other criteria may be relevant as well. So, for example, the absence of an express reference to compensation does not mean that the fair balance never requires compensation.

The second point is that some of the jurisprudence on proportionality developed with respect to other Convention rights can be applied to P1(1). Indeed, in *James*, the Court used the language of proportionality interchangeably with that of the fair balance, as it said that 'Not only must a measure depriving a person of his property pursue, on the facts as well as in principle, a legitimate aim "in the public interest", but there must also be a reasonable relationship of proportionality between the means employed and the aim sought to be realised.'[6] The 'fair balance' described in *Sporrong* merely expresses the requirement of a 'reasonable relationship of proportionality' in other terms.[7] Nevertheless, the fair balance/proportionality test under P1(1) is not identical to that under other Convention rights. For example, compensation has a role in determining the fairness of an interference with the right to property that it does not have in relation to other Convention rights. That is, the individual may consent to the interference with other fundamental rights, but the State cannot dispense with the necessity of obtaining consent simply by paying compensation for the interference. In effect, the State can buy out the right to property by taxing some to pay off others, without obtaining the consent of either. As the fair balance/proportionality test under P1(1) has distinctive aspects, this chapter is not intended to provide a general overview of the proportionality test; for that purpose, general works on the Convention are recommended. Instead, the remainder of the chapter highlights the way in which the proportionality test is applied in property cases.

---

[4] *James* (n 2) [37].
[5] Above [50].
[6] Above.
[7] Above.

THE FAIR BALANCE

The classic test of proportionality derived from the 'necessary in a democratic society' phrase incorporates several elements.[8] First, the interference must relate to a legitimate aim, and an aim is legitimate only if it corresponds to a 'pressing social need'. Hence, the courts must first evaluate the importance of the professed aim of the interference. Secondly, the interference must be rationally connected with that aim and, thirdly, the interference must be proportionate to the aim served. In some cases, the courts have applied a test of strict necessity, which means that the interference must be no more than necessary to achieve the aim. Whether this applies under P1(1) is doubtful, as explained below.

The division of the proportionality analysis into these elements provides a valuable guide, but it is no more than that: it does not provide a technical or mechanical scheme for resolving difficult issues. In many property cases, the most important issue is the level of scrutiny: how much leeway does the court allow other decision-makers in setting general policy and resolving specific cases? Accordingly, we begin by examining the approach regarding the intensity of review, before turning to the different elements of the proportionality analysis.

The analysis then turns to the first two elements of the proportionality test, where the Court asks only whether the interference is rationally connected with a legitimate aim. As it was probably the original intention of the member States and their delegates that P1(1) would not require more than this, at least in relation to regulatory measures, it will be asked whether the extension of the fair balance has been successful or even doctrinally coherent. Finally, the balancing process itself will be examined.

THE MARGIN OF APPRECIATION AND
THE AREA OF DISCRETION

In most P1(1) cases, whether in Strasbourg and the United Kingdom, the intensity of review has been quite low. In Strasbourg, the Court has developed the margin of appreciation to reflect its international and judicial aspects. The international aspect follows from the fact that the Convention was never intended to make national laws uniform, and hence States have some freedom in determining their own policies and the means of achieving those policies. The judicial aspect reflects the Convention aim of securing democracy, from which it follows that courts should show some deference to the decisions of democratic bodies.

---

[8] *Sunday Times v The United Kingdom*, Series A No 30 (1979–80) 2 EHRR 245 [62]–[68]; *Olsson v Sweden*, Series A No 130, 11 EHRR 259: 'notion of necessity implies that the interference corresponds to a pressing social need and, in particular, that it is proportionate to the legitimate aim pursued.'

Plainly, the international aspect does not apply to the UK courts applying the Human Rights Act 1998, but in recognition of their judicial character, the courts have stated that they will allow other decision-makers an area of discretion.

In the United Kingdom, the courts have said that the degree of deference depends on a number of factors.[9] First, it is said that it is appropriate to exercise greater deference to the decisions of Parliament than to those of ministers or administrative authorities.[10] This reflects the importance of democratic institutions in the Convention, both in the Statute of Europe and in the express limitations to some of the Convention rights. However, the courts (especially in the United Kingdom) are inclined to read a great deal into the democratic aspect of regulatory systems. For example, in *Marcic v Thames Water Utilities Ltd*,[11] it was significant that Parliament had delegated wide regulatory powers of the Director General of Water Services, because it led to the conclusion that private law remedies for nuisance were ousted by statutory remedies. However, as David Howarth points out, the Director General makes his decisions on the basis of the existing distribution of property rights, and there is no reason to suppose that Parliament assumed that the Director General is better able than the courts to determine questions on the legal content of property.[12]

Secondly, there is a greater need for deference where the terms of the Convention require a balance to be struck, as they do with the right to property.[13] Indeed, while some Convention rights are unqualified, P1(1) is strongly qualified (particularly in the third sentence). Accordingly, the courts should show more deference in relation to property issues (especially those dealing with controls on the use of property) than they might in respect of other issues.[14] In

---

[9] See P Sales and B Hooper, 'Proportionality and the Form of Law' (2003) 119 *Law Quarterly Review* 426; D Feldman, 'Proportionality and the Human Rights Act 1998' in E Ellis (ed), *The Principle of Proportionality in the Laws of Europe* (Hart Publishing, Oxford, 1999) 117, 124–26; I Leigh, 'Taking Rights Proportionately: Judicial Review, the Human Rights Act and Strasbourg' [2002] *Public Law* 265.

[10] *International Transport Roth GmbH v Secretary of State for the Home Department* [2003] QB 728 [83] (Laws LJ).

[11] [2004] 2 AC 42; see below 157ff and Chapter 7, 212–16.

[12] D Howarth, 'Nuisance and the House of Lords' (2004) 16 *Journal of Environmental Law* 233, 257–58. See also Chapter 7, 199–210 on planning regulation, centralisation and democratic institutions.

[13] *Director of Public Prosecutions, Ex Parte Kebeline* [2000] 2 AC 326, 380 (Lord Hope); *International Transport* (n 10) [84] (Laws LJ).

[14] *Blečić v Croatia*, Appl No 59532/00, 29 July 2004 [63]:

> The Court accepts that where State authorities reconcile the competing interests of different groups in society, they must inevitably draw a line marking where a particular interest prevails and another one yields, without knowing precisely its ideal location. Making a reasonable assessment as to where the line is most properly drawn, especially if that assessment involves balancing conflicting interests and allocating scarce resources on this basis, falls within the State's margin of appreciation.

But *cf Chassagnou v France*, Reports 1999–III 21 (2000) 29 EHRR 615, and in particular the dissenting opinion of Judge Zupančič; and *cf Connors v The United Kingdom*, Appl No 66746/01, 27 May 2004 [82], where the Court observed that there is narrower margin of appreciation in relation to Art 8.

the end, however, the need to defer arises because the fair balance has been extended to all forms of interference. That is, prior to the *Sporrong* judgment, it appeared that all interferences other than expropriations fell under the third sentence of P1(1); and under the third sentence, only a test of rationality was required. In particular, in *Handyside v United Kingdom*, the Court held that the third sentence 'sets the Contracting States up as sole judges of the "necessity" for an interference.' In such cases, the Court may only review the lawfulness and the purpose of the interference.[15] Now that the review also extends to the proportionality of the interference, the margin of appreciation has become more important.

Thirdly, the nature of the subject-matter is also important. In *International Transport Roth GmbH v Secretary of State for the Home Department*, Laws LJ remarked that 'greater deference will be due to the democratic powers where the subject-matter in hand is peculiarly within their constitutional responsibility, and less when it lies more particularly within the constitutional responsibility of the courts.'[16] Laws LJ also stated that 'greater or lesser deference will be due according to whether the subject matter lies more readily within the actual or potential expertise of the democratic powers or the courts.'[17] *International Transport* itself provides one example: it concerned measures taken to prevent illegal immigration, which Laws LJ regarded as falling within the expertise of the administrative and legislative branches.[18] Similarly, in relation to property, the courts in both Strasbourg and the United Kingdom have identified programmes relating to social justice,[19] social welfare provision,[20] economic planning,[21] public health and safety,[22] environmental protection,[23] planning

---

[15] Series A No 24 (1979–80) 1 EHRR 737 [62]; see also *Marckx v Belgium*, Series A No 31 (1979) 2 EHRR 330 [64].

[16] [2003] QB 728 [85].

[17] Above [87].

[18] *Yildirim v Italy*, Appl No 38602/02, 10 April 2003; *cf Lindsay v Customs and Excise Comrs* [2002] 1 WLR 1766.

[19] *James* (n 2); *Broniowski v Poland*, Appl No 31443/96, 22 June 2004 (Grand Chamber) [149]; *Antoniades v The United Kingdom*, Appl No 15434/89, 15 February 1990; *Pincová and Pinc v The Czech Republic*, Reports 2002–VIII; *Zvolsky and Zvolská v The Czech Republic*, Reports 2002–IX 163.

[20] *Kohls v Germany*, Appl No 72719/01, 13 November 2003: the amount, conditions for qualifying for social welfare generally within margin of appreciation (so long as not discriminatory); see also *Sevo v Croatia*, Appl No 53921/00, 14 June 2001; *Hadzic v Croatia*, Appl No 48788/99, 13 September 2001.

[21] *Gayduk v Ukraine*, Reports 2002–VI 405; *Trajkovski v The Former Yugoslav Republic of Macedonia*, Appl No 53320/99, 7 March 2002; *Posti and Rahko v Finland*, Appl No 27824/95, 24 September 2002; *Appolonov v Russia*, Appl No 47578/01, 29 August 2002; *Olczak v Poland*, Appl No 30417/96, 7 November 2002; *Gallego Zafra v Spain*, Appl No 58229/00, 14 January 2003; *GL & SL v France*, Appl No 58811/00, 6 March 2003; *Izquierdo Galbis v Spain*, Appl No 59724/00, 20 May 2003.

[22] See the series of cases on handgun controls, cited above, Chapter 4, n 56.

[23] *Fredin v Sweden*, Series A No 192 (1991) 13 EHRR 784; *Karayiannis v Greece*, Appl No 65607/01, 20 March 2003; *Trailer & Marina (Leven) Ltd; R (on the application of Trailer & Marina (Leven) Ltd) v Secretary of State for the Environment, Food and Rural Affairs* [2004] EWCA Civ 153.

controls,[24] consumer affairs,[25] tenancy protection,[26] fiscal laws relating to taxation or other contributions,[27] and the resolution of private disputes over property[28] as areas where greater deference should be shown to the policy choices of the administrative and legislative branches.[29] This does not mean, of course, that the courts have no supervisory role in these areas, but that they are far less likely to find that an interference with property for one of these purposes is incompatible with P1(1).

Conversely, there are some areas relating to property that can be identified as requiring less deference. In *International Transport*, Laws LJ referred to the 'doing of criminal justice';[30] similarly, the conduct of civil proceedings is within the special expertise of the courts. *Allard v Sweden*[31] is one example: Swedish authorities ordered the destruction of building without waiting for the final outcome of civil proceedings that could have required its preservation. It was this decision not to respect the civil process that was particularly serious, and in respect of which the Court would not defer to the judgment of the national

---

[24] *Pine Valley Developments v Ireland*, Series A No 222 (1992) 14 EHRR 319; *Frascino v Italy*, Appl No 35227/97, 11 December 2003; *Trailer & Marina* above.

[25] *Wilson v Secretary of State for Trade and Industry* [2004] 1 AC 816; *Olczak* (n 21).

[26] *James* (n 2); *Mellacher v Austria*, Series A No 169 (1990) 12 EHRR 391; *Spath Holme Ltd v The United Kingdom*, Appl No 78031/01, 14 May 2002; *R v Secretary of State for the Environment, Transport and the Regions ex parte Spath Holme Ltd* [2001] 2 AC 349 (Lord Bingham on the P1(1) issue); *Antoniadis* (n 19).

[27] *Hentrich v France*, Series A No 296–A (1994) 18 EHRR 440; *Gasus Dosier und Fordertechnik GmbH v The Netherlands*, Series A No 306–B (1995) 20 EHRR 403; *National & Provincial Building Society v The United Kingdom*, Reports 1997–VII 2325 (1998) 25 EHRR 127; *Finkelberg v Latvia*, Appl No 55091/00, 18 October 2001 (VAT levels); *Dangeville SA v France*, Reports 2002–III 71 (2004) 38 EHRR 32; *MA and 34 Others v Finland*, Appl No 27793/95, 10 June 2003; *Ardex SA v France*, Appl No 53951/00, 2 September 2003; *Balaz v Slovakia*, Appl No 60243/00, 16 September 2003; *Stockholms Forsakrings–Och Skadestandsjuridik AB v Sweden*, Appl No 38993/97, 16 September 2003; *Roshka v Russia*, Appl No 63343/00, 6 November 2003; *Hughes v Commissioners of Customs and Excise* [2003] 1 WLR 177 (CA); *Ogis–Institut Stanislas, Ogec St Pie X and Blanche de Castille v France*, Appl No 42219/98 and Appl No 54563/00, 27 May 2004; *Di Belmonte (No 2) v Italy*, Appl No 72665/01, 3 June 2004. This includes need to control budgets by, for example, cutting social welfare: *Saarinen v Finland*, Appl No 69136/01, 28 January 2003; *MV and U–M v Finland*, Appl No 43189/98, 28 January 2003; however, this would not justify a simple failure to honour an existing court judgment: *Prodan v Moldova*, Appl No 49806/99, 18 May 2004.

[28] *Islamische Religionsgemeinschaft EV v Germany*, Appl No 53871/00, 5 December 2002; *Synod College Of The Evangelical Reformed Church Of Lithuania v Lithuania*, (2003) 36 EHRR CD94; *Shestakov v Russia*, Appl No 48757/99, 18 June 2002 (public order reasons for delaying enforcement of private law judgments).

[29] Especially where schemes involve restructuring of economic or political systems: *Lithgow v The United Kingdom*, Series A No 102 (1986) 8 EHRR 329, and the German reunification cases: eg *Lenz v Germany*, Appl No 40862/98, 27 September 2001. In addition, as a related point, the European Court of Human Rights does not act as a court of 'fourth instance'. Hence, it defers to domestic tribunals on the interpretation of domestic law: see *Transado–Transportes Fluviais Do Sado, SA v Portugal*, Appl No 35943/02, 16 December 2003 (relating to the interpretation, by an arbitration panel, of a concession agreement from Govt to private party) and *Karstova v The Czech Republic*, Appl No 54407/00, 30 September 2003.

[30] *International Transport* (n 10) [86].

[31] (2004) 39 EHRR 14.

authorities.[32] Similarly, a number of cases from some of the eastern European States have concerned the overturning of final judgments in civil proceedings by administrative authorities or other courts.[33] While such a 'supervisory' power seems to be a part of the legal systems of these States, and conceivably may serve the interests of justice in some cases, the Court has not been willing to defer to the judgement of national authorities on the appropriateness of the exercise of such powers in specific cases.[34]

Most judges would accept that other decision-makers may have expertise beyond their own, and that they should take such expertise into account in determining when to defer to the judgements of others. However, they do not necessarily agree on how they should characterise the decision in question. In *International Transport*, for example, Laws LJ regarded the setting of penalties on those found guilty of carrying clandestine entrants as relating to the implementation of immigration laws. He was in the minority, however, and the majority regarded the setting of penalties as more closely related to issues of criminal justice.[35]

Although the issues of deference and the fair balance are conceptually distinct, it seems that they often run together. For example, in *International Transport*, Simon Brown LJ said that 'ultimately one single question arises for determination by the court: is the scheme not merely harsh but plainly unfair so that, however effectively that unfairness may assist in achieving the social goal, it simply cannot be permitted?'[36] Nevertheless, in Strasbourg, a distinction is sometimes made between the margin of appreciation shown in respect of the identification of a public interest and the margin shown in relation to the fairness of the treatment of victims of the policies taken in the public interest. The margin is very broad in relation to the public interest: indeed, there do not appear to be any P1(1) cases where the Court has rejected, on the facts, a State's claim that it acted in the public interest. However, the margin sometimes narrows in relation to the extent to which individuals are expected to bear the

---

[32] See also *Karstova* (n 29); *Frascino* (n 24); *Prodan* (n 27); *Sciortino v Italy*, Appl No 30127/96, 18 October 2001; *Zwierzyński v Poland*, Reports 2001–VI 203 (2004) 38 EHRR 6, and see the line of cases on Italian re-possession proceedings, cited below n 176. Note that there still is a margin of appreciation: *Fransson and Fransson v Sweden*, Appl No 8719/02, 16 March 2004: the imposition of costs of unsuccessful proceedings where authorised by domestic law ordinarily lies with the margin of appreciation (see also *Papakokkinou v Cyprus*, Appl No 20429/02, 7 January 2003).

[33] See S Djajic, 'The Right to Property and the *Vasilescu v Romania* Case' (2000) 27 *Syracuse Journal of International Law and Commerce* 363, on the structural deficiencies of the legal systems of some former communist States in relation to the vindication of private law rights, and the effect on Art 6 and P1(1) cases.

[34] See eg *Brumărescu v Romania*, Reports 1999–VII 201 (2001) 33 EHRR 35; *Burdov v Russia*, Reports 2002–III 317 (2004) 38 EHRR 29; *Piven v Ukraine*, Appl No 56849/00, 29 June 2004; *Zhovner v Ukraine*, Appl No 56848/00, 29 June 2004; *Bocancea v Moldova*, Appl No 18872/02, 6 July 2004. But *cf Kalogeropoulou v Greece and Germany*, Appl No 59021/00, 12 December 2002, where non-enforcement of a judgment could be justified, as enforcement would have violated principles of international law on State immunity.

[35] See also David Howarth's point concerning *Marcic*: above, text to n 12.

[36] [2003] QB 728 [26].

costs of measures taken to protect the public interest. For example, where property is expropriated for public use, the European Court of Human Rights has recognised that the national authorities must have a wide margin of appreciation in determining whether expropriation furthers the public interest. However, the margin of appreciation narrows considerably when it comes to the issue of proportionality and, to be more specific, the issue of compensation.[37]

RATIONALITY

The legitimate aim

The Court normally begins by asking whether an interference with a Convention right was intended to serve a legitimate aim. With other Convention rights, the express limitations give some guidance on the aims that an interference with that particular right may serve. Article 10(2), for example, provides that the right to freedom of expression may be subject to limitations 'in the interests of national security, territorial integrity or public safety, for the prevention of disorder or crime, for the protection of health or morals, for the protection of the reputation or rights of others, for preventing the disclosure of information received in confidence, or for maintaining the authority and impartiality of the judiciary.' In P1(1), however, the aims that may justify an interference with possessions are not defined: it says only that a deprivation of property must be 'in the public interest', and that the enforcement of controls on use must be 'in the general interest or to secure the payment of taxes or other contributions or penalties.'

The failure to restrict the purposes that justify an interference with the right to property means that this stage of the analysis does not present any real difficulties for States. Of course, if a State fails to provide any reason for an interference, it would follow that P1(1) had been violated.[38] However, there are no cases where the European Court has rejected the State's argument that its purpose was legitimate.[39] The only area of real controversy has been the redistribution of private property. Arguably, laws that benefit one private person at the expense of another serve a private interest, rather than the public or general interest.

---

[37] In *James* (n 2), it was accepted that there was a margin of appreciation in relation to both, but compensation was still required to maintain the fair balance; in more recent cases (such as *Katikaridis v Greece*, Reports 1996–V 1673 (2001) 32 EHRR 6) it appears that the margin relating to compensation is narrowing.

[38] There are cases where the aim or its legitimacy was not in issue: eg where the only issues are ones of fact, or where the State offers no justification for its acts (see eg *Brumărescu* and the other cases cited n 34).

[39] *Cf Former King of Greece v Greece*, Reports 2000–XII 119 (2001) 33 EHRR 21 [88], where Court did accept that the interference served a legitimate aim, but did not accept that it served all the aims put forward by Greece.

However, the European Court has taken a generous view of the public and general interest, with the result that redistribution schemes should normally satisfy P1(1). This is shown by the *James* case, which concerned the provisions of the Leasehold Reform Act 1967 that allow occupying tenants on long leases to acquire the freehold or an extended lease of the property, without the consent of the landlord. The applicants, who owned land that subject to the Act, claimed that a compulsory transfer of property for the private use of another individual could not be in the public interest. They accepted that the State may regulate private property for the purpose of redistributing wealth, but claimed that the transfer of private property was a different matter. Indeed, they pointed out that the second sentence of P1(1) only allows deprivations in the 'public interest', whereas the third sentence of P1(1) allows regulatory controls in the 'general interest'. In their view, the change in wording could only be explained by construing 'public interest' as a narrower expression than 'general interest'.[40]

The European Court of Human Rights did not agree. To begin with, it said that 'even if there could be differences between the concepts of "public interest" and "general interest" in Article 1 (P1(1)), on the point under consideration no fundamental distinction of the kind contended for by the applicants can be drawn between them.'[41] Moreover, the Court also stated that 'public interest' and the corresponding French expression, 'pour cause d'utilité publique', have an autonomous meaning.[42] Hence, it did not apply a potentially narrower interpretation of the French expression, which might have ruled out redistributions. It then said that this autonomous meaning is broad enough to support measures which require direct transfers of property from one private person to another, so long as the transfer is itself intended to pursue a broader aim that is in the public interest. In this case, it did not regard the purpose of this scheme as exclusively private. In a crucial passage, it said that:

> the fairness of a system of law governing the contractual or property rights of private parties is a matter of public concern and therefore legislative measures intended to bring about such fairness are capable of being "in the public interest", even if they involve the compulsory transfer of property from one individual to another.[43]

From this, it followed that the United Kingdom only had to show that the legislature had intended leasehold enfranchisement to bring about greater fairness in property relations.

Since *James*, the Court has identified other aims that can support transfers between private persons,[44] such as the regulation of the relations between company shareholders,[45] the consolidation of agricultural land to achieve

---

[40] *James* (n 2) [43].
[41] Above.
[42] Above [42].
[43] Above [40].
[44] See also *Bäck v Finland*, 37598/97, 20 July 2004, [53] and [60] (the adjustment of private debts as part of a process designed to avoid bankruptcy).
[45] *Bramelid and Malmström v Sweden* (1982) 5 EHRR 249 (Comm), 256.

greater efficiency,[46] and restitution schemes intended to redress infringements of human rights under communist governments.[47] In such cases, the Court has viewed redistributions only a means to an end, with the result that the public interest requirement has been satisfied quite easily.[48]

Rationality and the relationship of the interference to the aim

Once it is determined that the aim of the interference is legitimate, the next issue is whether the interference actually serves the aim. On this point, the level of scrutiny is again very low. This follows from the tendency of the Court to describe the aim of domestic laws in the widest terms possible. For example, it has described the objectives of specific laws as the furtherance of social justice,[49] the suppression of drug trafficking,[50] the enforcement of tax laws,[51] or even the avoidance of costs to public authorities.[52] Such broad descriptions make it unlikely that an interference would fail to serve the aim in some way. By contrast, in relation to the compulsory purchase of land, common law courts normally ask whether the ultimate use of the land is in fact necessary for the achievement of the legislative purpose. If, for example, land is to be taken for a purpose which is ancillary to the main purpose of the legislative scheme, some common law courts would refuse to sanction it on the grounds that the taking would not satisfy the legislative purposes.[53] Similar arguments have been made under P1(1), but the Court sees this as a question involving the final step of the analysis, where the purpose of the aim is balanced against need to protect fundamental rights. That is, if the connection of a specific taking with broad legislative purpose is very weak, there is a greater chance that the interference would be found disproportionate; however, it is unlikely that the Court would find that the taking bears no relationship to the legitimate aim.[54]

---

[46] *Erkner and Hofauer v Austria*, Series A No 117 (1987) 9 EHRR 464; *Poiss v Austria*, Series A No 117 (1988) 10 EHRR 231; and *Prötsch v Austria*, Reports 1996–V 1812 (2001) 32 EHRR 12; see also *Håkansson and Sturesson v Sweden*, Series A No 171 (1990) 13 EHRR 1 [44].

[47] *Zvolsky* (n 19) [67]–[68]; see also *Pincová* (n 19).

[48] See also *Wilson* (n 25) [28] (Lord Nicholls).

[49] See *Bäck* (n 44), where debt adjustment was justified even where the debt was almost totally extinguished.

[50] *Air Canada v The United Kingdom*, Series A No 316 (1995) 20 EHRR 150.

[51] *Gasus* (n 27).

[52] *Blanco Callejas v Spain*, Appl No 64100/00, 18 June 2002: it was legitimate to reduce (prospectively) pensions in light of budgetary constraints; see also *Ambruosi v Italy* (2002) 35 EHRR 5: the extinction of claims against State for payment of lawyer's fees was 'in the public interest', as it saved public expense.

[53] M Taggart, 'Expropriation, Public Purpose and the Constitution' in C Forsyth and I Hare (eds), *The Golden Metwand and the Crooked Cord: Essays on Public Law in Honour of Sir William Wade QC* (Clarendon Press, Oxford, 1998).

[54] *James* (n 2); *Motais de Narbonne v France*, Appl No 48161/99, 2 July 2002; *Papadopoulou v Greece*, Appl No 53901/00, 14 March 2002. It is not conclusive that the interference may frustrate another public interest relating to the same property *Allard* (n 92) [56].

The level of intensity is also affected by principles relating to the proof of the legitimacy of the aim and the rationality of the specific interference. In general, it appears that the burden on the State is not a heavy one, and once the State has provided some evidence of the aim and the suitability of the interference, the applicant faces a heavier burden of rebuttal.[55] For example, in *Mellacher v Austria*,[56] the landlords argued rent control was unnecessary, by producing evidence that there had been no shortage of reasonably-priced accommodation for tenants of average income. However, the Court rejected this argument, solely on the basis that an explanatory memorandum of the Austrian Parliament established both the purpose and rationality of the rent control legislation.[57] Similarly, in *James*, the applicants claimed that Leasehold Reform Act 1967 was purely a vote-seeking measure rather than a genuine attempt to act in the public interest. However, the Court did not look behind the evidence put forward by the United Kingdom, as it accepted that the debates in Parliament and the official papers showed that leasehold reform had long been a matter of public concern and that the Act was intended to address that concern. Moreover, it also stated that it would 'respect the legislature's judgment as to what is "in the public interest" unless that judgment be manifestly without reasonable foundation.'[58] This was particularly true in relation to housing and social justice, where it said that

> The margin of appreciation is wide enough to cover legislation aimed at securing greater social justice in the sphere of people's homes, even where such legislation interferes with existing contractual relations between private parties and confers no direct benefit on the State or the community at large.[59]

The effect is to make the degree of scrutiny of the legitimacy and rationality of an interference so low that it amounts to little more than a test of good faith, which is met by simple assertions on the part of the government. For example, the Court has stated that it is enough that the State 'may have considered it necessary' to resolve a problem.[60]

In the courts of the United Kingdom, these issues arose in *Wilson and others v Secretary of State for Trade and Industry*,[61] in which the House of Lords overturned the Court of Appeal's declaration of incompatibility in respect of s 127(3) of the Consumer Credit Act 1974. Section 127(3) provides that a lender's failure to disclose certain information in a credit agreement renders the

---

[55] *Håkansson* (n 46) [47]; *Phocas v France*, Reports 1996–II 519 (2001) 32 EHRR 11 [54]–[55]; *Tre Traktörer Aktiebolag v Sweden*, Series A No 159 (1991) 13 EHRR 309, [56]–[57]; *GL & SL v France*, Appl No 58811/00, 6 March 2003; *Elia srl v Italy*, Appl No 37710/97, 2 August 2001 (note the dissenting opinion of Judge Conforti).

[56] *Mellacher* (n 26).

[57] Above [47]; see also *Holy Monasteries v Greece*, Series A No 301–A (1995) 20 EHRR 1 [69].

[58] *James* (n 2) [46]; see also *Pressos Compania Naviera SA v Belgium*, Series A No 332 (1996) 21 EHRR 301 [37].

[59] Above [47].

[60] *Zvolsky* (n 19) [68].

[61] *Wilson* (n 25).

agreement unenforceable. First County Trust, a lender, claimed that s 127(3) violates P1(1), as it does not allow enforcement in cases where the consumer suffers no harm as a result of non-disclosure. The Court of Appeal agreed that s 127(3) serves a legitimate aim, as it was intended to secure consumer protection; moreover, the specific measures relating to disclosure and the bar on enforcement serve that aim.[62] However, it then assumed that the P1(1) proportionality test required the State to show that the interference no more than necessary to achieve its purpose.[63] As explained in the next section, it is doubtful that this is an element of the P1(1) test, especially in regulatory cases such as *Wilson*. In any case, the interesting point is the nature of the evidence the Court of Appeal considered in establishing necessity, since it has broader implications in relation to establishing or challenging the legitimacy of the aim of an interference. As the Court was asking whether the bar on enforcement was strictly necessary, it suggested that the aim of requiring disclosure would have been achieved if the courts had been given a discretion to allow enforcement where justice so required. It then sought to discover why Parliament excluded such a discretion from s 127(3). Neither the Crowther Report[64] nor the White Paper *Reform of the Law on Consumer Credit*[65] recommended an absolute bar on enforcement, and there was nothing in Hansard to explain why it had been included.[66] From this, the Court of Appeal concluded that the bar had not been justified: 'There is no reason that we can identify and . . . no reason has been advanced why an inflexible prohibition is necessary in order to achieve the legitimate policy aim. There is no reason why that aim should not be achieved through judicial control; by empowering the court to do what is just in the circumstances of the particular case.'[67] Accordingly, the Court of Appeal stated that a declaration of incompatibility should be issued.

This point was addressed at length in the House of Lords, where it was agreed that Parliamentary materials might, in some circumstances, provide evidence of the aim of legislation or the reasons for a specific interference with a Convention right.[68] However, the absence of such information does not mean that the interference cannot be justified. In any case, the statute itself embodies Parliament's intentions, and may provide evidence of the reasons for a particular interference. In this case, their Lordships implicitly found that the provisions of the Consumer Credit Act 1974 revealed that Parliament intended to protect consumers in loan transactions and that it believed that the bar on enforcement would help to achieve that end. Consequently, the Parliamentary record has little weight at this stage of the inquiry, if only because it should not be difficult

---

[62] [2001] 1 QB 407 (sub nom *Wilson v First County Trust Ltd*) [38]–[39].

[63] Above [39].

[64] United Kingdom, *Report of the Crowther Committee* (Cmnd 4596, 1971).

[65] United Kingdom, *Reform of the Law on Consumer Credit* (Cmnd 5427, 1973).

[66] *Wilson* (CA) (n 62) [35]–[37].

[67] Above [39].

[68] The UK's use of the Parliamentary record in *James* (n 2) (and Court's acceptance of the record as evidence of aim) would support this.

to establish the aim of legislation from the statute's preamble or its specific terms. Indeed, even the Court of Appeal in *Wilson* agreed that the bar on enforcement served a legitimate end, and it did so without searching for specific reasons to that effect in Hansard.[69]

Whether it is appropriate for courts to exercise such a high degree of deference on the rationality issue is doubtful, at least where the issue is one of fact. In practice, however, even where there is cogent evidence that an interference does not serve the professed aim, the courts tend to weigh this in the balance between the public and private interest.[70] Given the level of deference exercised by the courts, and the generality of the limitations to P1(1) (contrasted with, for exampled, Article 10(2)), it seems doubtful that there is any real chance of success for an argument that an interference does not serve a legitimate aim.[71] In jurisdictions where a right to property does not incorporate an open-ended balancing test, rationality can become more prominent. For example, in the United States, the constitutional analysis of 'exactions' (payments or benefits required as a condition for obtaining planning consents) often concentrates on rationality.[72] Similarly, in the United Kingdom, the limits on the powers of local authorities to impose conditions on a grant of planning permission developed without the application of the balancing of the proportionality test.[73] Under P1(1), however, the *Sporrong* judgment has had the effect of causing the rationality test to be sidelined in determining the justification for the interference.

A test of strict necessity?

The next question is whether the interference was necessary for the particular aim. A test of strict necessity would ask whether there was another, less drastic means of achieving the same end. While the test of strict necessity is part of the

---

[69] *Wilson* (CA) (n 62).

[70] For example, in *Chassagnou v France*, Reports 1999–III 21 (2000) 29 EHRR 615 the Court accepted France's claim that certain hunting laws served a legitimate public interest in conservation, without examining closely the applicant's argument that the laws did not in fact serve the purpose of conservation, but rather the purpose of managing hunting as leisure activity. Note also the dissenting opinion of Judge Foighel, in *Gasus* (n 27) [5] (joined by Judges Russo and Jungwiert) which doubts the public interest in the seizure of property belonging to third parties as a means of satisfying a tax debtor's liabilities, as it appeared that very little money was actually recovered in this way.

[71] Except where the State offers no justification for the interference, as in *Brumărescu* (n 34).

[72] In *Nollan v California Coastal Commission* 483 US 825 (1987) the Supreme Court held that an exaction is acceptable if it has an 'essential nexus' with a problem related to the initial reason for prohibiting the development in question (so long as the initial reason is also legitimate). Subsequently, in *Dolan v City of Tigard*, 114 S Ct 2309 (1994), it added a requirement of 'rough proportionality' to the Nollan test. See D Rhoads, 'Developer Exactions and Public Decision Making in the United States and England' (1994) 11 *Arizona Journal of International and Comparative Law* 469.

[73] *Tesco Stores Ltd v Secretary of State for the Environment* [1995] 1 WLR 759 (HL): the offer to provide funds to construct a road some distance from a proposed developed was not a material consideration in the grant of planning permission (it was not the developer that offered the funds that challenged the grant, but its competitor).

analysis under other Convention rights, there is some doubt that it is an element of the proportionality test under P1(1). In *James v United Kingdom*, the applicants argued that the deprivation of their possessions could be justified 'only if there was no other less drastic remedy for the perceived injustice that the extreme remedy of expropriation',[74] and then claimed that the objective of protecting tenants could be ensured without empowering them to purchase the freehold of the rented property. The Court rejected this argument:

> This amounts to reading a test of strict necessity into the Article, an interpretation which the Court does not find warranted. The availability of alternative solutions does not in itself render the leasehold reform legislation unjustified; it constitutes one factor, along with others, relevant for determining whether the means chosen could be regarded as reasonable and suited to achieving the legitimate aim being pursued, having regard to the need to strike a "fair balance". Provided the legislature remained within these bounds, it is not for the Court to say whether the legislation represented the best solution for dealing with the problem or whether the legislative discretion should have been exercised in another way.[75]

Although the majority of cases have followed this approach,[76] there are some specific circumstances where the Court has taken a stricter line. The first arises where the State has interfered both with property rights and with the judicial process. In such cases, the interference with property may serve a legitimate aim, but the Court is unlikely to accept that the aim could not have been served without respect for the rule of law. In that sense, it is likely to consider the availability of alternative means of achieving the same aim as a sign that the interference with property was disproportionate. For example, in *Allard*,[77] the applicant objected to a court-ordered destruction of a home she had constructed on land she held jointly with other members of her family. The destruction served a legitimate aim, since it was intended to enforce strict rules prohibiting the construction of building without the consent of joint owners. However, the joint owners were still embroiled in separate legal proceedings concerning a division of the land when the destruction occurred. The European Court regarded the execution of the order for destruction as a violation of P1(1), but not on the basis that the destruction itself was wrong. Indeed, the destruction would probably have been acceptable in the absence of the division proceedings or if their outcome had not been favourable to the applicant. It was the failure to take the

---

[74] *James* (n 2) [51].

[75] Above.

[76] For example, in *Mellacher* (n 26), the possibility of using a more flexible approach to rent controls did not make the controls disproportionate. Similar reasoning can be seen in *Tre Traktörer* (n 55) [62], where an alcohol licence was revoked in order to ensure that the aim of controlling consumption was achieved: other, less draconian measures might have succeeded, but the failure to apply them did not put the State in violation of P1(1). See also *Smits, Kleyn, Mettler Toledo BV et al, Raymakers, Vereniging Landelijk Overleg Betuweroute and Van Helden v The Netherlands*, Appl No 39032/97, 39343/98, 39651/98, 43147/98, 46664/99, 61707/00, 3 May 2001.

[77] *Allard* (n 31).

less drastic approach of waiting for the division proceedings to finish that was material.[78]

There are other cases where strict necessity has been applied, but whether these represent general categories of exceptions to P1(1) is doubtful. One example is *Hentrich v France*,[79] where legislation gave tax authorities a power of pre-emption that allowed them to buy land within three months of a sale. The price was fixed at 10% over the original purchase price. The power was intended for use against buyers who had avoided tax by making artificially low declarations of the purchase price. In holding that the exercise of the power against the applicants violated P1(1), the Court placed considerable weight on the possibility that the tax could have been collected by less drastic means.[80] However, this does not seem to represent a general principle in respect of tax enforcement. Indeed, *Gasus Dosier und Fordertechnik GmbH v The Netherlands*[81] is an example to the contrary. The applicants complained that the Dutch tax authorities had seized property of theirs that was in the possession of a third party, to satisfy the third party's tax liabilities; they argued that the State could have secured the payment of taxes by some means that would not have involved the seizure of the possessions of innocent third parties. The dissenting judges accepted this argument, as they stated that the seizure of the applicant's possessions was not 'indispensable' to the enforcement of the tax laws in question. However, the majority did not regard this as a significant consideration.[82] It is the approach in *Gasus*, rather than *Hentrich*, which is more widely followed in the Court's own case law.[83]

In the United Kingdom, the courts initially tended toward a view of P1(1) proportionality that incorporated the test of strict necessity. Indeed, in *Wilson v First County Trust*,[84] the Court of Appeal held that, since the Consumer Credit Act 1974 was intended to protect consumers from entering transactions without full knowledge of the terms of credit, there was no need to prohibit enforcement in every case where disclosure was not made. An alternative, less drastic solution was available, as the courts could be given a discretion to allow enforcement where justice so required. If, for example, the consumer would

---

[78] Above [58]–[59]. See also the cases where the extinction of a civil judgment has been found to violate P1(1): in such cases, the scrutiny is much closer (see eg *Burdov* (n 38) and the other cases cited at n 38).

[79] *Hentrich* (n 27).

[80] Above [47].

[81] *Gasus* (n 27) (Judge Foighel, joined by Judges Russo and Jungwiert) [5].

[82] Above [5] (of the dissenting opinion).

[83] See eg *Mellacher* (n 26); *Tre Traktörer* (n 55) [62]; *Blečić v Croatia*, Appl No 59532/00, 29 July 2004 [67].

[84] *Wilson* (CA) (n 62); see also *International Transport* (n 10) [51]–[52] (Simon Brown LJ) [193] (Jonathon Parker LJ), where the proportionality test set out in *De Freitas v Permanent Secretary of Ministry of Agriculture, Fisheries, Lands and Housing* [1999] 1 AC 69, 80 (adopting a passage from *Nyambirai v National Social Security Authority* [1996] 1 LRC 64, 75 (Zim SC; Gubbay CJ)) was applied to P1(1), although it was developed in the context of a constitutional right to freedom of expression.

have entered the loan even if disclosure had been made, the court could allow enforcement.[85] In the House of Lords, it was agreed that strict necessity was not part of the proportionality analysis under P1(1). It appears, therefore, that the approach of the UK courts on strict necessity is substantially the same as it is in Strasbourg.[86]

The public interest and coercive State power

The Court has made one important but implicit assumption regarding the characterisation of the interference with the individual's right to property. Arguably, the concern should not be with the interference with property as such, but with the coercive nature of that interference. In particular, in the case of a deprivation of possessions, it could be argued that a consensual, negotiated sale of property would always be a less intrusive means of obtaining the property than a forced sale. Hence, the State should normally be required to show that it made a reasonable attempt to obtain the property without resorting to its coercive powers. Indeed, the same could be said for many types of regulation: if the State could have obtained the victim's consent to the restrictions in question, there was no necessity for relying on the compulsory powers. Plainly, there may be cases where necessity could be established: if, for example, it would have been impossible to obtain consent because the number of affected property owners was too great or if, for example, the cost of obtaining consent would have been prohibitive for other reasons.[87] Nevertheless, it should normally fall to the State to establish that the use of compulsion was necessary.

This point was touched upon in *Lithgow*, where it was argued that taking property without compensation related to the actual value of the property could not be in the public interest.[88] This puts a different perspective on the public interest issue, since it concentrates on the public interest in resorting to the State's compulsory powers rather than the public interest in acquiring or regulating the property interest. However, in *Lithgow*, the Court rejected the argument because it found that, although deprivations of property normally

---

[85] Above [39].

[86] See also *Owen v Ministry of Agriculture, Fisheries and Food* [2001] EHLR 18 (QBD), where it was held it was not disproportionate to apply BSE regulations so as to destroy cow before birth of calf, even though waiting until birth might establish that there is no risk that BSE would have been transmitted from cow to calf.

[87] As in the case of an emergency: see *Burmah Oil v Lord Advocate* [1965] AC 75, and *cf* J Rowan-Robinson, 'Utility Wayleaves: Time for Reform' [2001] *Journal of Planning & Environment Law* 1247, 1256, on differences amongst utilities with compulsory powers in relation to the need to negotiate before relying on compulsory powers.

[88] *Lithgow* (n 29) [108]; M Mendelson, 'The United Kingdom Nationalization Cases and the European Convention on Human Rights' (1986) 57 *British Yearbook of International Law* 33, 50.

require compensation, the 'obligation to pay compensation derives from an implicit condition in Article 1 of Protocol No 1 (P1(1)) read as a whole'.[89]

It was also raised at first instance in *R (on the application of Trailer & Marina (Leven) Ltd) v Secretary of State for the Environment, Food and Rural Affairs*,[90] in which the owner of land that had been designated as an SSSI complained that it had not been compensated for the loss of future income from activities it was now prohibited from undertaking. It was particularly aggrieved because, until January 2001, it had been receiving compensation of £19,000 annually for agreeing to forego these activities. However, changes in the legislative framework meant that compensation was no longer available.[91] Hence, in this case, it was clear that the objective of protecting the environment could have been achieved by negotiating for the landowner's consent. Nevertheless, the Court held that the refusal to compensate was in the public interest, and did not upset the fair balance. Ouseley J observed that the policy makers had decided that it was inappropriate to compensate property owners who threatened to engage in activities that were harmful to the environment. Given the broad area of discretion afforded to the legislature and executive in determining policy objectives, he could not say that this was disproportionate. Although Ouseley J only considered the question of coercion briefly, it is interesting that he did so at all.

More generally, States are not asked to justify the choice of public or private law methods of achieving a legitimate aim. For example, the State need not justify the choice between using private law or public law rules as a means of achieving a legitimate aim. The courts have varied in their explanation for this: either the issue is ignored; or the choice falls within the margin of appreciation; or it is seen as a consequence of the nature of the fair balance test, as it does not incorporate a test of strict necessity. Hence, issues regarding the necessity for the interference relate only to the purpose of taking or regulating the property and not to the reasons for resorting to the State's coercive powers over property. Questions regarding the need to use coercion are left to the balancing test.

THE BALANCING TEST

Finally, the Court asks whether the interference was proportionate to the legitimate aim pursued, or, as it said in *Sporrong*, whether a fair balance was struck

---

[89] *Lithgow* above [109]. Note also that the argument on strict necessity is similar, as the victim may argue that a consensual sale would have been a less drastic means of achieving the same end. However, as explained in the previous section, the argument on strict necessity did not succeed in *James* (n 2) [51].

[90] [2004] EWHC 153 *affirmed* [2004] EWCA Civ 1580.

[91] Part of his land was notified as an SSSI under s 28 of the Wildlife and Countryside Act 1981. Amendments made by the Countryside and Rights of Way Act 2000 authorise English Nature to enter management agreements concerning the use of areas notified as SSSIs. However, according to Ministerial guidance effective from the beginning of 2001, English Nature can no longer agree to compensate for activities that the landowner is not currently undertaking.

between the 'demands of the general interest of the community and the requirements of the protection of the individual's fundamental rights'.[92]

The reason for shifting away from legality and rationality as the elements of
justification has never been fully explained by the Court. It ignores the drafting
history, as it was quite clear that many governments and delegates did not wish
P1(1) to become an instrument for reviewing regulatory controls on substantive
grounds. In fact, the case law has not strayed too far from this objective, but
doctrinally this is achieved by allowing a wide margin of appreciation and by
rejecting the test of strict necessity. Nevertheless, the adoption of the three-rule
structure of P1(1) suggests that it was not necessary to develop over-arching
rules of proportionality: instead, the Court could have concentrated on developing principles relevant to each Rule. However, as explained in chapter 4, the
structure set out in Sporrong has had little impact on the jurisprudence.
Although the metaphor of the balance suggests that a measure is taken of both
the 'demands of the general interest' and the impact of the interference on the
individual, and that an almost arithmetic comparison of each is then made, it is
applied in a much more impressionistic manner. In any given case, the Court
usually repeats the *Sporrong* statement and then isolates the specific facts which
are most influential to its decision, without suggesting that its decision on those
facts represents an elaboration or refinement of the *Sporrong* test itself. In general, there is very little discussion of the relevance of classifying the interference
under one Rule or another.

The application of the fair balance test to all interferences reflects a sense of
the purpose of the right to property. Perhaps there was a belief that, as long as
the doctrine took a formal view of applicability, and a limited view of the tests
of legality and rationality, human rights would not be fully protected.
Something about the fair balance test captures the essence of a human right to
property that the other tests do not. If this is the case, however, it leads to a further question: what is it that the fair balance test does protect?

As explained in chapter 2, applicability is usually determined by formal criteria, from which it follows that the P1(1) protects existing entitlements. For
example, a moral entitlement to property is an insufficient basis for a P1(1)
claim. The applicability doctrines therefore suggest that P1(1) is directed toward
a conservative agenda of protecting entitlements against modification or
change. It is possible, therefore, that the fair balance test brings other elements
into play. For example, although the test involves an assessment of the impact
on the victim, the assessment tends to focus on specific types of loss. This focus
reveals something of the Court's understanding of the purpose of a right to
property. So, for example, in some cases, the impact is described in terms of the
social function of property; more often, it is described in terms of economic loss.

In addition, there are a significant number of cases in which the fair balance
test appears to place little weight on either the public interest supporting the

---

[92] *Sporrong* (n 1) [69] (references omitted).

interference or the substantive impact on the individual who suffers the interference. In these cases, the focus shifts to rule-of-law issues. Concerns that might
have been relevant to the legality condition often arise in relation to the fair
balance, and, although insufficient to establish a failure to satisfy the legality
condition, they may be conclusive with respect to the fair balance. Again, this
reveals something of the Court's perception of the purpose of P1(1), since Article
6(1) would often be sufficient to prevent procedural abuses. Under P1(1), these
issues arise where the Court has a more general sense of the abuse of power by
State organs; and in that way, they affirm the value of stability that underlies the
case law on applicability

This section therefore examines how the fair balance test characterises the
impact in terms of the social function of property, and in terms of economic loss.
It then considers the test in relation to issues relating to the rule of law. Before
beginning, however, it is worth noting the Court has paid comparatively little
attention to the analysis of the public interest side of the balance. It would have
already considered the 'demands of the general interest of the community' in
deciding whether the interference was rationally connected to a legitimate aim
and whether the margin of appreciation (or area of discretion) should be narrow
or wide, but in relation to the fair balance, it must decide whether the specific
purpose of the interference justifies the interference. However, the assessment of
the public benefit only rarely incorporates an analysis of the practical effects of
the interference. In the vast majority of cases, the Court does not even go this
far: having already accepted that the aim of the interference is legitimate, and
that there is at least enough of a public benefit to satisfy the rationality test, it
does not go further and examine the significance of the actual benefit resulting
from the interference.[93]

The social function of property

Although the courts usually measure the impact on the victim in economic
terms, it is also clear that the impact on other interests may affect the fair balance. In some cases, this arises only in negative sense. For example, the Court
tends to be much less sympathetic to complaints concerning interferences with
property used for a commercial purpose. In *Gasus*,[94] for example, it indicated
that commercial operators may be expected to bear greater risks of at least some
types of State action than non-commercial operators.[95] In this case, Dutch tax
authorities satisfied the tax liabilities of a third party by seizing goods delivered
to him by a seller under a retention of title clause. The Court said that the risk
of seizure was one of the risks that the seller should be expected to bear, even

---

[93] Any such examination is more often found in dissenting judgments: see eg Judge Foighel,
joined by Judges Russo and Jungwiert in *Gasus* (n 27) [5] (of their opinion).

[94] *Gasus* (n 27).

[95] See also *Pine Valley* (n 24) [59].

though it did not have access to the information that would have enabled it to assess the buyer's tax liabilities and hence to determine the actual risk of seizure. Nevertheless, the Court said that the seller could have protected itself by refusing to sell on credit, by obtaining alternative security, or by increasing the price of the goods to reflect the risk of seizure. Consequently, it could not complain when the risk materialised and it suffered a loss thereby.[96]

It is clear that the distinction is based on a judgement of the value of using human rights to protect commercial property. That is, the discussion of risk in *Gasus* is more of a conclusion: to say that a commercial operator should expect these risks is merely another way of saying that human rights law is not directed to the reduction of these risks. It is not a matter of the victim's capacity for addressing these risks.[97] On this point, one can contrast *Gasus* with the *Hentrich* case, where the Court suggested that taking the victim's property was particularly harsh because they could not have predicted that the tax authorities would use its powers of pre-emption. This suggests that the question of risk and predictability has an objective basis. However, the sale contract in *Hentrich* included provisions to protect against the risk of pre-emption. On the facts, the only distinction of substance between the two cases was the commercial nature of the victim's interest in *Gasus*.

This point is also evident in the Court of Appeal's judgment in *Lindsay v Commissioners of Customs and Excise*,[98] which dealt with the forfeiture of a vehicle used to smuggle goods into the United Kingdom. Under the Customs and Excise Management Act 1979, goods imported without payment of duty are subject to forfeiture,[99] as are any vehicles used for the carriage of such goods.[100] The Commissioners have the discretion to restore anything forfeited or seized,[101] but recently they settled on a policy not to restore vehicles in the absence of 'exceptional circumstances'.[102] In *Lindsay*, the owner argued that forfeiture was disproportionate because he had not intended to resell the goods for a profit: he had either bought them for his own use or for reimbusement at cost by family members. The Court of Appeal agreed: where goods are smuggled without an intention to sell at a profit, there must be some consideration of the individual's culpability, including such factors as 'the scale of importation, whether it is a "first offence", whether there was an attempt at concealment or dissimulation, the value of the vehicle and the degree of hardship that will be caused by forfeiture.'[103] However, such consideration need not be given in cases where smuggling was for resale a profit.

---

[96] *Gasus* (n 27) [70].
[97] See also *Bäck* (n 44) [62].
[98] [2002] 1 WLR 1766.
[99] Customs and Excise Management Act 1979, s 49.
[100] Customs and Excise Management Act 1979, s 141.
[101] Customs and Excise Management Act 1979, s 152.
[102] The policy is described in *Lindsay* (n 98) [19]–[21].
[103] Above [64]; see also *R (Hoverspeed Ltd) v Customs and Excise Comrs* [2003] QB 1041 [187]; *Gascoyne v Customs and Excise Commissioners* [2004] EWCA Civ 1162 [95]–[101].

The point made in *Lindsay* about the commercial purpose of the victim is worth examining closely, as it seems that it was neither the effects of the commercial activity nor the nature of the interest in the property that were relevant. None of the judges said that stricter measures could be justified in the case of smuggling for resale at profit because, for example, it is somehow more difficult to deter or detect than it is in cases of non-profit smuggling, or that the losses are much greater. Neither was it suggested that the impact of seizure on non-profit smugglers is greater than it is on for-profit smugglers because, for example, non-profit smugglers are not in a position to assess the risk of forfeiture. Indeed, Customs and Excise went out of their way to warn all travellers of the risk of forfeiture. The relative financial impact might be greater in cases of non-commercial smuggling, but again there was no evidence of this. It seems that it was purely the commercial nature of smuggling that made a difference, and this is more of a moral judgement than a fact.

Plainly, *Lindsay* deals with a different situation than *Gasus*, but it is at least consistent with the European jurisprudence to distinguish between commercial and non-commercial operators. It is also evident in cases dealing with the family home,[104] such as *Venditelli v Italy*.[105] It concerned the sealing of the applicant's flat for a failing to obtain the required permits for building work. In 1990, the Italian courts held that a presidential amnesty applied to the applicant in respect of his conduct, but nonetheless the flat was not released to him for another year. The Court held that the P1(1) was violated, in part because the impact of the delay was exacerbated by the fact that the applicant was locked out of his home.[106]

A further example of the importance of social functions arises where property expresses or reflects an individual's personality or identity. In such cases, an interference may be more difficult to justify. The one notable example is *Chassagnou v France*.[107] Under French law, the right to hunt belongs exclusively to the landowner. However, a 1964 law required the owners of landholdings below a specified size to become members of any approved hunters' association set up in their municipality and to transfer the hunting rights over their land to the association. The hunting rights would then be used to create a

---

[104] And possibly in relation to other property necessary for subsistence: see eg *Azinas v Cyprus*, Appl No 56679/00, 20 June 2002 (Third Section), 28 May 2004 (Grand Chamber), where the Third Section said that the withdrawal of the pension was particularly harsh because it deprived the applicant and his family 'of any means of subsistence' (at [44]). The Grand Chamber overturned the judgment on the ground that the applicant had failed to exhaust domestic remedies. But *cf Vikulov v Latvia*, Appl No 16870/03, 25 March 2004; *Kohls* (n 20): the amount and conditions for qualifying for social welfare generally are within margin of appreciation (so long as the conditions are not discriminatory).

[105] Series A No 293–A (1995) 19 EHRR 464.

[106] Above [2] of the joint dissenting opinion of Judges Walsh, Spielmann, Palm And Loizou (concurring with respect to P1(1)). See also the series of cases dealing with Italian bankruptcy laws: eg *Luordo v Italy*, Appl No 32190/96, 17 July 2003; *Parisi v Italy*, Appl No 39884/98, 5 February 2004 and *Neroni v Italy*, Appl No 7503/02, 22 April 2004.

[107] *Chassagnou* (n 70).

municipal hunting ground. The applicants, who held small holdings and had been compelled to join an association, were opposed to hunting on ethical grounds. They claimed that the law infringed P1(1),[108] on the basis that the loss of their hunting rights constituted a disproportionate control over the use of their property, 'firstly in that they were obliged to tolerate the presence of hunters on their land, whereas they were opposed to hunting for ethical reasons, and secondly in that they could not use the land they owned for the creation of nature reserves where hunting was prohibited.'[109]

The Court held that the interference was disproportionate, on the basis that 'Compelling small landowners to transfer hunting rights over their land so that others can make use of them in a way which is totally incompatible with their beliefs imposes a disproportionate burden which is not justified under the second paragraph of Article 1 of Protocol No. 1.'[110] The emphasis on their beliefs is quite significant, because it shows that the Court was not concerned solely with the formal or economic of the interference. Indeed, the French Government argued that the actual interference with their land was slight, as hunting was only permitted for part of the year and was not permitted within 150 metres of dwellings. France also argued that the applicants enjoyed the offsetting benefit of a right to hunt on all land of the local hunters' association,[111] but the Court found that this was immaterial: the right to hunt on other land was of no value to anyone ethically opposed to hunting.

It is uncertain how far the reasoning in *Chassagnou* extends. While the Court took the applicants' ethical objections into account, it was clear that not every reason for retaining the right to exclude would be accepted: if, for example, the applicants had no objection to hunting, but did not wish to allow anyone from a particular race or nationality to enter the land, the Court would almost certainly have held that the interference was not disproportionate. On this point, the Court observed that the 'The applicants are opposed to hunting on ethical grounds and the Court considers that their "convictions" in this respect attain a certain level of cogency, cohesion and importance and are therefore worthy of respect in a democratic society'.[112] In any case, it is doubtful that ethical objections of the *Chassagnou* applicants would have weighed in the balance in the event of an expropriation of their land. For example, it seems unlikely that a landowner could object to the compulsory acquisition of land for the construction of an airport solely on the basis that he or she objected on ethical grounds

---

[108] As well as Arts 9 and 11 of the Convention.

[109] *Chassagnou* (n 70) [72].

[110] Above [85].

[111] In addition, the Government claimed that the law allowed applicants to prevent hunting by enclosing their land or by acquiring enough additional land to be exempt from the law. However, the Court observed that these measures were not practical alternatives for the applicants, as they would have required considerable expense.

[112] This statement was made in relation to the right to freedom of association, but it indicates the Court's approach under P1(1) (in support, the Court referred to *Campbell and Cosans v The United Kingdom*, Series A No 48 (1982) 4 EHRR 293 [36]).

to the environmental harm that would be caused. It is likely that compensation alone would be enough to maintain the fair balance.[113]

In conclusion, the social function of property operates as a kind of wild card in the balancing process: not only is it of indeterminate weight, but it is also unclear in the scope of its application. While it is reasonably clear that property used for a commercial purpose may suffer greater interference than property used for a non-commercial purpose, it is not at all clear that non-commercial interests can be ranked in the same way. One would expect the European Court to invoke the margin of appreciation in such questions, and similarly for the UK courts to consider such decisions as falling within discretionary area of judgment of legislature or executive. Indeed, *Chassagnou* itself is exceptional on this point. As Judge Zupančič pointed out in a dissenting opinion, laws often discriminate between different uses of property. In essence, the enactment of the hunting laws represented a choice between the interests of the owners in favour of hunting and the interests of those opposed to it. This kind of choice is often made by regulators, as regulation involves the weighing of the value of different social practices. Property is concerned with control over the material world, and the expression of social practices usually requires access to some material resources. Rights to property therefore often allow their holders some power to oppose and support social practices, and it is the extent to which the legislature may control this power that is the real issue. The question for the Court is therefore to determine how far P1(1) limits the powers of the legislature in this regard. To be more specific, why, in *Chassagnou*, did an international tribunal think it necessary, as a matter of human rights, to protect the interests of non-hunters?

Economic Loss

As explained in chapter 2, the Court sometimes dismisses applications solely on the basis that the victim cannot demonstrate any economic loss.[114] Moreover, in cases involving the imposition of financial liability, it assumes that economic loss alone is sufficient to engage the State's responsibility under P1(1). Plainly, this demonstrates that the Court sees a close connection between the right to property and the protection of economic power and wealth. In some cases, economic power is tied to the social function of property: for example, in the social welfare cases, the denial of assistance may affect the capacity to carry on an autonomous existence. However, in the majority of cases, the reasoning does not go this far. The protection of wealth is a valid objective by itself.

---

[113] Indeed, even in *Chassagnou* (n 70), it appears that this was the result: the Court made an award for non-pecuniary damage, but no evidence of pecuniary damage was submitted, and so no compensation under that head. It is not clear whether the payment of damages was a sufficient remedy for future entry on the applicants' land.

[114] Chapter 2, 82–83.

It seems that property is, once again, equated with the conservative value of stability, although stability is not specifically related to rights as rights. That is, the Court has not developed a 'core rights' theory of property in the manner of the American courts. The theory holds that any permanent taking of a 'core right' of property is a taking of property, for which compensation is required.[115] The right to exclude others is a core right; consequently, any permanent physical intrusion on land is normally presumed to require compensation, no matter how trivial the actual interference may be.[116] The core rights theory developed partly in response to the theory of 'conceptual severance', which holds that every right in the bundle of rights is itself property, and hence that any restriction on a right of property is effectively a taking of property for which compensation should be paid.[117] The theory represents a partial acceptance of the conceptual severance theory, since rights of property are themselves property. At the same time, the idea of a 'core' right rejects the notion that every right in the bundle of rights is equally deserving of protection. The right to exclude is singled out because it is central to any description of property or ownership. In relation to land, it is particularly important because it represents an interest more worthy of protection than, for example, the right to engage in certain kinds of trades on land.[118] In that sense, the core rights theory is not purely formal, as it reflects the importance of the social function of property.

Under P1(1), specific rights are not singled out for special protection. It may therefore appear that the impact on formal rights is not important under the P1(1) analysis. However, to the extent that this is accurate, it is only accurate in relation to the balancing test. As Chapter 4 shows, the difference between a Rule 2 deprivation of possessions and other interferences with property is usually described in terms of the impact on the formal rights of property.[119] There is, of course, the possibility that regulation may be so extensive that it amounts to a de facto deprivation of possessions, but this is only likely to be found where a public body has effectively taken over all rights of ownership. Since the Court is far more likely to say that the fair balance requires compensation in Rule 2 cases, the formal description of the interference can be important. Hence, the formal analysis may still be relevant to the outcome, but not conclusive.

---

[115] The constitutional right to be compensated for takings is provided by the Fifth Amendment to the Constitution, as follows: 'No person shall be . . . deprived of . . . property, without due process of law; nor shall private property be taken for public use, without just compensation.'

[116] *Loretto v Teleprompter Manhattan CATV Corp,* 458 US 419 (1982).

[117] See RA Epstein, *Takings: Private Property and the Power of Eminent Domain* (Harvard University Press, Cambridge, MA, 1985) 75: 'No matter how the basic entitlements contained within the bundle of ownership rights are divided and no matter how many times the division takes place, all of the pieces together, and each of them individually, fall within the scope of the eminent domain clause.' For a criticism, see MJ Radin, 'The Liberal Conception of Property: Cross Currents in the Jurisprudence of Takings' (1988) 88 *Columbia Law Review* 1667, 1676–78, who coined the phrase 'conceptual severance' to describe Epstein's position. For the most recent attempt to revive the theory, see *Eastern Enterprises v Apfel,* 524 US 498 (1998).

[118] *Loretto* (n 116) 435–38.

[119] Chapter 4, 112–18.

The economic measure is most rigorously analysed in cases involving the deprivation of possessions, as the Court has indicated that the fair balance normally requires monetary compensation in such cases. However, as the Court may also consider the extent of the economic loss in other cases, it is worth addressing two general questions concerning its use as the measure of the impact on the victim of the interference. The first relates to the measure itself: how is the loss calculated? The second arises once the loss is calculated: what does the fair balance require in respect of a specific loss?

Measuring the loss

Counter-balancing benefits

The assessment of the loss should take into account the availability of counter-balancing benefits. While the focus is usually on the amount and timing of compensation, it is clear that other benefits must be considered.[120] For example, in a series of cases on the consolidation of parcels of land, the Court has made it clear that the deprivation of one plot of land may be counter-balanced by the provision of a different plot of land, provided that there is a reasonable relationship in the value of each.[121] Similarly, in *Cooperativa La Laurentina v Italy*,[122] it was relevant to the assessment of the proportionality of a planning restriction that the applicant could have negotiated a development agreement with the local authority. And in *Wilson*, the House of Lords said necessary to consider the lender's gains and losses 'in the round', and so it asked whether the lender would have had a civil right to restitution of the principal advanced under an unenforceable loan.[123]

But while this is accepted in principle,[124] it appears that it is not always observed, particularly in Strasbourg. This is demonstrated by contrasting the

---

[120] In addition to the cases cited below, see also *Posti* (n 21); *Teuschler v Germany*, Appl No 47636/99, 4 October 2001.

[121] *Erkner* (n 46); *Poiss* (n 46); *Prötsch* (n 46).

[122] Appl No 23529/94, 2 August 2001.

[123] *Wilson* (n 25) [47]–[48] (Lord Nicholls) [171]–[172] (Lord Scott): the lack of a restitutionary (or other) claim which might have benefited the lender was relevant, although it did not make the interference disproportionate. See also *Wittek v Germany*, Reports 2002–X 43 [59]–[60].

[124] *Stevens and Knight v The United Kingdom*, Appl No 28918/95, 9 September 1998; *Irvine v The United Kingdom*, Appl No 29576/95, 9 September 1998; *Bass v The United Kingdom*, Appl No 30135/96, 9 September 1998: accident victims claimed that the operation of the Compensation Recovery Scheme under the Social Security Act 1989, represented a disproportionate interference with their possessions. The Scheme allows recovery of certain social security benefits paid out on injury or incapacitation, where that injury or incapacitation is caused by the negligence of a wrong-doer and the victim has recovered damage from the wrongdoer. In these cases, the victims claimed that the scheme effectively took from them the possibility of recovering general damages in the civil claim (ie against the part of the damages awarded for pain and suffering, loss of amenity and earning capacity, for which no benefits were paid). However, the Commission found that the scheme, taken as a whole, did not affect the victims in a way that was disproportionate. There were advantages from immediate, secure payment of the benefits: these, in effect, compensated for the risky, delayed payment of general damages.

judgment of the European Court in *Andrews v United Kingdom*[125] with that of the Court of Appeal in *Hughes & Ors v HM Customs & Excise*.[126] Both cases concern receiverships imposed to secure restraint orders issued under the Criminal Justice Act 1988. The Act allows receivers to charge their costs and remuneration to the defendant's estate. This is also the usual rule in insolvency proceedings, and it often has the effect of imposing the cost of receivership on the unsecured creditors. However, the creditors do not bear the costs if the assets are sufficient to cover their claims; hence, in such cases, charging the costs to the estate puts the entire burden on the debtor. In *Andrews* and *Hughes*, the defendants were acquitted, and yet they were still subject to the receivers' charges. In both cases, the courts found that there was an interference with possessions, but it did not upset the fair balance. In *Andrews*, the European Court simply noted that the applicant did not argue that there had been insufficient evidence to bring the criminal proceedings, or that there had been no need to preserve the assets pending the trial. From this, it seemed to follow that the charging of costs and remuneration to the applicant was not unfair under P1(1). A similar conclusion was reached in *Hughes*, but on different reasoning. Unlike the European Court, the Court of Appeal considered the overall impact of the receivership, and noted that there may be aspects of the process that produce some value to the defendant. For example, the receiver may insure or maintain the defendant's property, and the defendant may be able to bring a civil claim against the receiver for failing to safeguard the property properly.[127] By contrast, the European Court did not look beyond the domestic court's reasons for making the appointment of the receiver.[128] In other words, the appointment itself was not separated from the charging of the costs of appointment, and in that sense the Court did not take a close look at the overall impact of the interference on the victim.

The converse situation arises where the State does take offsetting benefits into account, but in a manner that is not sufficiently sensitive to the facts of the specific case. A series of cases from Greece have concerned expropriations of part of an owner's land for road improvements.[129] Plainly, in some cases, the remaining land would increase in value as a result of the improvements. However, under Greek law, an irrebuttable presumption of offsetting benefit applied in such cases, even where it could be shown that the remaining land had

---

[125] *Andrews v The United Kingdom*, Appl No 49584/99, 26 September 2002.

[126] *Hughes* (n 27); the Court of Appeal also discussed *Re Andrews* [1999] 1 WLR 1236, which was the basis of the application in *Andrews v The United Kingdom*.

[127] *Cf* Proceeds of Crime Act 2002, s 61. In *Andrews*, the European Court made a brief reference to the applicant's position as a director and shareholder of the company in receivership, but whether it meant that the applicant would have benefited from the management of the receiver is unclear.

[128] See also *Stockholms Forsakrings–Och* (n 27), where this question came up because a company was put into liquidation due to an error of the court. The applicant successfully argued that the imposition of the fee was disproportionate, but only on the basis that the liquidation had been unnecessary and was attributable solely to the fault of the Swedish courts (at [54]).

[129] *Katikaridis* (n 37) [49]; see Chapter 7, 172.

actually suffered a loss in value as a result of the construction of the road. Consequently, the European Court of Human Rights held that a flexible rule would have been compatible with P1(1), but a the fixed rule violated P1(1) because it took no account of the actual impact of the expropriation on the victim.

The extent to which the State may apply rules of general application to the assessment of economic loss is controversial. The Greek cases suggest that at least some consideration of the specific circumstances is needed; however, in *Lithgow* and *James*, the Court accepted the UK's arguments that valuation could be based on general criteria that did not necessarily reflect the true loss suffered by each victim. However, as explained below, the United Kingdom was able to raise special factors in these cases that justified a departure from the standard principles of valuation. In ordinary cases, the principle is becoming more rigid, and States are expected to avoid using blanket rules that exclude specific types of loss from consideration.[130]

Subjective or personal loss

Where no special issues arise in relation to the social function of property, valuation is normally determined objectively, without reference to the value of the property to the owner or to the acquiring body. While this is consistent with the rules applied in most national systems, it is questionable whether the objective market valuation reflects human rights principles better than subjective valuation. It may seem unfair to a property owner that the willingness of the average person to sell at the market price means that the State can force him or her to 'sell' at the same price. Moreover, except in the case of fungible commodities held purely for their exchange value, the payment of the market value does not always compensate for all associated losses.[131] For example, the homeowner in a small, unique community tied together by culture, language and religion may place a much higher value on the house than the average buyer.[132] Similarly, the cost of adaptations for a particular use are often not reflected in the market price.[133]

Arguably, the exclusion of subjective loss is consistent with the principle that P1(1) only requires a fair balance, but this only suggests that individuals may be required to accept some part of the losses arising from an interference with their possessions: it does not necessarily follow that special losses that they suffer are entirely irrelevant. Moreover, it is plain that the exclusion of subjective loss does not follow from any perceived difficulty in its measurement, as it is possible to

---

[130] See eg *Lallement v France*, Appl No 46044/99, 11 April 2002.

[131] Equally, there may be unusual cases where the transaction costs (to the owner) of a forced sale are lower than the ordinary, open–market transaction costs, with the result that the owner is actually better off.

[132] As in *Gerasimova v Russia*, Appl No 24077/02, 25 March 2004.

[133] See Chapter 6, 177–79.

measure some types of subjective loss (such as the cost of special adaptations). It appears that the principle was adopted without close examination, because most national authorities already apply a similar rule. Nevertheless, there are cases where the Court has been uncomfortable with the idea that subjective factors should be excluded, as shown by *Lallement v France*.[134] In this case, part of the applicant's farm land was expropriated, and he was paid reasonable compensation for it. However, as a result of the division of the farm, it became less profitable to farm the remaining land. The Court held that it was disproportionate not to provide compensation for this loss. The applicant had been given had the option of requiring the authorities to purchase the entire farm at its market value, but as he chose not to do so because he did not wish to give up the family home, he could not be reproached for failing to do so.

Compensation

Although P1(1) does not incorporate a right to compensation, in *Sporrong*, the Court found that the issue of expropriation permits for an unlimited period interfered with the applicants' possessions in a way which 'could have been rendered legitimate only if they had had the possibility of seeking a reduction of the time-limits or of claiming compensation.'[135] The reference to compensation was picked up in the *James* and *Lithgow* cases, where the Court stated that 'compensation terms are material to the assessment whether a fair balance has been struck between the various interests at stake and, notably, whether or not a disproportionate burden has been imposed on the person who has been deprived of his possessions.'[136] From this, the Court concluded, in both cases, that the 'the taking of property without payment of an amount reasonably related to its value would normally constitute a disproportionate interference which could not be considered justifiable' under P1(1).[137] Hence, it is now the position that P1(1) does provide a kind of compensation guarantee in at least some cases.

Chapter 6 offers a more detailed examination of the principles on compensation for a deprivation of possessions. At this point, there are two points that are worth mentioning. The first relates to the type of the interference and the necessity for compensation, and the second to the amount of compensation needed to maintain the balance.

---

[134] *Lallement* (n 130); see also *Poltorachenko v Ukraine*, Appl No 77317/01, 18 January 2005 [45], where the Court took into account 'the applicant's financial and social status, his age and state of health' in determining that 'the quashing of the final judgment given in his favour constituted a disproportionate interference with his right to the peaceful enjoyment of his possessions'.

[135] *Sporrong* (n 1) [73]; see also *Terazzi srl v Italy*, Appl No 27265/95, 17 October 2002.

[136] *James* (n 2) [54]; *Lithgow* (n 29) [120].

[137] *James*, above; *Lithgow*, above [121].

The type of interference

In most States, constitutional law only requires compensation for an expropri-ation of property (if it requires it at all).[138] In terms of the structure of P1(1), this corresponds to a Rule 2 deprivation of possessions. Since the *Sporrong* judg-ment recognises both de jure and de facto deprivations of possessions, the courts have some flexibility in determining whether compensation should have been provided in a specific case. However, as the *Sporrong* judgment also made it clear that the three rules are not distinct, and that all three reflect the fair balance, it follows that the availability of compensation is relevant in Rule 1 and 3 cases as well. Nevertheless, to date, the Court has only found compensation necessary in some of these cases. In particular, it has indicated that the fair bal-ance normally requires compensation for an expropriation of an interest short of full ownership,[139] and it may also be required where there has been an exces-sive delay in processes preliminary to expropriation (as in *Sporrong* itself).[140]

Whether compensation is required in cases involving other types of regulation is doubtful. Plainly, if compensation is provided, it is likely that the fair balance has been maintained.[141] However, there is no uniform practice of providing compensation, either across member States or within the United Kingdom itself. In some situations, the common law provided a right to compensation for the destruction of property in an emergency,[142] and there are statutory provisions for compensation in specific instances,[143] but the decision to provide compensa-tion is often determined by considerations relating to the implementation of the specific policy rather than constitutional principle.[144]

The absence of a common principle or practice of compensating for regula-tory losses makes it is unlikely that the courts in either Strasbourg or the United

---

[138] See AJ van der Walt, *Constitutional Property Clauses: A Comparative Analysis* (Juta, Cape Town, 1999).

[139] See eg *Iatridis v Greece*, Reports 1999–II 75 (2000) 30 EHRR 97.

[140] See also *Terazzi* (n 135). However, even in *Sporrong* (n 1), the Court only went as far as saying that compensation would have been one way of ensuring a fair balance. Accelerating the expropriation procedure would have been an alternative.

[141] For example, in *Owen* (n 86), the owner of a pedigree show cow sought an injunction to pre-vent MAFF from destroying the cow until after she had given birth. The injunction was refused, in part because compensation at market value was payable for cattle and accordingly an immediate slaughter would not be disproportionate. MAFF was acting under the BSE Offspring Slaughter Regulations 1998 (SI 1998 3070), which gave it a discretion whether to slaughter or not, but it insisted on an immediate slaughter so that the United Kingdom could satisfy the conditions for the resumption of beef exports to Europe. On this basis, the Court found that there was a public inter-est in slaughtering the cow, despite the owner's evidence that a delay would not present any risk to the health of humans or cattle.

[142] *Burmah Oil* (n 87).

[143] For example, see the BSE regulations discussed in n 141; and see also M Redman, 'Compulsory Purchase, Compensation And Human Rights' [1999] *Journal of Planning & Environment Law* 315, 322–23.

[144] With the BSE regulations (above), the likelihood of successfully eradicating the disease and regaining the export market was likely to be enhanced by guaranteeing compensation for any animals that were destroyed.

Kingdom would say that compensation is required for all such losses. Indeed, it is clear that the impact of regulatory measures can be very harsh without upsetting the fair balance. For example, in *Mellacher*,[145] the majority decided that Austrian rent control legislation did not breach P1(1), but without offering a clear sense of practical impact of the legislation. It was left to the dissenting judges to point out that rents had been reduced to the point that they did not correspond to any realistic assessment of the ordinary expenses of life. As they put it, 'The applicants do not seem to be far wrong when they say that the reduced [monthly] rent now corresponds to the price of a simple meal for two persons in a cheap restaurant.'[146] Nevertheless, the majority held that the interference was not disproportionate, in part because landlords were still permitted to pass on many of their costs to tenants, and more significantly because the needs of social justice could justify such strict measures: 'The fact that the original rents were agreed upon and corresponded to the then prevailing market conditions does not mean that the legislature could not reasonably decide as a matter of policy that they were unacceptable from the point of view of social justice.'[147] It is still conceivable that a combination of restrictions on the rights of landlords which had the effect of making it practically impossible to earn a profit from the property might upset the fair balance, but it appeared that landlords in *Mellacher* could still show a net profit from the rentals.

Other cases support the position taken in *Mellacher*. In *Pine Valley v Ireland*,[148] the annulment of a grant of planning permission reduced the value of land to one-tenth of its previous value, but this was not so drastic that P1(1) was violated. In *Gasus*,[149] the seizure of goods in which the applicant had a property interest effectively wiped out the entire value of that interest; again, there was no violation of P1(1). This is also reflected in the cases decided under the Human Rights Act 1998. In *Wilson*,[150] the creditor could not enforce the loan contract, and could not even claim restitution of the monies advanced under the loan. While the House of Lords agreed that the consequences for the lender were draconian, this did not mean that the relevant statutory provisions were incompatible with P1(1). Another recent example is provided by *Trailer & Marina (Leven) Ltd*.[151] Part of the applicant's land was designated as an area of special scientific interest under the Wildlife and Countryside Act 1981. The applicant had agreed to forego the development of fishing and boating on the Canal for annual compensation of £19,000. However, the statutory regime changed, and

[145] *Mellacher* (n 26).
[146] Above (joint dissenting opinion of Judges Cremona, Bindschedler-Robert, Gölcüklü, Bernhardt and Spielmann); see also *Spath Holme Ltd v The United Kingdom* (n 26); *R v Secretary of State for the Environment, Transport and the Regions ex parte Spath Holme Ltd* (n 26) (Lord Bingham); and *Morgan v Attorney-General of Trinidad and Tobago* [1988] LRC (Const) 468 (PC).
[147] *Mellacher* (n 26) [56].
[148] *Pine Valley* (n 24).
[149] *Gasus* (n 27).
[150] *Wilson* (n 25).
[151] [2004] EWCA Civ 1580.

from 2001 compensation was no longer available for the loss of potential income from future developments. In effect, an asset that had previously been sold was now taken without payment. Nevertheless, there was no incompatibility with P1(1).

It may therefore appear that the extent of the economic loss is not important in regulatory cases, as the severity of the loss seems to have no bearing on the proportionality of the interference. However, it would be more accurate to say that a severe loss is not enough, by itself, to lead the courts to conclude that the fair balance has been upset. In combination with other factors—such as the denial of procedural rights, or a prolonged period of uncertainty—the courts may treat the the severity of the loss as a crucial factor in deciding that P1(1) has been violated. *Sporrong* is the leading example: the fact that the expropriation permits were left outstanding for many years left the applicants in an uncertain position, in which they were denied any effect process for obtaining a remedy. The fact that the value of their property was affected was therefore relevant, although not conclusive on its own.[152]

The one group of cases that appear exceptional are those concerning penalties. In *Azinas v Cyprus*, the Third Section of European Court of Human Rights considered penalties too harsh (and hence incompatible with P1(1)) on the basis that they had stripped the victim of virtually all his wealth.[153] Similarly, the Court of Appeal in *Lindsay*[154] and *International Transport*[155] balanced the amount of monetary penalties against the degree of blame and decided that the rules in question were incompatible with P1(1). As a matter of principle, these cases do not seem objectionable: one cannot say if a penalty is disproportionate to the degree of blame unless one knows what the penalty is, and if the penalty is a fine, the measurement of the impact must be monetary. However, it does raise the questions concerning the relevance of the loss taken alone. That is, in other regulatory cases, it appears that some procedural flaw, or possibly some other aggravating factor, must be present before the courts will find that there has been a breach of P1(1). Arguably, fines and penalties differ from ordinary regulations because they are used for the sole purpose of imposing a burden, whereas the burden arising from regulations is a secondary effect of the pursuit of some other purpose. However, even in the criminal context, the Court has not used Article 6 or other Convention rights as a means of imposing substantive limits on sentencing powers where only a fine is involved. In this sense, *Azinas*, *Lindsay* and *International Transport* are anomalous, whether considered as regulatory or criminal cases.

---

[152] See text accompanying n 92.

[153] *Azinas* (n 104). On a referral to the Grand Chamber, the Court found for Cyprus on the basis that the applicant had failed to exhaust domestic remedies. Four of the fifteen judges expressed doubts over the majority judgment in the first hearing, but the remainder said nothing on the merits. See Chapter 9, n 79.

[154] *Lindsay* (n 98).

[155] *International Transport* (n 10).

The end result is therefore reasonably clear in doctrinal terms: compensation is normally required for the expropriation of a property interest, and not for other types of interference with property. Put differently, P1(1) does not incorporate a doctrine of substantive due process that would allow property owners to challenge regulatory controls solely on the basis that the impact is too severe. While justifications for the distinction that can be provided, these do not have their foundation in the idea of fairness. For example, it could be argued that cases involving the acquisition of property by public bodies for their own use creates a significantly higher risk of the abuse of power than the regulation of property use, and hence a compensation rule for acquisition can be justified as a means of reducing that risk.[156] However, this argument centres on the risk of an abuse of power, which does not appear to be central concern of the European Court of Human Rights. The idea of a fair balance seems to rest more on the allocation of burdens, and not so much on the nature of the power being exercised or even the purpose for which the property is taken or regulated.

Amount of compensation

In *James* and *Lithgow*, the Court laid down the 'reasonably related to its value' standard for compensation in Rule 2 cases. This is plainly not a strict standard: while it suggests that national authorities must take the value of the property into account when determining the amount of compensation to be paid, it does not suggest that the full value must be paid in every case.[157] However, it appears that at least some justification must be provided for paying something less than the full value. In *Lithgow*, for example, the Court agreed that economic restructuring justified both the nationalisation of the aircraft and shipbuilding industries and the application of valuation principles that did not necessarily provide full compensation to every shareholder. As the Court put it, 'Article 1 (P1(1)) does not . . . guarantee a right to full compensation in all circumstances, since legitimate objectives of "public interest", such as pursued in measures of economic reform or measures designed to achieve greater social justice, may call

---

[156] J Sax, 'Takings and the Police Power' (1964) 74 *Yale Law Journal* 36.

[157] See eg *Abrial v France*, Reports 2001–VI 339; and *De Dreux–Breze v France*, Appl No 57969/00, 15 May 2001: both concerned compensation paid for securities cancelled by the USSR in 1918, under terms of agreements made in 1996: the 1996 agreements created P1(1) possessions, but the fact that compensation was only at 1% of the face value of the securities was not disproportionate, given the length of time over which repayment on the securities had been unexpected (the actual value of the securities was not stated). Note that in *Motais de Narbonne* (n 54), even compensation at market value was judged not to be sufficient, given that the authorities held the land for 19 years without developing it as originally planned; but see *Papadopoulou* (n 54) and *cf Kolb, Holaus, Taxacher and Wechselberger v Austria*, Appl No 35021/97 and Appl No 45774/99, 21 February 2002. In relation to social justice and redistribution, see *Pincová* (n 19): Czech laws allowing restitution of land operated so as to require applicant to give up land bought from the State in 1967. The applicants would receive restitution of the price paid, with costs of upkeep in the intervening period. This was disproportionate in absence of market value compensation (see also *Zvolsky* (n 19)).

for less than reimbursement of the full market value'.[158] In several cases, including *James*, the Court has allowed States to depart from the ordinary standards where the victim's moral entitlement to the property may be doubted. For example, an acquiring body may be permitted to acquire property without paying for specific assets, if body has already provided the funds that enabled the present owner to acquire the property. Similarly, the State may acquire without compensation if it appears that the victim's interest arose purely by exploiting some technical loophole in the law.

These issues are covered in greater detail in the next chapter.[159] At this point, it is worth noting that there is a risk that the Court may allow States to avoid any substantive obligation to property owners if it accepts their assessments of moral entitlement without a close examination of its own. However, it also allows the Court to avoid potentially rigid applications of formal law. For example, although P1(1) does not protect the right to acquire property, the existence of a moral entitlement to acquire specific property may be realised by allowing the person so entitled to acquire it for something less than its full market value. Similarly, the potential extension of P1(1) in the *Sporrong* decision has been counter-balanced by the Court's refusal to adopt a rigid rule of compensation.

Rule of law issues

Factors that are relevant to the legality condition—such as the certainty, predictability and arbitrariness of the interference—may also be relevant to the fair balance. Indeed, it often seems that the Court would prefer to consider these situations under the fair balance test. For example, in *Broniowski v Poland*,[160] the Court noted that the Constitutional Court of Poland had described the situation under consideration as contrary to the rule of law, and yet it did not hold that the legality condition of P1(1) had been violated. Nevertheless, in deciding that the fair balance had been upset, it was strongly influenced by the uncertainty of the State's actions. As put by the Court, 'it should be stressed that uncertainty—be it legislative, administrative or arising from practices applied by the authorities—is a factor to be taken into account in assessing the State's conduct.'[161]

These issues arise in different circumstances, and the Court has not attempted to articulate unifying principles for all of them. Nevertheless, the cases do reveal a concern with the manner in which power is exercised, irrespective of the severity or nature of the impact on the individual. This section of the chapter therefore considers several categories of cases where this concern is evident. The

---

[158] *Lithgow* (n 29) [121].
[159] Chapter 6, 180–93.
[160] *Broniowski* (n 19).
[161] Above [154].

first concerns the use of powers that have an unpredictable, selective or uneven impact. The second concerns the collapse of administrative systems for handling the use of power; in particular, the failure to provide an adequate system for enforcing judgments raises specific issues relating to the rule of law. The third category relates to a situation that is not quite so dramatic, as it deals with the failure to satisfy legitimate expectations created by State conduct. Finally, this section closes with a brief review of the procedural requirements imposed by P1(1).

Selective, unpredictable or uneven impact

Where measures are taken against one person but not another, with no explanation for the difference, the courts may treat this as a factor tending to show that the fair balance has not been maintained.[162] In an extreme case, measures that operate in an unpredictably selective or arbitrary manner may fail to satisfy the condition of legality. However, even if the condition is satisfied (and it usually is),[163] the Court may treat consider these factors in its assessment of proportionality. This is clear in *Hentrich*,[164] where the Court found a breach of P1(1) in respect of a power of pre-emption that allowed tax authorities to buy land within three months of a sale. This was intended as a response to the problem of tax evasion arising from declarations of artificially low values on the sale, but it appeared that the tax authorities relied on the power in only a small proportion of the cases and did not explain the criteria by which they selected buyers to pre-empt. The Court was concerned that the right of pre-emption 'does not apply systematically—in other words, every time the price has been more or less clearly underestimated—but only rarely and scarcely foreseeably.'[165] The impact on the victim was therefore judged to be disproportionate.

In practice, cases involving unpredictable State action have been rare. More frequently, complaints concern regulatory schemes that may be fair in general terms but impose a severe impact on isolated individuals. In such cases, it seems that deference is given greater weight than the concern with arbitrary action. In the United Kingdom, the *Wilson* case provides an example of this. The facts are

---

[162] This may also raise issues under Art 14, as in *Pine Valley* (n 24) and *Darby v Sweden*, Series A No 187 (1991) 13 EHRR 774. The applicant in *Hentrich* (n 27) also brought a complaint under Art 14 (in combination with P1(1), Art 6 and Art 13), but in the light of its conclusion that there had been violations of P1(1) and Art 6 taken alone, the Court did not decide the Art 14 point (see [66]).

[163] *Špaček, sro v The Czech Republic* (2000) 30 EHRR 1010 is one example; see Chapter 3. However, in *Hentrich* (n 27) [42], the Court concluded that tax exemption provisions did not satisfy conditions of legality, although it then went on to consider proportionality; similarly in *Broniowski* (n 19) [154], the Court noted that the Polish Constitutional Court had described the situation under consideration as contrary to the rule of law, and yet the Court did not find that the legality condition had been violated: instead, it considered the facts under the fair balance.

[164] *Hentrich* (n 27).

[165] Above [47]. See also *Broniowski* (n 19) [151], on the importance of certainty: 'it should be stressed that uncertainty—be it legislative, administrative or arising from practices applied by the authorities—is a factor to be taken into account in assessing the State's conduct.'

described above: to recapitulate, the House of Lords applied a low level of scrutiny to provisions of the Consumer Credit Act 1974 which render certain consumer loan contracts unenforceable. Their Lordships stated that Parliament had a wide area of discretion to determine how to achieve the aim of consumer protection. Since it was possible that the legislature had decided that draconian measures were appropriate, the courts should not interfere.[166] Moreover, the generality of the prohibition suggested that Parliament had sought to balance the interests of classes rather than individuals, and hence that the courts should defer to its judgement.[167]

By characterising the issue as one of balancing the interests of classes, the focus shifts to the impact on a class rather than the specific victim. The broader the affected class, the more likely a court is to say that either the impact is not excessive or that it is appropriate to defer to the judgements of elected representatives. The real issue, therefore, is to determine whether a given case is likely to be seen in terms of its general or its specific impact. *Wilson* shows that the emphasis tends to be put on the general impact. Moreover, regulatory controls tend to be seen as the product of democratic bodies rather than administrative officials. This is clearly illustrated in *Marcic v Thames Water Utilities Ltd*,[168] in which a landowner complained of repeated flooding of his home caused by the back flow of foul water from the defendant's sewerage system. He claimed that the flooding was an actionable nuisance and that the defendant's failure to carry out works to end the flooding was violation of his rights under Article 8 and P1(1), for which he sought damages under the Human Rights Act 1998. His action in nuisance was dismissed, on the basis that the remedial scheme under the Water Industry Act 1991 was comprehensive. The Act gave a homeowner the right to bring proceedings for damages, but only where the independent regulator (the Director General of Water Services) had issued an enforcement order and the statutory undertaker had failed to comply with it. In this case, instead of issuing an enforcement order, the Director General approved the defendant's scheme of improvement, even though the scheme gave the improvement of the system serving plaintiff's property a low priority.

Lord Nicholls framed the issue in broad terms, as he said that balance took into account 'interests of customers of a company whose properties are prone to

---

[166] *Wilson* (n 25) [71]–[75] (Lord Nicholls), [138] (Lord Hobhouse), [169]–[172] (Lord Scott); see also *Spath Holme v The United Kingdom* (n 26); and *R v Secretary of State for the Environment, Transport and the Regions ex parte Spath Holme Ltd* (n 26), 396 (Lord Bingham):

It is an enduring and intractable problem of social policy that those who need relief cannot always be helped without giving relief to those who do not need it. Housing benefit is means-tested, and the allocation of public resources is a matter for ministers, not courts. The hardship which the Order imposed on landlords was a very relevant consideration, but it was for ministers to judge where the balance between the competing interests of landlords and tenants should be struck.

[167] This, of course, takes the very point that the Court of Appeal saw as most damning and turns it into an argument in favour of compatibility. That is, the Court of Appeal saw the lack of discretion as the central problem with the Consumer Credit Act 1974: in essence, Parliament should not have taken on this decision for itself.

[168] [2004] 2 AC 42.

sewer flooding and, on the other hand, all the other customers of the company whose properties are drained through the company's sewers.'[169] Framed in this way, the balancing process reduces the importance of the impact on the victim. In the Court of Appeal,[170] the fact that Mr Marcic had to endure years of flooding without compensation was given much more weight than it was in the House of Lords. Moreover, Lord Nicholls' approach also stresses Parliament's decision to set up the remedial scheme instead of the defendant's failure to take action. This approach makes it very unlikely that a regulatory scheme would be found incompatible, even if the impact on specific persons is very harsh. At most, there is a possibility of bringing judicial review of specific decisions. Indeed, under the Water Services Act 1991, a homeowner may request the Director General to issue an enforcement order against a statutory undertaker, and then bring an application for judicial review if the Director General refuses to do so. Mr Marcic did not take this route: perhaps if he had done so, he would have succeeded. However, even here the extent of a human rights review is unclear. While section 6 of the Human Rights Act 1998 requires public authorities to act compatibly with the Convention, the weight to be given to the substantive impact on a specific individual in the proportionality analysis is unclear. Indirectly, the discretion that was regarded as unnecessary in *Wilson* may yet prove to be necessary in a case such as *Marcic*.[171]

The issue of selectivity and discretion is particularly important in cases involving social justice. If the purpose of a scheme is to produce greater justice, can it survive scrutiny if its operation in specific cases produces injustice? In *Marcic* and *Wilson*, it could not be argued that a harsh impact in an isolated case would represent a contradiction of the purpose of the legislation. While such cases might go further than the purpose requires, they are not contrary to it. In that sense, the argument for discretion in specific cases is strongest where the purpose of legislation is to bring about a fairer distribution of wealth and property. In *James*, the landlords argued that, even if social justice justified allowing tenants the right to purchase the freehold, the legislation was drawn too broadly because some of the tenants would benefit unfairly. However, the Court accepted that there would be some 'anomalies' and 'windfall profits', but the scale of the anomalies was not so great so as to make the scheme as a whole

---

[169] Above [40].

[170] [2002] QB 929.

[171] This uncertainty is compounded by the ambivalence expressed by Lord Nicholls in both *Wilson* (n 25) and *Marcic v Thames Water Utilities Ltd* [2004] 2 AC 42. In *Wilson*, he stated that he might have come to a different conclusion if the Consumer Credit Act 1974 applied to loans up to £250,000 (instead of £25,000) (at [80]), and in *Marcic*, he suggested that the failure of some statutory undertakers to offer compensation for flooding should be considered by the undertakers and Director General (at [44]–[45]). Moreover, even the Strasbourg authorities are unclear: for example, against the *James* (n 2) case, one could raise *Sporrong* (n 1) or the cases cited below n 176. In both situations, the European Court said that there should have been some mechanism by which the victims could raise their special circumstances with the regulatory authorities, to ensure that the impact upon their property is neither arbitrary nor unforeseeable.

unreasonable.[172] Moreover, since it was the tenant who initiated the legal process which resulted in the compulsory transfer of the freehold, the Court stated that the United Kingdom's role in specific interferences was limited. All the Court felt that it could review was the enactment of the legislation itself; specific cases were only relevant as illustrations of the operation of the legislation.[173]

Administrative failures

As explained above, the margin of appreciation is narrowed when the court orders are not enforced. The example of *Allard*[174] was given, although in fact the applicant objected to the execution of a court order. However, the order was executed before an appeal had been heard, and it was this failure to allow civil proceedings to run their course that was significant.[175] A long series of cases on Italian tenancy laws illustrate how the failure of administrative systems to operate efficiently, or to operate at all, affects the fair balance.[176] Under Italian law, a tenant cannot be evicted without police assistance. Beginning in 1983, when rules on security of tenure were changed, landlords often obtained judicial orders for repossession but then found it took many years to evict the tenants, due to a system of rationing police assistance. According to the Italian government, the staggering of police assistance was intended to avoid the disruption that would be caused if large numbers of tenants were evicted at the same time, before alternative housing could be made available. Landlords could file a declaration of need with the police, and in theory this should have expedited the process. In any case, the Court has made it clear that the policy of staggered evictions serves the public interest. Initially, the Court held that a long delay in

---

[172] *James* (n 2) [69].

[173] See also: *Mellacher* (n 26), *James* (n 2); cf *Zvolsky* (n 19) [72]–[74].

[174] *Allard* (n 31).

[175] Above [58]–[59]; see also the cases cited in n 34 on the extinction of civil judgments.

[176] The cases first came before the Court in *Spadea and Scalabrino v Italy*, Series A No 315–B (1996) 21 EHRR 482; and *Scollo v Italy*, Series A No 315–C (1996) 22 EHRR 514. The number of cases increased steadily over the years, and the Court ultimately reached the point of issuing sets of formulaic, standard–form judgments to deal with the volume of applications. In 2003 alone, formulaic judgments were given in *Ciccariello v Italy*, Appl No 34412/97, 9 January 2003 and eight others on that date; *G and M v Italy*, Appl No 31740/96, 27 February 2003; *Ferretti v Italy*, Appl No 60660/00, 6 March 2003; *C Spa v Italy*, Appl No 34999/97, 3 April 2003 and seven others on that date; *PM v Italy*, Appl No 34998/97, 17 April 2003 and ten others on that date; *Voglino v Italy*, Appl No 48730/99, 22 May 2003 and two others on that date; *Onorato Ricci v Italy*, Appl No 32385/96, 17 July 2003 and four others on that date; *Miscioscia v Italy*, Appl No 58408/00, 31 July 2003 and nine others on that date; *Bonamassa v Italy*, Appl No 65413/01, 2 October 2003 and seven others on that date; *Tassinari v Italy*, Appl No 47758/99, 16 October 2003 and four others on that date; *Rispoli v Italy*, Appl No 55388/00, 30 October 2003 and three others on that date; *Gamberini Mongenet v Italy*, Appl No 59635/00, 6 November 2003 and two others on that date; *Nicolai v Italy*, Appl No 62848/00, 27 November 2003 and twenty others on that date; and *Di Matteo v Italy*, Appl No 37511/97, 11 December 2003 and two others on that date. On 8 December 2004, the Committee of Ministers issued a resolution (Interim Resolution ResDI I(2004)72) calling upon Italy to ensure that its law is compatible with Convention standards, and to honour the outstanding judgments against it.

obtaining police assistance did not necessarily upset the fair balance: in *Spadea and Scalabrino v Italy*,[177] the applicants had to wait about six years before obtaining possession of their flats, but the Court found that this was not disproportionate, particularly in light of the fact that the tenants were elderly and of modest means and had been waiting for the city council to allocate them low-cost housing. Given that the protection of tenants was one of the purposes of the policy and that the applicants had not claimed any special need, the Court found that the delay had not produced a disproportionate impact.[178] Conversely, in *Scollo v Italy*,[179] the applicants made the declarations of need, but received no response from the authorities; moreover, it did not appear that his tenant had greater need to occupy the property. Consequently, given the delay of over ten years, the Court held that interference with the applicant's rights was disproportionate.

As the flood of cases continued, the Court began to take a stricter line. It began to say that, even where it appeared that the tenants would not be able to afford alternative accommodation, an indefinite delay in obtaining possession could not be justified. The public authorities could not use their failure to provide low-cost housing as an excuse for failing to allow others to exercise their rights to property.[180] Finally, the Court moved to a fairly rigid position, in which a delay of more than four years in obtaining possession is almost certainly disproportionate and a delay of less than four years is almost certainly not disproportionate.[181] In effect, the open-ended balancing test that was seen in *Spadea* and *Scollo* has given way to a narrowly applied and rigid rule. Given the failure of the Italian authorities to respond to the Strasbourg judgments, it is difficult to see how the Court could have dealt with the situation differently. Had the legislation explicitly redefined the rights of ownership so as to make the right to occupy the property subject to a right of a tenant to continue in occupation where in need, and left it to the courts to make the determination of need in specific cases, the Court might have found that the policy was either proportionate or within the margin of appreciation. However, this was not the case. Judgments were being made by the courts that could not be executed. In addition, unlike *Mellacher*,[182] there was no suggestion that purpose of policy was to modify the behaviour of owners as a class to bring about a more socially just market. Neither was there any sense that the property owners were guilty

---

[177] Above.

[178] *Cf Libert v Belgium*, Appl No 44734/98, 8 July 2004, where a delay in obtaining possession was justified by policy allowing the occupant (the applicant's former spouse) time to find new accommodation.

[179] *Scollo* (n 176).

[180] *Immobiliare Saffi v Italy*, Reports 1999–V (2000) 30 EHRR 756; *AO v Italy*, Appl No 22534/93, 30 May 2000; see also *Prodan* (n 27): similar example of serious delays in the enforcement of judgments for repossession of flats. The State's excuse was that it lacked the funds to provide alternative accommodation for evicted tenants, but the Court did not regard this as a sufficient reason to find that the fair balance had not been upset.

[181] See eg the cases decided in 2003, above n 176.

[182] *Mellacher* (n 26).

of immoral or improper practices. And, unlike the *James* case, it was not said that the tenants had acquired a moral entitlement to continued occupation by having already paid for the property that was transferred to them. Ultimately, the eviction cases demonstrates how the fair balance test narrows when the Court believes that administrative failings jeopardise the institution of property itself.[183]

Administrative law and legitimate expectations

Pine Valley,[184] *Stretch v United Kingdom*[185] and *Rowland v Environment Agency*[186] show that P1(1) undermines the common law rules regarding legitimate expectations and ultra vires representations made by public authorities in relation to property.[187] However, the fair balance does not necessarily mean that public authorities are now bound by promises beyond their powers. The policy reasons for the strict rule still reflect a public interest, as the risk remains that public officials will extend their power by making unauthorised representations. In addition, Professor Craig identifies two other aspects of the public interest that are reflected in the case law:

> There is the argument that estoppel cannot be applied to a public body so as to prevent it from exercising its statutory powers or duty. There is also the argument that to allow an ultra vires representation to bind the public body would be to prejudice third parties who might be affected, and who would have no opportunity of putting forward their views.[188]

These reasons may still justify the departure from ultra vires representations. Indeed, in the P1(1) cases to date, the courts have stopped short of saying that public authorities are strictly bound by their representations.

For example, in *Pine Valley*, a landowner claimed that the annulment of an ultra vires grant of outline planning permission could not be proportionate in the absence of compensation or retrospective validation of the grant.[189] However, the Court simply concluded that 'The applicants were engaged on a commercial venture which, by its very nature, involved an element of risk'. Indeed, they should have been aware that the grant of planning permission was open to challenge.[190] Consequently, the annulment was not disproportionate.

---

[183] This opinion was shared by the Committee of Ministers: in its Interim Resolution (n 176) it stated that the repeated violations of P1(1) 'reveal the existence of a serious and persistent structural problem'.

[184] *Pine Valley* (n 24).

[185] (2004) 38 EHRR 12.

[186] [2004] 3 WLR 249 (CA).

[187] See Chapter 2, 67–71.

[188] P Craig, *Administrative Law*, 4th edn (Sweet & Maxwell, London, 1999) 641 (and see generally 635–50).

[189] *Pine Valley* (n 24) [58].

[190] Above [59].

Stretch v United Kingdom concerned the grant of a lease of 22 years with an option to renew for another 21 years. Both the applicant (the tenant) and the council honestly believed that the option was valid, but it was later determined that the council had not had the power to grant it. While the Court said that the refusal to grant another 21-year lease was an interference with the tenant's possessions, it did not say (as the tenant had argued) that the council was bound to grant a new lease or provide compensation equal in value to such a lease. There was a violation of P1(1), but the amount of damages was quite modest.[191] Although damages follows a violation, and in that sense does not define action that might have made the interference proportionate, it is worth noting that the amount was roughly equal to the amount of rent the applicant paid in the initial 22-year period. In effect, the council had to give the tenant back the money he had already paid on the contract.[192] Finally, in *Rowland v Environment Agency*,[193] the Environment Agency (and its predecessors) had mistakenly allowed the applicant (and her predecessors) to believe that a section of the River Thames was her private water. In fact, the relevant public authorities had never had the power to extinguish public navigation rights over that section, and consequently the Environment Agency sought to re-assert these rights. The Court of Appeal held that the applicant did have a legitimate expectation that were protected under P1(1); however, these were satisfied by the Environment Agency's promise that it would re-assert the public navigation rights in a way which would minimise the interference with her personal enjoyment of her adjoining estate.

In conclusion, the public interests furthered by the old common law rule remain legitimate public interests under P1(1). However, instead of expressing these interests by a strict rule excluding judicial review, they are expressed in the proportionality analysis. It may be the case that, as in *Pine Valley*, resiling from an ultra vires act is not disproportionate; or, as in *Stretch* and *Rowland v Environment Agency*, some steps must be taken to satisfy the proportionality requirement.

Procedural safeguards

The procedural aspect of P1(1) arises in two situations. The first concerns the deliberate frustration of the civil process, whether in the form of a refusal to adhere to a final judgment of the courts, or in the form of an interference with civil proceedings that have not yet reached their conclusion. The second

---

[191] *Stretch* (n 185) [42]–[51].

[192] Although this was plainly more symbolic than a measure of a real loss: eg there was no allowance for having lost the use of the money over that period, or for improvements to the property, which he might have benefited from during the renewal period.

[193] *Rowland* (n 186).

concerns cases where there is no attempt to frustrate civil proceedings, but a failure to provide adequate procedural safeguards in respect of the interference itself.

With the first type of case, the Court takes a very strict line. Where the State has ignored a judgment, the Court has sometimes refused to accept that the State has any justification for its actions.[194] Even where it accepts that there may be a legitimate aim to the interference, it is likely to say that the interference has been disproportionate.[195] However, there are exceptions. Indeed, there is some doubt that P1(1) is even applicable prior to the final judgment of the national courts.[196] Even where P1(1) is applicable, the Court has indicated that the interference may serve a legitimate aim, without inflicting a disproportionate loss on the applicant. In *National & Provincial Building Society and others v United Kingdom*,[197] for example, the Court found that the UK's interference with ongoing proceedings for the restitution of an unlawfully imposed tax was not disproportionate. As the Court saw it, the applicants were attempting to take advantage of a technical defect in legislation, and hence it was not disproportionate for Parliament to correct the defect, with retrospective effect. However, where there is no suggestion that the applicant's case is weak, the Court is more sympathetic. In *Dangeville SA v France*,[198] for example, the refusal to honour a claim for restitution of an improperly assessed tax was disproportionate, in part because there was no suggestion that the applicants were taking advantage of a loophole in the law.[199]

With the second type of case, the issue of proportionality concentrates on the procedure by which the interference occurs. This was discussed in *Hentrich*,[200] where the European Court considered the absence of any real opportunity to challenge a pre-emption as an important factor in determining the proportionality of an interference. The authorities had a statutory power to acquire land by pre-emption where it appeared that the declared taxable value was below the actual value. The Court found that the pre-emption procedures had a disproportionate impact, because (among other things) 'it was not attended by the basic procedural safeguards. . . . A pre-emption decision cannot be legitimate in

---

[194] Eg *Brumărescu* (n 34) (although it appears that Romania offered no justification).

[195] See *Frascino* (n 24): where the local authorities did not follow a court order in a planning case, there was a P1(1) violation; ie although there is normally a wide margin of appreciation in planning matters, it does not apply where orders of the national courts to the planning authorities are ignored. To similar effect, see also *Allard* (n 31); *Zwierzynski v Poland*, Appl No 34049/96, 19 June 2001; *Prodan* (n 27) and the line of Italian cases on the failure to allow landlords to repossess flats, discussed above, text to n 176ff.

[196] See Chapter 2.

[197] *National & Provincial* (n 27). *Kalogeropoulou v Greece and Germany*, Appl No 59021/00, 12 December 2002 is another example: it would have violated principles of customary international law relating to State immunity to allow a judgment to be enforced.

[198] *Dangeville SA* (n 27).

[199] See also *MA and 34 others* (n 27); cf *Ogis–Institut Stanislas* (n 27).

[200] *Hentrich* (n 27); see also *Chassagnou* (n 70) [84].

the absence of adversarial proceedings that comply with the principle of equality of arms'.[201]

How far this can be extended is unclear. As explained in Chapter 9, the adequacy of judicial review is an important consideration in cases involving penalties, especially in the light of failure to recognise proportionality as a distinct ground of review prior to the Human Rights Act 1998. However, in *AGOSI v United Kingdom*[202] and *Air Canada v United Kingdom*,[203] the European Court accepted the adequacy of judicial review in forfeiture cases, and with section 6 of the Human Rights Act 1998 it seems likely that judicial review would be regarded as an adequate protection in most property cases.[204] Nevertheless, in some of the cases on the inflexibility of compensation systems, the Court has stated that the real defect in the relevant legislation was the failure to provide property owners with the opportunity to challenge the valuation.[205] Delays in the assessment or payment of compensation may also be significant in determining whether the fair balance has been upset.[206] Procedural issues may, of course, also raise issues under Article 6, but there is a distinction between the analysis of under Article 6 and P1(1). For example, in *Poiss v Austria*,[207] the Austrian Government argued that, if the Court were to decide that a delay in determining compensation breached Article 6(1), there would be no basis on which to apply P1(1) to the same delay. The Court did not agree, because the same fact may fall foul of more than one provision of the Convention, and in any case Article 6(1) and P1(1) deal with different subject matter:

> Moreover, the complaint made under Article 6 § 1 (art. 6(1)) can be distinguished from the complaint relating to Article 1 of the Protocol (P1(1)). In the former case, the question was one of determining whether the length of the consolidation proceedings had exceeded a 'reasonable time', whereas in the latter case their length—whether excessive or not—is material, together with other elements, in determining whether the disputed transfer was compatible with the guarantee of the right of property.[208]

The 'other elements' that are taken into account under P1(1) would vary from case to case. In *Poiss*, the Court considered whether the applicant had received any compensating benefits during the period of delay. In that case, the scheme

---

[201] *Hentrich* (n 27) [42]. Contrast *Ardex* (n 27): the applicant's property was subject to security to enforce liabilities, but it had the right to apply to have security not exercised if the effects would be too harsh: hence the interference was not disproportionate.

[202] Series A No 108 (1987) 9 EHRR 1.

[203] Series A No 316 (1995) 20 EHRR 150.

[204] See *Alconbury* [2003] 2 AC 295 (discussed in Chapter 7, 205–10); and *Webb v The United Kingdom*, Appl No 56054/00, 10 February 2004.

[205] *Katikaridis* (n 37); see also *Hentrich* (n 27) [49].

[206] See Chapter 7; see also the series of cases dealing with Italian bankruptcy laws, cited above n 106; and *Angelov v Bulgaria*, Appl No 44076/98, 22 April 2004; *Karahalios v Greece*, Appl No 62503/00, 11 December 2003.

[207] *Poiss* (n 46).

[208] Above [66]; *Erkner* (n 46) [76]; but *cf Gavrielides v Cyprus*, Appl No 15940/02, 7 January 2003: a complaint relating to lengthy delays in civil proceedings to establish a right of access to the applicant's land were admissible with respect to Art 6(1) but not admissible with respect to P1(1).

was not flexible enough to allow the authorities to respond to cases of special hardship, and consequently the Court felt that the impact on the applicant was disproportionate.[209] By contrast, in *Phocas*, the interference was not disproportionate, in part because the procedures provided a remedy of 'abandonment' by which an owner could require the local authority to purchase land.[210]

CONCLUSIONS

The analysis of a set of facts in relation to P1(1) involves several elements: the applicability of P1(1), the legality of the interference, the identification of the relevant Rule, and the proportionality of the interference. In practice, the emphasis is on applicability and proportionality. The legality principle is so easily satisfied that the doctrine of proportionality now performs some of the functions that might have been left to it. Similarly, the identification of the Rule is of questionable importance, since it seems to have little impact on the outcome of the case. Instead, the breadth of the proportionality test is now so wide, in terms of the facts it takes into account, that the doctrines relating to legality and the differences between the Rules are rarely of any importance. The applicability test is merely a filter, and the tendency of the courts to bypass it in complex cases in order to review the State's acts under the proportionality test means that it is the most important consideration in the vast majority of P1(1) cases.

Even within the test of proportionality, the analysis emphasises only some issues. In particular, the focus often lies on the impact on the victim, in the sense that the rationality aspect of the test has become much less important than the balancing aspect. We therefore find that reasons for judgments are cast in an almost impressionistic way, where the courts seem to do little more than say that a particular interference imposed an excessive impact on the victim or not. This is not to say that the results on specific facts are wholly unpredictable. Indeed, in specific areas, the results can be quite predictable: in the cases on the Italian evictions and police assistance, it is reasonably clear that a delay of more than four years in obtaining possession would be considered disproportionate, and anything less than that would not be; and that other, potentially relevant factors are being ignored (even if said to be relevant in earlier cases). Yet in none of the cases has the Court expressly stated that there is a four-year 'rule', and there had been well over 100 judgments by January 2004. Similarly, in relation to regulatory takings, the European Court has not seen anything like the American obsession with laying down rules on regulatory takings, even though the American debated was provoked in part by the vagueness of tests put forward by the Supreme Court to identify regulatory controls that should be

---

[209] *Poiss*, above [67]–[70]. For example, in *Sporrong* (n 1) [70]–[72].
[210] *Phocas* (n 55) [60]; *cf Lallement* (n 130).

treated as compensatable takings. However, while this means that the doctrinal analysis in Europe has not descended into narrow debates over 'categorical' takings, 'as applied' takings, and 'conceptual severance' that seem to dog the American jurisprudence, it also means that the European jurisprudence does not come to grips with questions that might usefully be addressed.

More generally, it leads to doubts over the value of extending the fair balance test to all forms of interference. On the one hand, it provides a doctrinal justification for requiring compensation for the expropriation of property, whether classified as deprivations of possessions under Rule 2 or appropriations of intangibles and interests short of ownership under Rule 1. However, it seems that the practical effect on Rule 3 cases is negligible, at least as a form of substantive due process. That is, the breadth of the margin of appreciation and the absence of a strict necessity doctrine mean that the results are the same as they would be under the legality and rationality tests. While there have been hints that the Court would use the fair balance test as a means of using P1(1) as something other than a further support for existing entitlements, in fact the concentration on economic loss as the measure of the impact seems to take the right to property even further from the usual focus of human rights on autonomy and dignity.

6

Compensation and Expropriation

⟫⟫∘⟨⟨

W HILE THE PRINCIPLE that compensation must be paid on
expropriation is widely accepted, it proved impossible to reach
agreement on its place in the right to property. As explained in
Chapter 1, early drafts of Article 17 of the Universal Declaration of Human
Rights would have protected against the deprivation of property without 'just
compensation', but the final version states only that 'No one shall be arbitrarily
deprived of his property.'[1] In the Council of Europe, there were proposals to
guarantee 'fair compensation which shall be fixed in advance',[2] or 'such compensation as shall be determined in accordance with the conditions provided for
by law'[3] or simply 'compensation', without any qualification.[4] In addition,
some delegates believed that a guarantee against 'arbitrary compensation'
would necessarily include a guarantee of compensation on expropriation.[5]
Eventually, agreement was reached only by dropping all references to compensation and arbitrary confiscation: the final version of P1(1) states only that a
deprivation must be 'in the public interest and subject to the conditions
provided for by law and by the general principles of international law.' Precisely
what it was that this provided was unclear, but that was the key to its acceptance: it was sufficiently ambiguous that no State could find it objectionable.

The inclusion of the reference to international law was particularly attractive
to those States (like the United Kingdom) that were anxious to protect their
investments abroad, but wished to preserve their legislative powers at home.
The reference is to customary international law, which allows a State to protest
against the expropriation of its nationals' property by another State. While
there has been some controversy over the circumstances in which a State may
raise a protest, the States signing up to the Protocol in 1950 would have said
that right of protest arises where an alien's property is taken without prompt,

---

[1] Art 17(2); see Chapter 1, 18.
[2] Council of Europe, *Collected edition of the 'Travaux Préparatoires' of the European
Convention on Human Rights: Recueil des Travaux Préparatoires de la Convention Européenne des
Droits de l'Homme* (M Nijhoff, The Hague, 1975–85) vol 7, 194.
[3] Above vol 7, 222–24, 230.
[4] Above vol 7, 206–8.
[5] Above.

adequate and effective compensation.[6] P1(1) is therefore significant because it expresses these rules as human rights of the individual, rather than a right of the State to intervene to protect an individual.

The lack of an express guarantee for nationals did not discourage arguments in favour of implied guarantees. It has been argued, for example, that the reference to international law should extend to both national and aliens;[7] and that a deprivation of property without compensation would not be in the public interest;[8] and that it might not fulfil the requirement of legality, but these arguments were not accepted.[9] The Court has rejected all of these arguments, but ultimately accepted the principle that expropriation without compensation may violate the human rights of the property owner. Doctrinally, this has been expressed through the proportionality principle. In *Sporrong and Lönnroth v Sweden*,[10] *James v The United Kingdom*[11] and *Lithgow v The United Kingdom*,[12] the Court declared that the doctrine of proportionality applied to P1(1) (although in its the weaker 'fair balance' formulation), and that the availability of compensation was a material factor in determining whether a given deprivation had a disproportionate impact on the victim. Accordingly, the Court concluded that the 'the taking of property without payment of an amount reasonably related to its value would normally constitute a disproportionate interference which could not be considered justifiable' under P1(1).[13] At the same time, the Court stated that there may be circumstances where something less than full compensation may satisfy the fair balance. Indeed, in principle, even the complete denial of any compensation may be justified.

In the end, we have a kind of compensation guarantee, but only through the application of the fair balance test. This chapter therefore examines how this 'guarantee' arises, and what it promises the property owner. It begins by examining the development of the modern law of the United Kingdom on compensation, before considering the European principles and, in particular, the normative assumptions that underpin the present situation.

---

[6] See HR Fabri, 'The Approach Taken by the European Court of Human Rights to the Assessment of Compensation for "Regulatory Expropriations" of the Property of Foreign Investors' (2002) 11 *New York University Environmental Law Journal* 148, 162–63, who observes that when Portugal entered a reservation to P1(1) ((1978) 21 *Yearbook of the European Convention on Human Rights* 16), the United Kingdom, Germany and France submitted made declarations that the general principles of international law require prompt, adequate and effective compensation ((1979) 22 *Yearbook of the European Convention on Human Rights* 16–22).

[7] *Gudmundsson v Iceland* (1960) 3 *Yearbook of the European Convention on Human Rights* 394.

[8] *Lithgow v The United Kingdom*, Series A No 102 (1986) 8 EHRR 329 [108], [109].

[9] Above.

[10] Series A No 52 (1983) 5 EHRR 35.

[11] Series A No 98 (1986) 8 EHRR 123.

[12] *Lithgow* (n 8).

[13] *James* (n 11) [54]; *Lithgow*, above [121].

THE SCOPE AND SOURCE OF THE COMPENSATION STANDARD

The background in national law[14]

Legislation on compulsory purchase began to acquire its present form in the early nineteenth century, as private Acts of Parliament were granted to canal and railway companies to enable them to purchase land for the construction of works.[15] The conditions on which these compulsory powers were granted were codified and extended in the Land Clauses Consolidation Act of 1845,[16] which provided a standard set of clauses for inclusion in the private Acts. In particular, the Act's clauses required compensation on the basis of 'the value of the land'.[17] However, the Act did not lay down detailed rules or even general principles for determining the value of land: this was left to the courts to develop. Nevertheless, it soon became clear that the value of the land was its value to the owner, rather than the acquiring body.[18] The landowner was entitled to compensation for its loss, but for no more than that; and the loss was measured by the value that the land would have in the absence of the exercise of the taker's statutory powers. For example, the acquiring body could not reduce the amount of compensation by pointing to an enhancement in the value of the remaining land caused by the completion of the scheme.[19] As seen above, this is almost certainly compatible with the Strasbourg cases, although it would also be legitimate to take such enhancements into account.

While the 1845 Act excluded the value to the taker, the valuation could take into account the potential value of the land for development. Indeed, the fact that the land had potential for the very purposes for which the compulsory powers were being exercised did not mean that that potential had to be excluded from consideration. In addition, the fact that the compulsory powers were usually exercised by commercial companies tended to lead to generous awards. While public perceptions of the generosity of compensation under the 1845 Act varied,[20] the fact that most compulsory purchasers were private bodies meant that public funds were not at stake. However, following World War I, there was a real concern that the compensation provisions of the 1845 Act could hamper

---

[14] See generally Law Commission of England and Wales, *Towards a Compulsory Purchase Code: (1) Compensation* (Law Com Consultation Paper No 165, 2002) 11–22 and *Towards a Compulsory Purchase Code: (1) Compensation* (Law Com No 286, 2003) 151–221; and M Redman, 'Compulsory Purchase, Compensation and Human Rights' [1999] *Journal of Planning & Environment Law* 315.

[15] See generally, RW Kostal, *Law and English Railway Capitalism, 1825–1875* (OUP, Oxford, 1994).

[16] 8 Vict, c 18.

[17] Above s 63.

[18] *Stebbing v Metropolitan Board of Works* (1870) LR 6 QB 37, 42 (Cockburn CJ).

[19] *South Eastern Railway Company v London CC* [1915] 2 Ch 252.

[20] See Kostal (n 15), ch 4.

reconstruction by public authorities. In particular, it was believed that public authorities should not necessarily be subject to the same rules as commercial companies. Section 2 of the Acquisition of Land Act 1919 therefore contained a set of six rules on compensation to be applied where land was acquired by a public authority. Although these rules also reflected the 'value to the owner' principle, they were intended to put stricter limits on the consideration of spec- ulative values and, in particular, to exclude the consideration of the impact of the acquiring authority's scheme on the value of the land.

The system was radically changed again with the enactment of the Town and Country Planning Act 1947, which sought to integrate the rules of compulsory purchase with the new rules on planning law. The State took over all develop- ment rights relating to land, and those wishing to develop their land had to pay a charge to do so. A fund was set up to compensate all owners for the loss of development rights. Consequently, compensation at market value should have excluded the development value of land, and there should have been no need to apply special rules excluding the consideration of the value of the land to the taker. In practice, however, the new scheme did not work well, and the six Rules of the 1919 Act were restored by section 5 of the Land Compensation Act 1961. In addition, new rules relating to the relevance of associated development and planning assumptions were introduced to reflect the planning system of the 1947 Act.

A further review of compensation resulted in the Land Compensation Act 1973. While it provided for compensation for other losses connected with the compulsory purchases and the execution of works, it affirmed the principle the owner should only receive compensation for the value of the land, as determined objectively and without reference to the value of the land to the taker. The model is not one that seeks to extract the 'enrichment' from the acquiring authority. Moreover, the operation of the principles has meant that the English law has not allowed compensation to be reduced by consideration of offsetting benefits. Indeed, although compensation for harm caused to any remaining land is available, it is treated as a separate head of the claim.

The statutory rules on compensation were recently the subject of an extensive review. In November 2003, the Law Commission presented its final report on the compensation provisions of a new compulsory purchase code. The code has not been enacted yet, but in any case, the report states that the code is intended only to 'maintain, and build on, the main features of the existing law within a simpler and more logical structure, using more accessible labels. Its essential objective is clarification of principle.'[21] Hence, one can say that the legislative practice has remained reasonably stable over a lengthy period; a balance has been struck, and it is one that bases compensation on the value as objectively determined.

---

[21] Law Commission (2003) (n 14), xiii.

The meaning and determination of value under P1(1)

The *Lithgow/James* formulation states that fair balance normally requires payment of an amount 'reasonably related' to the 'value' of the property, but without offering a definition of 'value'.[22] It is clear that compensation is not 'reasonably related' to the value of property if it is based solely on the owner's cost.[23] However, it is not clear how far it requires a particular standard of valuation. For example, distinctions can be made between market value of property, the current market value, and the fair value, and all of these can be distinguished from the 'best price' obtainable on a sale.[24] In both *James* and *Lithgow*, the Court remarked that special circumstances may call for payment of less than 'the full market value' of the property.[25] The possibility that 'value' and 'full market value' may be distinct was not addressed. Similarly, in *Pincová and Pinc v The Czech Republic*, the Court stated that the fair balance 'is generally achieved where the compensation paid to the person whose property has been taken is reasonably related to its "market" value, as determined at the time of the expropriation.'[26] Again, the Court did not elaborate on the possible differences between 'value' and 'market value', or that both may differ from 'full market value'.[27]

Lithgow demonstrates how the choice of a valuation standard can affect the outcome.[28] It concerned the valuation of shares taken as part of the nationalisation of the aircraft and shipbuilding industries. Shares listed on the London Stock Exchange were valued primarily on the basis of the quoted prices over a 'Reference Period'. Unlisted shares were valued on the basis of the price that they would have had if they had been listed over the Reference Period. All of the complaints concerned the unlisted shares. The applicants argued that the use of the hypothetical share price model was inappropriate, and that the model of a

---

[22] Above 165 n 35: 'The term "full compensation" does not appear to be used in any precise sense; the term "full market value" is also used. Generally, the case law of the European Court of Human Rights on damages adopts the principle of equivalence (or *restitutio in integrum*), but does not lay down any consistent principles for assessment'.

[23] *Hentrich v France*, Series A No 296–A (1994) 18 EHRR 440; *Pincová and Pinc v The Czech Republic*, Appl No 36548/97, 5 November 2002.

[24] Gerald Eve Chartered Surveyors and the University of Reading, *The Operation of the Crichel Down Rules* (Office of the Deputy Prime Minister, London, 2000) [5.5.28].

[25] *James* (n 11) [54] (emphasis added); *Lithgow* (n 8) [121].

[26] *Pincová* (n 23) [53].

[27] See also *Holy Monasteries v Greece*, Series A No 301–A (1995) 20 EHRR 1 [71], referring to the passage in *James* (n 11) about justified departures from 'market value'; *Håkansson and Sturesson v Sweden*, Series A No 171 (1990) 13 EHRR 1, [51]–[55]; *Beyeler v Italy*, Reports 2000–I 57 (2001) 33 EHRR 52 [121]; *Broniowski v Poland*, Appl No 31443/96, 22 June 2004 (Grand Chamber) [182].

[28] For a detailed analysis of *Lithgow*, see M Mendelson, 'The United Kingdom Nationalization Cases and the European Convention on Human Rights' (1986) 57 *British Yearbook of International Law* 33; and RA Salgado, 'Protection of Nationals' Rights to Property under the European Convention on Human Rights: *Lithgow v The United Kingdom*' (1987) 27 *Virginia Journal of International Law* 865.

sale by private treaty between a willing seller and a willing buyer would have produced a more accurate valuation. The willing seller—willing buyer model would have taken into account, among other things, the premium that is usually paid to acquire a controlling block of shares.[29] In effect, the hypothetical share price model treated the ownership of these companies as though it were divided amongst a diverse body of shareholders when in fact it was not.

Other aspects of the case also demonstrate how the working model for value affected the outcome. For example, the Court did not criticise the United Kingdom for giving little consideration to the book values of company assets, as it would have been 'costly and time-consuming' to determine them for every company.[30] In addition, the fact that the cash reserves of some of the target companies exceeded the amount paid in compensation was of little weight.[31] Having decided that the hypothetical share price model was acceptable, it followed that the existence of substantial book values or cash reserves could be disregarded.

While *Lithgow* suggests that the failure to articulate a clear conception of 'value' allows the State to limit compensation, it should be noted that the Court treated the nationalisation as an exceptional measure. As explained below, this justified a departure from the general principle that compensation must be reasonably related to the value of the property;[32] in addition, it led the Court to allow the United Kingdom a very wide margin of appreciation in relation to compensation. Nevertheless, it is clear that 'value' itself remained undefined.

Cases subsequent to *Lithgow* have not clarified the meaning of 'value' or 'market value'. If national law sets compensation at market value, the Court is unlikely to examine closely whether the calculation of compensation reflected market value in fact, or whether the valuation rules reflect some international understanding of market value.[33] It is only likely to say that compensation is inadequate where specific assumptions were made that contradict the conception of value that appears to be required by national law itself.[34] This is demonstrated by a series of Greek cases concerning the use of presumptions for valuing land.[35] Under the relevant Greek laws, full compensation was given for the expropriation of land; however, where that land was used for the construction of a major road, there was a presumption that any adjoining land retained by the owner had increased in value, and that increase was subtracted from the

[29] The applicants had evidence showing that the premium averaged 34% at the time of vesting: *Lithgow* (n 8) [98].

[30] Above [125].

[31] Above [174].

[32] Below, 180–93.

[33] See eg *S v The United Kingdom*, Appl No 13135/87, 4 July 1988.

[34] In addition to cases discussed below, see *Scordino v Italy*, Appl No 36813/97, 17 March 2003: Art 42 of the Italian constitution requires compensation at market value for the expropriation of land; however, the facts demonstrated that the award of compensation was only about half of the value as ordinarily determined.

[35] *Katikaridis v Greece*, Reports 1996–V 1673 (2001) 32 EHRR 6; *Tsomtsos v Greece*, Reports 1996–V 1699; *Papachelas v Greece*, Reports 1999–II 1 (2000) 30 EHRR 923; see also *Serghides v Cyprus* (2003) 37 EHRR 44.

compensation payable for the expropriated land.[36] This rule was inflexible: it applied even where the facts showed that the adjoining land had declined in value. Consequently, the amount of compensation would be reduced in cases where, if anything, it should have been increased.

The Court did not question the general principle behind the Greek rules, as it found that 'it is legitimate to take into account the benefit derived from the works by adjoining owners.'[37] However, the inflexibility of the rules upset the fair balance: their application was 'manifestly without reasonable foundation' and hence the expropriations had a disproportionate effect on the applicants.[38] At the very least, landowners should have had the opportunity to show that the presumption should not apply in their case.[39]

Ultimately, it appears that the Court has not closely examined the principle that compensation must be reasonably related to the value of the property. There are at least two reasons for this. The first is that the standard of P1(1) reflects the constitutional standards of the member States in any event, and hence its application is unlikely to be controversial in the ordinary case. The second is that the P1(1) standard does not necessarily apply to every case: where its application might prove controversial, the Court can always say that the facts are exceptional and hence the standard does not apply. In the end, however, it has meant that fundamental questions of principle have not been addressed. Since the European Court has not justified its position on compensation, it is worth asking why the standard should not require more than the market value. On the one hand, it is not clear that the public interest necessarily favours the minimisation of the amount of compensation. As a matter of sound administrative policy, the compulsory power should only be used to ensure that transactions that produce a net overall benefit to the public will go ahead. Since the decision to acquire specific property is normally made by the body that will use the property, rather than a central planner, the compensation rules should ensure that it has the incentive to exercise the power when it is in the public interest to do so, and to refrain from exercising the power when it is not. However, this does not necessarily lead to the conclusion that the public interest is best protected by setting compensation at the market value. Some economic analysts argue that a system that denies any compensation to the former owner would be efficient; others argue that compensation should normally

---

[36] These owners were deemed to derive a benefit from construction, and compensation was reduced by an amount equal to the value of land of an area equal to half that of the road built, provided that it did not exceed half the surface area of the property concerned. In *Katikaridis*, above, compensation was by reduced by an amount equal to the value of an area fifteen metres wide.

[37] *Katikaridis*, above [49].

[38] Above.

[39] And this should not require further proceedings to be brought by the landowner: see *Efstathiou v Greece*, Appl No 55794/00, 10 July 2003; *Interoliva ABEE v Greece*, Appl No 58642/00, 10 July 2003; *Konstantopoulos AE v Greece*, Appl No 58634/00, 10 July 2003; *Biozokat AE v Greece*, Appl No 61582/00, 9 October 2003.

exceed market value.[40] In any case, it is quite clear that the Court would not question a government that insists that a higher level of compensation would be contrary to the public interest. Any argument for greater compensation must be based on the impact suffered by the applicant.

Since the European Court has indicated that market value is normally required, the first question is whether this is indeed fair to the property owner. The market value thesis holds that the property owner has no ethical entitlement to any of the surplus generated from the transfer of the property. Even if the owner had some claim to the surplus, the acquiring body has a stronger claim because it has earned it through its own efforts in identifying a more profitable way to use the property. Moreover, there is nothing about the compulsory nature of the purchase entitles the owner to receive more for the property than he or she would have obtained on the market. At the most, the property owner may have a claim for the costs of being forced to sell not at the time of his or her own choosing, but these are costs rather than compensation for the property.

Accordingly, since any entitlement of the owner to the surplus is weak, at best, the fair balance is not upset if he or she only receives the market value for the property. While it is doubtful that the courts in Strasbourg or the United Kingdom would question the validity of this position, there are three arguments that might carry weight in exceptional circumstances.

(1) One might argue that the use of compulsion is undesirable in itself. Put differently, even if the payment of the market value does compensate for the loss of the property, it does not address the infringement in the property owner's autonomy arising from the coercive nature of the interference. Accordingly, the compensation rules should be set so that the compulsory purchaser has the strongest possible incentive to obtain the owner's consent to the transfer. Hence, compensation should be at the maximum price that still allows the compulsory purchaser to retain enough of a benefit to induce it to go ahead with the purchase.

While it is plain that the Court would not accept this as a general principle, there are cases where it has been concerned that compulsory powers are not being exercised for an appropriate purpose. One difficult area concerns the disposition of land discovered to be surplus to the requirements of the purchaser. Under the English rules, the impact of the scheme on land is normally excluded from valuation. Consequently, the compulsory purchaser would gain if it could compulsorily purchase all the land that would be affected by the scheme, even if much of the land is not actually necessary for the scheme. Since the purchase price would disregard the impact of the scheme, any land not actually used could be resold on the market at a profit.

---

[40] For a review of the literature, see TJ Miceli and K Segerson, 'Takings' in B Bouckaert and G De Geest (eds), *Encyclopedia of Law and Economics* (Elgar, Cheltenham, 1999) (online at <http://encyclo.findlaw.com/> and <http://allserv.rug.ac.be/~gdegeest/>).

Arguably, the ethics of securing the capital gain are not the concern in such cases, since it is considered legitimate for the compulsory purchaser to secure the gain when it does use the property in the scheme. That is, there would be no objection to its retention of the surplus if it bought the property on the open market. Rather, it is the use of coercion as a means of obtaining the gain that is objectionable. In theory, it should be possible to control the such uses of coercion by a rigorous application of the public interest tests: arguably, taking property merely for the purpose of securing a capital gain does not satisfy the test, and would violate P1(1). However, the courts are unlikely to take this view of P1(1): in practical terms, the State could easily justify the purchase by saying that property may be used for the scheme at some future point, and it is in the public interest to acquire the property immediately in order to save public funds. Put this way, the purpose is likely to satisfy the P1(1) requirements.[41]

In the United Kingdom, this issue is addressed as a matter of administrative law and practice. When public authorities determine that land that was compulsorily acquired is surplus to their requirements, they normally give the former owner the first opportunity to re-purchase it. In some cases, this practice is required by statute, but often they apply by ministerial guidance. In addition, in some circumstances, such as the acquisition of land for a street or highway, there is an automatic reverter of land to the former owner where it is no longer used for the purpose for which it was acquired. The failure to apply these principles led to the Crichel Down affair in 1954, which in turn led to the promulgation of the Crichel Down Rules on the disposition of lands surplus to requirements.[42]

The Rules reflect a feeling that the former owners have a strong moral claim to any gain in value in the intervening period. However, in the absence of specific statutory rules, the Rules operate only as administrative guidance. Even as administrative guidance, they are only mandatory for Government departments and their agencies, and are only commended to local authorities and privatised bodies to which public sector land holdings were transferred the owner. Moreover, there is no obligation to provide the opportunity to repurchase if the land has changed materially in the meantime. In any case, research commissioned by the Department of the Environment, Transport and the Regions showed that a significant proportion of Government departments and their agencies mistakenly believed that they were not required to follow the Rules, or were not even aware of their existence.[43] Conversely, many local authorities were under the mistaken impression that they were bound by the Rules. Even

---

[41] See eg *Motais de Narbonne v France*, Appl No 48161/99, 2 July 2002.

[42] For the development of the Rules, see Gerald Eve Chartered Surveyors and the University of Reading, *The Operation of the Crichel Down Rules* (Office of the Deputy Prime Minister, London, 2000); and R Gibbard, 'The Crichel Down Rules: Conduct or Misconduct in the Disposal of Public Lands' in E Cooke, (ed), *Modern Studies in Property Law, Vol 2* (Hart Publishing, Oxford, 2003) 329.

[43] Gerald Eve, above 43–83.

where the Rules were applied, there was often no sense of the purpose which they were intended to serve. Consequently, they were applied in a mechanical way, with the result that there were differences in their application from one Government body or authority to another.

While these misunderstandings may suggest that the Rules no longer serve any useful purpose,[44] they still have strong supporters amongst Members of Parliament and senior judges. For example, in *Blanchfield*, a Privy Council case from Trinidad and Tobago, Lord Millett remarked that granting former owners the first opportunity to re-purchase was demanded by 'elementary fairness'.[45] However, if the statutory power of compulsory purchase was not expressly subject to such a condition, none would be implied.[46] This raises an interesting question: does P1(1) have any relevance where the Crichel Down Rules may operate?

In *Motais de Narbonne v France*,[47] the applicants complained that they had been unfairly deprived of a capital gain when land lay unused for nineteen years after its expropriation. The applicants made demands for the return of the property, or alternatively for a payment representing its capital appreciation over that period, but were refused by the French authorities and courts. In Strasbourg, the Court held that P1(1) had been violated. It was not suggested, however, that the initial expropriation violated P1(1): the amount of compensation was acceptable at the time, and the expropriation furthered the public interest. The property had been expropriated with no specific project in mind, but under French law, certain public authorites may assemble a land reserve for future development. Nevertheless, the failure to allow the applicants a share of the capital gain upset the fair balance.

The case plainly raises many questions concerning the scope of P1(1). For example, since the expropriation of property is not a continuing event, it should follow that no issue should arise if the initial expropriation complied with P1(1). There was no suggestion that French law gave the applicants an interest in the land that entitled them to a share of the capital gain; nor was it said that P1(1) requires States to make every exercise of a power of compulsory purchase subject to a right of reverter or similar condition. In any case, the complaint that the applicants missed out on a potential capital gain makes little sense, as they had had the opportunity to invest the compensation received on the expropriation in other property, and to earn a similar capital gain thereby.

All of these points suggest that the judgment is inconsistent with other P1(1) principles, and indeed there are other cases where the Court has taken a more

---

[44] Whether the Rules have any continued role has been questioned, particularly in the light of changes in compensation. At the time the Rules were promulgated, compensation did not include development value.

[45] *Blanchfield v Attorney General of Trinidad and Tobago* [2002] UKPC 1 [21] (Lord Millett).

[46] Above [13]: 'in the absence of an express reverter clause in the enabling legislation or in the conveyance or order by which the land was conveyed to or vested in the acquiring authority, none can be implied.' (At [16], Lord Millett listed specific exceptions to this rule.)

[47] *Motais de Narbonne* (n 41).

conservative view. In particular, in *Papadopoulou and Others v Greece*,[48] the applicants complained that twenty years had passed since their land was expropriated and it was still not being used for the purpose for which it was taken. However, the Court did not find this unacceptable: the initial compensation was reasonable, the authorities had not abandoned their original purpose, and the delay was not intolerable. Nevertheless, even if *Motais de Narbonne* is treated as anomalous, it demonstrates that the neither the public interest nor the compensation requirements address all the Court's concerns over the potential abuse of power. The facts raised questions of fairness because it seemed that the power of compulsory purchase had been unnecessary: the authorities should have ensured that the specific plans were formulated with a reasonable period of time, and should not have rushed in assembling the property before doing so. It was clear that there was a sense that the formation of the land reserve allowed the State to speculate on property values, and this risk of such speculation had to be controlled by a generous application of P1(1).[49]

(2) Alternatively, it could be argued that compensation should be set at the value of the property to its owner.[50] As discussed above, valuation normally excludes consideration of the special value of the property to both the purchaser and the owner. While payments are sometimes made for losses associated with the transfer, these are not seen as payments for the property itself. As some commentators have noted, the payment of the market value 'undercompensates landowners, possibly by a large amount, since owners do not generally view land and wealth as perfect substitutes, whereas market value compensates them as if they did.'[51] This is particularly true in the case of the home. Often, owners place a higher value on factors relating to the neighbourhood, especially where it reflects a cultural or social group that the owner cannot easily find elsewhere.[52]

There is some recognition of the importance of subjective factors in *Lallement v France*.[53] A part of the applicant's farm was expropriated at

---

[48] Appl No 53901/00, 14 March 2002. In *Kolb, Holaus, Taxacher and Wechselberger v Austria*, Appl No 35021/97 and Appl No 45774/99, 21 February 2002, the Court rejected the suggestion that compensation ought to take into account any changes in land values after a provisional transfer in a land consolidation scheme (although it concerned a provisional rather than a final transfer).

[49] See *Motais de Narbonne* (n 41) [21]: 'L'article 1 du Protocole n° 1 oblige en effet les Etats contactants à prémunir les individus contre le risque d'un usage de la technique des réserves foncières autorisant ce qui pourrait être perçu comme une forme de spéculation foncière à leur détriment.'

[50] This could be justified on the basis that no owner should be worse off as a result of the exercise of the compulsory power over property. One might also argue that it secures efficiency, as the loss of such subjective values are significant to the economy as a whole: the fact that others would not be able to derive similar value from the same property does not mean that it does not exist. Failing to take these subjective values into account would mean that acquisitions may go forward that will result in a net loss to the economy. Moreover, such cases would not be the exception: in many cases, compulsory powers are exercised because owners do not wish to sell at the market price, and they do not sell at the market price because it does not represent the value they derive from the property.

[51] Miceli and Segerson (n 40) 331.

[52] As in *Gerasimova v Russia*, Appl No 24077/02, 25 March 2004.

[53] Appl No 46044/99, 11 April 2002.

market value. The applicant could have required the authorities to purchase the entire farm, but he decided against it because the remaining land contained the family home. However, the profitability of the remaining land fell considerably as a result of the division of the farm, and he sought compensation for the loss of this profit. France argued that the interference had not been disproportionate: in effect, the loss of profit was caused by his decision to stay in the home rather than the expropriation itself. The Court did not accept this, on the basis that the applicant could not be 'reproached' for wishing to stay in the home. Further compensation should have been provided to maintain the fair balance.

Although *Lallement* reflects the view that the family home may have a subjective value above the market value, it does not state that this subjective value must be considered in all cases. Indeed, in *Lallement* itself, it was the failure to compensate for the loss of profitability that was material, as the applicant never lost the home. Hence, it represents an acknowledgement of the value of the home to its owner, but not that there is any claim to compensation for the loss of that value.

In the United Kingdom, there is some acknowledgement of the value of the home in the present compensation rules. Payments to landowners usually include both compensation for the property and additional amounts for other losses associated with the fact that the expropriation is compulsory.[54] These payments are made on a fixed scale, which means that home-loss payments do not cover all costs suffered by every homeowner. In a report published in 2000 by the Department of the Environment, Transport and the Regions acknowledged that expropriation raises special difficulties for owners of low-value homes, especially where values collapsed relative to the general market. Market value compensation may not be enough to enable them to buy another home, even with a home-loss payment. The Report stated that there is 'a need, in human rights terms, to ensure that such displaced owner-occupiers are not made to bear a disproportionate burden as a result of the compulsory purchase of their homes.'[55] The principle that compensation should be reasonably related to the value of property is not in issue, since these owners do receive the market value for their homes. The issue is therefore whether the payment of only the market value is itself disproportionate. Hence, it was suggested that the Canadian idea of home-for-a home payments should be considered, where the scheme would be 'more closely based on the concept of equivalence, with scope for loans (possibly interest free) and equity shares to avoid betterment being achieved at public expense.'[56] Although this was supported by the Parliametary Committee on Transport, Local Government and the Regions,[57] the regulations

---

[54] Home Loss Payments (England) Regulations 2003 (SI 2003 No 1706).

[55] Compulsory Purchase Policy Review Advisory Group, *Fundamental Review into the Laws and Procedures relating to Compulsory Purchase and Compensation* (Transport and Regions Department of the Environment, London, 2000) [169].

[56] Above.

[57] Committee on Transport, Local Government and the Regions, *Sixth Report* (HC Paper (2002) No 240–I) [124]–[128].

that were finally implemented did not incorporate this suggestion.[58] Since the issue of human rights was raised, it is worth asking whether it would be disproportionate to deprive these owners of a home without providing them with the means to acquire another similar home for personal occupation.

Ultimately, it seems that the Government concluded that the problem had been over-stated, as it concluded that the home-loss payments and other allowances

> would be sufficient to enable the vast majority of displaced owner-occupiers to rehouse themselves adequately. We therefore see it as unnecessarily cumbersome to devise a separate compensation regime applicable to all owner-occupiers, whilst it would also be unfair to treat one group of homeowners on a different basis from all others.[59]

While it might be questioned whether it is unfair to treat one group differently when that group is in different circumstances, it is worth noting that there are no Strasbourg cases requiring the home-for-a-home principle. In *Pincová and Pinc v The Czech Republic*, the Court noted that the compensation paid for the applicants' home left them in an 'uncertain, and indeed difficult, social situation,' as it was not enough to enable them unable to buy somewhere else to live.[60] This failure to take into account their 'personal and social situation' supported the conclusion that the fair balance had been upset.[61] However, in *Pincová*, the compensation was based on the price the applicants had paid for the property many years earlier: if they had been paid the current market price, the fair balance would not have been upset. More generally, the Court has said that P1(1) does not entitle those without property to have or to acquire property;[62] neither has it suggested that P1(1) entitles anyone to a home or even to basic subsistence.[63] This suggests that it would regard these owners of low-value homes as victims of poverty rather than victims of State action, which again supports the view that it is enough to limit compensation to the value of the property itself.[64] Finally, there is the broader concern that a home-for-a-home principle might actually constrain the alleviation of poverty, since low-value homes are often bought as part of regeneration schemes. The difficulties faced by low-value homeowners arise because of a general deterioration of the economic base and other social conditions in their wider neighbourhood, and so

---

[58] Home Loss Payments (England) Regulations 2003 (SI 2003 No 1706).

[59] Department of Transport, Local Government and the Regions, *Compulsory Purchase and Compensation: the Government's Proposals for Change* (Office of the Deputy Prime Minister, December 2001), [3.30] (also available at <http://www.odpm.gov.uk/stellent/groups/odpm_planning/documents/p/odpm_plan_605835.hcsp>).

[60] *Pincová* (n 23) [62].

[61] Above [63], [64].

[62] *Marckx v Belgium*, Series A No 31 (1979) 2 EHRR 330 [50]; *Rieberger and Engleitner v Austria*, Appl No 8749/02, 7 October 2004.

[63] *Sardin v Russia*, Appl No 69582/01, 12 February 2004; see Chapter 2, n 136.

[64] See also the cases on inflation, Chapter 2, n 35 (the State has no responsibility under P1(1) to safeguard the value of assets against inflation).

requiring higher compensation might have perverse effect of hindering regeneration by increasing its cost.

(3) Finally, it could be argued that a distinction ought to be made between compulsory purchases by public authorities and commercial companies. Where two private parties are concerned, as with the purchase by a commercial operator, the public interest is neutral as between the distribution of the gain arising from the transaction. The public interest would be served if the acquisition when ahead when there is a net gain to the public, and in order to ensure this, it would be necessary to provide the purchaser with a sufficient profit incentive. However, the incentive need only be the minimum necessary to encourage the compulsory purchaser to exercise its powers. While the owner may have no expectation of sharing the gain, one could argue that it should not be required to suffer a loss in order to provide a gain to the commercial operator (or its shareholders). Indeed, the restrictions of the 1919 Act were brought in to ensure that public authorities were not subject to the same compensation provisions as commercial companies. It does not follow the obligations of commercial companies should also be relaxed.

In practice, however, the European Court of Human Rights has not made this distinction. Indeed, in *Bramelid*, the compulsory purchasers were private persons, and yet the fair balance was not upset when they paid only the market value for the property. Similarly, in *James*, although the tenants were not commercial operators, the surplus went entirely into their hands.[65] To date, the courts in the United Kingdom have also failed to make this distinction. For example, although *Marcic v Thames Water Utilities Ltd*[66] did not deal with an expropriation, the House of Lords did not discuss the status of a privatised utility as a profit-making commercial enterprise. Indeed, the cases cited in support of a finding of no liability for flooding all dealt with public authorities.[67] The commercial status of a party is considered when it is a victim of an interference: in some cases, the courts have said that owners of property held for commercial purposes should accept a higher degree of risk of State interference. However, this does not seem to apply where the commercial party is the source of the interference.

DEPARTURES FROM THE 'REASONABLY RELATED' STANDARD

The *James/Lithgow* cases permit a departure from the 'reasonably related to the value' standard in exceptional cases. Before considering these cases, it is worth noting that the Court is not likely to treat compensation as 'reasonably related' to the value of the property if it is a fraction of the value. For example, a State

---

[65] *James* (n 11).

[66] [2004] 2 AC 42.

[67] Above [32]–[33], where Lord Nicholls briefly refers to the Court of Appeal's consideration of the profits made by Thames Water, but does not suggest that it is relevant (*cf Marcic v Thames Water Utilities Ltd* [2002] QB 929 (CA) [38] and [83]).

that pays compensation at a rate of 80% of the value of the property could not argue that this met the ordinary standard, although the amount of compensation is plainly 'related' to the value. The Court would treat this as a departure from its usual rule, and expect the State to provide some justification for falling below full compensation. That is, the idea that compensation need only 'reasonably' related to the value of the property seems to mean that the Court does not wish to engage in a close examination of the valuation rules applied in the case, and not that only a 'reasonable' proportion of the value may be paid.[68]

Plainly, any property owner who receives less than he or she could receive on the market is bound to feel that they have been treated unfairly. In addition, the risk of abuse of power increases if purchaser is permitted to pay less than the market value. To take an extreme example, there is the risk that the compulsory purchaser will use the power to acquire property at a price below the market price, with a view to resale at profit; or to acquire property at the market price, with a view to not to its exploitation for some public use, but simply to hold it for capital appreciation. To some extent, such abuses would be prevented by the requirement that expropriations serve the public interest; similarly, the Crichel Down Rules prevent an immediate resale. However, the public interest requirement is rarely applied in human rights law with any force and, as explained above, it is not even clear that the Crichel Down Rules have any weight at all in human rights law.[69] Hence, the rule requiring compensation at market price ensures that the purchaser has no incentive to abuse its powers.

To date, the Court has identified a number of specific circumstances that may justify a departure from the ordinary principles, without attempting to provide a comprehensive list of such circumstances. In some cases, the Court has focused on the proposed use of the property, by accepting that an important public interest could not be achieved if full market value were payable. In others, the focus has fallen on the owner's ethical entitlement to compensation, as it is adjudged too weak to require full market value. However, beyond this, there is no set of general principles tying these different categories together, and hence each must be examined on its own.

Economic restructuring

In several cases, States have argued that programmes involving a radical economic restructuring justify takings of property without compensation, or at least with compensation that does not necessarily reflect the property's

---

[68] See eg *Yiltas Yildiz Turistik Tesisleri AS v Turkey*, Appl No 30502/96, 24 April 2003, where a violation was found on the basis that the valuation used by the Turkish authorities was only about 5% of the values produced by independent experts; and *Scordino* (n 34), where a violation was found when compensation represented only about 50% of the value of the property and no compelling reason was put forward paying less than the full value.

[69] Above 175–77.

full value. The *Lithgow* case is the leading example, as the United Kingdom persuaded the Court that economic restructuring justified the application of valuation principles that did not necessarily provide full compensation to every shareholder.[70] As explained above, the use of the hypothetical share price model raised specific objections. In some cases, the amount of compensation did not even equal the cash reserves of some of the companies. Indeed, even after taking over the nationalisation process in 1979, the Conservative Government described the valuation rules as 'grossly unfair to some of the companies'.[71] Nevertheless, both the Commission and Court found that there had been no violation of P1(1).

The Court explained its decision both in terms of proportionality and the margin of appreciation. In relation to the fair balance, it stated that 'the valuation of major industrial enterprises for the purpose of nationalising a whole industry is in itself a far more complex operation than, for instance, the valuation of land compulsorily acquired and normally calls for specific legislation which can be applied across the board to all the undertakings involved.'[72] Hence, by this broad description of the requirements of the fair balance, the Court avoided the need to lay down specific rules on valuation. Indeed, the flexibility of the fair balance seems to make it unnecessary to rely on the margin of appreciation. However, the Court also stated that, in relation to the margin of appreciation, it would 'be artificial in this respect to divorce the decision as to the compensation terms from the actual decision to nationalise, since the factors influencing the latter will of necessity also influence the former.'[73] Consequently, it would accept 'the legislature's judgment in this connection unless that judgment was manifestly without reasonable foundation.'[74] Moreover, in this specific case, the extent of the debates in Parliament demonstrated that the very issues that were before the Court had received careful consideration when the legislation was formulated. It may have also been significant that, despite its objections while in opposition, the Conservative Government elected in 1979 decided not to change the valuation rules.[75] This support from different governments may have given the legislation a kind of legitimacy that it might not have otherwise had.

In any case, the combination of the relaxed view of proportionality and the wide margin of appreciation made it apparent that the shareholders were given

---

[70] *Lithgow* (n 8) [121].

[71] Above [17], quoting statements to House of Commons by Secretary of State for Industry 7 August 1980 (although the Conservative Government decided against amending the compensation formula, and defended it before the European Commission and Court of Human Rights).

[72] Above [121].

[73] Above [122]; see also *Almeida Garrett, Mascarenhas Falcão v Portugal*, Appl No 29813/96, 30229/96, 11 January 2000 [52].

[74] Above.

[75] The Conservative Government's position was discussed, but only to dismiss the possibility that its statements in Parliament that the legislation had produced some 'grossly unfair' results was not binding on it in litigation in Strasbourg.

very little protection: in the abstract, the rules for determining compensation only had to be 'reasonably related' to the value of the property, and in practice, the application of the rules could leave some owners with less than the value of their shares; and even so, a challenge would be successful only if the rules were 'manifestly without reasonable foundation'. In the end, it is difficult to imagine how any set of valuation rules could have been challenged, so long as some compensation had been provided.[76] Accordingly, the Court rejected complaints that the hypothetical share price model did not represent the value of the companies because it did not allow for a premium for control. As explained above, the United Kingdom was permitted to treat the ownership as divided when in fact it was concentrated.

Plainly, the State cannot normally reduce the amount of compensation by choosing to describe a single asset as a collection of assets that, taken singly, are worth less than they are collectively.[77] As a corollary, the State should not be required to increase compensation when it assembles property that it has acquired from a number of different owners to form a single asset of greater value than its parts: in such cases, it is the State that has 'earned' the surplus that arises from concentrating ownership. This is consistent with the general principle that the valuation of property should ignore the value to the taker. However, in *Lithgow*, the applicants argued that the property was already a single asset at the time of acquisition: in effect, the State appropriated the surplus that the applicants had already generated. Nevertheless, the Court dismissed the applicants' arguments with little trouble, as it stated that the choice of the hypothetical share price model was not so unreasonable so as to put the legislation outside the margin of appreciation. While the model had an element of artificiality about it, so would the willing buyer-willing seller model, as it assumed that there would have been a single buyer for any of the companies.[78] Still, it must have been less artificial to regard the property as the blocks of shares that they were in fact, rather than a number of unconnected smaller holdings. Moreover, it would not contradict the principle against compensating for the value to the taker, as the value of a block of shares depends on its size of relative to all issued shares. Finally, the Court also accepted that the United Kingdom had sought to treat all shareholders alike; from this, it seemed to follow that, since some shareholders did not receive the premium, none of them should. Again, it is not so obvious that equality ought to prevail in such cases.

In the end, the compensation fell far short of the price that the applicants

---

[76] Note that the margin of appreciation would not extend to a clear error: in *Platakou v Greece*, Reports 2001–I 21 a violation of P1(1) was found where valuation had proceed on the basis of a mistake of fact that the applicant had not had a real opportunity to correct (and that the relevant public officials may have deliberately hidden) (see [56]–[57]).

[77] Indeed, the choice of a share price valuation demonstrated a belief that it was the shares, rather than the company's assets, that were being acquired.

[78] *Lithgow* (n 8) [129]: 'a degree of artificiality would also have been involved in an assumption that there would have been a willing buyer for large shareholdings in a company engaged in the particular industries concerned.'

would have expected on a sale of their holdings to a private buyer, and yet there was no violation of P1(1). Not surprisingly, the judgment was heavily criticised.[79] Nevertheless, although the margin of appreciation was plainly very wide, it did not entirely exclude any assessment of the fairness and proportionality. In this respect, it seems that the fairness/proportionality standard was satisfied by showing that the compensation bore *some* relationship with the value of the shares. Despite the questionable validity of the valuation model, compensation was not based on factors entirely divorced from the value of the shares: for example, it was not based on the length of time that the owner had held the shares, or on some other factor bearing no relationship with the value of the shares (however 'value' was described).

This was regarded as an exceptional case, and it remains a difficult case because two separate factors made it exceptional. Both the scale and complexity of valuing property on a nationalisation and the support given to the legislation by (ultimately) two governments were significant, but it is not easy to determine the significance of each factor taken alone.

Moral entitlements

In *James*, the Court stated that the furtherance of social justice could justify a departure from the general principle that the fair balance normally requires expropriation to be accompanied by compensation. The case concerned powers given to long-lease tenants to purchase the freehold of the property at a price that only reflected the value of the land. As no compensation was paid for the buildings, the landlords argued that the fair balance had been upset. The United Kingdom maintained that, since most tenants would have been contractually obligated to maintain the buildings, many of them would have paid an amount equivalent to the current value of the buildings over the period of the lease.[80] The Court agreed that this meant it was not unfair to allow them to exclude the value of the buildings from compensation.

However, in the majority of cases where the social justice argument has been accepted, it is the manner in which the applicant acquired the property that has been relevant. This is supported by *James*, and it is confirmed in cases where applicants complain that causes of action have been extinguished without compensation. These cases raise difficult issues concerning the existence of P1(1) possessions[81] and (assuming that P1(1) is applicable) the identification of the

---

[79] See eg Mendelson (n 28) 74: 'The broad scope given to the Government's "margin of appreciation" apparently leaves it open for governments to pay compensation at whatever level they feel is compatible with the social objectives of the nationalizing legislation, without much fear of condemnation from Strasbourg.' See also Salgado (n 28) 912: 'The Court has failed to appreciate one of the most fundamental goals of the Convention: to set up a system of checks to prevent the reemergence of totalitarian regimes.'

[80] *James* (n 11) [57].

[81] Chapter 2, 46–64.

Rule to be applied to the facts.[82] Nevertheless, if it appears that the applicant is seeking to exploit a technical defect in legislation, the State may be justified in remedying the defect with retroactive effect. Depending on the facts, the applicant's cause of action may be extinguished, without compensation. For example, in *National & Provincial Building Society and others v The United Kingdom*,[83] the applicants argued that P1(1) was violated by the extinction of a claim to restitution of an unlawfully imposed tax. However, the Court held against the applicants, primarily for the reason that it believed that the applicants were seeking to take advantage of an inadvertently created loophole in transitional tax arrangements. In effect, the weakness of the applicants' moral claim to restitution meant that it took very little for the United Kingdom to justify its interference with the applicants' claims.[84]

While the Court in *James* and *National & Provincial* readily accepted the State's argument that the victims could not expect full compensation, it was less sympathetic in *Jahn and others v Germany*.[85] In this case, the applicants' claim related to agricultural land in the former German Democratic Republic. Prior to re-unification, the GDR passed the 'Modrow Law' in order to facilitate the transition to a market economy, and specifically to enable those in possession of agricultural land to transfer or otherwise deal with the land after re-unification. In effect, the law converted personal usufructuary interests to full ownership. The applicants should not have qualified to receive title under the Modrow Law, since they were not in occupation of agricultural land. However, due to administrative failures, they succeeded in being registered as owners of land on the basis of a formal title to land that had been taken over by the State many years earlier. After re-unification, the Federal Republic of Germany passed legislation to reverse the failures to administer the Modrow Law properly. Consequently, land could be vested in the tax authorities, without compensation, if it was determined the beneficiaries had not in fact satisfied the conditions of the Modrow Law. The German courts subsequently determined that the applicants fell into this category; the applicants claimed that this violated P1(1).

---

[82] Chapter 4, 114–16.

[83] *National & Provincial Building Society v The United Kingdom*, Reports 1997–VII 2325 (1998) 25 EHRR 127.

[84] See also *MA and 34 others v Finland*, Appl No 27793/95, 10 June 2003; and *Roshka v Russia*, Appl No 63343/00, 6 November 2003; and *Ogis–Institut Stanislas, Ogec S Pie X and Blanche de Castille v France*, Appl No 42219/98 and 54563/00, 27 May 2004, concerning claims filed in the French administrative courts for reimbursement in full of social-security contributions. A 1992 case of the Conseil d'Etat stated that technical defects in the existing legislation entitled them to such a claim. Legislation was subsequently enacted to remedy the defect, and to bring about greater equality in the rules on and it thereby denied them the right to full reimbursement. The Court in Strasbourg assumed for the sake of argument that the applicants' claims constituted 'possessions' in the form of acquired rights to reimbursement. However, as it appeared that the possibility of claiming full reimbursement arose due to an unintended technical defect in the legislation, and it was clear that the legislature would act to correct the defect, the fair balance was not upset when the defect was remedied.

[85] Appl No 46720/99, 72203/01, 72552/01, 22 January 2004.

Germany argued that the applicants' title was uncertain, illegitimate, and purely formal, and it followed the interference was minimal. Accordingly, the denial of compensation was justified. However, the Court stated simply that the Modrow Law had taken effect before the Convention was extended to the former GDR; hence, the applicants had held full ownership at the time the Convention did take effect. While the Court acknowledged that P1(1) does not require compensation in every case, it stated that:

> In the instant case, if the German legislature's intention was to correct *ex post facto* the—in its opinion unjust—effects of the Modrow Law by passing a new law two years later, this did not pose a problem in itself. The problem was the content of the new law. In the Court's view, in order to comply with the principle of proportionality, the German legislature could not deprive the applicants of their property for the benefit of the State without making provision for them to be adequately compensated. In the present case the applicants evidently did not receive any compensation at all, however.[86]

This passage does not explain why the Court did not treat this case in the same way as *National & Provincial*. Indeed, *Jahn* seems an even stronger case for denying compensation, as it was suggested that the applicants had exploited a situation of administrative confusion and incompetence, whereas the applicants in *National & Provincial* had lawfully exploited a loophole in the written law. Nevertheless, the Court rejected the suggestion that the manner of acquisition can affect the fair balance:

> The Court cannot, however, agree with the Government's reasoning in the instant case regarding the concept of 'illegitimate' ownership, which is an eminently political concept. As the Court has already stated above, regardless of the applicants' situation before the entry into force of the Modrow Law, there is no doubt that they legally acquired full ownership of their land when that Law came into force.[87]

In this passage, the Court seems to deny the arguments underpinning *National & Provincial*, and even *James* itself.[88] Moreover, the reasoning is inconsistent with that in *Zvolsky and Zvolská v The Czech Republic*[89] and *Pincová and Pinc v The Czech Republic*,[90] both of which concerned individuals who had acquired land in Czechoslovakia during the socialist era. After the change in government, the Czech Republic enacted laws allowing many of those who had lost land in the socialist era to obtain its restitution, even from private individuals. In *Zvolsky*, the courts rescinded the original transaction by which the applicants had obtained the property, even though it appeared that the former owners had consented to the transaction and received a fair payment under it. In *Pincová*, the applicants had acquired the land from a State enterprise, in good faith and without knowledge of the manner in which the land had been

---

[86] Above [91].
[87] Above [90].
[88] See also *Forrer–Niedenthal v Germany*, Appl No 47316/99, 20 February 2003.
[89] Reports 2002–IX 163.
[90] Appl No 36548/97, 5 November 2002.

taken from its original owner. While the law allowed the applicants to recover the price they paid for the property, with further allowances for the maintenance of the property during their occupation, the amount fell far below the market value of the land at the time the restitution orders took effect. Hence, it fell to the Czech government to justify its position.

In these cases, the Court accepted that the denial of market value compensation could be fair if the current owner had acquired property in questionable circumstances. However, it was disproportionate not to consider the specific facts of each case, as the Court concluded had happened in these two cases. Indeed, it appears that the Czech courts did review the manner in which each applicant had acquired its property; nevertheless, the Court still felt that the Czech Republic had not clearly shown that compensation should fall so far short of the ordinary standard.

In comparison with *Jahn*, the judgments in *Pincová* and *Zvolsky* confirm that compensation may be denied where the circumstances of the acquisition cast doubt on the applicant's moral entitlement to the property. Moreover, the judgments also confirm that it should not be readily assumed that the circumstances are exceptional. However, contrary to *Jahn*, it seems that the Court has accepted an idea of 'illegitimate' ownership, although it has not put it in such terms. Hence, it is uncertain whether *Jahn* has any significance beyond its facts, especially since the majority left the issue of just satisfaction for resolution at a later date.[91] In a separate judgment, Judge Cabral Barreto stated that the finding of a violation was sufficient to provide just satisfaction. Perhaps the majority will ultimately decide that just satisfaction does not require an award that would reflect the value of the lost property (as in *Former King of Greece v Greece*, below). Until then, however, the judgment on the merits casts some doubt on the relevance of the moral entitlement to compensation and the fair balance.

The source of funds for acquisition

A related consideration concerns the source of funds used to acquire property. While *James* was concerned with an expropriation by private persons, similar issues concerning the source of the value arises in cases involving expropriation by a public body. This point has not been clearly resolved.[92] In *Holy Monasteries v Greece*,[93] Greece argued that land held by monasteries had a

[91] Note that the passage quoted above (n 86) emphasises the lack of *any* compensation, which suggests that the Court left open the possibility that something less than full value may be awarded.

[92] In *Stran Greek Refineries v Greece*, Series A No 301-B (1995) 19 EHRR 293, Greece argued that, since the applicant had acquired possessions from the former military regime, it was legitimate for the new regime to deprive him of those possessions without compensation. The Court held for the applicant, but on the grounds that the possessions in question had in fact been acquired after the military regime had fallen.

[93] Series A No 301-A (1995) 20 EHRR 1.

public character, and therefore the fair balance did not require it to pay full compensation for it. This was accepted by the Commission, as it stated that exceptional circumstances can justify a departure from full compensation. In this case, it considered how the monasteries had acquired and used the property, and their dependence on the Greek Church and the State. The Commission's decision was overturned by the Court, but with very little discussion. The Court merely observed that the monasteries had been compensated for property nationalised as recently at 1952. However, as the Court noted, the compensation paid in 1952 amounted to only one-third of the value of the land. Whether this meant that it would have been legitimate to pay only one-third in 1987 was not explained. Nevertheless, it suggests that there is a possibility of recovering public investment, or otherwise taking a public aspect of the value into account, when settling compensation terms.

The issue of State contributions was addressed once more in the *Former King of Greece v Greece*,[94] which concerned the claims of the former King and members of his family regarding several large estates which had been expropriated without compensation. Greece argued that no P1(1) issue arose, because the land was held by the royal family in its public capacity: in effect, the land was already public property, and P1(1) only applies to private property. As explained in chapter 2,[95] the European Court did not accept this argument, partly because at least some of the land had been acquired by the ancestors of the former King through the ordinary private law processes, and partly because the previous dealings between the State and the royal family had been conducted on the basis that the land was held privately. In any event, Greece also argued that it was not under a duty to compensate the applicants because of the manner in which the land had been acquired and maintained. For example, Greece claimed that much of the land had been donated to the applicants' ancestors by the State, and that the estates were subsequently maintained at State expense. Moreover, the royal family had enjoyed special tax exemptions and other advantages. These benefits, it was argued, exceeded the current value of the property: hence, there was no entitlement to any compensation. While the applicants questioned whether the State support had been as significant as Greece claimed, they also argued that the manner of acquisition and the availability of tax privileges had no relevance to the issue of proportionality and compensation.

While this case plainly concerns a unique situation, the general issue of State contributions and support arises in many contexts. The expropriation of the property of companies, such as the privatised utilities, that have benefited from subsidies (direct or indirect), tax advantages, or other support involves such questions. Hence, the case is of broader interest than the facts might suggest.

The proceedings in *The Former King of Greece* ultimately led to two separate judgments. In its judgment on the merits, the Court found that the lack of com-

---

[94] Reports 2000–XII 119 (2001) 33 EHRR 21 (merits), (2003) 36 EHRR CD43 (just satisfaction).
[95] See Chapter 2, 69.

pensation made the expropriation disproportionate. Subsequently, the parties failed to reach a settlement, and then, in the just satisfaction judgment, Court then found that the Greece should pay a total of €13.2 million in pecuniary damages to the former King and his family. In both judgments, the Court rejected Greece's argument that the manner of acquisition and subsequent State support made it unnecessary to compensate the applicants, but without making its reasons entirely clear.

In its judgment on the merits, the Court began by observing that 'at least part of the expropriated property was purchased by the applicants' predecessors in title and paid out of their private funds.'[96] This suggests that a State contribution to value would have been relevant, but perhaps that such a contribution had not been proven. However, the Court then referred to an expropriation of royal estates which had occurred in 1973: since compensation had been paid for that expropriation, it followed that the 'applicants had a legitimate expectation to be compensated by the Greek legislature for the taking of their estates.'[97] This suggests that the existence of contributions or other support is not relevant, as long as an expectation of compensation had been established by past practice.[98] Finally, the Court stated that:

> The privileges afforded in the past to the royal family or the tax exemptions and the writing off of all the taxes owed by the former royal family have no direct relevance to the issue of proportionality, but could possibly be taken into account in order to make an accurate assessment of the applicants' claims for just satisfaction under Article 41 of the Convention.[99]

In the just satisfaction judgment, the Court stated that, assuming that Greece would not restore the property to the applicants, it would be 'appropriate to fix a lump sum based, as far as possible, on an amount "reasonably related" to the value of the property taken, i.e. an amount which the Court would have found acceptable under Article 1 of Protocol No. 1, had the Greek State compensated the applicants.'[100] The Court now referred to *James*, and stated that although this case was not framed in terms of social justice, 'less than full compensation may be equally, if not a fortiori, called for where the taking of property is resorted to with a view to completing "such fundamental changes of a country's constitutional system as the transition from monarchy to republic" '.[101] It referred to the passage quoted above, but now said that 'the manner of acquisition of the

---

[96]   (2001) 33 EHRR 21 [98].

[97]   Above.

[98]   This point is not persuasive, as the payment of compensation may have (and probably was) part of a political settlement, rather than an acknowledgement of a duty to compensate.

[99]   31 EHRR 21 [98].

[100]   (2003) 36 EHRR CD43 [79]: 'the Court deems it appropriate to fix a lump sum based, as far as possible, on an amount "reasonably related" to the value of the property taken, ie an amount which the Court would have found acceptable under Art 1 of Protocol No 1, had the Greek State compensated the applicants.'

[101]   Above [78] (the reference is to para 87 of the principal judgment); see also *Broniowski v Poland*, Appl No 31443/96, 22 June 2004 (Grand Chamber) [149].

properties cannot deprive the first applicant of his *right* to compensation; it may, though, be taken into account for the determination of the *level* of compensation.'[102] It followed that the Court would adjust the amount of pecuniary damage downwards 'in view of the privileges and other benefits awarded in the past to the properties in question.'[103] This seems to contradict the passage quoted above, as the Court had made it clear that these privileges and benefits 'have no direct relevance to the issue of proportionality'. Nevertheless, the effect on the outcome was significant, as the amount awarded by the Court was far less than the amount claimed by the applicants. The Greek Government's own valuation of the property was in excess of €70 million, and this excluded part of the 'Tatoi' estate, which Court had found belonged to the applicant: had this been included, the Government's own valuation would have produced a figure of over €200 million. In the end, however, the award of €13.2 million was determined on an 'equitable basis', without real indication of its relationship to the value of the property or the events prior to the expropriation.

Plainly, it would have been helpful if the Court had explained in some detail how it arrived at the figure of €13.2 million, particularly in relation to the question of the source of value. It seems safe, however, to conclude that States may adjust compensation to reflect value that has accrued as a result of public support. How far the State is free to do so remains uncertain.

Administrative complexity and legal certainty

In the cases cited above, the Court also accepted that the scale and complexity of the legislative scheme may justify a variation of the ordinary principles. Hence, in *Lithgow*, the Court stated that the valuation of the company shares did not need to consider the book values of the company's assets, since the investigation into the value of each asset would have been too costly and time-consuming.[104] Similarly, in *James*, where some applicants argued that there should have been independent consideration of the reasonableness of each proposed enfranchisement, the Government pointed out that it had not provided for such consideration to avoid 'the uncertainty, litigation, expense and delay that would inevitably be caused for both tenants and landlords under a scheme of individual examination of each of many thousands of cases.'[105] This was accepted by the Court as a legitimate reason for reducing the level of scrutiny in individual cases.

---

[102] Above [85] (emphasis added).

[103] Above [96]; see also [98]: 'in order to make an accurate assessment of the applicants' claims for just satisfaction, the Court cannot ignore the special circumstances surrounding the abolition of the monarchy'.

[104] *Lithgow* (n 8) [125]ff.

[105] *James* (n 11) [68].

In such cases, the need to achieve a degree of certainty outweighs the need to ensure that every victim is treated with an equal degree of fairness. In effect, by accepting that a scheme of broad application does serve the public interest, the Court must also accept that the risk that requiring States to achieve perfect fairness in each case would frustrate the objects of the scheme. This point also arises in a different context, where there is a strong public interest in ensuring legal certainty and stability in a period following a radical transformation of the economic or political system. It is not clear, however, how far such transformations may justify the taking of property without full compensation. For example, in *Jahn*, the Court recognised that the public interest in regularising land titles in the former GDR could justify interferences with possessions; however, it seems that the Court doubted that the reversal of the some of the effects of the Modrow Law was an appropriate way to achieve this. Similarly, in *Broniowski v Poland*,[106] where the Court also recognised that the need for stability and certainty may justify some modification of entitlements, it was also reluctant to it to become an excuse for a wholesale re-adjustment of existing expectations.

Browniowski concerned guarantees given to people who had been displaced from the former Soviet Union to Poland at the end of World War II. Poland promised to provide them with either land or compensation, and then periodically re-affirmed the promise throughout the socialist period and after. Over this period, some claims were satisfied, others were paid in part, and still others never received anything.

However, the land originally set aside for the claimants was exhausted; while some monetary compensation was provided, many claimants received almost nothing. The potential expense of satisfying all the outstanding claims was so great that the legislature decided to pay only a proportionate amount of some claims and to cancel the rest. Those claimants who had never had any compensation would receive 15% of the value of their claim; those who had received some compensation would not receive anything further. For example, in *Broniowski*, the applicant had only received about 2% of the value of his claim when it was extinguished, and his position was not unusual: as the Court estimated that there were another 80,000 or so claimants in a similar position.

The Court recapitulated the principle that there could be no guarantee of full compensation, and the State had a wide margin of appreciation 'in situations such as the one in the present case, involving a wide-reaching but controversial legislative scheme with significant economic impact for the country as a whole'.[107] However, it did not suggest that no compensation could be provided: while 'The choice of measures may necessarily involve decisions restricting compensation for the taking or restitution of property to a level below its market value',[108] it is still the case that compensation should be 'reasonably related'

---

[106] *Broniowski* (n 101).
[107] Above [182].
[108] Above.

to the value of the property. The Court would not say precisely how far compensation could fall below market values, but given that the applicant had only received 2% of the amount due, the interference with his possessions was disproportionate. There was a suggestion, however, that it would be legitimate to limit compensation to the 15% to be paid to those who had previously received nothing. There were other factors as well: concern that the administration of the claims had not always met the requirements of the rule of law; and that the criteria for extinguishing without any compensation seemed arbitrary.[109] Consequently, it is difficult to draw out principles that would be relevant in other cases.

Concluding comments

The case law gives us very little indication on the scope for arguing that special circumstances justify a departure from the ordinary principles. Moreover, the uncertainty is exacerbated by the two judgments in *Former King of Greece*, as it seems that the factors that would be relevant to the merits of the case (and specifically to the fair balance and compensation) may still prove to be important in the just satisfaction proceedings. Arguably, these cases simply represent ad hoc responses in cases of particular sensitivity, in which the Court takes a prudential line that avoids controversy.

In addition, it is impossible to identify general principles on the extent to which special circumstances justify a departure from ordinary principles of valuation. Since the Court has accepted the possibility that a deprivation of property need not be accompanied by any compensation at all, in principle it should be possible to base compensation on some factor other than the value of the property. In practice, however, the Court has yet to sanction a deprivation accompanied by compensation that has no relationship with the value of the property.[110] While it might be argued that the just satisfaction judgment in *Former King of Greece* suggest that the connection with the value of the property may be very weak, the *Broniowski* reasoning suggests that compensation must be based on the value of property, even though it need not be the full value. Similarly, in *James* and *Lithgow*, the compensation bore some relationship with the value of the property: the existence of special circumstances meant only that valuation could ignore some factors that would otherwise be relevant. In addition, in *James*, the

---

[109] Those who had never received anything would be entitled to compensation for 15% of the value of their claims; but those who had received something would get nothing more, even if (like the applicant) they had received far less than 15%.

[110] Whether it would be properly described as compensation is questionable, but the point is that it would preserve the fair balance: see eg *Hentrich* (n 23); and *Pincová* (n 23), where violations were found because compensation had been based on the price paid by the buyer (although these cases were not treated as raising special circumstances).

exclusion of those factors was tied directly to the special circumstances: that is, the tenants' moral entitlement to the buildings would not have justified a departure from the ordinary principles relating to the valuation of the land.

DELAYS IN THE PAYMENT OF COMPENSATION

Complaints regarding delays are often made in relation to both Article 6 and P1(1), and the same facts may represent violations of both.[111] However, under Article 6, the Court asks whether the proceedings exceed a reasonable time, whereas under P1(1), the length of proceedings is one of the many factors relevant to determining whether a fair balance has been maintained.[112] In *Guillemin v France*, in relation to Article 6 and compensation delays, the Court has stated that 'The reasonableness of the length of proceedings must be assessed in the light of the particular circumstances of the case'.[113] This calls for an overall assessment of the reasons for the delay, including the complexity of the case and the conduct of the applicant and of the relevant authorities. In relation to P1(1), the Court categorically stated that 'Compensation for the loss sustained by the applicant can only constitute adequate reparation where it also takes into account the damage arising from the length of the deprivation. It must moreover be paid within a reasonable time.'[114] Consequently, excessive delay in the payment of compensation may upset the fair balance, even where the original assessment of compensation was appropriate.

The effect of a delay is particularly significant during inflationary periods, or where any interest that is paid is well below the ordinary market rates. In *Akkuş v Turkey*, the Court found that a delay in payment of only 17 months upset the fair balance, in part because interest accrued at 30% annually over this period while inflation was up to 70% annually.[115] Similar conclusions have been reached in the substantial number of cases from Turkey concerning delays in compensation payments,[116] as well as cases involving other States.[117]

However, the relevance of inflationary loss is not entirely clear. In a dissenting opinion in *Akkuş*, Judge Vilhjálmsson[118] argued that P1(1) cannot establish

---

[111] *Erkner and Hofauer v Austria*, Series A No 117 (1987) 9 EHRR 464 [76]: 'one and the same fact may fall foul of more than one provision of the Convention and Protocols'; see also *Poiss v Austria*, Series A No 117 (1988) 10 EHRR 231 [66].

[112] *Erkner* above; *Poiss* above.

[113] *Guillemin v France*, Reports 1997–I 149 (1998) 25 EHRR 435 [38].

[114] Above [54].

[115] Reports 1997–IV 1300 (2000) 30 EHRR 365.

[116] See *Aka v Turkey*, Reports 1998–VI 2668 (2001) 33 EHRR 27; *Kayihan v Turkey*, Appl No 42124/98, 8 April 2004; *Dönmez v Turkey*, Appl No 48990/99, 29 April 2004; *Koçak v Turkey* Appl No 42432/98, 19 May 2004; and *Cibir v Turkey*, Appl No 49659/99, 19 May 2004.

[117] See eg *Sporrong* (n 10); *Almeida Garrett* (n 73); *Satka v Greece*, Appl No 55828/00, 27 March 2003; *Jorge Nina Jorge v Portugal*, Appl No 52662/99, 19 February 2004; *Mora do Vale v Portugal*, Appl No 53468/99, 29 July 2004.

[118] Joined by Judge Mifsud Bonnici.

a claim to be insulated from the effects of inflation. During a period of inflation, many individuals suffer financially (such as those living on unindexed State benefits), and yet it would go too far to read P1(1) as providing some kind of general protection against inflation (or other losses arising from general economic conditions). This view did not command the majority in *Akkuş*, and it is consistent with the reasoning in *Lithgow*. The hypothetical share price was determined over the Reference Period, which ended several years before the vesting day. Since the 1970s were a period was one of unusually high inflation, the value of the compensation was steadily eroded from the end of the Reference Period to vesting and thereafter. Nevertheless, the Court did not find this disproportionate, for a number of reasons. First, the impact of inflation was mitigated by the payment of interest, and advance payments of compensation were made in some cases.[119] Second, the Court found that the choice of the Reference Period was reasonable, as the Government wished to avoid the potential distortion in the market that would have been caused by the announcement of its intention to acquire the shares. Accordingly, since the intention to nationalise had been announced in the Labour Party's election manifesto, the reference period ended on the date of the election: 'the date on which the prospect of nationalisation became a reality'.[120] As a general principle, the Court did not accept that taking and valuation had to be simultaneous, and the choice of the date of valuation fell within the margin of appreciation.[121] Nevertheless, there seems to be no compelling reason to allow the United Kingdom to ignore the impact of economic conditions from the end of the Reference Period to the Vesting Day. The Court simply accepted the United Kingdom's argument that the fixing of the share prices (or hypothetical share prices, in the applicants' case) could have benefited either side: that is, if either share prices or the retail price index had dropped, the shareholders would have benefited. In fact, however, Parliament always retained the power to modify the compensation terms. Indeed, it withdrew from nationalising one company that became insolvent between the Reference Period and the Vesting Day. Moreover, the rule was set with hindsight: when the legislation was passed, it was already known that the fixing of the price at the Reference Period would work to the Treasury's advantage.

THE VALUATION PROCESS

The primary concern of the European Court has been to see that the valuation process is not subject to the acquiring authority's control. Since valuation

---

[119] Shareholders were entitled to continue to receive dividends until vesting, although the legislation restricted dividend payments so as to safeguard company assets before vesting. After vesting, compensation attracted interest, at rates set by the Treasury, until payment.

[120] *Lithgow* (n 8) [132].

[121] Above [134].

determines a civil right, the process must satisfy the minimum requirements of Article 6. However, *Alconbury*[122] confirms the valuation itself need not be carried out by a court, if judicial review of the valuation process is available. *Alconbury* is discussed in more detail in chapter 7,[123] but in connection with compensation it is worth mentioning *Håkansson and Sturesson v Sweden*.[124] The applicants bought land at auction, but in the knowledge that they could be forced to sell the land at a public auction if they did not obtain certain permits from the County Agricultural Board. The Board refused the permits, so the auction went ahead.[125] Auctions were subject to a estimated minimum 'market price' which, at the applicants' request, the Board appointed two special valuers to set. The valuers were required to act in consultation with the Board, and it turned out that the Board put in the only bid at the auction. While this may raise suspicions of bias, the Court stated simply that there was 'no reason to doubt the impartiality of the two special valuers who made the final estimate',[126] and that there was 'no substantiated allegation that the valuation, or any other decision regarding the 1985 auction, was not in accordance with the [relevant legislation]'.[127] From this, it followed that the valuation must have been 'reasonably related to the value' of the property.[128] Moreover, there was no violation in respect of the manner of the valuation. While this may appear very favourable to the State, the valuation merely set a minimum price. There was an open auction, and it may have been this factor that persuaded the Court that the price was not unfair under P1(1). Moreover, there was a right of appeal to a court, which was exercised in this case. Hence, there was no violation of Article 6.

CONCLUSIONS

The compensation standard of P1(1) has developed with very little consideration of the specific values of human rights law, as the European Court of Human Rights seems to have been borrowed from national and international rules without examining whether they were intended to reflect the values of human autonomy and dignity that are central to human rights. It seems that the flexibility is at least partly attributable to the failure in 1950 to reach agreement on

---

[122] *Alconbury* [2003] 2 AC 295.

[123] Below, 206–10.

[124] Håkansson (n 27).

[125] There was a separate issue whether officials of the CAB had promised that the permits would be granted, and whether any such promises would have legal effect: this was resolved against the applicant.

[126] *Håkansson* (n 27) [49] (although this related to legality).

[127] Above [54].

[128] Above [53]–[55]. While the Court did conclude that there had been a violation of Art 6, this was in relation to the refusal to grant the permit and not the valuation. Swedish law provided a right of appeal to the courts for all issues relating to the compulsory sale, and an appeal by the applicant was dismissed. There was some doubt whether the appeal was public, but the Court decided that the applicant had waived his right to a public hearing.

principles of compensation, as the Court has doubted the scope of its own role in subjecting compensation terms to a close review. Consequently, there is a high degree of flexibility, both in relation to the principle that the fair balance requires nothing more than compensation that is reasonably related to the value of the property (with departures permitted in exceptional cases) and in relation to the willingness of the Court to extend the margin of appreciation in determining the terms on which compensation will be granted. In practice, a property owner would only be confident that a human rights challenge would have a chance of success in two circumstances: (1) where it is apparent on the face of the national principles on compensation reveal that there is no relationship between the amount of the payment and the property's value (however defined), and (2) where the national principles are consistent with the principle set out by the Court, but in application it is clear that the specific rules by which compensation is determined produce payments that bear little or no relationship with the value of the property.

7

Controls on the Use of Land

———⋙⋄⋘———

REGULATING THE USE of land has become an important function of modern government. Planning controls, environmental restrictions, and heritage and scientific designations are obvious examples of controls on the use of land; others include rent controls and the opening of private land to public access. Under the standard analysis, the imposition and enforcement of all controls on the use of land falls under the third sentence of Article 1 of Protocol No 1 (P1(1). When P1(1) was drafted, it was thought that the third sentence would insulate regulatory laws from judicial scrutiny, except on the grounds of legality and possibly rationality.[1] However, with the judgment in *Sporrong v Sweden*,[2] it became clear that the limitations in the third sentence were subject to the general principle of the fair balance. It therefore appeared at least possible that the State's power to impose and enforce controls on the use of property could be subject to substantive limits.

Three different situations involving controls over land use are considered in this chapter. The first arises where a landowner claims that restrictions on its use of land violate its rights under P1(1). Such cases are commonly seen as involving a conflict between the public and private interests, and the owner's argument begins from the premise that the rights of ownership include an unrestricted right to use and develop the land in any way he or she sees fit, and hence anything that restricts the use of land is necessarily an interference with possessions. There is, of course, an alternative conception of land that does not accord the owner such absolute rights of use: if the courts accepted this conception in human rights law, it would mean that at least some forms of regulation would not be regarded as P1(1) interferences with possessions.[3] This argument was made in *Frascino v Italy*,[4] where Italy claimed that the ownership of land did not include an absolute right to build upon it. In English law, landowners do not have an unrestricted right to develop land without planning permission, and

---

[1] See the discussion of *Handyside v The United Kingdom*, Series A No 24 (1979–80) 1 EHRR 737, Chapter 4, 119.

[2] Series A No 52 (1983) 5 EHRR 35.

[3] See S Coyle and K Morrow, *The Philosophical Foundations of Environmental Law: Property, Rights and Nature* (Hart Publishing, Oxford, 2004) for the historical development of the dominant view.

[4] Appl no 35227/97, 11 December 2003.

hence it might also be argued that a specific denial of permission does not interfere with property in land.[5] However, in *Frascino v Italy*, the European Court held (with very little discussion) that P1(1) was applicable, thereby leaving the question of compatibility to be resolved by the application of the fair balance test.[6]

The second type of case concerns the right of one person to control the use of land belonging to others. Traditionally, private law provided the power to exercise such control, but with the increasing use of statutes that grant powers and impose duties on statutory undertakers, Parliament and the courts began to restrict the scope of nuisance and other common law actions. This raises issues for human rights law, at least in circumstances where property owners are left with no legal means for protecting their property from damage caused by third parties. More recently, with privatisation of the utilities, there has been an emphasis on the use of regulatory systems for controlling all claims relating to damage to land. As discussed below, such systems often require all private claims to be channelled through a regulatory body, which (ideally) then considers the best means of satisfying the claim in the light of the potential impact on the full range of competing interests that would be affected by satisfying it. The possibility that individuals may bypass the regulatory system by appealing directly to the courts may therefore have an unpredictable and potentially destabilising impact on the regulatory process. Nevertheless, it is necessary to ask whether the process of regulatory control over such claims complies with P1(1), especially where the regulatory response does not provide any substantive satisfaction to the complainant.

Finally, the chapter closes with a brief examination of an issue relating to the social function of property rights. In several cases, individuals have argued that the exercise of their human rights entitles them to obtain access to land belonging to others. There has been some recognition of similar rights under the common law[7] and modern statutory law.[8] In the United States, similar claims under the Bill of Rights have had limited success,[9] but the courts in England and Strasbourg have been more conservative. While P1(1) does not prevent States from legislating to require access to land, it appears that is no general Convention obligation to do so.

---

[5] Town and Country Planning Act 1990, s 57(1).

[6] *Frascino* (n 4); *cf ISKCON v The United Kingdom* (1994) 18 EHRR CD 133, where the Commission expressed some doubt that the enforcement of planning restrictions that were in place when property was acquired was an interference, but assumed that it was.

[7] *Constantine v Imperial Hotels Ltd* [1944] KB 693.

[8] See the Race Relations Act 1976, Part III (see especially ss 20–24); Sex Discrimination Act 1975, Part III (see especially ss 29–32); Disability Discrimination Act 1995, Part III (see especially ss 19–21, and *Manchester City Council v Romano* [2004] 4 All ER 21).

[9] See eg *Pruneyard Shopping Center v Robins* 447 US 74 (1980).

CONTROLS ON THE USE OF ONE'S OWN LAND

Where the complaint relates to the substantive nature of the regulatory controls, rather than the process of their imposition or enforcement, the focus is usually on proportionality: is the impact so severe that it cannot be justified? Put differently, is the interference unfair in the absence of some counter-balancing advantage, such as monetary compensation?[10] In practice, the courts are likely to answer this question in the negative. As explained in the Chapter 4, compensation is generally required for a Rule 2 deprivation of possessions, but not for a Rule 3 control on the use of property. A Rule 2 deprivation normally involves a transfer or vesting of the owner's full interest in the property, but as it applies to both de jure and de facto deprivations of possessions, some regulatory measures may be treated as deprivations. However, the Court's conception of a de facto deprivation is a narrow one: it would not include regulatory controls on land use unless they have the effect of allowing a public authority to assume the position of owner.[11] Even in *Fredin v Sweden*, where the cancellation of a permit to exploit a gravel pit left the applicant's land with practically no other economic use, the Court held that there had been no deprivation of possessions because the gravel pit was part of a larger landholding that still had valuable use.[12]

While there is a general principle that compensation is required for a Rule 2 deprivation, the Court has not ruled out the possibility that compensation may also necessary in other cases.[13] However, it is clear that regulations may have a very harsh impact without violating P1(1). In *Fredin*, *Pine Valley Developments v Ireland*,[14] *Mellacher v Austria*,[15] *ISKCON v The United Kingdom*,[16] and other cases,[17] the Court has refused to say that regulatory controls violated P1(1) solely on the basis that they were very restrictive or resulted in serious economic

---

[10] There may be issues concerning the legality of the interference: see eg *Frascino* (n 4).

[11] Chapter 4, 112–14.

[12] Series A No 192 (1991) 13 EHRR 784 [41]–[47]; see also *Trailer & Marina (Leven) Ltd; R (on the application of Trailer & Marina (Leven) Ltd) v Secretary of State for the Environment, Food and Rural Affairs* [2004] EWCA Civ 1580.

[13] See eg *Bramelid and Malmström v Sweden* (1982) 5 EHRR 249 (Comm); *Erkner and Hofauer v Austria*, Series A No 117 (1987) 9 EHRR 464; *Poiss v Austria*, Series A No 117 (1988) 10 EHRR 231; *Prötsch v Austria*, Reports 1996–V 1812 (2001) 32 EHRR 12; *Iatridis v Greece*, Reports 1999–II 75 (2000) 30 EHRR 97; *Chassagnou v France*, Reports 1999–III 21 (2000) 29 EHRR 615.

[14] Series A No 222 (1992) 14 EHRR 319 (withdrawal of planning permission; note that, although there was no breach of P1(1), there was a breach of Art 14 in combination with P1(1)). See also *Goletto v France*, Appl No 54596/00, 12 March 2002; *Steck–Risch v Liechtenstein*, Appl No 63151/00, 10 October 2002; *Orion Breclav SRO v The Czech Republic*, Appl No 43783/98, 13 January 2004; *Haider v Austria*, Appl No 63413/00, 29 January 2004.

[15] Series A No 169 (1990) 12 EHRR 391 (rent controls; see also *Spath Holme Ltd v The United Kingdom*, Appl No 78031/01, 14 May 2002 and *R v Secretary of State for the Environment, Transport and the Regions ex parte Spath Holme Ltd* [2001] 2 AC 349).

[16] *ISKCON* (n 6).

[17] *Cooperativa La Laurentina v Italy*, Appl No 23529/94, 2 August 2001; *Majorana v Italy*, Appl No 75117/01, 3 June 2004.

loss.[18] The position is therefore that, although the European Court has stated that the fair balance may require compensation in some regulatory cases, there are no cases where it has done so solely on the basis that the economic loss is too severe.[19] This should not be surprising, as it reflects the position under the constitutional laws of most States.[20] It is clear that the Court has been reluctant to impose substantive limits on regulatory powers in the absence a similar consitutional rule emerging from State practice. Nevertheless, it may seem odd that the Court would normally find that the fair balance is upset if compensation were not paid for the expropriation of land only worth 10% of the value of the entire plot, and yet it would not expect compensation to be paid if regulatory controls reduced the value of the land by 90%.[21]

It is therefore worth asking whether the cases reveal a principled basis for this distinction between deprivations and regulations, other than the desire not to move further than national law. Several possibilities can be suggested and dismissed. First, in some cases, the Court has explained its decision by reference to the margin of appreciation,[22] which suggests that it doubts that it is better-placed that the national authorities to judge the factors affecting the fairness of regulatory decisions.[23] The Court has made this point in several ways, but none of them are convincing. First, while it is understandable that deference is shown in respect of the decision to regulate, it is not so clear that an equally high degree of deference should be shown in respect of the balance struck between the interests: in other words, the decision to regulate can be separated from the decision to compensate, and the degree of deference shown in respect of each decision should not necessarily be the same. This is the approach with deprivations of possessions: while the European Court has allowed States a wide margin of appreciation in relation to the decision to expropriate, it often narrows the margin in relation to the decision to compensate and the terms on which compensation is paid.[24]

Secondly, the distinction does not depend on the difficulty of ascertaining the victim's loss. That is, it might be argued that compensation is normally required for a deprivation because the loss is easier to calculate than it is with regulatory losses, but even if this were true in many cases, it is not true in every case. If the

---

[18] See Chapter 5, 151–54.

[19] Note that in *Cooperativa La Laurentina* (n 17), the Court considered it relevant to the assessment of the impact of a planning restriction that the applicant could have negotiated a development agreement with the local authority.

[20] See generally AJ van der Walt, *Constitutional Property Clauses: A Comparative Analysis* (Juta, Cape Town, 1999).

[21] As in *Pine Valley* (n 14).

[22] *Mellacher* (n 15) [45]–[57]. See also, in relation to Art 8: *Buckley v The United Kingdom* (1997) 23 EHRR 101 [75]; and *Chapman v The United Kingdom* (2001) 33 EHRR 18 [92].

[23] This is also reflected in the breadth of the area of discretion accorded to the executive and legislature by UK courts in regulatory matters.

[24] See *Katikaridis v Greece*, Reports 1996–V 1673 (2001) 32 EHRR 6; *Tsomtsos v Greece*, Reports 1996–V 1699; *Papachelas v Greece*, Reports 1999–II 1 (2000) 30 EHRR 923; see also *Serghides v Cyprus* (2003) 37 EHRR 44.

difficulty of ascertaining loss were the reason for the distinction, we would expect to see at least some cases where the Court would say that the regulatory loss is sufficiently ascertained that the State should have offered compensation to maintain the fair balance.

Finally, the scope of the margin of appreciation should not depend solely on the formal distinction between the taking of a full bundle of rights and the restrictions on the exercise of specific rights in that bundle. Since the fair balance applies to both deprivations and regulations, and since the usual measure of the impact is economic, any formal distinctions that can be made do not explain the differences in the application of the fair balance.

Underlying these invocations of the margin of appreciation there is, however, a more defensible concern relating to the breadth of the losses suffered. Regulations tend to affect broad classes of individuals, unlike the typical expropriation. In most situations, the funds for compensation would need to be raised from taxation, and there is no guarantee that the courts would be able to formulate or implement a set of human rights principles on the incidence of taxation that would be fairer than the allocation of loss that results from the current principles. That is, the spreading of the loss works in the typical expropriation, but there is no guarantee that it would work with the typical regulation. Hence, the distinction may reflect the Court's desire to put a clear limit on the types of recoverable losses arising from the exercise of State power. From its point of view, it is appropriate to leave it to States to determine when regulation is necessary and when compensation will be provided. Similarly, from the point of view of the courts in the United Kingdom, it is also appropriate to leave this to the executive and legislature.

In some cases, the Court has not invoked the margin of appreciation, but has simply concluded that the regulations do not have a disproportionate impact on the victim. This can be seen in a number of cases relating to land use controls. For example, in *Pine Valley*[25] and *ISKCON*,[26] the Court stated that the annulment of planning permission fell within the category of risks that the applicants had accepted as part of running a business. In some other cases, courts have found that the burden is not excessive, given the impact of the regulatory scheme as a whole. For example, in *Marcic v Thames Water Utilities Ltd*,[27] the House of Lords found that repeated flooding of the claimant's land was an interference with P1(1), but the balance struck under the relevant legislation was not unfair when consideration was given to the full range of interests affected by the regulatory scheme and the remedies available to the victim under the scheme.

To these general observations, several exceptions should be noted. The first relates to the requirement of legality. There are a handful of cases where controls have been imposed or continued without any apparent regard for procedures

[25] Eg *Pine Valley* (n 14).
[26] *ISKCON* (n 6).
[27] [2004] 2 AC 42.

imposed by national law. The most serious cases involve administrative inaction in the face of clear judicial orders.[28] In these cases, the breakdown in the rule of law has lead the European Court to conclude that P1(1) has been violated, although the controls would probably not have been considered disproportionate if the legal process had been properly observed. However, it is unusual to find such clear threats to the rule of law: in most cases concerning regulatory controls on land use, the substantive issues tend to be presented in terms of conflicting interests, with the public interest pitted against private property rights, with the usual outcome in favour of the public interest.

The second concerns complaints that are not related to the loss in economic value caused by the controls. *Chassagnou v France*[29] is the leading example, as the applicants objected to regulations that required them to allow access to their land for hunting on ethical grounds, rather than economic grounds. The Court concluded that the fair balance had been upset, but in doing so, it took the unusual course of assessing the impact with a view to the personal characteristics of the owners. However, it is not unique: in *Chapman v The United Kingdom*, the Court has said that regulatory controls should take into account the traditions of the members of a minority with a lifestyle different from that of the majority of a society.[30] Nevertheless, where the landowner's real objection is cast in economic terms, it seems that only the uncompensated appropriation of all value (as seen in de facto deprivation) is likely to upset the fair balance.

The third exception relates to the process by which the regulatory balance has been struck by domestic decision-makers. This is apparent in *Hatton v The United Kingdom*,[31] which concerned Article 8 applications regarding the decision of the Secretary of State for Transport to move to a system of noise quotas for regulating night flying at Heathrow airport. In 2001, the Third Section held

---

[28] See eg *Hornsby v Greece*, Reports 1997–II 495 (1997) 24 EHRR 250 (Art 6 only); *Antonetto v Italy*, Appl No 15918/89, 20 July 2000; *Fuchs v Poland*, Appl No 33870/96, 11 December 2001; *Frascino v Italy*, Appl No 35227/97, 11 December 2003; *Kurkchian and Kurkchian v Bulgaria*, Appl No 44626/98, 22 January 2004.

[29] Reports 1999–III 21 (2000) 29 EHRR 615.

[30] *Chapman* (n 22) [96]:

> although the fact of being a member of a minority with a traditional lifestyle different from that of the majority of a society does not confer an immunity from general laws intended to safeguard assets common to the whole society such as the environment, it may have an incidence on the manner in which such laws are to be implemented. As intimated in the *Buckley* judgment [cited above, n 22], the vulnerable position of gypsies as a minority means that some special consideration should be given to their needs and their different lifestyle both in the relevant regulatory planning framework and in arriving at the decisions in particular cases. To this extent there is thus a positive obligation imposed on the Contracting States by virtue of Art 8 to facilitate the gypsy way of life (citations omitted).

See also *Connors v The The United Kingdom*, Appl No 66746/01, 27 May 2004 [84]–[95]; for a UK authority, see *Wrexham County Borough Council v Berry* [2003] UKHL 26 and see J Maurici, 'Gypsy Planning Challenges in the High Court' [2004] *Journal of Planning Law* 1654.

[31] (2003) 37 EHRR 28 (Grand Chamber), (2002) 34 EHRR 1 (Third Section); and see also *Marcic v Thames Water Utilities Ltd* [2004] 2 AC 42 (discussed below, text accompanying n 81 ff).

that the process by which the decision had been reached was flawed because the Secretary of State had not gathered enough information to assess either the benefit to the general interest from night flights or the impact on individuals.[32] The case was then referred to the Grand Chamber, which accepted that 'a governmental decision-making process concerning complex issues of environmental and economic policy such as in the present case must necessarily involve appropriate investigations and studies in order to allow them to strike a fair balance between the various conflicting interests at stake.'[33] However, the Grand Chamber made it clear that national authorities are not debarred from making decisions in the absence of 'comprehensive and measurable data' on 'each and every aspect of the matter to be decided.'[34] In this case, the investigations of the impact and economic effect of night flying were sufficient, particularly since the quota system was periodically reviewed.

While *Hatton* opens door to arguments that the process of striking the balance has not sufficiently rigorous, it did not arise under P1(1). Moreover, it does not focus on the structural issues that might influence the level of scrutiny and the approach to the fair balance. This point has been made in relation to planning law in the United States, where commentators have often focused on the counter-majoritarian aspect of judicial review under the Bill of Rights.[35] It has been argued that judicial review is particularly valuable where there is a greater risk that democratic institutions may be dominated by specific interest groups, which then use their power to gain advantages at the expense of others. In relation to planning law in the United States, it is said that the risk is greatest at the local level.[36] The structure of local government varies from State to State, but in general, rules relating to the development of local neighbourhoods are set at the municipal level, with only a limited amount of control in the State or national authorities. Moreover, in some States, it is possible for neighbourhoods to secede from their municipalities, thereby allowing a local group to develop its own rules on property development. Consequently, there is a real risk that 'not-in-my-backyard' groups of landowners may control development by controlling local democratic power, and thereby capture additional value for their land while remaining accountable only to themselves. Put differently, the availability

---

[32] (2002) 34 EHRR 1 [102]–[103].

[33] (2003) 37 EHRR 28 [128].

[34] Above [128].

[35] AM Bickel, *The Least Dangerous Branch: The Supreme Court at the Bar of Politics* (Bobbs-Merrill, Indianapolis, 1962); H Wechsler, 'Toward Neutral Principles of Constitutional Law' (1959) 73 *Harvard Law Review* 1.

[36] See especially W Fischel, *Regulatory Takings: Law, Economics and Politics* (Harvard University Press, Cambridge, MA, 1995); *cf* C Rose, 'Takings, Federalism and Norms' (1996) 105 *Yale Law Journal* 1121. For background on zoning in the United States, see W Fischel, 'Zoning and Land Use Regulation' in B Bouckaert and G De Geest (eds), *Encyclopedia of Law and Economics*, ch 2200 (Elgar, Cheltenham, 1999) (online at <http://encyclo.findlaw.com/> and <http://allserv.rug.ac.be/~gdegeest/>) (see especially 407–8); for Europe and the United States, see MG Faure, 'Environmental Regulation' in B Bouckaert and G De Geest (eds), *Encyclopedia of Law and Economics*, ch 2300 (online at <http://encyclo.findlaw.com/> and <http://allserv.rug.ac.be/~gdegeest/>), 478–81.

of political power at the local level may indirectly allow some landowners to translate their private property rights into governing power, which is then used to protect and enhance the value of those private rights. Those without land, and those landowners whose interests put them in the minority, must look to the courts or other administrative or political processes to prevent the majorities from regulating in a way that indirectly appropriates the value of their property. By contrast, the risk of a capture of regulatory power is attenuated at the national level, as it is less likely that any groups with similar interests will be able to sustain control over national democratic institutions for an extended period. In effect, the ordinary political processes of the democratic state often provide the minority groups with the protection they need. The role of a constitutional bill of rights in such cases is therefore limited to more dramatic or serious cases, where, for example, there is an abuse of majoritarian government which cannot be left to be resolved by the ordinary give-and-take of the democratic process. This, of course, depends on the allocation of political power between local, regional and national bodies, but the point is that the securing of political power by a relatively small group may be easier at the local level than the regional or national level. Accordingly, it has been argued that there is greater need for an independent body to ensure that the local political process does not result in long-term exclusion from the benefits of government, especially when those benefits include the power to exercise compulsory powers over others. Hence, the impact on rights of property may be the same whether the source of the regulatory controls is local, State or national, but the opportunities available to individuals to protect those rights through the mechanisms of accountability or ordinary political processes may vary considerably. Accordingly, judicial review is more likely to be necessary in respect of decisions made at the local level.

In the member States of the Council of Europe, policy-making in planning and environmental matters is generally more centralised than it is in the United States.[37] However, to state the obvious, policy formation in some of European countries operates on a small scale, both in terms of the size of the population and the territory.[38] Moreover, the effectiveness of the judicial process varies considerably: indeed, some P1(1) cases concern repeated failures of local officials to comply with judgments of administrative courts.[39] Nevertheless, one can say that the degree of centralisation in many of the member States suggests that there may be less concern with majoritarian abuse at local level, and hence less reason to use judicial review as a means of controlling local democratic bodies. However, this must be counter-balanced against the possibility that there may be doubts concerning the effectiveness of democratic or legal mechanisms

---

[37] MA Heldeweg, RJGH Seerden and KR Deketelaere, 'Public Environmental Law in Europe: A Comparative Search for a *ius commune*' [2004] *European Environmental Law Review* 78.

[38] And conversely the EU policies are obviously set on a grander scale.

[39] *Frascino* (n 28) and *Antonetto* (n 28). See JM Sellers, 'Litigation as a Local Political Resource: Courts in Controversies over Land Use in France, Germany, and The United States' (1995) 29 *Law and Society Review* 475, for a detailed study of the role and effectiveness of litigation in land use.

for accountability in all situations. This suggests that the strengthening of judicial review, through human rights, may be desirable as a means of protecting those affected by planning decisions. Indeed, the European Court has done so, by emphasising the importance of the legality condition and the rule of law in cases where judgments of adminstrative courts are not implemented.

In the United Kingdom, the planning system is far more centralised than it is in the United States.[40] As a general principle, planning permission is required for any development of land. Applications for planning permission are made to development control authorities. These authorities are local, and applications submitted to them are decided either by elected councillors or local authority officers who are accountable to them. The local authorities also prepare local development schemes for consideration when determining applications. From this, it may appear that the local authorities have considerable power over the development of their areas. However, they are subject to fairly tight controls from the Secretary of State, who has extensive powers to control the content of local development schemes,[41] and hears appeals from a refusal to give planning permission.[42] There is also a power to 'call in' an application from a local authority for his/her own determination.[43] In general, the Secretary of State exercises this power for major or particularly sensitive developments, or developments where the local authority proposes to depart from its own plan. Finally, there are wide default powers to impose a particular course of action on a local planning authority.[44]

The Planning and Compulsory Purchase Act 2004 has brought some changes to this system, although the theme of centralisation has not changed.[45] Indeed, the Secretary of State's powers have not been significantly weakened, and there are still signs of caution in relation to the the democratisation of the planning process. For example, the Secretary of State may recognise Regional Planning Bodies (RPBs); once recognised, they will have responsibility for preparing statutory Regional Spatial Strategies (RSSs).[46] In the House of Lords, the Bill was amended by the inclusion of a clause that would have limited recognition to

---

[40] See Lord Hoffman's summary in *Alconbury*, [2003] 2 AC 295 [94]–[95], where he describes how the system has become more centralised over time.

[41] See eg Planning and Compulsory Purchase Act 2004, ss 10, 21, 27; and the Town and Country Planning Act 1990, ss 13(5), 17(1), 18(1), 33(5), 35(2), 35A(1), 40(6), 43(4) and 44(1). The Secretary of State also issues Planning Policy Statements (replacing the Planning Policy Guidance) that must be taken into account in determining planning applications.

[42] Town and Country Planning Act 1990, s 78.

[43] Above s 77.

[44] Above ss 51, 100, 104.

[45] On the Act generally, see P Thomas, 'The Planning and Compulsory Purchase Act 2004: The Final Cut' [2004] *Journal of Planning & Environment Law* 1348; 'Planning and Compulsory Purchase Act: The Democratic Deficit' [2004] *Journal of Planning & Environment Law* B25. Centralisation is also the norm in relation to the designation of buildings as listed buildings or scheduled ancient monuments, and the designation of land as a Site of Special Scientific Interest or SPA: see the discussion in *R (on the application of Trailer & Marina (Leven) Ltd) v Secretary of State for the Environment, Food and Rural Affairs* [2004] EWHC 153 (affirmed [2004] EWCA Civ 1580).

[46] Planning and Compulsory Purchase Act 2004, Part I (see especially ss 2, 3).

elected regional bodies.[47] This was overturned before the Bill was finally passed into law, but not without a concession from the Government that the recognition would only be given to a body unless at least 60 per cent of its membership are members of a district, county or metropolitan district council, a National Park authority, or the Broads Authority in the RSB's area.[48]

The end result is that planning policies and decisions are set by both elected and non-elected officials, but the real power is held by non-elected officials in the Secretary of State's office. It is reasonably clear that one of their primary objectives is to ensure compatibility of local decisions with central policies, and to ensure some consistency from one authority to another. The contrast with the American system is therefore quite marked. In this respect, the threat of a 'capture' of the decision-making process by local property owners is much less in the United Kingdom than it is in the United States. This, alone, suggests that there is less reason to subject local decisions to close judicial scrutiny.

In the United Kingdom, the leading case on the planning system is *Alconbury*,[49] which involved three appeals on related aspects of the planning system. Briefly, the House of Lords considered whether Article 6 was violated in cases where the Secretary of State had called in planning decisions for resolution or disposed of appeals from local planning boards.[50] The issue arose because the scope of judicial review of the Secretary of State's decisions is limited: in particular, there is no review based on a question of pure fact. Since factual matters are therefore not determined by an independent tribunal, there was some doubt as to whether the determination of the civil rights arising on planning cases satisfied the Article 6 of the Convention.

Before considering the judgment in *Alconbury*, it is worth pointing out that planning decisions that have the effect of limiting the use of land are treated as determinations of civil rights, and hence come within the scope of Article 6(1).[51] At first impression, this would suggest that the administrative decision itself must comply with the Article 6(1) procedural safeguards. However, in *Albert*

---

[47] Planning and Compulsory Purchase Bill, HL Bill 45 (16 March 2004), clauses 1, 3.

[48] Planning and Compulsory Purchase Act 2004, s 4.

[49] *Alconbury* (n 40); see P Craig, 'The Courts, The Human Rights Act and Judicial Review' (2001) 117 *Law Quarterly Review* 589, 596 –603; M Poustie, 'The Rule of Law or the Rule of Lawyers? Alconbury, Article 6(1) and the Role of Courts in Administrative Decision-Making' [2001] 6 *European Human Rights Law Review* 657; D Elvin and J Maurici, 'The Alconbury Litigation: Principle and Pragmatism' [2001] *Journal of Planning & Environment Law* 883. On accountability within the planning system, see M Grant, 'Human Rights and Due Process in Planning' [2000] *Journal of Planning & Environment Law* 1215.

[50] The first case, *Regina (Alconbury Developments Ltd) v Secretary of State for the Environment, Transport and the Regions*, concerned the recovery of applications for planning permission by the Secretary of State, under para 3 of Schedule 6 to the Town and Country Planning Act 1990. The second case, *Regina (Holding & Barnes Plc) v Secretary of State for the Environment, Transport and the Regions*, concerned the Secretary of State's calling in of an application under section 77 of the 1990 Act. The third case, *Secretary of State for the Environment, Transport and the Regions v Legal and General Assurance Society Ltd*, concerned an improvement scheme proposed by the Highways Agency (a branch of the Secretary of State's department), which would require the compulsory purchase of land belonging to the applicant company.

[51] *Bryan v The United Kingdom*, Series A No 335–A (1995) 21 EHRR 342.

and Le Compte v Belgium, the Court held that Article 6(1) is satisfied if either the administrative body itself complies with the Article 6(1) safeguards, or if it is 'subject to subsequent control by a judicial body that has full jurisdiction and does provide the guarantees of Article 6(1).'[52] This principle was examined in greater detail, in relation to the decisions of planning inspectors, in *Bryan v The United Kingdom*.[53]

The case arose after Mr Bryan constructed two buildings on his land without planning permission, in a Green Belt and conservation area. The planning authority served an enforcement notice on him requiring the demolition of the buildings. He appealed to the Secretary of State on the grounds (amongst others) that there had been no breach of planning control, and that permission should be granted for the buildings in any event. The appeals were dismissed by an inspector appointed by the Secretary of State, whereupon Bryan appealed to the High Court, essentially on the ground that planning permission should have been granted. The High Court dismissed his appeal, on the basis that it raised issues that lay within the judgment of the inspector. In Strasbourg, the European Court held that the review by the inspector 'does not of itself satisfy the require- ments of Article 6 of the Convention, despite the existence of various safeguards customarily associated with an "independent and impartial tribunal".'[54] Hence, it was necessary to consider whether appeal to the High Court satisfied Article 6. The European Court noted that the High Court's jurisdiction was limited: it only extended to points of law, and hence the High Court could not take into account all aspects of the inspector's decision.[55] In particular, there was no re- hearing of the complaints, and the 'High Court could not substitute its own decision on the merits for that of the inspector; and its jurisdiction over the facts was limited.'[56] Was this limited jurisdiction sufficient?

---

[52] Series A No 58 (1983) 5 EHRR 533 [29]. See the series of cases on Swedish planning law, where violations of Art 6 were found on the basis that there were insufficient judicial controls: *Sporrong and Lönnroth v Sweden*, Series A No 52 (1983) 5 EHRR 35; *Pudas v Sweden*, Series A No 125–A (1987) 10 EHRR 380; *Bodén v Sweden*, Series A No 125–B (1987) 10 EHRR 367; *Tre Traktörer Aktiebolag v Sweden*, Series A No 159 (1991) 13 EHRR 309; *Jacobsson v Sweden*, Series A No 163 (1989) 12 EHRR 56; *Skärby v Sweden*, Series A No 180–B (1990) 13 EHRR 90; *Zander v Sweden*, Series A No 279–B (1993) 18 EHRR 175.

[53] Series A No 335–A, (1995) 21 EHRR 342. See also *Zumtobel v Austria*, Series A No 268–A (1993) 17 EHRR 116, where the applicants complained that an administrative court did not have 'full jurisdiction' over an administrative authority's decision to purchase their land compulsorily, because the court could not substitute its decision for that of the authority. However, at [32], the Court stated that the administrative court did have sufficient jurisdiction, given the 'the respect which must be accorded to decisions taken by the administrative authorities on grounds of expedi- ency and to the nature of the complaints made by the [applicants]'.

[54] *Bryan* (n 51) [38]. Mr Bryan applied to the Commission on the basis that his Art 6 rights had been violated, both in relation to the finding that the building was not agricultural, and in relation to the decision to refuse planning permission. In the Commission, there were minority and concur- ring judgments, but it is clear that there was a consensus that Art 6 does not require the State to ensure that a court has the power to substitute its decisions for those of the administrative authori- ties on matters of planning policy or 'expediency'.

[55] Above [44].

[56] Above.

To answer this question, the Court returned to Bryan's original complaints. It held that the appeal regarding the refusal of planning permission 'went essentially to questions involving "a panoply of policy matters such as development plans, and the fact that the property was situated in a Green Belt and in a conservation area".'[57] It was not so much a question of fact as a matter of policy, and hence High Court's jurisdiction was sufficient to satisfy Article 6. However, the issues relating to Bryan's argument that the buildings did not contravene the planning controls were different, as they involved findings of fact. However, the Court still concluded that the system was satisfactory. To begin with, the planning inspector did not act in a purely administrative capacity, as the Court noted 'the uncontested safeguards attending the procedure before the inspector: the quasi-judicial character of the decision-making process; the duty incumbent on each inspector to exercise independent judgment; the requirement that inspectors must not be subject to any improper influence; the stated mission of the Inspectorate to uphold the principles of openness, fairness and impartiality.'[58] And while the High Court could not substitute its own findings of fact, it did have 'the power to satisfy itself that the inspector's findings of fact or the inferences based on them were neither perverse nor irrational'.[59] On this basis, it concluded that 'Such an approach by an appeal tribunal on questions of fact can reasonably be expected in specialised areas of the law such as the one at issue, particularly where the facts have already been established in the course of a quasi-judicial procedure governed by many of the safeguards required by Article 6(1). It is also frequently a feature in the systems of judicial control of administrative decisions found throughout the Council of Europe member states.'[60] Hence, there was no violation of Article 6(1).

In *Alconbury*, the complaint focused on the role of the Secretary of State, rather than that of the planning inspector. However, their Lordships did not regard this as a material distinction from *Bryan*, and their views on the Secretary of State's position parallel those of the European Court in *Bryan* regarding the position of the planning inspector.[61] It accepted the Secretary of State's argument that, although he could not act as an independent or impartial tribunal in called in or recovered matters, there was sufficient judicial control of his decisions to satisfy the Article 6 requirment for a determination by an independent and impartial tribunal. In relation to matters of policy and planning judgement, there was no requirement under Article 6 that a court would substitute its determination for that of planning inspectors or the Secretary of State.[62] Similarly, in relation to judicial review and findings of fact, their Lordships saw

---

[57] Above [47].
[58] Above [46].
[59] Above [47].
[60] Above.
[61] See eg in *Alconbury* (n 40) [162] (Lord Clyde).
[62] Above [117]: Lord Hoffman stated that 'No one expects the inspector to be independent or impartial in applying the Secretary of State's policy'.

little difference from the situation in *Bryan*. Their Lordships noted that the Secretary of State must accept the findings of the inspector unless he has first notified the parties and allowed them to make representations,[63] and from this concluded that there is no real issue. As put by Lord Hoffman, 'the *Bryan* case is authority for saying that the independent position of the inspector, together with the control of the fairness of the fact-finding procedure by the court in judicial review, is sufficient to satisfy the requirements of Article 6.'[64] This was supported by *Chapman v The United Kingdom*,[65] where the complaint concerned the High Court lack of jurisdiction to review questions of fact or the weight given to specific factors affecting the planning decision. The European Court held, following *Bryan*, 'that in the specialised area of town planning law full review of the facts may not be required by Article 6 of the Convention' and that the opportunity to challenge the decision 'on the basis that it was perverse, irrational, had no basis on the evidence or had been made with reference to irrelevant factors or without regard to relevant factors' afforded adequate judicial control of the administrative decisions in issue.[66]

Since *Alconbury* is only concerned with Article 6 and the powers of the Secretary of State, it is not directly relevant to the issues relating solely to the severity of planning restrictions. Nevertheless, to return to the importance of the division of power in planning matters, it is worth noting that their Lordships commented on the fact and importance of central control over the planning process. They accepted that a central authority must have the power to resolve cases and appeals, and that it was consistent with democratic principle to confer this power on a minister accountable to Parliament.[67] The centralisation of control also means that there should be a reduced risk of self-interested acts by groups of local landowners intent on controlling future development to protect their own property. *Why* control must lie in the hands of a central administrative authority is not so clear: it seems equally consistent with democratic principle to leave the power in the hands of elected local bodies, with only a limited power of review in the national executive. However, it seems as firmly set in the political culture of the United Kingdom that land use policies are determined centrally as it is set in American political culture that the same policies are made locally. In any case, the end result is that the judgment in *Alconbury* reflects the appropriate level of deference for substantive as well as procedural issues.

---

[63] In accordance with rule 17(5) of the Town and Country Planning (Inquiries Procedure) (England) Rules 2000.
[64] *Alconbury* (n 40) [128].
[65] *Chapman* (n 22).
[66] Above [124].
[67] See *Alconbury* (n 40) [140]–[141] (Lord Clyde).

CONTROLS ON THE USE OF ANOTHER'S LAND

To some extent, private law already allows individuals to control the use of land by their neighbours, whether by actions for nuisance, negligence or the rule in *Rylands v Fletcher*, or for breach of a contract or restrictive covenant. The availability of these remedies raises two issues for human rights law: first, are the remedies sufficient for the protection of Convention rights? And secondly, to what extent may the State abolish or restrict the private law remedies in favour of public regulatory systems for the control of land use? These two questions may be regarded as aspects of the same issue, since both are concerned with the adequacy of the rights, public or private, that an individual has under national law for controlling the use of land. However, in answering these questions, it is useful to begin by considering the adequacy of private law remedies on their own.

The adequacy of private law remedies

One area where the common law remedies may not provide sufficient protection is in relation to the Convention rights of occupiers. In *Hunter v Canary Wharf Ltd*,[68] the House of Lords made it clear that nuisance only protects possessory interests in land; hence, a mere occupier cannot bring an action for nuisance. However, it is doubtful that a mere occupier holds a P1(1) possession in any event. While the European Court of Human Rights has treated some interests that are classified as personal rights under national law as possessions for the purposes of P1(1), the applicants in these cases had at least a contractual interest in property under their national law.[69] Hence, while one might argue that a contractual licensee has a P1(1) possession, it may be more difficult to persuade the courts that a bare licensee also has a P1(1) possession in respect of the land.[70] If the individual occupies the property as a home, he or she may argue that a neighbour's use of land interferes with his or her rights under Article 8. However, it is unlikely that a violation would be found unless the interference is so severe that the property cannot be occupied as a home. *Hatton* is an example: against the applicants, the Grand Chamber observed that their houses remained saleable without any apparent loss of value due to night flying, and so the interference was not disproportionate on that ground alone.[71] Plainly,

---

[68] [1997] AC 655, but *cf* 714 (Lord dissenting Cooke).

[69] Eg Iatridis (n 13), *Gasus Dosier und Fordertechnik GmbH v The Netherlands*, Series A No 306–B (1995) 20 EHRR 403.

[70] Especially since the interests in these cases (*Iatridis*, above and *Gasus*, above) would be recognised as proprietary interests under English law.

[71] *Hatton* (n 31); *cf S v France* (1990) 65 D&R 250, 262, 264: the payment of compensation for a nuisance-like interference meant that the impact was not disproportionate.

despite the noise, many people still felt that houses in the Heathrow area would make adequate homes. By contrast, a violation of Article 8 was found in *López Ostra v Spain*,[72] where fumes, noise and smells from a waste treatment plant were so severe that nearby residents had to be evacuated and temporarily re-housed.

A second area of concern involves the State's responsibility in nuisance or negligence for the acts of third parties. The Court decided in *López Ostra*[73] that the State's positive obligations may extend to controlling interferences caused by third parties. The waste treatment plant was operated by a third party, but Spain was held responsible because, in breach of existing regulations, 'the town allowed the plants to be built on its land and the State subsidised the plant's construction'.[74] Subsequently, the local authorities not only failed to respond to the obvious environmental problems, but resisted judicial orders requiring it to take steps to alleviate the problems.[75]

In the United Kingdom, issues similar to those in *López Ostra* arose in several cases on the acts of tenants or occupiers of land belonging to local authorities.[76] With tenants, the local authority is only liable in nuisance where it has authorised their acts. That is, in the absence of such authorisation, it is not liable for failing to exercise its powers to evict the tenants. For example, in *Hussain v Lancaster City Council*,[77] owners of a shop and residence brought claims in nuisance and negligence against Lancaster County Council after suffering repeated and serious acts of racial harassment from tenants of neighbouring council houses. However, the Court of Appeal held that there could be no liability in nuisance, because the Council as landlord had not authorised the tenants to commit the nuisance, and the acts of harassment did not arise from the tenants' use of the rented property. Similarly, there was no basis for imposing a duty of care in negligence for the failure to use its statutory powers against the tenants: the Council had not acted irrationally, and it would not be fair, just and reasonable to impose a duty, given the practical difficulties and choices involving in housing cases. By contrast, liability is more easily imposed where the local authority has retained legal possession of land. In *Lippiatt v South Gloucestershire Council*,[78] for example, a landowner was repeatedly harassed by occupants of council land. The council argued that the claim should be struck out, on the basis of the *Hussain* judgment. However, in this case, the Court of Appeal said that no rule of law precluded liability for the acts of independent third party occupiers of land, where the defendant knew of the harmful conduct.

---

[72] Series A No 303–C (1994) 20 EHRR 277.
[73] Above.
[74] Above [52].
[75] Above [56]–[57].
[76] See generally S Bright, 'Liability for the Bad Behaviour of Others' (2001) 21 *Oxford Journal of Legal Studies* 311 (see 327–30 for the human rights implications).
[77] [2000] QB 1 (CA); see also *Mowan v Wandsworth LBC* [2000] EWCA Civ 357.
[78] [2000] QB 51 (CA).

The distinction between *Lippiat* and *Hussain* lies in the capacity of the defendant: in *Lippiat*, the Council had not granted a lease to the third parties. The basis for this distinction seems to lie in the greater degree of control retained by a landowner who has not given up possession under a lease. However, as council landlords normally have the power to evict tenants who are guilty of harassing their neighbours, the distinction is not convincing. Hence, it seems that the position in English law on licensees probably satisfies the Convention requirements, but there is room to doubt the position regarding tenants, as set out in *Hussain*. Indeed, in *López Ostra*, it appears that the third party held the land under a lease, and the enforcement of the law would have been no more difficult in *Hussain*. That is not to say that Spanish and English law regarding the rights and powers of landlords are the same, but these technical distinctions between responsibility for the acts of tenants and those of licensees are likely to carry little weight in Strasbourg.

The abolition or restriction of private law remedies

P1(1) is applicable where regulatory schemes restrict or abolish the private law right to bring an action relating to the use of land by another person. Either the interference that would have supported an action in nuisance or negligence is itself an interference with possessions under P1(1), or the restriction on taking action against the nuisance is an interference with P1(1). On the face of it, however, it is doubtful that human rights law would make a difference in most cases. As in *Alconbury*, the courts are likely to say that States have a wide margin of appreciation (or area of discretion) when setting up regulatory schemes that adjust property rights and liabilities across broad cross-sections of the public.[79] It is therefore unlikely that the State would fail to establish that the scheme serves the public interest, or that the balance between public and private interests is not fair.[80] Hence, the courts would probably hold that the abolition of private law remedies in favour of public law remedies is not incompatible with P1(1) solely for that reason. There may be specific issues regarding the procedures adopted by the regulatory body and the availability of judicial review, but if Parliament has designed the regulatory system in the belief that the independent use of private law actions would interfere with its operation, the courts are likely to accept that as a valid reason for excluding or restricting such actions. Hence, in the English context, the Human Rights Act 1998 does not enhance the existing common law actions relating to land use in areas where regulatory bodies hold sway. If anything, the human rights analysis makes it even less likely that private remedies will continue. To see this, it is necessary to review the recent litigation in *Marcic v Thames Water Utilities Ltd.*[81]

---

[79] See Chapter 5, 125–30.
[80] See eg *Pine Valley* (n 14); and *Mellacher* (n 15).
[81] *Marcic* (n 27); see M Stallworthy, 'Environmental Liability and the Impact of Statutory Authority' (2003) 15 *Journal of Environmental Law* 3; D Howarth, 'Nuisance and the House of Lords' (2004) 16 *Journal of Environmental Law* 233.

In *Marcic*, the claimant brought claims in nuisance and under the Human Rights Act 1998 for damage caused by repeated flooding from the back flow of foul water from the sewerage system operated by the defendat, the statutory sewerage undertaker under the Water Industry Act 1991. The 1991 Act makes no express reference to common law liability for nuisance; neither does it create a statutory right for compensation for nuisance.[82] Statutory undertakers are subject to specific duties under section 94 of the 1991 Act, but in the first instance, only the Secretary of State or the Director General of Water Services (the regulator) may enforce those duties.[83] The status of the common law actions is not as clearly set out as it might have been, as section 18(8) provides that

> 18(8) Where any act or omission constitutes a contravention of a condition of an appointment under Chapter I of this Part or of a statutory or other requirement enforceable under this section, the only remedies for that contravention, apart from those available by virtue of this section, shall be those for which express provision is made by or under any enactment and those that are available in respect of that act or omission otherwise than by virtue of its constituting such a contravention.

The key part of this subsection is the scope of 'a statutory and other requirement enforceable under this section'. In this regard, subsection (6) of section 18 provides that:

> 18(6) For the purposes of this section and the following provisions of this Act—
> (a) the statutory and other requirements which shall be enforceable under this section . . . shall be such of the requirements of any enactment or of any subordinate legislation as
>> (i)   are imposed in consequence of that appointment; and
>> (ii) are made so enforceable by that enactment or subordinate legislation.

It therefore appears that the common law actions are not expressly excluded by section 18; nor, for that matter, are they excluded by any other provision of the 1991 Act. Consequently, the Court of Appeal concluded that the action for nuisance survived the passage of the Act. However, the Court also applied the general principle that a person under a statutory duty is only liable for nuisance to the extent that it is an inevitable result of carrying out the duty.[84] In that sense, the Court of Appeal accepted that the regulatory system had curtailed the liability of the defendant.

Despite the wording of section 18, the House of Lords held that the 1991 Act completely excluded the action for nuisance, irrespective of the inevitability of

---

[82] Sections 111, 114, 117 of the Water Industry Act 1991 state that certain functions are to be exercised so as not to create a nuisance, but without imposing liability for that nuisance at common law or otherwise.

[83] See also section 18 of the Water Industry Act 1991. (Although described as an 'independent' regulator in the case reports, he/she could only act to enforce the undertaker's statutory duty 'with the consent of or in accordance with a general authorisation given by the Secretary of State': s 94(3).)

[84] *Marcic v Thames Water Utilities Ltd* [2002] QB 929.

harm, because the remedial scheme was intended to be comprehensive.[85] Their Lordships felt that the Act must have been intended to leave the task of balancing the different interests affected by the regulation of water services to the Director General of Water Services. They did not feel that the procedure by which the Director General balances these interests was inherently unfair: in particular, homeowners are entitled to request the Director General to issue an enforcement order against a statutory undertaker, and then to apply for judicial review if he or she refuses their request. Once the enforcement order is in place, the homeowner may bring proceedings against the undertaker to have it enforced. Moreover, in terms of its substantive merits, the balance that had been struck was appropriate: Thames Water was fulfilling its statutory duties regarding the maintenance of the sewerage system and had agreed a programme of investment with the Director General. While the scheme gave low priority to the improvement of the sewers in the claimant's area, it was also the case that investment was made first in areas where flooding was more serious. To enable individual homeowners to bring private actions for nuisance threatened to upset the balance that had already been struck by the Director General (with the authority of Parliament), and the House of Lords could see no reason to allow this.

Several points follow from this. First, would the continued availability of the nuisance action really set the regulatory scheme to nought, as asserted by Lord Nicholls?[86] As David Howarth has pointed out, the imposition of liability in negligence would not have the left the Director General unable to help Thames Water avoid insolvency, as he could have adjusted the burdens between Thames Water and its customers by allowing it to increase the charges for water services.[87] That is, while the specific regulatory solution of rationing sewer improvements (and letting losses lie where they fell) may no longer have been feasible, the regulatory scheme of allowing the Director General to allocate costs through customer charges would still have been effective.

Secondly, Lord Hoffman questioned the competence of the courts to determine questions of capital expenditure. As he put it, in the typical nuisance case between neighbours, the court decides what is reasonable as between the two parties. However, the situation here is not the same:

> But the exercise becomes very different when one is dealing with the capital expenditure of a statutory undertaking providing public utilities on a large scale. The matter is no longer confined to the parties to the action. If one customer is given a certain level of services, everyone in the same circumstances should receive the same level of services. So the effect of a decision about what it would be reasonable to expect a sewerage undertaker to do for the plaintiff is extrapolated across the country. This in turn

---

[85] See *Marcic* (n 27) [22] (Lord Nicholls): 'The closing words of section 18(8) expressly preserve remedies for any causes of action which are available in respect of an act or omission otherwise than by virtue of its being a contravention of a statutory requirement enforceable under section 18.'

[86] Above [35].

[87] Howarth (n 81) 257.

raises questions of public interest. Capital expenditure on new sewers has to be financed; interest must be paid on borrowings and privatised undertakers must earn a reasonable return. This expenditure can be met only be charges paid by consumers. Is it in the public interest that they should have to pay more? And does expenditure on the particular improvements with which the plaintiff is concerned represent the best order of priorities?[88]

By characterising the central issue as a question of capital expenditure rather than compensation for loss, Lord Hoffman effectively undermines the competence of the courts not only in relation to statutory undertakers, but indeed in any case where the liability arises from the provision of services or goods to a cross-section of the public. This passage is particularly striking because of the extent to which the analysis of the private law claims mirrors the human rights analysis. That is, the broader public interest may enter into the private law balance, but the fact that shareholders' profits may be reduced or that other customers may need to pay more for water services is only of secondary importance (if any).

Is *Marcic* therefore a case where the application of human rights values had the effect of restricting individual property rights? While the House of Lords did not suggest that P1(1) requires the exclusion of the action for nuisance, its application of the proportionality test led it to conclude that private law rights could be restricted because it was not unfair to do so. Admittedly, it would be dangerous to read too much into this case, as the nuisance claim turned on the interpretation of an unclear statute: that is, if section 18 of the 1991 Act had explicitly removed common law actions, there would have been no real issue of statutory interpretation. Furthermore, even if the human rights analysis did creep into private law, it did no more than reinforce the existing tendency of the English courts to favour regulatory solutions over private law solutions in relation to controls on the use of land.[89] Indeed, there is an interesting contrast with Canadian developments in the law of nuisance, where the courts have tended to restrict the scope of defences based on statutory authority. Courts in both countries apply the principle that a nuisance is not actionable if it is the inevitable result of exercising a statutory power or the non-negligent fulfilment of a statutory duty.[90] In England, the courts apply the test of inevitability as a kind of negligence test, as they only require the statutory undertaker 'to carry out the work and conduct the operation with all reasonable regard and care for the interests of other persons'.[91] By contrast, in Canada, the nuisance-creator must show that it was 'practically impossible to avoid the nuisance' and that there were no

---

[88] *Marcic* (n 27) [63].

[89] See generally Stallworthy (n 81).

[90] See *City of Manchester v Farnworth* [1930] AC 171, 183 (Viscount Dunedin); *Department of Transport v North West Water Authority* [1984] 1 AC 336, 359–60 (Lord Fraser); G Kodilinye, 'The Statutory Authority Defence in Nuisance Actions' (1990) 19 *Anglo-American Law Review* 72.

[91] *Allen v Gulf Oil Refining Ltd* [1981] AC 1001, 1011 (Lord Wilberforce).

'alternate methods of carrying out the work'.[92] This position was reached in absence of a constitutional protection for the right to property, and yet it is stronger than the position that now seems to prevail in England. Consequently, while one might say that the approach to private law in *Marcic* is compatible with human rights values, it is doubtful that it represents a real change, given the existing lack of faith in private law as even an adjunct to regulatory law in relation to land use controls.

Public law remedies

If private law remedies are abolished or restricted, the adequacy of the substitute remedies must be considered. Are there any situations where the authorities must impose or enforce restrictions on the use of land so as to prevent harm to property or personal interests arising from (for example) environmental hazards? From *Marcic* and *Hatton*, it is clear that the public interest may override specific rights, but in neither case was the impact so severe that the property lost all its utility or economic value. By contrast, in *López Ostra*, a violation of Article 8 was found where it became impossible to occupy the property as a home: however, the Court also noted that the authorities had not applied the environmental laws that were already in place, even in the face of court orders requiring action. It remains the case that the Court is reluctant to intervene in cases where the State has adopted and adhered to a regulatory regime which may involve intrusions on some interests. Accordingly, the strongest cases are those where the individual is only seeking the enforcement of existing laws in respect of a clear default, as in *López Ostra* (and not *Marcic* or *Hatton*). For example, in planning cases, P1(1) has been found applicable where failings in administrative or judicial procedures allow neighbouring land owners to flout the law in a manner that affects the applicant's enjoyment of its possessions.[93] It is clear, however, that P1(1) is not applicable in respect of third party acts unless there is such a failing: the fact that a third party has broken the law is not, by itself, enough to engage the State's responsibility.[94]

Even where the State's responsibility is engaged, its failure to take action is unlikely to violate the Convention unless the public authorities had clear warnings of the risk of harm to the claimant, whether or not the conduct of third parties created the risk. This is apparent from *Öneryildiz v Turkey*,[95] which concerned a landslide at a tip that killed thirty-nine people and destroyed ten

[92] *Tock v St John's Metropolitan Area Board* (1989) 64 DLR (4th) 620, 651 (Sopinka J); *Ryan v City of Victoria* [1999] 1 SCR 201; *cf Sutherland v Canada (Attorney General)* (2002) ACWSJ LEXIS 2840; 2002 ACWSJ 4266; 114 ACWS (3d) 982 (BCCA).

[93] See the cases cited above n 28. It appears that more than a simple complaint to the authorities must be made: see eg *Josephides v Cyprus*, Appl No 2647/02, 24 September 2002.

[94] See the discussion of *López Ostra v Spain*, text accompanying n 73ff; and *Novoseletskiy v Ukraine*, Appl No 47148/99, 11 March 2003: the State's responsibility is not engaged by the mere fact that an individual is a victim of a property crime.

[95] Appl No 48939/99, 30 November 2004 (Grand Chamber).

homes. The tip was the responsibility of the local city council, but it had failed to respond to an official report warning of the specific risks that led to the landslide. The Court found that the failures of the city council amounted to a breach of the positive obligations arising under Article 2 and P1(1). In relation to P1(1), the Court stated that the 'real and effective exercise' of the right to the enjoyment of possessions may require positive measures of protection, and 'This obligation will inevitably arise, inter alia, where there is a direct link between the measures which an applicant may legitimately expect from the authorities and his enjoyment of his possessions.'[96] In this case, the knowledge of the specific risks was sufficient to engage the State's responsibility, and the failure to do anything about the risks amounted to a breach of its obligations. It was implicit that the State's responsibility would not have been engaged without the specific warnings of the risk, or at least that its failures to act would not have amounted to a breach without the warnings.

Even where Article 8 is applicable, it does not necessarily follow that the balance of interests will favour the victims of the interference. There is no duty on the State to provide a clean and safe environment for everyone within its borders:[97] the duty is only to strike a fair balance between the competing interests of the victims of the interference and the community as a whole.[98] As discussed above, in *Hatton*, the Grand Chamber held that the process by which the Secretary of State adopted a noise quota system for Heathrow airport was compatible with Article 8. When it came to the substantive merits of the quota system, the Grand Chamber accepted the United Kingdom's claim that night flying had important economic benefits, even though it was difficult to isolate the general benefit from the specific benefit accruing to the airlines. It also noted that the impact on the applicants was not as severe as it is in some Article 8 cases: in particular, the applicants' homes had not become more difficult to sell as a result of night flying, and there was no need to give environmental rights a special status under Article 8. Consequently, the State had a wide margin of appreciation on the substantive merits. In any case, the applicants' concerns had not been completely disregarded: indeed, the system of noise quotas was intended to address their concerns. Hence, given the margin of appreciation, the Grand Chamber could not say that a fair balance had not been struck.

Consequently, although both P1(1) and Article 8 do give rise to positive obligations regarding environmental or other interferences with the enjoyment of possessions or the home, it seems that the Court is unlikely to find that a fully-considered, lawful decision to allow the interference to continue has upset the

---

[96] Above [145].

[97] *Hatton* (2003) 37 EHRR 28 (Grand Chamber) [96]; see generally R Desgagne, 'Integrating Environmental Values into the European Convention on Human Rights' (1995) 89 *American Journal of International Law* 263; MT Acevedo, 'The Intersection of Human Rights and Environmental Protection in the European Court of Human Rights' (2000) 8 *New York University Environmental Law Journal* 437.

[98] Above [98].

fair balance under either right. In broad terms, this is consistent with the approach taken in P1(1) cases where property owners object to the impact of regulatory measures, as it confirms that the State has a broad discretion in choosing whether to regulate or not to regulate.

Access to land belonging to others[99]

The non-interventionist approach in other land use cases is also evident where individuals claim that the enjoyment of their Convention rights requires access to land belonging to others. Unless national law confers a proprietarial right of access over the land, the individuals would have no possessions on which to base a P1(1) argument. Hence, it would be necessary to argue that the exercise of some other Convention right requires access to land. This has proved to be a difficult case to make. In *Botta v Italy*[100] and *Zehnalova and Zehnal v The Czech Republic*,[101] disabled applicants argued that their States had a positive obligation under Article 8 to enforce laws requiring landowners to facilitate access to property open to the public. In *Botta*, the applicant complained that no steps were being taken to enforce statutory provisions intended to guarantee disabled people effective access to private buildings and establishments. The law put mayors under a duty to ensure that the certain work would be carried out at the request of the disabled, and funds were set aside for that purpose. However, while on holiday, the applicant discovered that a private beach in Ravenna had not undertaken the prescribed work (such as providing access ramps and separate changing facilities for the disabled). Despite making repeated requests to the local mayor to enforce the law, nothing was done. He eventually applied to Strasbourg, complaining that his Article 8 right to respect for private life had been breached, on the basis that he was unable to enjoy a normal social life which would enable him to participate in the life of the community and to exercise essential rights.

While the Court agreed that Article 8 included some positive obligations on the part of the State, it also stated that there must be 'direct and immediate link between the measures sought by an applicant and the latter's private and/or family life'.[102] However, in this case, 'the right asserted by Mr Botta, namely the right to gain access to the beach and the sea at a place distant from his normal place of residence during his holidays, concerns interpersonal relations of such

---

[99] See K Gray and SF Gray, 'Civil Rights, Civil Wrongs and Quasi-Public Space' [1999] 1 *European Human Rights Law Review* 46; K Gray and SF Gray, 'Private Property and Public Propriety' in J McLean, (ed), *Property and the Constitution* (Hart Publishing, Oxford, 1999); A Grear, 'A Tale of the Land, the Insider, the Outsider and Human Rights (an Exploration of some Problems and Possibilities in the Relationship between the English Common Law Property Concept, Human Rights Law, and Discourses of Exclusion and Inclusion)' (2003) 23 *Legal Studies* 33.

[100] Reports 1998–I 412 (1998) 26 EHRR 241.

[101] Reports 2002–V 337.

[102] *Botta* (n 100) [34].

broad and indeterminate scope that there can be no conceivable direct link between the measures the State was urged to take in order to make good the omissions of the private bathing establishments and the applicant's private life.'[103] Consequently, Article 8 had no application, and hence the failure to comply with national law was immaterial.

The applicants' position in *Zehnalova* seems even stronger, as it concerned the failure to enforce laws requiring better access to public buildings. Nevertheless, the Court again held that Article 8 did not apply. There had to be evidence that the lack of access 'affects her life in such a way as to interfere with her right to personal development and her right to establish and develop relationships with other human beings and the outside world'.[104] This evidence would need to relate to the actual obstacles to entry and the particular needs of her private life. Indeed, the fact that she complained that a large number of buildings were inaccessible weakened her case, since the Court concluded that her complaint did not relate to any specific aspect of the services provided in the buildings.

Plainly, *Botta* and *Zehnalova* discourage anyone from arguing that the State's positive obligations extend to the regulation of the private law right of exclusion. However, these cases centred on the State's reluctance to enforce laws which it had already passed: there was no suggestion that there is a general positive obligation to limit the private right of exclusion. Indeed, the laws in question were intended to facilitate access, rather than limit a private law right of exclusion. The property owners in *Botta* nor *Zehnalova* had not purported to exercise a property right to exclude the applicants on the basis of their disability: if they had, the legal issue may have been different.

Nevertheless, even in cases of deliberate exclusion, the Court has taken a conservative line. This question has come up in several cases from the United Kingdom, and the results indicate that there is very little chance of persuading the courts in the United Kingdom or Strasbourg that there is a positive obligation to allow access. The private law issues were squarely before the Court of Appeal in *CIN Properties Ltd v Rawlins*,[105] in which the leaseholder of Swansgate Shopping Centre obtained a permanent injunction prohibiting a group of young men from entering the Centre. The exclusion had a severe effect on the lives of the young men, as the Centre occupies about three-fifths of the town centre of Wellingborough and contains its main shopping facilities, including the Electricity Showroom[106] and the Co-operative Bank.[107] The shops in the Centre also constituted one of the main sources of employment. As Kevin Gray and Susan Gray point out, 'the impact of arbitrary exclusion on the life chances of the young men was not merely potential, but actual and far-reaching.'[108]

---

[103] Above [35].
[104] *Zehnalova* (n 101).
[105] [1995] 2 EGLR 130.
[106] Where the applicant bought their electricity cards.
[107] Where one of the young men had an account.
[108] Gray and Gray (n 99) 50.

Nevertheless, the Court of Appeal held that the leaseholder could rely on its private law right to exclude anyone from land in their possession. Hence, the case did not turn on its justification for excluding the young men, but on the absolute nature of its right to do so.[109]

As a matter of private law, it may be questioned whether the Court of Appeal's decision was correct. At the very least, it demonstrates that the Court had no interest in using the existing doctrines on common callings to reflect modern concerns. It is a long-standing rule that property used for certain types of business must be open to the public generally. For example, at common law, an innkeeper could not refuse to accommodate someone solely on the basis of race, even if the prospective customer could obtain other suitable accommodation elsewhere at the same cost. At one time, the idea of a common calling was applied widely, to any sort of business affected with a public interest; in more recent years, as shown by *CIN v Rawlins*, the courts have let the doctrine atrophy. Innkeeper, common carriers and ferrymen are the only remaining categories of common callings. Even so, the legislature has intervened to put these limitations on private property on a statutory footing. However, as Peter Benson[110] and Amnon Reichman[111] have argued, the statutory aspect does not mean this is a field of public law, in the sense that the foundation for these limitations lies in private law concerns.[112] That is, it is not a matter of pitting the property owner's private interests against the public interest in access, but simply a matter of recognising that the property owner has accepted the limitations as a result of dedicating the property to a common calling. As such, it can be seen in the same light as the rules that prevent an owner from using their property to harm others: one does not need to invoke public law considerations to see that private law does not confer such powers on property owners. However, it seems that the rise of statutory rules on race and sex discrimination, or on the specific professions concerned, has suggested to the courts that the

---

[109] The position was not put in such stark terms in *Porter v Commissioner of Police for the Metropolis* (CA, 20 October 1999), where a woman refused to leave a London Electricity Board showroom until her complaints regarding service were addressed to her satisfaction. The Court stated that 'Having allowed her every opportunity to do what she was entitled to do in their premises, the LEB could reasonably withdraw her permission to remain.' On the facts, the LEB had acted reasonably, but the judgment hints at the possibility that the LEB might not have been able to withdraw her permission unreasonably, or without providing some explanation for the withdrawal. (The claim was brought against the police, for battery, wrongful arrest, false imprisonment and malicious prosecution, all related to force used in removing her from LEB premises.) However, as Grear notes, the emphasis remains on absolute rights of exclusion: see Grear (n 99) 51–52, and *R (on the application of Fuller and others) v Chief Constable of Dorset Police* [2003] QB 480 [61]–[66].

[110] P Benson, 'Equality of Opportunity and Private Law' in D Friedmann and D Barak-Erez (eds), *Human Rights in Private Law* (Hart Publishing, Oxford, 2001) 201–43.

[111] A Reichman, 'Property Rights, Public Policy and the Limits of the Legal Power to Discriminate' in D Friedmann and D Barak-Erez (eds), *Human Rights in Private Law* (Hart Publishing, Oxford, 2001) 245–82.

[112] See also K Gray, 'Property in Thin Air' (1991) 50 *Cambridge Law Journal* 252 on moral limits as conditioning the extent of excludability and property.

development of the law of common callings is now solely the preserve of the legislature and human rights law. That is, limitations on the property owner's use of property are not justified solely by reference to private law ideas that property cannot be used to harm others; instead, we must now invoke legislative or human rights norms to achieve the same end (or not, as in *CIN v Rawlins*). As in the decision in *Kaye v Robertson*,[113] it is the unnecessary contraction of the private law which now compels the extension of public law, and particularly the law of human rights.

Several of the young men in *CIN v Rawlins* applied to the European Commission for relief, on the basis that the United Kingdom had not fulfilled its positive obligation to allow them to exercise their Article 11 right of peaceful assembly. In *Anderson v The United Kingdom*,[114] the Commission found their case inadmissible, on the basis that freedom of assembly does not 'guarantee a right to pass and re-pass in public places, or to assemble for purely social purposes anywhere one wishes', and the applicants had not shown that they had used the Centre 'for any form of organised assembly or association.'[115] As in *Botta* and *Zehnalova*, the Court did not rule out the possibility that the enjoyment of a Convention right might require access to private land, but such a right would be probably limited to specific purposes, and hence to specific times and places. However, in these cases, the Court held that there had been no interference with a Convention right.

Subsequently, in *Appleby v The United Kingdom*,[116] the applicants argued that their Article 10 right to freedom of expression had been interfered with when they were denied access to a shopping mall in which they wish to campaign on local development issues.[117] The owners informed them that it maintained a policy of strict neutrality on all political and religious issues, and accordingly it refused entry. The applicants claimed that the denial of access interfered with their right to freedom of expression. Hence, the case could be distinguished from *Anderson*, as the applicants were not seeking entry to assemble for purely social purposes. However, the outcome was the same, as the Court held that there had been no breach of the Convention. Nevertheless, unlike *Anderson*, the Court did acknowledge that there had been an interference with freedom of expression, although in balancing the applicants' Article 10 right against the owner's rights under P1(1), it found that the rights of the owner prevailed. It is therefore difficult to judge the lasting significance of *Appleby*. In practical terms, it seems unlikely that Article 10 would ever prevail over P1(1), as the Court said that the State's positive obligation to regulate property rights would only be engaged where 'the bar on access to property has the effect of preventing any effective exercise of freedom of expression or it can be said that the

[113] [1991] FSR 62.
[114] (1998) 25 EHRR CD172.
[115] Above CD174.
[116] (2003) 37 EHRR 38.
[117] Ironically the campaign concerned the loss of public playing fields.

essence of the right has been destroyed'.[118] The positive obligation would come into play only where, for example, 'an entire municipality was controlled by a private body.'[119] That was not the case here: although the shopping mall occupies most of the town centre of Washington, the Court still found that the applicants could campaign elsewhere. By this reasoning, it is virtually impossible to imagine a case in the United Kingdom that would satisfy the Court's requirements. Nevertheless, it did not dismiss the case out of hand: it remarked that the applicants were not barred from campaigning in individual shops that had given their consent.[120] As the Court also remarked that the applicants could campaign elsewhere in town, the observation regarding access to other shops should have been entirely irrelevant. Perhaps, in future, the Court might view another case more favourably.[121]

Two points emerge from this series of cases: the first is that the common law right of the person in possession to exclude others is virtually unrestricted by P1(1) or other Convention rights, even where the use of the land has a public aspect. By public aspect, it is meant only that the possessor has invited the general public to enter the land for commercial purposes, and access to that land has then become a place of community life. This is admittedly very vague,[122] but given the current state of the law, it seems that there is no need to be more precise: however we define 'public aspect', it seems that there is neither a general right of access, nor specific rights to enter for the purpose of obtaining a service or to exercise a Convention right. Moreover, the reasoning in *Anderson* and *Appleby* shows that the Convention rights have almost no impact on the absolute nature of this right. One might argue that the cases could have been put in different terms: in particular, the general invitation to enter that was extended by the owners to potential customers might have constituted a possession under P1(1), thereby giving the applicants some basis for a case under P1(1) or at least Article 14 in combination with P1(1). However, in *Anderson*, the Commission suggested that it was not interested in engaging in judicial creativity of this kind, as it observed that the United Kingdom had not ratified Article 2 of Protocol 4 to the Convention, which guarantees the right to liberty of movement within the territory of a State. Perhaps access cases would receive a more favourable hearing under P4-2, and consequently the Commission was

---

[118] *Appleby* (n 116) [47].

[119] Above.

[120] Presumably the applicants were not barred from entering and passing through the mall to get to such shops.

[121] Note also that the Human Rights Act 1998, s 12 (special regard for freedom of expression), but *cf Monsanto v Tilly and Others* [2000] Env LR 313. It is significant that, in *Appleby*, the Court accepted that Art 10 was applicable. Hence, unlike the *Botta*, *Zehnalova* and *Anderson* cases, *Appleby* raises the possibility that it may possible to challenge an exclusion if the reason was discriminatory under Art 14. See Grear (n 99) p 57, at n 108.

[122] Reichman (n 111), 250, offers a description of a common calling that is more precise: 'except for associational commerce (such as identity-sensitive clubs or other associations that require meaningful membership), all business is "common"' (footnotes omitted).

unwilling to interpret P1(1) (or Art 11) generously for those States which have not ratified it.

Hence, the Convention says almost nothing about the privatisation of public space, except possibly in extreme cases. While it does not prohibit States from regulating the exercise of the right to exclude, the usual effect of privatisation is to remove the decision to exclude from any judicial scrutiny. In *Appleby*, it was at least recognised that this may have some impact on the exercise of other Convention rights, but it seems there is no real possibility that the exclusion from such quasi-public spaces is itself an interference with human rights. In any case, it is odd that an exclusion for other reasons, unrelated to Article 10, might not engage Article 14.

Plainly, it is discouraging that human rights law has so little to say about the use of private property and social exclusion, but the cases are consistent with the general reluctance of the courts to intervene in either the public or private aspects of land use on human rights grounds. That is not to say that it is entirely irrelevant to the human rights analysis: where the State does decide to require access and the landowner objects, the courts are likely to find that the State was entitled to take the social case for access into account, with the result that the interference with possessions can probably be justified.[123] However, except in limited cases, the claim to access is seen as a moral claim without a basis in any of the Convention rights, and the Convention says very little about the arbitrary and discriminatory exclusion of people from spaces that are privately owned but nonetheless constitutive of community.[124]

CONCLUSIONS

The cases on land use controls demonstate that the Court tends to take a conservative and deferential view of its powers. Regulations are not subject to a close scrutiny, and in general the State remains free to regulate property as it sees fit. There are some exceptions, but these arise where the Court has concerns that decision-making process has not been observed.

The position is therefore similar to that found under the constitutional laws of most States, even though the conception of land ownership is one that

[123] Although the need for allowing access is only a factor to be weighed: see eg *Chassagnou v France*, Reports 1999–III 21 (2000) 29 EHRR 615.

[124] The position may be better under the Twelfth Protocol, on free-standing discrimination, or Art 2 of the Fourth Protocol ('P4(2)'): see eg *Östergren v Sweden*, Appl No 13572/88, 1 March 1991, where barring access to traditional grazing land of Sami people raised no appearance of a violation; *Van de Vin v The Netherlands*, Appl No 13628/88, 8 April 1992, where it was held that there was no guarantee of a right to a specific place of residence in the absence of title to reside there; *Van den Dungen v The Netherlands*, Appl No 22838/93, 22 February 1995, where P4(2) was applicable to an injunction prohibiting the applicant from coming within 250 metres of a named abortion clinic, but given his previous conduct, the interference was not disproprotionate; and *Santoro v Italy*, Appl No 36681/97, 1 July 2004, where a police supervision order limiting movement violated P4(2) due to a failure to comply with the legality condition.

suggests that the owner has an unrestricted right to use the land in whatever way he or she sees fit. There appears to be no recognition of the notion that property (especially land) may be subject to obligations, or that the scope of the property bundle of rights is constituted by State power and therefore may be limited by State power. However, it is equally apparent that this expansive conception of ownership is limited to the applicability question. Justifications for land use controls may be necessary, but in most cases, the courts are likely to find that controls do not violate the right to property, either on the fair balance principle or the basis that they ought to defer to the legislature or executive in relation to planning matters.

8

Private Law and the
Right to Property

⟶•◦•⟵

THE EUROPEAN CONVENTION on Human Rights does not bind individuals and provides no procedure for making individuals to accountable to either the Council of Europe or their own States. Nevertheless, it is also clear that the exercise of property and other private law rights may affect the interests protected by Convention rights. To give just two examples already recognised by the courts, the denial of access to private land may restrict right to freedom of expression and association,[1] and the use and disposition of property may interfere with the right to respect for private life and the confidentiality of correspondence.[2] While it does not necessarily follow that Convention rights are enforceable in private litigation, it does suggest that substantive aspects of private law may be incompatible with Convention rights. For example, *Tolstoy Miloslavsky v The United Kingdom*,[3] the European Court of Human Rights found that an award of £1.5 million in damages for libel was a disproportionate interference with the defendant's rights under Article 10.[4] Conversely, private law may provide the mechanisms by which individuals may protect the interests protected by Convention rights: for example, a private right to bring an action for trespass fulfils (in part) the State's obligation to ensure that the right to property is effective, and the right to bring an action for breach of confidentiality fulfils (in part) the State's obligations in respect of privacy.[5] It is possible, therefore, that the Human Rights Act 1998 requires new limits on existing rights of private property, or even the creation of new private law mechanisms for the protection of interests covered by Convention rights.

This chapter begins by asking whether the exercise of private property rights would engage the State's responsibility under P1(1) or other Convention rights. While it is (reasonably) clear that other Convention rights may be applicable

---

[1] *Anderson v The United Kingdom* (1998) 25 EHRR CD172.
[2] *Haig v Aitken* [2001] Ch 110.
[3] Series A No 316–B (1995) 20 EHRR 442.
[4] Above [51] and [55].
[5] *Campbell v MGN* [2004] 2 WLR 1232; *Earl Spencer v The United Kingdom* (1998) 25 EHRR CD105.

when property rights are exercised, this cannot be said with certainty with respect to P1(1). If a Convention right is applicable, it would be necessary to consider how the proportionality and fair balance tests would operate. As both human rights law and private law seek to protect human autonomy and dignity (amongst other things), the exercise of private law rights should not normally violate Convention rights. However, as *Tolstoy Miloslavsky* demonstrates, this cannot be assumed. Finally, the chapter closes by examining the responsibility of the United Kingdom courts under the Human Rights Act 1998 in those cases where private law is incompatible with a Convention right.

THE APPLICABILITY OF CONVENTION RIGHTS WHERE PROPERTY OR CONTRACTUAL RIGHTS ARE EXERCISED

In relation to P1(1), British lawyers at the time the Convention was drafted probably believed that Convention rights would encroach on private law, and hence that it would be necessary to draft explicit limitations to rights if private law rules were not to be affected. Indeed, the possibility that constitutional property rights could have some impact on private relationships had been assumed in Parliamentary debates concerning the Government of India Act, 1935[6] and then again in 1962, in the debates on the repeal of the right to property in the Government of Ireland Act, 1920.[7] This concern is also evident from the drafting of constitutional rights to property in the Commonwealth, as the draftsmen often found it difficult, if not impossible, to distinguish between the compulsory acquisition of property for public purposes and the enforcement of the civil judgments of regarding contracts, property, trusts and other civil relationships. Accordingly, although the Nigerian Bill of Rights was based on the European Convention on Human Rights, the right to property includes express limitations for a number of matters, including those relating to private law.[8] There was no suggestion that the private law of property should be subject to constitutional review, but it was only by including express limits on the right to property that this could be achieved with certainty.

---

[6] See T Allen, *The Right to Property in Commonwealth Constitutions* (CUP, Cambridge, 2000) 44–46.

[7] Above 42–43.

[8] Above 60–69; section 31(3) of the Constitution provided that

> Nothing in this section [containing the right to property] shall be construed as affecting any general law . . . (c) relating to leases, tenancies, mortgages, charges, bills of sale or any other rights or obligations arising out of contracts; (d) relating to the vesting or administration of property of a person adjudged bankrupt or otherwise declared bankrupt or insolvent, of persons of unsound mind, of deceased persons and of companies, other bodies corporate and unincorporated societies in the course of being wound up; . . . (e) relating to the execution of judgments or orders of courts; . . . (h) relating to trusts and trustees; (i) relating to the limitation of actions; (j) relating to property vested in bodies corporate directly established by any law in force in Nigeria.

Are rights other than P1(1) applicable?

Where the State confers special powers over property or other interests that would not arise in private law, the exercise and enforcement of those powers may interfere with Convention rights. For example, the exercise of a power of compulsory purchase engages the State's responsibility under P1(1) and, if the property is a home, under Article 8 as well. The real issue is whether the ordinary exercise of a private law right can interfere with Convention rights. As the Convention provides that it only binds States, it is not immediately obvious that the exercise of property rights by a private person can interfere with the Convention rights of another. However, the wording of some of the Convention rights suggests that it was assumed that the exercise of property or other private law rights could interfere with right itself.[9] For example, while Article 8(1) sets out the right of everyone 'to respect for his private and family life, his home and his correspondence', Article 8(2) restricts it as follows:

> (2) There shall be no interference by a public authority with the exercise of this right except such as is in accordance with the law and is necessary in a democratic society in the interests of national security, public safety or the economic well-being of the country, for the prevention of disorder or crime, for the protection of health or morals, or for the protection of the rights and freedoms of others.

Arguably, the wording in the first line of Article 8(2) suggests that there is a distinction between an interference by a public authority and an interference by a private person, and hence that it is possible for a private person to interfere with the right. Similarly, the reference to the protection of the rights and freedoms suggests that private law rights may be exercised and enforced in a way that interferes with the Article 8 right; and that public authorities, including the courts, may find it necessary to uphold private rights over the Article 8 right.[10]

In any case, it is clear that the State's responsibility may be engaged if it fails to provide a means for vindicating existing private law rights, as it has a positive obligation to ensure that the acts of private persons do not interfere with the interests protected by Convention rights. For example, Article 8 has been found applicable where the State has failed to protect individuals from pollution caused by a third party,[11] and even the failure to investigate a theft may engage the State's responsibility under P1(1).[12] Hence, the judicial enforcement of a

---

[9] See D Beyleveld and S Pattinson, 'Horizontal Applicability and Horizontal Effect' (2002) 118 *Law Quarterly Review* 623, 641ff for a detailed textual analysis of the effect of different Convention provisions on the horizontality of rights.

[10] Even if the 'rights and freedoms of others' refers only to other Convention rights and freedoms, a restriction on the exercise of property rights would be an interference with P1(1).

[11] *López Ostra v Spain*, Series A No 303–C (1995) 20 EHRR 277 [58]; *Guerra v Italy*, Reports 1998–I 210 (1998) 26 EHRR 357 [57] (and see MT Acevedo, 'The Intersection of Human Rights and Environmental Protection in the European Court of Human Rights' (2000) 8 *New York University Environmental Law Journal* 437); cf *S v France* (1990) 65 D&R 250.

[12] *Novoseletskiy v Ukraine*, Appl No 47148/99, 11 March 2003: a P1(1) claim regarding the failure of the authorities to investigate theft of property was admissible.

private law right may engage the State's responsibility, where the enforcement leads to an interference with the interests protected by a Convention right. For example, the enforcement of an exclusive arbitration clause interferes with the Article 6 right of access to the courts (although there is no violation if the consent to the clause was not forced).[13] Similarly, the granting of an injunction or other remedy in private law proceedings for defamation or breach of confidence would raise issues under Article 10.[14] Even the exclusion of an individual from private property may interfere with rights of freedom of association or freedom of expression, if access was sought for those purposes.[15] Plainly, in any of these cases, the State may be able to justify its actions, but it does indicate that the conception of rights under the Convention does not entirely rule out the possibility that the exercise of property rights may raise human rights issues.

The one area of confusion relates to the Article 8 right to respect for the home and the eviction of an occupant without a legal right to possession. Since a dwelling can be a 'home' even if it is illegally occupied,[16] an order vindicating the landlord's exercise of a lawful right to possession should engage Article 8.[17] Whether an eviction can be justified under Article 8(2) raises other issues, but it should be clear that Article 8 is engaged. Nevertheless, there was some confusion on this point in the House of Lords' judgment in *Qazi v Harrow LBC*,[18] where an occupier of a council house argued that allowing an owner to exercise his right to repossess the property would violate his Article 8 right to respect for the home. Mr Qazi, the occupier, and his wife held a joint tenancy of a house owned by the London Borough of Harrow. They separated, and she served notice on Harrow Council to end the tenancy, thereby also bringing Mr Qazi's tenancy to an end.[19] His application for a new tenancy was refused, whereupon Harrow brought proceedings for possession. In his defence, Mr Qazi's counsel argued that Harrow had failed to give effect to his Article 8 right to respect for the home and that the court should have taken that right into account before making an order for possession.[20]

Before the House of Lords, it was claimed that there were no circumstances in which either a public authority landlord or a court would breach Article 8 by

---

[13] See *Suovaniemi v Finland*, Appl No 31737/96, 23 February 1999; *Halsey v Milton Keynes General NHS Trust; Steel v Joy* [2004] 4 All ER 920 (CA) [9]; *Placito v Slater* [2004] 1 WLR 1605 (CA) [51].

[14] *Tolstoy* (n 3).

[15] Chapter 7, 218–223.

[16] *Qazi v Harrow LBC* [2004] 1 AC 983 [61]–[69] (Lord Hope).

[17] The issue regarding difference between public authority landlords and private landlords is discussed below (although it seems from *Ghaidan v Godin-Mendoza* [2004] 3 WLR 113 that this is no longer an issue).

[18] *Qazi* (n 16); see I Loveland, 'The Impact of the Human Rights Act on Security of Tenure in Public Housing' [2004] *Public Law* 594.

[19] It was therefore his wife, a private person, who brought his tenancy to an end rather than a public authority (such as Harrow or the court); S Bright, 'Ending Tenancies by Notice to Quit: The Human Rights Challenge' (2004) 120 *Law Quarterly Review* 398.

[20] It was not argued that there were Convention issues regarding the termination of the tenancy.

seeking or ordering the eviction of a former tenant after the lawful termination of the lease. However, the majority in *Qazi* agreed that repossession would engage Article 8. On the facts, the judgment could have confined itself to the position of public authority landlords; however, the reasoning applies equally to private landlords. Lords Hope and Millett stated that, since Article 8(2) allows an interference with the right conferred by Article 8(1) where necessary to protect the rights and freedoms of others, a landowner's unqualified right to possession would always prevail and there would be no breach of Article 8. As Lord Millett put it, the limitation in Article 8(2) applies because eviction is 'plainly necessary' to protect the landowner's property rights.[21] There is no need for any further inquiry or balancing of interests: in every case, the balance is on the side of the landowner.[22] By this reasoning, it seems that there is not even a theoretical possibility that Article 8 would be breached by allowing a landowner to exercise its right to possession. Nevertheless, since a majority of the judges[23] clearly indicated that there is at least an interference with the respect for the home, there may be cases where an Article 14 discrimination argument may arise in respect of the exercise of a property right to repossession.[24] However, even this limited recognition of the applicability of Article 8 was doubted by Lord Scott, as shown by his analysis of *Sheffield City Council v Smart*.[25] In that case, occupiers of premises held non-secure tenancies which were duly determined by their local authority landlords. The local authorities sought possession, and the Court of Appeal stated that possession orders would interfere with the occupiers' right to respect for their homes.[26] Lord Scott disagreed with this conclusion:

> Each home had been established on the basis of a proprietary interest in the premises obtained under the contractual tenancy granted by the landlord. How could the termination of that tenancy in a manner consistent with its contractual and proprietary incidents be held to constitute a lack of respect for the home that had been thus established? The home was always subject to those contractual and proprietary incidents. The contrary view seems to me to treat a "home" as something ethereal, floating in the air, unconnected to bricks and mortar and land.[27]

---

[21] *Qazi* (n 16) [100].

[22] Above [50] (Lord Hope): 'Article 8(1) does not concern itself with the person's right to the peaceful enjoyment of his home as a possession or as a property right. Rights of that kind are protected by article 1 of the First Protocol.' Nevertheless, repossession is bound to affect his interest in the privacy of his home; however, that does not necessarily mean that there is a serious issue to be tried merely arising from the fact of eviction (see also [100]–[103] (Lord Millett)).

[23] Lords Hope and Millett, who held that there was no further issue to try (ie the landowners' rights must prevail) and Lords Bingham and Steyn, who held that there was an interference and there should be further consideration of the balance of interests in allowing repossession.

[24] Eg *Larkos v Cyprus*, Reports 1999–I 557 (2000) 30 EHRR 597, where tenants of private landlords were entitled to statutory protection that tenants of public authority landlords, although the leases granted by public authority landlords were in the form of private law leases. There was a violation of Article 14 in conjunction with Article 8.

[25] [2002] HLR 639.

[26] Above [26]–[27].

[27] *Qazi* (n 16) [145].

Lord Scott is plainly right about the home not being 'unconnected to bricks and mortar and land'; indeed, the Convention meaning of 'home' links it to the physical dwelling actually occupied by the individual.[28] However, he seems to say that the connection with the physical dwelling is established by holding property rights over the dwelling, although it is quite clear that this is not necessary. Nevertheless, the thrust of this passage is clear: Article 8(1) cannot be used to defeat or limit a property right to the dwelling, and the scope of the Article 8(1) right is necessarily limited by property rights held by third parties. Put more generally, his *dicta* holds that the Convention does not confer new property rights, and hence Article 8 cannot confer a new defence against repossession. In support of this, the European Court of Human Rights has said that P1(1) protects rights *of* property, not rights *to* property.[29]

The other Law Lords in *Qazi* held that Article 8 was engaged, and they must be correct on this point: even if the proportionality balance normally lies on the side of the landlord's rights, there may be other cases where it is not, particular where Article 14 is invoked. This is illustrated by the more recent decision in *Ghaidan v Godin-Mendoza*.[30] Here, a tenant argued that the protection provided to spouses and co-habitees in a heterosexual relationship should also apply to co-habitees in a homosexual relationship. The Rent Act 1977 provides that, on the death of a protected tenant, a surviving spouse who is living in the property becomes a statutory tenant by succession. Schedule 1, paragraph 2(2) provides that this includes anyone living with the original tenant 'as his or her wife or husband'.[31] In 2001, in *Fitzpatrick v Sterling Housing Association Ltd*,[32] the House of Lords decided that paragraph 2(2) did not extend to those in a same-sex relationship. However, the Human Rights Act 1998 was not applicable in *Fitzpatrick*, and in *Ghaidan v Godin-Mendoza*,[33] their Lordships were invited to reconsider their interpretation in the light of the 1998 Act.

The House of Lords held that Article 14, in conjunction with Article 8, would be violated if a fresh interpretation of the Rent Act 1977 were not adopted; hence, in reliance on section 3 of the Human Rights Act 1998, it allowed Mr Godin-Mendoza to acquire the status of a statutory tenant. But since the landlord sought to exercise a lawful right to repossession, it is clear that Article 8 was also engaged and that Lord Scott's position is incorrect. Indeed, it is worth noting how far *Ghaidan v Godin-Mendoza* extends: it did not involve a public authority landlord, and unlike *James*, the relevant legislation extended the

---

[28] Above [61]–[69] (Lord Hope).

[29] *Marckx v Belgium*, Series A No 31 (1979) 2 EHRR 330; see Chapter 2.

[30] *Ghaidan* (n 17).

[31] Sch 1, '2(1) The surviving spouse (if any) of the original tenant, if residing in the dwelling–house immediately before the death of the original tenant, shall after the death be the statutory tenant if and so long as he or she occupies the dwelling–house as his or her residence. (2) For the purposes of this paragraph, a person who was living with the original tenant as his or her wife or husband shall be treated as the spouse of the original tenant'.

[32] [2001] 1 AC 27.

[33] *Ghaidan* (n 17).

private law rights protecting family home (although on a discriminatory basis). It therefore suggests that the courts in the United Kingdom will readily conclude that the Convention is engaged where the enforcement of private law rights interferes with practical enjoyment of the interests protected by the Convention rights.

Is P1(1) applicable?

P1(1) does not contain the reference to the 'rights and freedoms of others' that appears in Articles 8-11. It was probably assumed that P1(1) would not require changes in the substance of private property law, but the mechanism by which this would be achieved was not discussed. The Convention procedures only allow individuals to bring a claim against a State.[34] However, as the jurisprudence on other Convention rights shows, the enforcement of private property may interfere with the interests protected by Convention rights, and thereby engage the State's responsibility. In relation to P1(1), it may have been thought that the third sentence was so widely drawn that the State would be able to justify the enforcement of any right of private property that interferes with the property of another. Or, there may have been a belief that the lawful exercise of a contractual or property right cannot interfere with the property of another, as one person's entitlements are delimited by another's. So, for example, even if the lawful exercise of a right to repossession conflicts with the Article 8 right to the home, arguably it cannot conflict with the tenant's proprietary rights because either the landlord or the tenant must have a superior right to possession at any time. This is supported by numerous cases in which the European Court has stated that P1(1) is not concerned with the resolution of property disputes in civil proceedings in the domestic courts.[35] It appears that neither the breach of contract[36] nor the exercise

---

[34] Article 34: 'The Court may receive applications from any person, non-governmental organisation or group of individuals claiming to be the victim of a violation by one of the High Contracting Parties of the rights set forth in the Convention or the protocols thereto. The High Contracting Parties undertake not to hinder in any way the effective exercise of this right.'

[35] See eg *Skowronski v Poland*, Appl No 52595/99, 28 June 2001; *Kranz v Poland*, Appl No 6214/02, 10 September 2002; *Pado v Poland*, Appl No 75108/01, 14 January 2003; *Hagman v Finland*, Appl No 41765/98, 14 January 2003 (not applicable to enforcement of security in a private transaction; but *cf Tsironis v Greece*, Appl No 44584/98, 6 December 2001); *Popovici and Dumitrescu v Romania*, Appl No 31549/96, 4 March 2003; *Karstova v The Czech Republic*, Appl No 54407/00, 30 September 2003; *Eskelinen v Finland*, Appl No 7274/02, 3 February 2004.

[36] *Gustafsson v Sweden*, Reports 1996–II 637 (1996) 22 EHRR 409 [60]:

the State may be responsible under Art 1 (P1(1)) for interferences with peaceful enjoyment of possessions resulting from transactions between private individuals . . .. In the present case, however, not only were the facts complained of not the product of an exercise of governmental authority, but they concerned exclusively relationships of a contractual nature between private individuals, namely the applicant and his suppliers or deliverers. In the Court's opinion, such repercussions as the stop in deliveries had on the applicant's restaurant were not such as to bring Art 1 of Protocol No. 1 (P1(1)) into play.

of a contractual or property right[37] by a private party engages the State's responsibility under P1(1). More generally, in *Zohiou v Greece*, the Court said that 'there is no interference with the right to peaceful enjoyment of possessions when, pursuant to a pre-existing law, a court orders one individual party to a civil-law relationship to pay compensation to another'.[38] Similarly, in *Tormala v Finland*, the Court stated that the 'domestic court regulation of property disputes according to domestic law does not, by itself, raise any issues under Article 1 of Protocol No. 1 to the Convention'.[39] The corollary is that P1(1) cannot be used as a basis for enhancing contractual or property rights under national law. This follows from the statement in *Marckx* that P1(1) protects existing property rights only; as noted above, P1(1) protects rights of property, not rights to property.[40]

Although these judgments indicate that disputes concerning the content of private law interests do not engage P1(1), there are some Strasbourg cases where it seems that the Court takes a different view. One example is *Sesztakov v Hungary*,[41] which concerned a court-ordered division of matrimonial property. The Court declared the application inadmissible, on the basis that 'the court decisions provided a solution to a civil-law dispute between private parties' and hence they 'cannot of themselves engage the responsibility of the respondent State under Article 1 of Protocol No. 1'.[42] While this seems to confirm that P1(1) is not applicable in private law property disputes, the Court also said that its conclusion was reinforced by the absence of any appearance of 'arbitrariness in

---

[37] *Öztürk v Turkey*, Appl No 44126/02, 2 October 2003.

[38] Appl No 40428/98, 23 March 2000 (in support, the Court referred to *JW and EW v The United Kingdom*, Appl No 9776/82, 3 October 1983, although that case deals with discrimination in the provision of State pensions). See also *Mairitsch v Austria* (1989) 11 EHRR CD46, 46: an application regarding a marriage settlement and the transfer of property was declared manifestly ill–founded. P1(1) did apply, but the interference did not 'unjustly or arbitrarily deprive' one person in favour of another: 'in such cases the passing of property, resulting from legal limitations inherent in particular property rights, should not be considered as constituting a deprivation of possessions for the purposes of the second sentence of Article 1'.

[39] Appl No 41258/98, 16 March 2004. This even applied to winding up and wasted costs orders; see also *Papakokkinou v Cyprus*, Appl No 20429/02, 7 January 2003: costs order from private law proceedings is also outside P1(1); but *cf Fransson And Fransson v Sweden*, Appl No 8719/02, 16 March 2004: P1(1) is applicable, but the imposition of costs in unsuccessful proceedings normally lies with the margin of appreciation.

[40] *Marckx* (n 29). For a UK example in relation to P1(1), see *Nerva v The United Kingdom* (2003) 36 EHRR 4, in which the applicants complained when their employer, who ran a restaurant, included tips left by customers as part of their remuneration in satisfaction of his obligation to pay them the minimum wage, under the Wages Act 1986. The Court of Appeal had decided that the tips did not belong to the staff and hence could be used by the employer as it wished (see *Nerva v RL & G Ltd* [1996] IRLR 461 (CA)). The applicants complained that this ruling violated P1(1), on the basis that it deprived them of their possessions in the form of their statutory entitlement to the minimum wage. The majority in the European Court rejected their application, on the basis that ([43]) 'it was for the applicants to come to a contractual arrangement with their employer as to how the tips at issue were to be dealt with from the point of view of their wage entitlement . . . they cannot rely on Article 1 of Protocol No. 1 to base a claim to a higher level of earnings.'

[41] *Sesztakov v Hungary*, Appl No 59094/00, 16 December 2003.

[42] Above [38]; see also *Mlynar v The Czech Republic*, Appl No 70861/01, 10 December 2002 (arbitrary resolution of private disputes would be contrary to P1(1)); *Synod College of the Evangelical Reformed Church of Lithuania v Lithuania* (2003) 36 EHRR CD94.

the decisions reached or in the procedures followed'. Similarly, in *Voyager Limited v Turkey*, another admissibility decision, the Court remarked that 'the State could be held responsible for losses caused by such determinations by its courts if their decisions amounted to arbitrary and disproportionate interference with possessions'.[43] Again, the application was inadmissible, but these statements suggest that P1(1) is applicable, although the circumstances where it would be violated are very limited.

The British position is not entirely clear. Where the property or contractual rights have their source in common law or equity law, it seems that P1(1) is not engaged. The leading example is *Aston Cantlow and Wilmcote with Billesley Parochial Church Council v Wallbank*,[44] which concerned obligations owed by the owners of rectorial land. The owners, the Wallbanks, bought land which was subject to a potential liability to contribute to the repair of the chancel of the local parish church.[45] The Parochial Church Council with responsibility for the church served the Wallbanks with a notice to contribute for repair, and objected that the service of the notice was incompatible with P1(1). The Court of Appeal agreed, and required the Council not to proceed further with its demand for payment. The Council then appealed to the House of Lords, whose judgment concentrated almost entirely on the status of the Parochial Church Council: was it a public authority and, if so, was it required to consider the impact that the exercise of chancel repair rights would have on the Wallbanks' P1(1) rights? These issues were decided against the Wallbanks, and hence it was not strictly necessary to consider whether P1(1) would be engaged by the Parochial Church Council's exercise of its rights, or by a court order enforcing those rights. Nevertheless, Lords Hope and Hobhouse did say that the exercise of the right to demand a contribution for chancel repair did not interfere with the Wallbanks' possessions. According to Lord Hope, chancel repair liability was an incident of ownership, and so the enforcement of the liability could not amount to a P1(1) interference with their possessions.[46] More generally, Lord Hobhouse stated that it is 'clear that [P1(1)] does not extend to grant relief from liabilities incurred in accordance with the civil law.'[47]

Aston Cantlow dealt with rights arising at common law, and the position may be different in relation to rights conferred by statute. It is clear that the State's responsibility under P1(1) is engaged when it grants a private person the power to acquire property compulsorily. This was established in *James v The United*

---

[43] Appl No 35045/97, 4 September 2001: 'While the State could be held responsible for losses caused by such determinations by its courts if their decisions amounted to arbitrary and disproportionate interference with possessions, this is not the case here.'

[44] [2004] 1 AC 546.

[45] Ferris J, the trial judge, at [2000] 2 EGLR 149 [23] noted that, although chancel repair liability is an incident of ownership of rectorial land, it is 'an unusual incident because it does not amount to a charge on the land, is not limited to the value of the land and imposes a personal liability on the owner of the land.'

[46] *Aston Cantlow* (n 44) [69]–[72].

[47] Above [91].

Kingdom, in relation to the Leasehold Reform Act 1967 and its conferral on tenants of the power under to acquire the freehold interest from private landlords.[48] This suggests that P1(1) is applicable if a statute modifies existing property rights, but arguably not if a statute modifies the rules of private law by which property rights are acquired or the range of property interests that may be created. For example, should Parliament decide to restrict the types of security interests that lenders could take from borrowers, but without changing security interests already in existence, P1(1) would not be applicable.

Under the current law, it is not always possible to distinguish clearly between legislation that affects existing rights and that which does not. In some cases, the emphasis is based on timing: if the property interest is subject to the specific risk of interference from the time of its creation, there is no interference if the risk materialises. This is the approach taken by Lord Hope in *Wilson and others v Secretary of State for Trade and Industry*,[49] which concerned a prohibition on the enforcement of an otherwise valid contract. Section 127(3) of the Consumer Credit Act 1974 provides that consumer loan contracts are unenforceable if prescribed information is not disclosed in the contract. The lender claimed that section 127(3) interfered with P1(1). However, Lord Hope stated that section 127(3), where it took effect, did not engage P1(1), for a distinction had to be made 'between cases where the effect of the relevant law is to deprive a person of something that he already owns and those where its effect is to subject his right from the outset to the reservation or qualification which is now being enforced against him.'[50] Although he did not discuss *James* in relation to this point, his position is consistent with it on the facts, as the applicants in *James* complained of the effect of the Leasehold Reform Act 1967 on existing leases.[51] By this reasoning, the Leasehold Reform Act 1967 does not interfere with leases

---

[48] *James v The United Kingdom*, Series A No 98 (1986) 8 EHRR 123; *Bramelid and Malmström v Sweden* (1982) 5 EHRR 249. In *JA Pye (Oxford) Ltd v Graham* [2001] Ch 804, at 821, Keene LJ accepted that the operation of limitation periods may fall within P1(1). Mummery LJ (at 821) also regarded this as a matter of access to the courts, rather than an interference with possessions, although it is clear that this is incorrect: see eg *Holy Monasteries v Greece*, Series A No 301–A, (1995) 20 EHRR 1. In any case, both expressed the opinion that the loss of land due to the expiry of the limitation period under the Limitation Act 1980 s 15(1) was not disproportionate. JA Pye has taken their case to Strasbourg, where the Court has declared their application admissible: *JA Pye (Oxford) Ltd v The United Kingdom*, Appl No 44302/02, 8 June 2004. (The House of Lords did not discuss the issue, as it stated that the Human Rights Act 1998 did not have had retrospective effect in this case ([2003] 1 AC 419 [65])).

[49] [2004] 1 AC 816.

[50] Above [106] (Lord Hope); see also Lord Scott, at [168]: 'No authority has been cited to your Lordships for the proposition that a statutory provision which prevents a transaction from having the quality of legal enforceability can be regarded as an interference for article 1 purposes with the possessions of the party who would have benefited if the transaction had had that quality.'

[51] See *James* (n 48) [31]: the applicants complained, *inter alia*, that the Leasehold Reform Act 1967: '(i) interfered with agreements between the applicants and their tenants freely made before it came into effect; (ii) frustrated the expectations with which the applicants entered into the agreements, and on which the terms of such agreements were based'.

created after it came into force.[52] In effect, P1(1) is applicable if legislation affects the exercise of vested rights, but not otherwise.

By contrast, in *Wilson*, Lord Nicholls said that it would go too far to say that a 'person who acquires property subject to limitations under national law which subsequently bite according to their tenor cannot complain that his rights under Article 1 of the First Protocol have been infringed'.[53] Whether P1(1) is engaged is 'a matter of substance rather than form.'[54] Accordingly, section 127(3) of the 1974 Act should be seen as 'a statutory deprivation of the lender's rights of property in the broadest sense of that expression [rather] than as a mere delimitation of the extent of the rights granted by a transaction.'[55] In that sense, he accepts Lord Hope's view that a distinction should be made between statutory provisions that define the content of a property interest and those that modify the content of an existing interest, but differs on how that distinction should be made. Lord Nicholls concentrates on the character of the legislation, as he describes the 1974 Act as 'overriding legislation'.[56] By doing so, he suggests that the section 127(3) did not define the contractual rights, but that they were created and existed independently of it. Presumably, if the requirements of s 127(3) had been met, P1(1) would not apply if the borrower were compelled to pay the debt according to its terms; neither could the lender complain if it were compelled to pay over the the borrower any surplus achieved on the sale of the secured goods. Although Lord Nicholls did not elaborate on this point, it seems that the crucial factor is the coercive nature of the legislation. As such, his approach also appears consistent with *James*, for if the power to acquire the freehold been freely negotiated and included in the lease as an additional right of the tenant, the exercise of the right probably would have been treated as as an incident of a contract and hence outside P1(1). There is also some support for this approach in *Gustafsson v Sweden*,[57] where the owner of a business was put under a 'blockade' by a union, with the result that his suppliers stopped making their ordinary deliveries to him. The Swedish authorities refused to help, on the basis that the performance of the suppliers' contracts was a private matter, for which remedies were available in ordinary civil proceedings for breach of contract. The Strasbourg Court agreed: while it accepted that *James* shows that P1(1) may apply to 'interferences with peaceful enjoyment of possessions resulting from transactions between private individuals', in this case 'not only were the facts complained of not the product of an exercise of governmental authority, but they concerned exclusively relationships of a contractual nature

---

[52] There is some support for this in the case law: *Athanassoglou v Switzerland*, Reports 2000–IV 173 (2001) 31 EHRR 13 (although decided on Art 6); see also *Duke Power Co v Carolina Environmental Study Group, Inc* 438 US 59 (1978).

[53] *Wilson* (n 49) [40].

[54] *Wilson* (n 49) [44].

[55] Above.

[56] Above [41].

[57] *Gustafsson* (n 36).

between private individuals, namely the applicant and his suppliers or deliverers.'[58] While the focus was on responsibility for the acts of third parties, the judgment also supports the idea that P1(1) is only engaged when the State power is used to modify the terms of a relationship agreed by the parties. Indeed, a particularly significant aspect of Lord Nicholls' judgment is that it is not necessarily limited to statutes that operate on vested rights: as in *Wilson* itself, it may apply to an agreement made subject to a prior overriding rule that prevents it from taking effect according to terms.

Neither the approach of Lord Hope nor of Lord Nicholls can be said to be firmly established, and indeed there are cases where the view of applicability is broader than either one of these tests would suggest. *Bramelid v Sweden*[59] is one example. Here, the Commission held that P1(1) applied to provisions of Swedish company law allowing the holders of more than 90% of the shares of a company to force the minority to sell to them. Unlike the freehold interests in *James*, the shares in *Bramelid* were always subject to the possibility that the compulsory purchase procedure would be invoked.[60] In that sense, Lord Hope's test would suggest that there was no interference with the shares as possessions. Lord Nicholls' test also seems to come to the same conclusion, since the legislation defined the content of the rights that could be obtained by acquiring shares. In effect, it created a standard form of contract which individuals could choose to enter (or not to enter), and could not be described as 'overriding' legislation that altered a freely negotiated distribution of rights and obligations.

In the United Kingdom, this uncertainty can be seen in several recent cases from the Court of Appeal. These cases concern a business tenant's rights, under the Landlord and Tenant Act 1954, to continue a tenancy after the term has ended. In order to continue the tenancy, the tenant must give the appropriate notice to the landlord within a set period. In *CA Webber (Transport) Ltd v Network Rail Infrastructure Ltd*,[61] the tenant did not return a notice within the required time; in *Pennycook v Shaws (EAL) Limited*,[62] the tenant mistakenly

---

[58] Above [60]; but see *Kurkchian and Kurkchian v Bulgaria*, Appl No 44626/98, 22 January 2004: the applicants complained under P1(1) that the excessive length of the proceedings had allowed their neighbours to finish the construction which prevented the access of sunlight to their house: admissible. See also *Josephides v Cyprus*, Appl No 2647/02, 24 September 2002: a neighbour did construction work which applicant claimed interfered with land the applicant complained to public authorities about construction work done by a neighbour that interfered with his land; the Court rejected any claims against State as not responsible (applicant believed the authorities should have taken more action because he was out of the country). See also *MS v Bulgaria*, Appl No 40061/98, 17 May 2001: there was a flawed auction sale of applicant's property, who had but failed to pursue a civil action; hence inadmissible.

[59] *Bramelid* (n 48).

[60] Although the legislation in question had been enacted after the shares were issued (and acquired by the applicant), earlier legislation had contained substantially similar provisions. The primary change in the legislation was to allow a company holding shares to include the holdings of its subsidiaries. This turned out to be a material change, as the acquiring company only met the 90% threshold by including the shares held by a subsidiary.

[61] [2004] 1 WLR 320.

[62] [2004] 2 WLR 1331.

returned a notice stating that it would not exercise its statutory right before giving a second notice stating that it would. According to the established interpretation of the 1954 Act, the tenants in both cases lost their statutory rights as a result of these acts and omissions. Both tenants claimed that the loss of their statutory rights was incompatible with P1(1), and hence the Human Rights Act 1998 required the courts to adopt a different interpretation of the 1954 Act. But if, as Lord Hope maintained in *Wilson*, P1(1) is not applicable where a right is exercised or lost according to terms of contract, then arguably it should not be applicable to the exercise or loss of a statutory right relating to the contract, according to the terms of the statute. And, to turn to Lord Nicholls' test, the 1954 Act created a form of contract that parties could choose to enter or not to enter; as such, the Act does not seem to be 'overriding' legislation. Nevertheless, both Longmore LJ in *CA Webber* and Arden LJ in *Pennycook v Shaws (EAL) Ltd* concluded that P1(1) was applicable.[63]

Concluding comments on applicability

In conclusion, it seems that guidance on the resolution of difficult cases is thin. Although the scope for applying P1(1) is ill-defined, it is clear that it is narrower than it is with other Convention rights. It appears that there are two explanations for this position: the first is the reliance on the formal view that property interests delimit each other, from which it seems to follow that the vindication of one person's rights cannot 'interfere' with those of another; the second is the belief that the private law of property is entirely distinct from the public law of property.

In relation to the first, it is doubtful whether the efforts to come up with a formal test for limiting the application of P1(1) will be successful. Indeed, there is a parallel with the attempts of the common law courts to clarify the presumption of interpretation that a statute is not intended to impair vested rights. In *Wilson*, Lord Rodger commented that 'The courts have tried, without conspicuous success, to define what is meant by "vested rights" for this purpose.'[64] On reviewing the cases on the identification of vested rights, he concluded that 'It is not easy to reconcile all the decisions. This lends weight to the criticism that the reasoning in them is essentially circular: the courts have tended to attach the somewhat woolly label "vested" to those rights which they conclude should be protected from the effect of the new legislation.'[65] It seems unlikely that circular reasoning will be avoided under P1(1) if the courts attempt to formal tests for

---

[63] Both Longmore LJ and Arden LJ concluded, with little difficulty, that the interference was not disproportionate. See also *Kissova v Slovakia*, Appl No 57232/00, 14 June 2001: with similar Slovakian legislation, the failure to allow a renewal engaged P1(1), although the interference was not disproportionate on the facts.

[64] *Wilson* (n 49) [196] (Lord Rodger).

[65] Above.

distinguishing between legal rules that modify existing property and rules that modify the ways in which property may be acquired.

The second point concerns the belief that private law and human rights are distinct. This can be seen in the extra-judicial writing of Lord Justice Buxton, who argued that Convention rights are only concerned with the relationship between the State and the individual, and as such they say nothing about relationships between individuals. Indeed, they have little or no impact even as a source of values guiding the development of private law, since they reflect 'values whose content lives in public law.'[66] It is also reflected in Lord Nicholls' reasoning in *Wilson*, in his focus on 'overriding' legislation: it seems that individual choices that create private relationships are beyond the scope of P1(1), and the values of P1(1) do not assist in determining the legal incidents of such relationships. But is it correct to say that the values of human rights law are entirely distinct from those of private law? The human rights concern with autonomy and dignity are reflected principles such as contractual freedom and the freedom to exercise one's property rights as one sees fit.[67] Indeed, one might say that property and contract law preserve a sphere of autonomy and dignity in the field of private relationships, both in broad sweep of preserving freedom of contract and in relation to narrower and specific rules, such as those relating to restraint of trade and common callings. While the relationships regulated by public and private law are different, and the manner in which interests are balanced in each are different, that is not to say that the fundamental values are different. There is no sense that private law should be developed without reference to the value of autonomy and human dignity; plainly, other values are relevant as well, but it would be inaccurate to say that the values of human rights law have no relevance to private law. Hence, to the extent that there is a common concern with autonomy and dignity, it would make sense for a judge dealing with a rule of private law at least to consider whether human rights law can provide any guidance on the conceptions of autonomy and dignity that have been developed in other contexts. But whether this means that P1(1) is applicable and hence must considered in private law cases is another issue.

Two pragmatic arguments can be put forward for a broad view of applicability. That is, on the basis that both private law and public law share a concern with the protection of human autonomy and dignity, it would better serve this objective if P1(1) were considered applicable in doubtful cases.

(1) The first is an institutional or structural argument, and it is simply that courts involved settling private law disputes are likely to reach better conclusions if they consider the work of public law courts in human rights disputes. By way of comparison, it has been argued that the judicial expansion of civil rights

---

[66]   R Buxton, 'The Human Rights Act and Private Law' (2000) 116 *Law Quarterly Review* 48, 59.

[67]   See D Oliver, 'The Human Rights Act and Public Law/Private Law Divides' [2000] *European Human Rights Law Review* 343, 344: the values underlying both public and private law 'have in common recognition of the importance of respect for the vital interests of individuals in their autonomy, dignity and security.'

law in the United States (and its limited application in private law) can be explained partly by the institutional structure of the legal system at that time. State legislatures and courts have the constitutional power to reform most aspects of private and public law, but they often failed to exercise that power. At the national level, the jurisdiction of Congress and the President over State matters are strictly constrained. Hence, only the federal courts, and especially the Supreme Court, were both willing and able bring about change. The judicial activism of the Supreme Court could be explained as the product of, first, a strong belief that change was necessary; and second, an equally strong belief that no other institution of government was able or likely to bring about these changes. Hence, in cases like *Shelley v Kraemer*,[68] it was the federal courts that took action in the field of civil rights, with the Bill of Rights as their constitutional backing.

This suggests that the desirability of holding that P1(1) is applicable is not determined solely by its content, but also by the character of the tribunals that decide its content. In that sense, section 2 is as important as sections 3 or 6 or the remedial provisions of the 1998 Act. Before the acceptance of the right of petition and the jurisdiction of the Court (and Commission) in 1966, even if one could say that both public and private law of England and Wales shared the objective of protecting dignity and autonomy, all national issues relating to both were resolved by the same courts in the United Kingdom. Within the judicial system itself, there was no system of checks and balances that might produce a more rigorous approach to the realisation of fundamental objectives of law. The 1966 developments still left the national and international tribunals applying different rules, and with limited power to the international tribunals. Now, with the 1998 Act, they interpret the same human rights rules, and rough system of checks and balances is being created within the judicial system itself.[69] There is therefore the potential for influence that did not exist previously. Of course, to state that there is potential for influence does not suggest that it is necessarily a positive influence. Indeed, the American experience provides its own warning in this respect, as the Supreme Court in the early twentieth century used constitutional law as a means of limiting State power in fields of employment law and social reform.[70] The European jurisprudence is quite restrained where private law arises, and there is no evidence that the Court believes that either protecting or constraining choice is the only means of protecting autonomy and dignity. There is, of course, always the risk that judicial intervention will fall entirely out of step with public expectations on the role of law in protecting autonomy and dignity. As Brownsword and Feldman have pointed out, even in private law,

[68] 334 US 1 (1948).

[69] Section 2 subjects UK courts to Strasbourg; Strasbourg bound in terms of limited review of private law, but also takes into account developments in national courts on ECHR; and there have been proposals to extend.

[70] See Chapter 1, n 70 and accompanying text.

these ideas may be applied so as to extend individual choice or to restrain it.[71] The pragmatic argument therefore offers no continuing guarantee that introducing an international tribunal will, over the long run, strengthen the protection of autonomy and dignity in English private law in a manner that is considered appropriate in the domestic context.

The foregoing merely suggests that a broad view of applicability may have an impact on private law, but it does not necessarily follow that the impact would be beneficial. Some argument therefore needs to be made to demonstrate that, at the present time, it would be. This relies on the state of English private law prior to the 1998 Act. Although there are areas where developments in private law fulfilled human rights concerns, it has just as frequently failed to do so. *Kaye v Robertson*[72] is one striking example: the failure to protect privacy adequately in the past provided the justification for failing to remedy the situation in the present. Modern concerns over harassment, the protection of an occupier's interest in the home, obtaining access rights to quasi-public space, and almost the entire field of discrimination are also areas where the judge-made rules of private law do little to help victims. Overall, the record demonstrates a lack of coherent response to the modern concerns relating to autonomy and dignity.

Lord Nicholls' views of 'overriding' law reveal a belief that traditional areas of private law currently protect autonomy and dignity in private relationships in the most appropriate manner and hence any intervention by the legislature in formation of contract, or use of property, should be seen as potentially compromising that the autonomy or dignity of the individual. Human rights law therefore operates against a belief that private law currently provides appropriate protection, and the role of a human rights tribunal is to restore that position where it has been upset by the legislature, unless the State can provide justification to the contrary.

(2) The second point returns to the judicial approach to vested rights. As explained in chapter 1, the principles of statutory interpretation, including the presumption that Parliament does not intend to interfere with vested rights, have provided a kind of unwritten bill of rights in many common law jurisdictions. However, the presumption does not apply strictly: in practice, it means only that any Parliamentary interference with vested rights must be subject to closer scrutiny. Moreover, it appears that the scrutiny focuses on the fairness of the interference, rather than its formal description. As Lord Rodger observed in *Wilson*, the attempts to distinguish between the interference with vested rights and other forms of interference have proved unsuccessful. He also approved of a recent statement of Lord Mustill, who remarked that the basis of the presumption against the impairment of vested rights cannot be found in a formal description of vested rights, but rather it 'is no more than simple fairness, which

---

[71] R Brownsword, 'Freedom of Contract, Human Rights and Human Dignity' in D Friedmann and D Barak-Erez, (eds), *Human Rights in Private Law* (Hart Publishing, Oxford, 2001) 191–93 (referring to D Feldman, 'Human Dignity as a Legal Value: Part I' [1999] *Public Law* 682, 685).
[72] [1991] FSR 62.

ought to be the basis of every general rule.'[73] Ultimately, the objective of protecting fundamental rights produced a result-driven analysis in relation to the nature of the rights and interference, in order to express the more fundamental principle of fairness. Under the Convention, the same position would be achieved by extending applicability in such cases, in order to allow the courts to apply the tests of legality and, in particular, the fair balance. Indeed, the cases that present difficult issues in terms of applicability are often not so difficult to resolve in terms of the fair balance. That is, in *Aston Cantlow*, *Wilson*, *Bramelid*, *CA Webber* and *Pennycook v Shaws (EAL) Ltd*, the courts readily concluded that any interference with P1(1) had not upset the fair balance. The fact that the claimants had acquired property subject to a discoverable risk that others had rights that might be exercised against them was the significant point, as the victim could not complain that it was unfair that the risk subsequently materialised.

THE FAIR BALANCE AND PROPORTIONALITY TESTS

If the exercise of a property or contractual right does engage P1(1) or another Convention right, the analysis would move to the State's justification for the interference. While the State would be required to show that the interference satisfied the condition of legality, the focus is likely to fall on the proportionality/ fair balance test. In this respect, there are two different situations to consider: (a) the justification where the enforcement or exercise of a property right interferes with a Convention right other than P1(1) and (b) the justification in cases involving an interference with P1(1).

Proportionality and other Convention rights

It is clear that Convention rights do not necessarily override property rights. For example, the right to respect for the home does not provide an absolute right to remain in occupation as against a person with the legal right to possession,[74] and the right to freedom of expression does not necessarily prevail over copyright or the civil right to bring an action for defamation. It is not so clear, however, how far the courts will apply the limitations in favour of the rights and freedoms of others, or the specific limitations in favour of copyright or other civil rights. In *Qazi*, Lord Millett and Lord Hope indicated that the limitation in Article 8(2) would always operate in favour of an unqualified right to

---

[73] Lord Rodger in *Wilson* (n 49) [196], referring to *L'Office Cherifien des Phosphates v Yamashita-Shinnihon Steamship Co* [1994] 1 AC 486, 525 (Lord Mustill).

[74] *P v The United Kingdom*, Appl No 14751/89, 12 December 1990; *Wood v The United Kingdom* (1997) 24 EHRR CD69; *Ure v The United Kingdom*, Appl No 28027/95, 27 November 1996.

possession: when a home is lost as a result of a lawful exercise of a right to repossession, the interference cannot be disproportionate.[75] Whether this is supported in the Strasbourg decisions and judgments is doubtful. The limitation can be justified only where 'necessary in a democratic society', which imports the proportionality test. For example, in *Marzari v Italy*,[76] the Court noted that the public authorities had made a real attempt to find alternative accommodation before evicting a tenant who was 100% disabled. While there was no violation of the tenant's right to respect of the home, it seems that it was also relevant that the tenant's personal circumstances were taken into account by the authorities. Another example is *Ure v The United Kingdom*:[77] like *Qazi*, it dealt with a tenant of a council house who was evicted after his wife (the joint tenant) served a notice to quit. Here, the Commission observed that replacement housing accommodation had been found for the applicant, and in any case, his housing needs had changed. Again, there was no violation but, as in *Marzari*, it seems that the consideration given to the position of the applicant was relevant. *Marzari* and *Ure* suggest that there is a balance to be struck; while it may ordinarily fall on the side of property rights, it need not always do so.[78] However, although these cases were cited in *Qazi*, the majority only considered the outcomes: that is, the determination that Article 8 had not been violated on the specific facts of each case was extrapolated to a general principle that an eviction of an unlawful occupant by the person with the right to possession can never breach Article 8.[79]

The Strasbourg cases concern public authority landlords, and hence the Court did not consider the position of tenants of private landlords. For the majority in *Qazi*, it made no difference: the property rights of both public and private landlords are unaffected by Article 8. However, the position becomes more favourable to tenants (whether renting from public or private landlords) where Article 14 is raised in conjunction with Article 8 (or another Convention right). There is no express limitation in favour of the rights and freedoms of others, and the balance tends to be resolved in favour of the Article 14 right rather than the protection of private property. This depends, of course, on the nature of the discriminatory acts, as well as the impact on property that would result from prohibiting the acts. Nevertheless, it is recognised, perhaps more explicitly than it is with Convention rights standing alone, that there is a balance to be struck. For example, in *Ghaidan v Godin-Mendoza*, Lord Nicholls remarked that 'Parliament has to hold a fair balance between the competing interests of tenants and landlords, taking into account broad issues of social and

---

[75] *Qazi* (n 16).

[76] (1999) 28 EHRR CD 175.

[77] *Ure* (n 74).

[78] *Qazi* (n 16) [25] (Lord Bingham). Indeed, in his dissenting judgment in *Qazi*, Lord Bingham acknowledged that local authorities would not ordinarily violate Art 8 if they acted lawfully and in accordance with a scheme for allocating public housing.

[79] See especially *Qazi* above [75]–[77] (Lord Hope) and [102]–[103] (Lord Millett).

economic policy.'[80] He continued by saying that 'even in such a field, where the alleged violation comprises differential treatment based on grounds such as race or sex or sexual orientation the court will scrutinise with intensity any reasons said to constitute justification. The reasons must be cogent if such differential treatment is to be justified.'[81] The majority could not find a principled justification for the discrimination against same-sex couples: indeed, even Lord Millett, who dissented on the application of section 3 of the Human Rights Act 1998, accepted that the relevant provisions of the Rent Act 1977 violated Article 14.[82]

It is noteworthy that there was no discussion of the landlord's rights under P1(1) in *Ghaidan*. However, the adoption of a new interpretation of the Rent Act 1977 engages the United Kingdom's responsibility under P1(1), as it had the effect of restricting the landlord's property rights. Where a Convention right is pitted against a property right, the problem of balancing becomes more complex: not only must the interference with the Convention rights be considered, but the potential interference with property (and hence P1(1)) must also be considered. This was not done in *Ghaidan v Godin-Mendoza*. Moreover, it seems that there was little recognition of this in *Wilson*; indeed, Lord Rodger remarked that, while Convention cases involve the balancing of interests,

> when deciding whether the order sought by one private party would infringe a Convention right of the other, a court must balance the interests of both parties. If the court finds that the order would infringe the Convention right of the party against whom it would be made, this can only be because the court has concluded that his interests are to be preferred to any competing interests of the party seeking the order. In particular, the court must have concluded that the Convention right of the party resisting the order is to be preferred to the other party's common law or statutory right to obtain it.[83]

Lord Rodger did not explain how it is determined that one party's interests are to be preferred to the others. This should be done by considering whether it is possible to arrive at a solution that protects the essence of each right, while possibly allowing some interference with the more marginal aspects of one or both rights.[84] Such an approach can be seen in the recent Canadian case, *Syndicat Northcrest v Amselem*,[85] on the conflict between the human right to religious freedom and the human right to property under the law of Quebec. The appellants were occupiers and divided co-owners of units in residential buildings in Montreal. As Orthodox Jews, they were under an obligation to erect and dwell

---

[80] *Ghaidan* (n 17) [19].
[81] Above.
[82] Above [55].
[83] *Wilson* (n 49) [181].
[84] See LE Weinrib and EJ Weinrib, 'Constitutional Values and Private Law in Canada' in D Friedmann and D Barak-Erez, (eds), *Human Rights in Private Law* (Hart Publishing, Oxford, 2002) 54 61.
[85] [2004] *SCC* 47.

in small temporary huts ('succahs') over the nine-day festival of Succot. They wished to do so on their balconies,[86] but the respondent, a legal person representing the co-owners collectively,[87] claimed that the erection of the succahs violated the the declaration of co-ownership signed by all owners, including the appellants. Ultimately, the Quebec courts granted the respondents a permanent injunction against the erection of succahs.

The dispute therefore arose as a purely private matter concerning the interpretation of the declaration of co-ownership. However, the appellants claimed that the injunction infringed their right to freedom of religion, as guaranteed under Quebec's Charter of Human Rights and Freedoms.[88] In response, the respondents raised their right to property, also guaranteed by the Charter.[89]

The Supreme Court of Canada allowed the appeal. It recognised that both the appellants' right to religious freedom and the respondents' right to property were affected, but upholding the injunction would impair religious freedom more than denying it would impair property rights. In particular, denying the appellants the right to erect the succahs on their balconies would strike at the core of their beliefs,[90] and hence destroy the essence of their right to religious freedom. However, it would be possible to put conditions on the erection of the succahs that would preserve the core interests that the right to property was intended to protect.[91] While the Court recognised that the erection of the succahs would affect the co-owners' aesthetic, economic, and security interests in the property, and that they had sought to protect those interests in the declaration of co-ownership, the actual impact would be minimal. For example, it would be possible to ensure that safety was not compromised, and that the impact on the aesthetics of the buildings would be minimised for the short period that the succahs would be in place. Moreover, there was no proof that they would not be affected in any case. Hence, despite the apparent consent given by the appellants to the conditions in the declaration of co-ownership, they were permitted to erect the succahs.[92]

The Canadian approach takes both rights into account and, for each right, it asks whether accommodating that right would cause a serious infringement of

[86] Each co-owner of a unit was entitled to the exclusive use of the balcony attached to their unit, although the legal title to the balcony formed part of the common portions of the building.

[87] Under the Quebec Civil Code, Art 1039, 'Upon the publication of the declaration of co-ownership, the co-owners as a body constitute a legal person, the objects of which are to preserve the immovable, to maintain and manage the common portions, to protect the rights appurtenant to the immovable or the co-ownership and to take all measures of common interest.'

[88] Charter of Human Rights and Freedoms, Revised Statutes of Quebec, ch C–12, s 3 ('Every person is the possessor of the fundamental freedoms, including freedom of conscience, freedom of religion, freedom of opinion, freedom of expression, freedom of peaceful assembly and freedom of association.')

[89] Above s 6 ('Every person has a right to the peaceful enjoyment and free disposition of his property, except to the extent provided by law.')

[90] Syndicat Northcrest (n 85) [65]–[81].

[91] Above [82]–[90], [103]–[104].

[92] The majority also concluded that the signing of the declaration did not constitute a waiver of the right to freedom of religion: above [91]–[102].

the other. The reasoning in both *Ghaidan* and *Wilson* lacks this careful approach to balancing rights. Whether this is due to the manner in which the cases came before the House of Lords is unclear: in *Ghaidan*, it appears that the landlord did not raise the P1(1) issue, and in *Wilson*, neither one of the private parties appeared before the House.[93] In future, the right to property may be given a more thorough consideration in cases where it comes into conflict with other Convention rights.

The fair balance and P1(1)

If the exercise or enforcement of a private right over property engages the State's responsibility under P1(1), it becomes necessary to identify the circumstances in which the fair balance would be upset. To date, the courts in both Strasbourg and the United Kingdom have indicated that circumstances would need to be very exceptional for them to reach this conclusion.

The Court has already held that the State has a wide margin of appreciation when regulating property in furtherance of goals of social justice, the protection of consumers and tenants, or generally to further broadly-defined economic programmes and the like.[94] This point is discussed in more detail in chapter 5, but *Bäck v Finland* illustrates the scope given by the Court to national authorities in private law.[95] Here, the Court considered a claim that a debt adjustment scheme violated a creditor's rights under P1(1).[96] The scheme was enacted after the debt arose, and in this case, the adjustment reduced the debt almost completely. The Court accepted that the retroactive effect of the laws should be taken into account in determining whether the fair balance had been upset, but stated that 'in remedial social legislation and in particular in the field of debt adjustment . . . it must be open to the legislature to take measures affecting the further execution of previously concluded contracts in order to attain the aim of the policy adopted.'[97] Moreover, it has said that those who hold property for

[93] *Wilson* (n 49) [2], Lord Nicholls noted that 'the Attorney General appeared on behalf of the Secretary of State for Trade and Industry. The Speaker of the House of Commons and the Clerk of the Parliaments intervened. They were represented by leading and junior counsel. The Finance and Leasing Association also intervened, as did four insurance companies which are among the largest providers of motor insurance in this country. And leading and junior counsel also appeared as amicus curi.'

[94] Chapter 5, pp 125–30.

[95] Appl No 37598/97, 20 July 2004.

[96] The applicant had guaranteed loans of a third party debtor who ultimately defaulted; the applicant paid the debts, and then sought to recover the payment from the third party. Under Finnish law, the applicant had this right.

[97] *Bäck* (n 95) [68]. Although the legislation in *Bäck* was described as retroactive, it did not seek to change the legal effect of completed acts. It did not provide that the debt had never come into existence, or that payments that had had the effect of discharging the debt were henceforth to be treated as never having discharged it. In the common law, a distinction is made between laws that alter the legal effect of completed acts and those that alter existing rights. The common law principle that a statute should not applied retroactively unless the language clearly so requires does not

commercial gain should accept the general risk of some degree of regulation, even where the specific regulatory measures are harsh and unexpected.[98] Accordingly, it would be unusual to find that the State's private law rules would violate P1(1).

This is borne out in the domestic cases. In *Wilson*, there was no real doubt that the aim of protecting consumer lenders was legitimate, or that requiring disclosure of terms was rationally linked to that aim. The real issue was whether the impact of s 127(3) of the Consumer Credit Act 1974 was excessive. The Court of Appeal held that it was, as contracts were rendered unenforceable even where disclosure would have had no effect on the borrower. The provision would have been compatible with P1(1) if it had allowed enforcement in such cases, but it did not.[99] However, in the House of Lords, there was a consensus that the fair balance was not upset, even though some consumers might have received a 'windfall' as a result of s 127(3).[100] Indeed, the draconian nature of s 127(3) may have contributed to its effectiveness in reforming industry practices. It followed that proportionality did not require fair treatment to both parties to every consumer loan. Moreover, it was not necessary to show that there were less intrusive ways of achieving justice in some cases.

Wilson indicates that it is likely that regulatory schemes that are intended to intervene in the ordinary market can be justified fairly easily. In most cases, it would not be difficult to identify some link with the control over private property to social justice, consumer protection, or a broader social or economic programme. For example, in *Marcic v Thames Water Utilities Ltd*, the House of Lords found that the exclusion of the common law right to bring an action for nuisance for flooding in favour of statutory remedies did not violate P1(1), as the statutory scheme was intended, in part, to ensure that resources available for the improvement of sewer systems were allocated appropriately.[101] Once the link between the broad aim and the specific interference with property is established, the fair balance is likely to operate in favour of the State.

Cases such as *Bäck* and *Wilson* suggest that it is very difficult to imagine circumstances where the substantive principles of private law of property would not satisfy P1(1). Nevertheless, it is interesting that some judges have been careful to leave the door open to this possibility. For example, in *Wilson*, Lord Nicholls noted that the relevant provisions of the Consumer Credit Act 1974 only apply to a loan up to £25,000, and then remarked that he might have come to a different conclusion if the limit had been £250,000.[102] Similarly, in *Bäck*, the

---

arise in cases involving facts similar to those of *Bäck*. This would still be regarded as an example of a law that interferes with a vested right, but as shown by Lord Rodger in *Wilson* (n 49), such laws should not require justification as strong as that for truly retroactive laws.

[98] Chapter 5, 141–45.
[99] *Wilson v First County Trust Ltd (No 2)* [2002] QB 74 [38]–[40].
[100] *Wilson* (n 49) [72] (Lord Nicholls).
[101] [2004] 2 AC 42; see Chapter 7, 212–16.
[102] *Wilson* (n 49) [80].

Court also noted that the applicant had already accepted the risk that the debtor would become insolvent and hence that the debt would not be paid:[103] perhaps if the legislation had the effect of imposing liability in the absence of consent, the result would have been different.

THE CONVENTION AS A SOURCE OF NEW PRIVATE RIGHTS

Judgments of the European Court of Human Rights do not dictate how national law must be changed to ensure compatibility with Convention rights. In property cases, the State is normally expected to effect a reparation of what has been lost, where that is possible.[104] In practice, it is frequently not possible to do so, and in such cases, the Court may declare that the State is under an obligation to pay damages to the victim.[105] In neither situation, however, would the Court state that the State must make changes to specific aspects of its private law of property. Consequently, a State may find that it can satisfy its obligation to protect Convention rights by modifying its private law, but there are also likely to be other methods of satisfying its obligations. It is also within the power of the State to decide which political organ should work out the details of such modifications and, in particular, whether or not it should be left to the courts to do so.

While the Human Rights Act 1998 provides a framework for implementing Convention rights, the courts are still working out the extent of their powers and responsibilities under it. Prior to the Act, the Convention had no real impact on the judicial development of private law: it was only raised in a handful of cases and was dismissed as a largely irrelevant consideration.[106] It is therefore worth asking how far the Human Rights Act 1998 has (i) determined Convention rights should be protected by means of private law, and (ii) how far the courts have been required to effect this protection through private law (or, if not required to do so, whether they have been authorised to do so). In practice, the two questions are often linked, so that the issue is whether the 1998 Act requires or allows the court give horizontal effect to Convention rights in civil proceedings.

Where the outcome of private law proceedings turns on the interpretation of a statutory provision, section 3 of the 1998 Act comes into play. However, it is only section 3 that comes into play: in *Wilson*, their Lordships indicated that, if it had been determined that s 127(3) of the Consumer Credit Act 1974 was

---

[103] *Bäck* (n 95) [62].
[104] Eg *Former King of Greece v Greece*, Reports 2000–XII 119 (2001) 33 EHRR 21 (merits) (2003) 36 EHRR CD43 (just satisfaction).
[105] As in *Former King*, above.
[106] *Hunter v Canary Wharf Ltd* [1997] AC 655, 714 (Lord Cooke, dissenting); *Blathwayt v Lord Cawley* [1976] AC 397, 425–26 (Lord Wilberforce, dissenting); *Rantzen v Mirror Group Newspapers (1986) Ltd* [1994] QB 670, 690–92.

incompatible with P1(1), the court's obligation to ensure compatibility would arise only under section 3 of the 1998 Act, and not under section 6. The court would need to decide whether, under section 3, it was able to adopt a new interpretation of the offending provision; and if not, whether, under section 4, it should issue a declaration of incompatibility. If the court decides that it cannot avoid the incompatibility, it would be bound to apply the existing intrepretation of the relevant statutory provisions. Section 6(2)(a) would apply and it would not then be acting unlawfully under section 6(1) of the Act.

The position becomes more complicated where the incompatibility arises solely from the application of a judge-made rule of common law. Here, section 6 is in play, and its effect has been debated at length.[107] Most commentators and courts have rejected the argument that the Act requires direct horizontality; that is, they do not accept that it gives Convention rights effect in the form of new substantive rights exercisable both against public authorities and against other private persons.[108] Even if Convention rights were intended to impose duties on private persons, the 1998 Act does not directly incorporate Convention rights into national law. It gives 'further effect' to Convention rights, but section 6 does not impose duties on private persons and the remedies provided in sections 7 and 8 for action deemed unlawful under section 6 are only available against public authorities.[109] In the absence of some breach of recognised duty by a private person, there would be no cause of action available to an aggrieved individual. Moreover, while section 6 provides that a court in a private action is a public authority, it is plainly not the defendant in that action.[110] Hence, there is no way for one private person to get a claim against another private person into court unless it is based on some existing cause of action. As put by Baroness Hale in *Campbell*, 'The 1998 Act does not create any new cause of action between private persons'[111] and 'the courts will not invent a new cause of action to cover types of activity which were not previously covered'.[112] In such cases,

---

[107] See eg M Hunt, 'The "Horizontal Effect" of the Human Rights Act' [1998] *Public Law* 423; G Phillipson, 'The Human Rights Act, "Horizontal Effect" and the Common Law: a Bang or a Whimper?' (1999) 62 *Modern Law Review* 824; HWR Wade, 'Horizons of Horizontality' (2000) 116 *Law Quarterly Review* 217; Buxton (n 66); N Bamforth, 'The True "Horizontal Effect" of the Human Rights Act 1998' (2001) 117 *Law Quarterly Review* 34; Beyleveld and Pattinson (n 9); D Nicol, 'Remedial and Substantive Horizontality: the Common Law and *Douglas v Hello! Ltd*' [2002] *Public Law* 232.

[108] The rejection of direct horizontality does not mean that section 3 cannot be used to justify the creation of new causes of action (or property rights). Indeed, the House of Lords did so in *Ghaidan* (n 17). Nevertheless, the Human Rights Act 1998 is not the source of the cause of action or property right: in *Ghaidan*, for example, it is the Rent Act 1977 that is the source of the property right.

[109] Phillipson (n 107) 826–27; Hunt (n 107) 438; the section 6 focus on public authorities was particularly important in *Aston Cantlow* (n 44).

[110] Phillipson, above 828–29; 840.

[111] *Campbell* (n 5) [132].

[112] Above [133]; see also Lord Hoffman [49]: 'Although the Convention, as an international instrument, may impose upon the United Kingdom an obligation to take some steps (whether by statute or otherwise) to protect rights of privacy against invasion by private individuals, it does not follow that such an obligation would have any counterpart in domestic law.'

it is left to Parliament and the executive to address the incompatibility: Convention rights have no direct horizontal effect.

Nevertheless, the court is a public authority under section 6, and it is accepted that it has some responsibility to ensure that the outcome in private proceedings is compatible with Convention rights. There is no doubt that this includes the procedural and remedial aspects of the judicial power, and it is now clear that section 6 does extend to the judicial development of substantive principles of the common law. As such, the Act does require indirect horizontality, but it is the nature of the duty imposed by section 6 that is the focus of attention. Two alternatives are usually suggested.[113] A stronger version of indirect horizontality holds that, while Convention rights do not take effect against other private persons directly, the courts are obligated to develop existing substantive rights in a way that ensures compatibility with Convention rights.[114] A weaker version of indirect horizontality holds that the courts do not seek compatibility with Convention rights *qua* rights, but with the values underpinning those rights. As Gavin Phillipson argues, only the weaker version is consistent with Parliament's refusal to incorporate Convention rights directly.[115] Convention rights cannot be elevated to the category of overriding rules that exclude all rules of private law, as this would amount to a full incorporation of the rights into national law. This position has been adopted by the House of Lords, as it has said that, although the Act does not create new private law rights and obligations, it does provide values that ought to influence the ordinary common law development of those rights and obligations. In *Campbell v MGN Limited*, for example, Lord Nicholls stated that 'The time has come to recognise that the values enshrined in articles 8 and 10 are now part of the cause of action for breach of confidence.'[116] In direct contradiction to Lord Justice Buxton's thesis that Convention rights reflect 'values whose content lives in public law' and hence can have no application in private law,[117] Lord Nicholls stated that these values are 'as much applicable in disputes between individuals or between an individual and a non-governmental body such as a newspaper as they are in disputes between individuals and a public authority.'[118] By extension, the values reflected in all Convention rights are relevant in all cases concerning private law rights and obligations. It may be that, in specific cases, the values are virtually the same as the values that underpin private law, but (as *Campbell* shows) this is not necessarily the case.

As Convention values are now relevant, it is necessary to identify the values that might affect the development of the private law of property. It is apparent

---

[113] See Phillipson (n 107) 835ff for a detailed analysis.

[114] Hunt (n 107).

[115] Phillipson (n 107).

[116] *Campbell* (n 5) [17]. (The House previously decided in *Wainwright v Home Office* [2003] 3 WLR 1137 that there is no general tort of invasion of privacy.)

[117] Buxton (n 66) 59.

[118] *Campbell* (n 5) [17].

that senior judges do not always agree on the nature of Convention values, and in particular on how sharply Convention values differ from traditional private law values. For example, in *Campbell*, Lord Hope doubted that Article 8 or the 1998 Act had brought about a real shift in the action for breach of confidence. While the 'language has changed', as 'We now talk about the right to respect for private life and the countervailing right to freedom of expression',[119] and the European Court's jurisprudence 'offers important guidance as to how these competing rights ought to be approached and analysed',[120] this balancing exercise was already an integral part of the determination of claim for breach of confidence. Ultimately, the 'exercise to which that guidance is directed is essentially the same exercise'.[121] While it is 'plainly now more carefully focussed and more penetrating',[122] it seems that Convention values have not in fact had a significant independent impact on the development of the law.

The judgment of Lord Hoffman in *Campbell* accords Convention values a greater influence in the development of the law of confidence. He remarked that:

> Instead of the cause of action being based upon the duty of good faith applicable to confidential personal information and trade secrets alike, it focuses upon the protection of human autonomy and dignity—the right to control the dissemination of information about one's private life and the right to the esteem and respect of other people.[123]

This shifts the emphasis from the conduct of the holder of the information to the interests of the claimant that the cause of action ought to protect. Human rights law has identified 'private information as something worth protecting as an aspect of human autonomy and dignity.'[124] This leads him to the same conclusion as Lord Nicholls: it must be relevant in proceedings against both public and private persons. Moreover, it has led to a 'a shift in the centre of gravity of the action for breach of confidence when it is used as a remedy for the unjustified publication of personal information.'[125]

This leaves the central question open: what are the values that may affect the development of substantive principles of the private law of property? In the discussion on the applicability of P1(1) and other Convention rights, it was said that human autonomy and dignity are values in both human rights law and private law. Similarly, both human rights and private law often require a balance to be struck between competing interests. However, if values only take effect at a very high level of generality, alongside other private law values such as certainty, fairness, and the like, the effect of human rights law is unlikely to be significant. It may add a new rhetorical dimension to the reasoning in private

---

[119] Above [86] (Lord Hope).
[120] Above.
[121] Above.
[122] Above.
[123] Above [51] (Lord Hoffman).
[124] Above [50].
[125] Above [51].

law cases, but without changing the outcome. But once values are identified at a high level of generality, it should be possible to move to two more specific aspects relating to the development of private law doctrines where human rights law may prove significant (and is already proving significant). The first relates to the nature of the balancing process, and the second to the interests that private law seeks to protect.

The balancing process

As explained above, the courts have not adopted a particularly sophisticated method of balancing the Convention rights of individuals against each other in cases where they come into conflict. The example of the Canadian analysis in *Syndicat Northcrest v Amselem*[126] was raised as a more nuanced approach to resolving such issues. Hence, one may begin by doubting that the application of the Convention jurisprudence on balancing interests will make a difference in domestic litigation, given that it seems relatively undeveloped as it stands. Nevertheless, some general comments on the potential differences, and contributions, of Convention law are appropriate.

The Convention balance is more concerned with the balance between the State and private actors, whereas the private law balance is more concerned with the relationship between private actors. As Lorraine and Ernest Weinrib argue, in private law, the value of human dignity is reflected at the general level through the principle that individual are free to act as they wish, provided that they do not interfere with another's rights.[127] In setting the legal rules that determine their rights and liabilities against each other, the law treats them as equals, in the sense that the justification for the legal rule that applies to one of them also applies to the other. Neither party is responsible for the rules that apply to them, and hence neither party is under any obligation to justify the rule by reference to interests of those outside the relationship. By contrast, in public law, 'the element of relationship is concerned not with maintaining the transactional equality between the doer and the sufferer of a harm, but with negotiating the tension between specific rights and general values within the constitutional scheme.'[128] The State, as a party, does have a responsibility to justify the legal rules it seeks to invoke, and in justifying those rules it may argue that interests of other persons and groups must carry weight. For example, in Strasbourg, the balancing test under P1(1) conceives of State action as an interference with private relationships that already determine the distribution of resources, whereas the private law balance usually asks how legal rules ought to be formulated and applied so as to determine that distribution.

---

[126] *Syndicat Northcrest* (n 85).
[127] Weinrib and Weinrib (n 84) 43–72; see also D Oliver (n 67).
[128] Above p 53.

Although there is a distinction in principle, the end result is often the same. While the courts in private litigation are often wary of considering broader interests, there are many acknowledged examples of situations where they do consider such interests. The laws of nuisance are conditioned by notions of reasonable use, and even the rules of trespass may be subject to similar constraints.[129] In this sense, there is little to separate the two balancing tests. However, the Convention balance sometimes allows the State to identify the public interest solely in terms of the relevant public authority's interest in protecting its financial resources. The compensation issue also raises the possibility that there is a more fundamental distinction between the balancing tests. Arguably, the balance struck in private cases is between private interests, where the public interest is no more than the aggregation of private interests; by contrast, the public interest in human rights cases may be more than the aggregation of private interests. This would be the case if, for example, the human rights public interest included a kind of environmental interest which included more than the consideration of the impact of environmental laws on individuals. Alternatively, even if the public interest in human rights cases is indeed merely the aggregation of private interests, it may be the case that those interests are given different weight in human rights cases; in particular, it could be argued that private law gives greater weight to the interests of those who would be most immediately and directly affected by the decision, whereas human rights law gives relatively greater weight to the interests of more remotely and less specifically affected individuals, possibly over a different time span. Either way, the balancing process in private cases would differ significantly from the balancing process in human rights cases.

Although it is possible to imagine how these distinctions between the nature of the public interest might affect the balancing process, it is not at all clear that the judges on the European Court of Human Rights accept such distinctions. The difficulty here is that it is very difficult to determine the precise nature of the balancing process from the P1(1) jurisprudence of the European Court of Human Rights. The Court has done little more than say that the 'public interest' is very broad. Indeed, one could say the same about the traditional balancing process in private law. The decisions where judges discuss the nature of the public interest relevant to defining the scope of private property are rare; as in *Bernstein v Skyviews*, judges tend to find simply that a claimed right of use is reasonable or not, without examining the principles which determine why the claim is reasonable.

The identification of interests

In *Campbell*, Lord Hoffman's approach suggests that Convention values may be used to alter the standard description of the interest protected by a given

---

[129] *Bernstein v Skyviews and General Ltd* [1978] QB 479, 488.

cause of action. Article 8 protects privacy, and hence the action for confidence should be oriented to the protection of privacy. The Strasbourg jurisprudence is useful because it gives further precision to the meaning of privacy (as well as other interests, such as the nature of the home and correspondence).

However, this use of Convention values is limited by the position taken on the 1998 Act in relation to new causes of action. That is, ordinary incremental development of the common law sometimes produces new causes of action and new forms of property, and there is no suggestion that the 1998 Act has changed this. Indeed, if Convention values are relevant to the development of the common law, they ought to be available in directing and justifying the creation of new causes of action and forms of property. As such, the 1998 Act may not create new statutory causes of action, but the courts may still create new common law causes of action that reflect Convention values. However, it is reasonably clear that the courts are reluctant to go this far at present: indeed, it is significant that Baroness Hale's remarked in *Campbell* that the 1998 Act does not create new causes of action *and* that 'the courts will not invent a new cause of action to cover types of activity which were not previously covered'.[130] The second proposition does not necessarily follow from the first. Nevertheless, it is plain that judicial conservativism will govern the incremental development of the common law, at least in this area and at this time. While the courts may use the Strasbourg cases to identify interests that should be protected by private law with greater precision, they intend only to do so where they can say that those interests were already protected by private law. Indeed, the reasoning in *Campbell v MGN* is consistent with this approach: even though the action for breach of confidentiality protects privacy, it cannot cover the field completely if it retains its link to the communication of information. As Lord Hoffman states, the shift in the 'centre of gravity' did not change the nature of the cause of action: it is still limited to the protection of information rather than privacy as such.[131] Plainly, there is some room to extend the scope of interests that are not clearly defined: in *Campbell*, the notion of confidential information was sufficiently flexible that human rights values could be invoked to discount the requirement of a prior confidential relationship. However, it also seems that the action for confidentiality could not be divorced from its roots in the protection of the claimant's interest in private information, as opposed to privacy generally, even with the invocation of Convention values.

The protection of the home, under Article 8, raises similar issues. At common law, the protection of the home is usually achieved through the possessory actions of nuisance and trespass. To some extent, these could be adapted to cover some of the issues addressed by Article 8: for example, the action for nuisance already covers much of the ground of Article 8 in respect of the State's

---

[130] See above, n 112.
[131] *Campbell* (n 5); compare with *Von Hannover v Germany*, Appl No 59320/00, 24 June 2004, [2004] EMLR 21.

positive obligations to protect against interferences arising from the acts of third parties. However, just as the Convention idea of privacy is not the same as the common law idea of private information, the Convention idea of the 'home' is not the same as the common law idea of possession. Under Article 8, it is not necessary to be in legal possession of the dwelling for it to qualify as a 'home'.[132] Hence, the actions for nuisance and trespass would only cover all Article 8 cases if they were reconstructed so as to do away with the requirement for possession. *Hunter v Canary Wharf* already establishes that this cannot be done within the confines of the existing actions.[133] Consequently, the human rights values relating specifically to the protection of the home are not likely to influence the common law in this area.

This brings out the difficulty in identifying the scope of the 'no new causes of action' principle, because an incompatibility may arise as a result of a combination of statutory and judge-made rules. In both *Wilson* and *Ghaidan v Godin-Mendoza*, a statutory provision could be clearly identified as the source of the interference with possessions: in *Wilson*, s 127 of the Consumer Credit Act 1974 was the sole impediment to the enforcement of the contract; in *Mendoza*, the existing interpretation of Schedule 3 of the Rent Act 1977 plainly barred the claim to a statutory tenancy. However, in other cases, the distinction between statutory and judge-made law might not be so clear. Ian Loveland gives the example of a private landlord who wishes to recover possession of property let under an assured shorthold tenancy because the tenant is discovered to be gay.[134] The Housing Act 1988 provides that the landlord is entitled to an immediate possession order as long as he or she follows the procedure laid down in the Act.[135] If this is sufficient to bring section 3 of the Human Rights Act 1998 into play, it would be possible to confer a property interest on a claimant that would not have otherwise had one. However, if it is not, the courts would probably regard the claim as a new cause of action. Since it is doubtful that there is a common law action against discrimination, the claim would fail. If, however, values do allow creation of new causes of action, then it would be possible to arrive at the same conclusion, whether statutory law is involved or not. That is, as in *Ghaidan v Godin-Mendoza*, the source of the new right is not the 1998 Act, although in this case the source would be found in the jurisdiction of the courts to develop the common law, rather than the provisions of a specific statute (such as the Rent Act 1977).

In any case, other elements of a cause of action—such as those relating to the defendant's conduct or causation—are less likely to be seen as the identifying characteristics of the cause of action. For example, it has been suggested that current rules on the degree of knowledge or participation required before a

---

[132] See *Qazi* (n 16) (except Lord Scott).

[133] [1997] AC (*cf* Lord dissenting at 714 Cooke) 655.

[134] I Loveland, 'Making It Up as They Go Along? The Court of Appeal on Same Sex Spouses and Succession Rights to Tenancies' [2003] *Public Law* 222, 231.

[135] Section 21.

director can be held liable for wrongs committed by their companies are too lax, and that the protection of the human rights of the victims requires the rules to be made stricter.[136] If a claim based on a lower standard of knowledge were successful, the elements of the cause of action would plainly be modified, but the neither the nature of the interest protected nor the injury required to established the claim would have changed. At present, the paucity of cases makes it impossible to say whether the courts would treat this as a violation of the 'no new causes of action' rule. However, it is worth noting that, in *Campbell v MGN*, the House of Lords noted that the requirement of a prior relationship of confidentiality had been discarded, at least in case where the claimant's privacy was at stake, and yet this was not regarded as the creation of a new cause of action. Arguably, this element of confidentiality related only to the conduct of the defendant, rather than the nature of the interest or harm covered by the cause of action.

CONCLUSIONS

When the text of P1(1) was finally settled, the delegates hardly expected the recognition of a human right to property to require radical changes in the private law of property in their own States. The right to property, whether found in an international instrument or a constitutional instrument, tends to be a conservative force on lawmaking. Judicial decisions affecting private relationship which appear to be attributable to an international or constitutional right to property often demonstrate only that the courts have shifted from relying on the traditional balancing process to the constitutional/human rights balance. In effect, the courts believe that the constitutional/human rights balancing process has greater legitimacy. Nevertheless, there are still some significant differences which may lead to different results in specific cases. Even if both the human rights and traditional balances weigh similar facts against similar 'public interest' standards, the standard of proof and treatment of facts and interests differ. In public law, there are real differences between balancing tests which require the State to establish that its objectives are necessary, as opposed to merely expedient; similarly, there are differences between tests which ask whether the interference with the protected interest is the minimum necessary to achieve the stated objective, and those which only require that there should be a rational connection between the interference and the objective. Plainly, these differences are important. Under P1(1), the general position is that the Court does not

---

[136] PT Muchlinski, 'Holding Multinationals to Account: Recent Developments in English Litigation and the Company Law Review' (2002) 23 *Company Lawyer* 168, 174. It is doubtful, however, that this is required by human rights law in any event, given the acceptance of the corporate form. It is more likely that considerations of fault are likely to be employed by those who would be liable under ordinary law, as an argument that their rights under P1(1) have been violated. See also Oliver (n 127) 355.

require States to pursue the least intrusive means of achieving an end, although there are some P1(1) cases where it appears that it has done so. In private law, the balancing process is so vague that it cannot be said that there are principles regarding or the necessity and expediency of objectives or the degree of interference permitted to achieve those ends. The flexibility of the private law balance may allow an English court to reach the same result whether it relies on the Human Rights Act or on the traditional private law balance, but that does not mean that the two tests are merely different expressions of the same principle.

9

The Forfeiture and Confiscation of Property

T HIS CHAPTER EXAMINES the impact of P1(1) in circumstances where the State uses its powers over property as a response to criminal acts. This involves both actions directed against specific property and the imposition of fines or other monetary liabilities. Such acts often have harsh effects, and may operate on the basis of presumptions of fact or other evidential rules that compound the appearance of unfairness. Of course, the response of law enforcement agencies is often that they have no choice but to take dramatic action, and given that criminals are not likely to be forthcoming with evidence of their own activities, the ordinary rules regarding burdens of proof are not always appropriate.

Many such cases raise issues under Article 6 of the Convention, particularly in relation to the guarantees regarding the conduct of criminal proceedings. However, as this chapter demonstrates, not all measures directed against property are enforced in criminal proceedings. Indeed, most of the controversial cases concern measures that are enforced in civil proceedings, primarily to avoid the guarantees regarding criminal trials in Article 6. In particular, in civil proceedings, there is no need to wait for a criminal conviction to take action against property, and neither the right to remain silent nor the criminal standard of proof apply. Article 6 is relevant, as there are guarantees in civil proceedings, but these are generally more favourable to the State than the criminal guarantees.[1] Consequently, the potential for avoiding the criminal process seems to have caught the imagination of lawmakers in recent years. In the United States, civil forfeiture is used both as a means of controlling crime and as a means of funding law enforcement agencies. In Italy, forfeiture and confiscation have been used for many years to break down the financial strength of criminal organisations. In the United Kingdom, civil forfeiture has been a part of the law for many years, especially in relation to smuggling offences. Beginning in the 1980s, the confiscation of the proceeds of crime has been used in specific areas

---

[1] Although, as noted by Simon Brown LJ in *International Transport Roth GmbH v Secretary of State for the Home Department* [2003] QB 728 [33], this depends less on the classification as civil or criminal, but on the nature and effect of the proceedings.

(especially drug trafficking). The current trend is to use it for all forms of criminal or wrongful activity. This is part of the general trend to the use of informal or civil proceedings, such as anti-social behaviour orders, and to some extent, all of these measures raise similar human rights concerns.[2] In relation to property, however, P1(1) offers a further check on the use of the civil process as a response to crime.

This chapter is organised in terms of the purpose of the interference with property. While all the types of interference have the general aim of responding to wrongful activity, the nature of that response varies, and should affect the human rights analysis. The first section therefore examines measures taken to prevent crime, such as the seizure or forfeiture of property to be used as an instrument of crime. These should be regarded in a similar way to any measures intended to avoid a danger to the public, whether or not criminal wrongdoing is threatened. In such cases, one would expect the courts to ask whether the impact on the individual has been balanced against the risk to the public, where the risk is determined by both the likelihood and severity of the potential harm. However, so long as the danger is proven and sufficient, the public interest lies on the side of the seizure of the property. There may be issues regarding the duration of the seizure, but general principle should be in its favour. The crucial point is that the inquiry is not directed toward the personal guilt of the property owner, except to the extent that it may indicate the degree of the risk to the public that would exist if the property was not seized.

The second section concerns measures taken for a compensatory or reparative purpose. A specific loss is identified as the product of wrongdoing, and a liability is imposed to compensate for that loss. Given the scale of some criminal activity, the liability may be very great. However, in principle, the idea that a wrongdoer should compensate for an identified loss caused by their wrongful acts does not seem to violate the principle of proportionality. Neither does it seem inappropriate, in principle, to use the civil process to obtain compensation. There is an issue of guilt here, but more in the civil sense that liability should not be imposed without establishing causation. In practice, this has not been the point of controversy: the real issues arise where it appears that the State is seeking a kind of double-recovery, where compensatory measures are added to, or take no account of, penalties or forfeitures of property imposed in criminal or other civil proceedings.

The next section examines measures which have a deterrent or punitive function. It is in these cases that the classification of proceedings as criminal or civil are most likely to arise. Even in proceedings found to be civil, there may be questions over the use of presumptions of fact that effectively deny the victim an opportunity to present a real defence. In addition, the balance between the guilt (if any) of the victim and the severity of the penalty is also likely to raise

---

[2] See *R (on the application of McCann) v Manchester Crown Court; Clingham v Kensington and Chelsea RLBC* [2003] 1 AC 787 on anti-social behaviour orders and Article 6.

questions, whether or not the proceedings are criminal. To some extent, the principles on the classification of such proceedings have been worked out by the courts: as explained below, they are unlikely to find that proceedings are criminal unless they can result in a conviction or imprisonment. However, there is no clear indication on the substantive side: that is, is it necessary to make some finding of guilt before imposing a penalty? And must the penalty be commensurate with the wrongful act?

Finally, the chapter closes by looking at the remedy of 'civil recovery' created by the Proceeds of Crime Act 2002. This allows the Director of the new Assets Recovery Agency to bring a civil claim for the recovery of property representing the proceeds of crime. Civil recovery works outside the criminal process: indeed, the intention is that is should only be used where criminal proceedings are unlikely to be brought, or they were brought but resulted in acquittal. According to the Home Office, the Act was intended to introduce the principle that there is no right to enjoy property derived from criminal conduct. Consequently, it appears to have a reparative function; however, it is also the case that it is hoped to have a preventive and even punitive effect.

PREVENTIVE MEASURES

Property is often taken or destroyed to avoid a direct danger to safety, public health, the environment or the like. The danger may be connected with criminal activity, but in many cases the victim is innocent of any wrongdoing. Where compensation is provided, or the impact is slight, it is likely that the fair balance test would be satisfied.[3] However, there is no general principle, either under constitutional law or P1(1), that compensation must be provided. There may be a question of proportionality where the impact of the seizure is serious and the risk of harm is trifling, but in general, the courts are likely to exercise deference in such matters.

In the criminal context, these principles were confirmed in *Raimondo v Italy*.[4] The applicant, a suspected member of a 'mafia-type organisation', was charged with serious criminal offences but ultimately acquitted. Before his committal for trial, the Italian courts ordered the seizure of land and vehicles with a view to

---

[3] See eg *Owen v Ministry of Agriculture, Fisheries and Food* [2001] EHLR 18 (QBD). In some specific situations, the common law provided a right to compensation for the destruction of property in an emergency (*Burmah Oil v Lord Advocate* [1965] AC 75) but in practice, the decision has often been determined by pragmatic considerations relating to the effectiveness of the policy goal.

[4] Series A No 281–A (1994) 18 EHRR 237 (see also the earlier Commission decision in *M v Italy*, Appl No 12386/86, 15 April 1991). For an interesting discussion of the position taken by the European Court of Justice, see E Drewniak, 'Comment: The Bosphorus Case: The Balancing of Property Rights in the European Community and the Public Interest in Ending the War in Bosnia' (1997) 20 *Fordham International Law Journal* 1007, on *Bosphorus Hava Yollari Turizm ve Ticaret AS v Minister for Transport, Energy and Communications, Ireland*, Case C–84/95, [1996] ECR I–3953, [1996] 3 CMLR 257.

their possible confiscation. The seizure was recorded in the relevant property registers. Some of the land was then made the subject of a court order for confiscation, on the basis that there was no proof that it had been lawfully acquired. Subsequently, applicant was acquitted of all charges on the ground of insufficient evidence, and the Italian courts annulled the seizure and confiscation orders and ordered the restitution of the property to the applicant. The restitution order was entered into the relevant property registers in 1987, with the exception of the land which had been confiscated. For unexplained reasons, this entry was not made until 1991.

The applicant claimed that Italy had breached P1(1) in respect of the initial seizure of the property, the confiscation, and the delay in the cancellation of the confiscation. The crucial point concerns the confiscation.[5] The Court recognised the legitimacy and importance of the aim of fighting criminal organisations by controlling their assets, especially since it appeared that suspect capital was being moved into real property. Accordingly it held that 'Confiscation, which is designed to block these movements of suspect capital, is an effective and necessary weapon in the combat against this cancer.'[6] The preliminary seizure could therefore be justified as a measure intended to ensure that confiscation would be effective.

What is particularly interesting about *Raimondo* is the absence of real consideration of alternative measures or the impact of the interference; instead, the analysis concentrated entirely on the rationality of the measures.[7] Moreover, the case report does not suggest that the Italian authorities had identified any particular criminal plan for which the property was to be used.[8] In this context, the Court seemed to accept several points put forward by the Italian government. The first is that proof of previous criminal activity in 'mafia-type organisations' is sufficient to establish the risk of criminal activity in future, and the second that confiscating and freezing proceeds of crime is likely to frustrate future criminal activity. However, the Court looked closely at the Italian rules regarding the degree of risk needed to justify a seizure. It seems, from the Court's summary of the Italian rules, that the inquiry in the Italian courts concentrates solely on the defendant's previous criminality and the fact that the property in question

---

[5] The issue regarding the delay was not complex: the Italian authorities could not explain why it had occurred and hence there was a violation of P1(1) on this point.

[6] *Raimondo* (n 4) [30].

[7] See above [33]: the Court also stated that the fact that there had been some vandalisation of the property while under the seizure and confiscation orders did not change matters, because 'any seizure or confiscation inevitably entails damage.'

[8] The Italian legislation provided that property could be seized 'when there is sufficient circumstantial evidence, such as a considerable discrepancy between his lifestyle and his apparent or declared income, to show that the property concerned forms the proceeds from unlawful activities or their reinvestment' (from above [18]). The Court noted (above [19]) that the Italian Constitutional Court had held that 'it is not enough for the law to indicate vague criteria for the assessment of danger; it must set them forth with sufficient precision to make the right of access to a court and adversarial proceedings a meaningful one'.

represents proceeds of crime. This, it seems, is sufficient to establish a risk of harm that justifies the seizure of the property (both in Italy and in Strasbourg).

In the United Kingdom, this issue arises under Part 5 of the Proceeds of Crime Act 2002, as it allows for the seizure, detention and forfeiture of cash 'intended by any person for use in unlawful conduct'.[9] These are civil proceedings and may be taken independently of any criminal proceedings. Similar provisions under the Criminal Justice (International Co-operation) Act 1990 were considered in admissibility decision in *Butler v The United Kingdom*,[10] in which about £240,000 of the applicant's money was seized while being carried to Spain by his partner's brother. The Crown Court found, on balance of probabilities, that cash was to be used in drug trafficking, although it did not say that the applicant would have been responsible for using the money. In Strasbourg, the applicant challenged the forfeiture under both Article 6 and P1(1), and failed on both grounds. In relation to Article 6, the Court declared that the proceedings were not criminal because the 'forfeiture order was a preventive measure and cannot be compared to a criminal sanction, since it was designed to take out of circulation money which was presumed to be bound up with the international trade in illicit drugs.'[11] In relation to P1(1), the preventive purpose was such that, given the wide margin of appreciation and the serious harm caused by drug trafficking, the impact was not disproportionate. Although the Court did not elaborate on the importance of distinguishing between preventive and punitive forfeiture, it seems that preventive forfeiture need not be linked with blame: the probability of use in serious crime is generally enough to justify seizure.[12]

In one sense, the *Butler* decision is no more favourable to the State than *Raimondo*, since the British courts had established, on the balance of probabilities, a specific risk that the property was to be used to commit a serious offence. However, the forfeiture of the cash was not linked to any criminal proceedings; indeed, criminal proceedings were never brought against the applicant or anyone else (even for an attempt).[13] Moreover, as the domestic court had not found that the cash would be used in drug trafficking by either the applicant or his partner's brother, but only by some unidentified third party, it seems arguable that the risk of criminal activity had largely dissipated. That is, there may have been sufficient risk to justify a temporary seizure of the cash, but not necessarily a permanent forfeiture.[14]

---

[9] Ss 294(1)(b) and 294(2)(b) (seizure), s 295 (detention), and s 298(2)(b) (forfeiture); these are similar to (but broader than) Drug Trafficking Act 1994 c 37, Pt II s 42.

[10] Reports 2002–VI 349. *See also Webb v The United Kingdom*, Appl No 56054/00, 10 February 2004 (cash forfeiture under s 25 of the Criminal Justice (International Co-operation) Act 1990).

[11] Above 362.

[12] See also *Riela v Italy*, Appl No 52439/99, 4 September 2001: even the confiscation of proceeds of crime may be regarded as preventive.

[13] Although n that under the domestic law considered in *Riela*, above, it is clear that a conviction is not required, as criminal proceedings were not brought against all of the applicants.

[14] By contrast, in *Raimondo* (n 4), the confiscation orders were annulled once the main criminal proceedings came to an end without a conviction. Indeed, an unexplained delay in failing to lift one of the orders was itself a breach of P1(1).

Some support for the position in *Butler* can be seen in other Strasbourg cases on the Italian laws, decided after *Raimondo*. From *Riela v Italy*[15] and *Arcuri v Italy*,[16] it appears that Italian law does not require the order for preventive seizure to be limited to the period where criminal proceedings are active; similarly, orders may be made in respect of property that is owned by individuals who have not been directly involved in criminal acts. However, in *Riela* and *Arcuri*, the Italian courts had established a relationship was shown between the property owners and the members of the criminal organisation: in particular, the property in question had probably been given by members of the criminal organisations, and had probably been derived from criminal activities. Moreover, there was evidence that the criminal organisation still exercised some control over the property in question. In that sense, the risk was more immediate than it was in *Butler*.

Butler therefore illustrates how the function of a forfeiture can be unclear. On the facts, there seems to have been no justification for a permanent seizure of the cash, and yet it also seems clear that this had been the motive for seizure. Indirectly, the applicant was punished, quite severely, for failing to prevent the money from being used by some unknown person. Whether the punitive element should make a difference is discussed below, but it demonstrates that a proportionality analysis predicated on the preventive use of a power is inappropriate.

Seizure as security

The seizure of property as security for the payment of a criminal fine or a civil debt may be regarded as a preventive measure. As such, the preceding discussion suggests that the European Court is not likely to subject such measures to close scrutiny, provided they are used for the purpose of security and not as another form of deterrent or punishment. In practice, however, it is not always so clear that security is the purpose. This can be shown by comparing the provisions of the Proceeds of Crime Act 2002 on restraint orders and receivership with those of the Customs and Excise Management Act 1979 on the seizure and detention of goods liable to forfeiture.

Under the Proceeds of Crime Act 2002, restraint orders are used to prevent defendants from avoiding confiscation or civil recovery orders by concealing or hiding their assets. The Crown Court may issue a restraint order where it appears that criminal investigation or proceedings are underway and there is reasonable cause to believe that the alleged offender has benefited from his criminal conduct (and hence that a confiscation order may be issued in future). The Act also provides for the appointment of a receiver to manage the property

---

[15] *Riela* (n 12).
[16] Reports 2001–VII 517.

pending the outcome of the criminal proceedings. While it does not appear that it is necessary to show that such orders are only available where there is a risk of dissipation of assets, the Act does state that the receiver's powers should be exercised for the purpose of maintaining the value of the property available to satisfy any potential order.[17] In addition, cases under similar provisions of the Drug Trafficking Act and Criminal Justice Act indicate that the courts balance the need to preserve the property against the defendant's right to continue his or her ordinary life while still presumed innocent.[18] If this is carried through to the Proceeds of Crime Act 2002, it would appear that restraint orders and receivership do serve a protective function.

There are elements of these procedures that may operate harshly, especially where no confiscation or civil recovery order is made. For example, there is no appeal from the Crown Court's initial decision to grant a restraint order; instead, an application to vary or discharge the order must first be made to the Crown Court, and from that decision an appeal may be made to the High Court.[19] Restraint orders are issued without a cross-undertaking in damages from the prosecutor, and while the Court Crown 'may order the payment of such compensation as it believes is just', it may do so only where there has been 'serious fault.'[20] Moreover, the receiver may charge its expenses and remuneration to the property under its control.[21] Under P1(1), it seems that there is no basis to resist the receiver's claims for costs and remuneration. This conclusion was reached by the Court of Appeal in *Hughes v Commissioners of Customs and Excise*[22] and the European Court of Human Rights and *Andrews v The United Kingdom*.[23] Not only did the courts in these two cases consider the appointment of a receiver a proportionate means of securing a potential confiscation order, but also that it was proportionate to leave the costs of the receivership on the shoulders of a victim who was not convicted or made subject to a confiscation order.

Other aspects of the Proceeds of Crime Act 2002 suggest that restraint and receivership orders are likely to be found compatible with P1(1). In particular, it is clear that neither is granted without some evidence that they are needed to reduce a proven risk of the dissipation of assets.[24] By way of comparison, section 139(1) of Customs and Excise Management Act 1979 provides a power to seize or detain goods liable to forfeiture under the Act.[25] While it appears that

---

[17] See s 69(2) (especially s 69(2)(a)).

[18] *Re P (Restraint Order: Sale of Assets)* [2000] 1 WLR 473.

[19] Proceeds of Crime Act 2002, ss 42(3) and 43.

[20] Above s 72.

[21] T Millington and MS Williams, *The Proceeds of Crime: Law and Practice of Restaint, Confiscation and Forfeiture* (OUP, Oxford, 2003) 42–46.

[22] [2003] 1 WLR 177 (CA).

[23] Appl No 49584/99, 26 September 2002 (the restraint order was made on the *ex parte* application of Customs and Excise under sections 77 and 78 of the Criminal Justice Act 1988).

[24] Millington and Williams (n 21) 108–16.

[25] Ultimately, it falls to the court to determine whether the goods should be condemned: see Sch 3, para 6.

seizure or detention must be based on reasonable grounds, these grounds relate only to the liability to forfeiture rather than the need to secure the payment of excise duties or the preservation of the goods for condemnation. In that sense, there is no real consideration of the need to seize or detain goods as a means of securing payment of outstanding duties or penalties.

In strict terms, however, the powers of seizure and condemnation under the Customs and Excise Management Act 1979 are not limited to securing existing or potential obligations. Indeed, from *R v Smith*, it is clear that goods may be seized and condemned even where the duties are paid.[26] Moreover, it appears that the forfeiture is sometimes used as a means of putting pressure on the individual to pay a penalty, as the Act allows the Commissioners to release the goods against a penalty.[27] However, the statutory scheme does not provide that forfeiture is a security for the penalty, as the penalty is merely a substitute for forfeiture. The leading human rights case on the use of these powers is *Air Canada v The United Kingdom*,[28] which involved the seizure and condemnation as forfeit of an aircraft found to have been carrying drugs.[29] The aircraft was released after Air Canada paid a penalty of £50,000.[30] Air Canada argued that the seizure violated P1(1), but the Court held that it was not disproportionate, given the importance of combating international drug trafficking.[31] However, there was no indication that Air Canada would not pay the fine, or that the fine could not have been satisfied from Air Canada's other assets in the United Kingdom. Neither was there was any evidence suggesting that the seizure of this specific aircraft was necessary to reduce the immediate threat of drug trafficking. Indeed, since the aircraft was released once the fine was paid, it seems that the imposition of the fine had always been regarded as a sufficient penalty. Hence, there was a reasonable argument that the seizure was never intended to preserve assets, but merely to obtain payment of a penalty of £50,000 without establishing that there was any risk that a validly imposed penalty would not be paid without the forfeiture.[32]

---

[26] [2002] 1 WLR 54.

[27] Section 152(b) provides that the Commissioners, 'may, as they see fit' restore any thing, 'subject to such conditions (if any) as they think proper'; and under Schedule 3, they may deliver any thing to a claimant 'upon his paying to the Commissioners such sum as they think proper, being a sum not exceeding that which in their opinion represents the value of the thing' and any unpaid duties or taxes thereon.

[28] Series A No 316 (1995) EHRR 150.

[29] It was seized under s 139 as liable to forfeiture under s 141, which provides that . . .

> where any thing has become liable to forfeiture under the Customs and Excise Acts—a) any ship, aircraft, vehicle, animal, container (including any article of passengers' baggage) or other thing whatsoever which has been used for the carriage, handling, deposit or concealment of the thing so liable to forfeiture, either at a time when it was so liable or for the purpose of the commission of the offence for which it later became so liable; . . . shall also be liable to forfeiture.

[30] Pursuant to powers under Sch 3 para 16 of the Customs and Excise Management Act 1979.

[31] *Air Canada* (n 28) [41]–[42], [47].

[32] See the dissenting judgments of Judge Pekkanen and Judge Walsh.

Air Canada shows that the focus in cases involving detention as a form of security tends to be on the proportionality of the penalty whose payment it is intended to secure: so long as the imposition of the penalty satisfies P1(1), it is generally assumed that the detention also satisfies P1(1); and if the penalty does not satisfy P1(1), then it follows that the detention cannot satisfy it. Even where there are provisions relating to detention as a 'pure' security, the courts tend to view them in conjunction with the substantive penalties. For example, in *International Transport Roth GmbH v Secretary of State for the Home Department*,[33] which concerned the fixed penalties imposed on carriers found to be carrying 'clandestine entrants' on their vehicles,[34] the majority in the Court of Appeal found the detention provisions particularly worrying when taken in combination with the fixed nature of the penalty and the reversal of the burden of proof. However, although they distinguished *Air Canada*, their emphasis was on the substantive aspects of the penalty in *Air Canada*, rather than the seizure of the aircraft. On balance, however, the provisions on detention do not seem that far different from those in *Air Canada*: indeed, in *International Transport*, no detention was permitted unless there was a 'significant risk' that the fine would not be paid and no satisfactory alternative security for payment was provided.[35] In addition, the detention could be appealed to a court, which had the power to release the vehicle if the penalty had been paid, or alternative security provided, or if there was 'significant doubt' that the penalty was payable and the applicant had a 'compelling need' to have the transporter released.[36] By contrast, in *Air Canada*, the relevant statutory provisions did not specify the level of risk or any other factors that would justify a seizure: it only provided that the Commissioners had a discretionary power to seize goods liable to forfeiture. While Air Canada could apply for judicial review, the doctrine of proportionality was not part of English administrative law at that time. Hence, the basis on which a seizure could be challenged was very limited, and did not seem to offer a real opportunity to challenge the seizure on the basis that the risk of non-payment of the penalty was minimal.[37]

The failure to distinguish the proportionality of taking security over property to secure a potential obligation from the proportionality of the obligation itself is a sign that the deference exercised by the courts is too broad. By contrast, a public authority making a civil claim for damages cannot obtain a freezing order simply on the basis that its claim may result in an award that would be compatible with P1(1). It seems that this is recognised in part, in the rules relating to receivership

---

[33] *International Transport* (n 1).
[34] The penalties are imposed under s 32 of the Immigration and Asylum Act 1999; the power to detain is under s 36.
[35] Immigration and Asylum Act 1999, s 36(2).
[36] Above s 37(3).
[37] In *Customs and Excise Commissioners v Air Canada* [1991] 2 QB 446, reversing [1989] QB 234, the Court of Appeal held that liability to forfeiture under s 141(1) is absolute: it does not require the Commissioners to show that the defendants knew or ought to have known that the goods were on the aircraft.

under the Proceeds of Crime Act 2002 and those relating to the 'significant risk' of non-payment of the fine under the Immigration and Asylum Act 1999 (whether the imposition of the fine is compatible with P1(1) is considered below). However, it is not recognised as a distinct issue in the leading cases from Strasbourg.

COMPENSATORY AND REPARATIVE MEASURES

It is clear that P1(1) does not restrict the State's power to enact and enforce laws allowing it to bring proceedings to recover losses caused by private persons, even if those losses are significant. This is illustrated by *Porter v The United Kingdom*,[38] which concerned the £26 million surcharge imposed on the former leader of Westminster City Council in relation to losses arising from the sale of council homes.[39] The surcharge was imposed by the Council's Auditor, under powers granted by the Local Government Finance Act 1982. Section 20(1)(b) allows the liability to be imposed where 'a loss has been incurred or deficiency caused by the wilful misconduct of any person', and the liability is limited to the amount of the loss.[40]

The applicant claimed that her rights under both Article 6 and P1(1) were violated. In relation to Article 6, the Court found that the compensatory nature of the surcharge proceedings meant they were civil, and as such, the procedure satisfied the Convention requirements.[41] It might have decided differently if there had been an additional fine or penalty in default. For example, in *Bendenoun v France*,[42] proceedings were found to be criminal, as a tax surcharge was subject to a 200% punitive increase and for that reason could not be regarded as compensatory. Moreover, the applicant would have been liable to committal to prison if he had failed to pay. Similarly, in *Garyfallou AEBE v Greece*, the directors of a company risked detention if their company failed to satisfy the liability imposed upon it.[43]

---

[38] Appl No 15814/02, (2003) 37 EHRR CD 8. In addition to *Porter*, see the cases on the post-unification conversion of currency in Germany, where the European Court of Human Rights held that it was legitimate to require proof of provenance of funds and to deny conversion where appears funds obtained by misuse: *Islamische Religionsgemeinschaft EV v Germany*, Appl No 53871/00, 5 December 2002; *Honecker, Axen, Teubner and Jossifov v Germany*, Reports 2001–XII 187.

[39] The applicant, with others on Westminster City Council, developed a plan to sell council property in certain areas at reduced prices to applicants who, it was hoped, would be more likely to vote Conservative.

[40] Since repealed by the Audit Commission Act 1998, Sch 5 para 1.

[41] But see *Third Report of the Nolan Committee on Standards in Public Life: Standards of Conduct in Local Government in England, Scotland and Wales* (1997) (Cm 3702–1) [214]–[224], where the Committee noted that, since the surcharge could be applied where the individual has not acquired any property of the local authority, it was not restitutionary. From this, it seemed to conclude that the surcharge could only be a penalty. It recommended changes so as to remove the power of the auditor to certify liability, but it did not object to the principle that the local authorities should have a compensatory claim. (The Committee's recommendations were implemented for England and Wales by Part III of the Local Government Act 2000.)

[42] Series A No 284 (1994) 18 EHRR 54.

[43] Reports 1997–V 1821 (1999) 28 EHRR 344 [34].

In *Porter*, the analysis of P1(1) was brief, but it demonstrates that purely compensatory measures do not, in principle, violate the right to property simply because the liability is substantial. The Court stated that there was no indication that the surcharge was an inaccurate or arbitrary reflection of the losses for which the victim was responsible (together with another member of the Council), and it was sufficient that the applicant had had the opportunity to challenge the calculation of the surcharge in the courts.

This suggests that the State may create new forms of action to enable it to recover misappropriated funds or to obtain compensation for losses caused by individuals.[44] In such cases, however, the State is seeking compensation for actual losses, on the basis of a clear chain of causation (and, at least in *Porter*, on clear proof of a serious default). In recent years, the emphasis has shifted to the 'recovery' of the proceeds of crime. In the United Kingdom, the use of civil recovery has a punitive element to it, and hence it will be examined after a consideration of punitive measures.

PUNITIVE MEASURES

The taking of property or imposition of monetary liability as a penalty raises difficult issues relating both to the process and to the severity of the measures. In many cases, the relevance of guilt is controversial. This is partly due to the development of civil forfeiture as a form of proceedings against property, rather than persons, which meant that the guilt of the owner did not necessarily affect the liability of goods to forfeiture. Under P1(1), it could be argued that the public interest behind penalising those innocent of wrongdoing is advanced so slightly that forfeiture is disproportionate. However, the position is unclear.

One of the earliest cases, *AGOSI v The United Kingdom*,[45] concerned the seizure of gold coins being smuggled into the United Kingdom. The coins belonged to AGOSI, but had been delivered to buyers who had not yet received title under the terms of their contracts with AGOSI. The Commissioners had a statutory discretion to return the coins to AGOSI, but refused to do so.[46] On AGOSI's application for judicial review, the Court of Appeal refused to say that the discretion had to be exercised in its favour.[47] AGOSI then proceeded to Strasbourg, where it claimed that the forfeiture breached P1(1) because they had never been convicted of smuggling.

---

[44] Or to require compensation for injuries caused to third parties: *De Lorenzo v Italy*, Appl No 69264/01, 12 February 2004.

[45] Series A No 108 (1987) 9 EHRR 1 (sub nom *Allgemeine Gold und Silberscheideanstalt v The United Kingdom*).

[46] The discretion was given under s 288 of the Customs and Excise Act 1952.

[47] See *Allgemeine Gold und Silberscheideanstalt v Customs and Excise Commissioners* [1980] QB 390 (CA), 404 (Lord Denning MR): 'It is entirely a matter for the discretion of the customs and excise to consider whether the claim of the German company is so good that they should see fit in this case to release them to the German company or retain them and pay them some compensation.'

The Court accepted that the forfeiture served the legitimate aim of prohibiting the importation of gold coins; hence, the real question was whether the absence of fault made the forfeiture disproportionate.[48] While the Commission stated that an owner who is innocent of any wrongdoing should be entitled to recover the goods,[49] the Court was not willing to go this far. While it observed that all the member States permit the confiscation of smuggled goods, no common principle regarding the degree of fault had emerged. However, the Court did say that 'The striking of a fair balance depends on many factors and the behaviour of the owner of the property, including the degree of fault or care which he has displayed, is one element of the entirety of circumstances which should be taken into account.'[50] Because of this, there must be procedures in place to ensure that 'reasonable account . . . be taken of the degree of fault or care of the applicant company or, at least, of the relationship between the company's conduct and the breach of the law which undoubtedly occurred'.[51] In *AGOSI*, the Court concluded that this was the case. While AGOSI's fault was irrelevant to the initial proceedings to condemn the coins, it was entitled apply to the Customs and Excise Commissioners for restoration of the coins. At this point, it was conceded by the United Kingdom that, as a practical matter, the forfeiture of the property of a person who is free of any fault would be unlikely to further the objectives of the legislation, and hence would not be permitted to stand.[52] This was enough to satisfy the Court.[53]

A variation on this issue arose in *Air Canada*.[54] As explained above,[55] one of Air Canada's jets was found to have been carrying a container holding cannabis resin. Under section 141(1) of the Customs and Excise Management Act 1979, a vehicle (including an aircraft) is liable to forfeiture if found to be carrying contraband. Consequently, officers of the Customs and Excise Commissioners seized the aircraft, only to return it on payment of a penalty of £50,000.[56] Air Canada disputed the liability of the aircraft to forfeiture, but the Commissioners

---

[48] AGOSI (n 45) [52].

[49] (1985) 7 EHRR CD314 [77]–[79].

[50] AGOSI (n 45) [54].

[51] Above [55].

[52] The Government objected (above [53]) that it was enough that it is enough to show that forfeiture fulfils a legitimate purpose under P1(1). However, it also conceded that, 'as a practical matter, where a person is free of any fault which could relate in any way to the purpose of the legislation, it is likely that the forfeiture of that property could not on any sensible construction of the legislation further the object thereof.'

[53] However, it seems that no decision on AGOSI's conduct was ever made, or at least ever communicated to them. AGOSI's solicitors wrote to the Commissioners on 1 April 1980 (ie after being refused to appeal the Court of Appeal's judgment to the House of Lords) to request the return of the goods. The report of the European Court of Human Rights discloses that the 'solicitor for the Commissioners replied in the negative on 1 May 1980, without giving any reasons.' There is no report of a subsequent application for judicial review of this response.

[54] Air Canada (n 28).

[55] Text to n 28.

[56] Acting under ss 139(5), 152 and Sch 3, para 16: the Commissioners may 'if they see fit' return 'the thing' seized as liable to forfeiture to the owner 'upon his paying . . . such a sum as they think proper, being a sum not exceeding that which in their opinion represents the value of the thing . . .'.

brought condemnation proceedings which, ultimately, were successful before the Court of Appeal. Before the Court of Human Rights, Air Canada claimed that its rights under P1(1) had been violated, in respect of both the seizure and the penalty subsequently imposed.

The Court found against the applicant. It did not consider a penalty of £50,000 to be disproportionate, as it noted that the victim had been criticised for failing to adhere to security procedures (although this was not cited as a reason for forfeiture before the national courts). The Court only stated that, given the importance of combating international drug trafficking, neither the seizure nor the fine were disproportionate.[57] *Air Canada* therefore seems even more favourable to the State than *AGOSI*, for the United Kingdom did not make any concession that an innocent third party would normally have their goods restored to them. This concession was made, and regarded as material, in *AGOSI*. However, *Air Canada* was only decided by a narrow majority (5-4), and the dissentients maintained that Air Canada's innocence should have made the forfeiture and penalty disproportionate.[58] Given the narrow margin, it is fair to say that the issue of culpability is not resolved.

More recently, in *Yildirim v Italy*,[59] the Court indicated that the victim's behaviour is relevant, although the margin of appreciation is very wide. In this case, a Turkish national hired a bus to a company for one year. Two days after concluding the hire agreement, the company's drivers were arrested in Brindisi while illegally transporting 32 clandestine immigrants from Iraq. The drivers were convicted, and the same court also ordered the confiscation of the bus. Italian law allowed the owner to apply for return of the bus, if he could establish his 'good faith'. However, the Italian court dismissed his application, on the basis that he had not dispelled doubts regarding his conduct arising on the facts.

The Court indicated that the balance between the applicant's fundamental rights and the legitimate aim of preventing clandestine immigration and human trafficking depends on many factors, including the owner's conduct. Hence, the Court asked whether the Italian authorities 'had regard to the applicant's degree of fault or care or, at least, the relationship between his conduct and the offence which had been committed', and whether the applicant had an opportunity to make his case to the authorities. On the facts, the opportunity to apply for the return of the vehicle was sufficient to maintain the fair balance. Accordingly,

---

[57] *Air Canada* (n 28) [40]–[48].

[58] See eg of the dissenting opinion of Judge Martens (joined by Judge Russo) [5]:

> Confiscating property as a sanction to some breach of the law—however important that breach may be and, consequently, however weighty may be the general interest in preventing it by severely penalising the offence—without there being any 'relationship between the behaviour of the owner or the person responsible for the goods and the breach of the law' is definitely incompatible both with the rule of law and with the right guaranteed in Article 1 of Protocol No 1 (P1(1)).

(The quotation is from the speech made by Mr Frowein in his capacity as Delegate of the Commission during the oral hearings in the AGOSI case Series B No 91, p 103.)

[59] Appl No 38602/02, 10 April 2003; see also *CM v France*, Appl No 28078/95, 26 June 2001.

having regard to the margin of appreciation, the Court declared his application inadmissible.

While *Yildirim* seems to re-affirm the importance of the owner's conduct, it is not clear where this leaves punitive measures of the type seen in *Air Canada*. The Italian courts regarded the confiscation of the bus as a preventive measure, in that restoring the bus to the applicant would represent a 'danger', and this was accepted by the European court. Once the existence of a danger to the public is accepted, the question of blame becomes less important: indeed, if the removal of a danger is the purpose of confiscation, the owner's conduct is only relevant to the extent that it is evidence of the danger. This seems to have been the case in *Yildirim*, although it is not clear to what extent the prosecutors cited evidence beyond the owner's title as proof of the danger.[60]

The issue has become particularly important with the introduction of the Single Market and the rise in the evasion of Customs and Excise duties.[61] Recent policies demonstrate the determination of the Government to use civil forfeiture as a means of combating smuggling. Under the Customs and Excise Management Act 1979, goods imported without payment of duty are subject to forfeiture,[62] as are any vehicles used for the carriage of such goods.[63] The Commissioners have the discretion to restore anything forfeited or seized,[64] but recently they settled on a policy not to restore vehicles in the absence of 'exceptional circumstances'.[65] The sanction was intended to be as tough as possible, in order to discourage smuggling.[66] Indeed, the policy provided that vehicles would be restored only in cases of smuggling for personal use only where it would be 'inhumane' not to do so.[67] While forfeiture is sometimes used as a means of securing the payment of specific debts, it can operate cumulatively. There are cases where both the vehicle and the contraband have been forfeited and the duties have remained owing.[68]

Not surprisingly, there have been a number of cases on the compatibility of different aspects of the policy with P1(1). *Lindsay v Commissioners of Customs*

---

[60] The European Court of Human Rights also referred to the owner's failure to seek guarantees from the hirers regarding the use of bus in other countries, as well as some doubt about dates of hire contract and other details.

[61] In *Lindsay v Customs and Excise Comrs* [2002] 1 WLR 1766 [19], there is a reference to evidence of a Customs officer that 'In 1993 when the Single Market was introduced the revenue eroded on smuggled excise goods brought into the UK was in the region of £30–£40 million. By the year 2000 this had escalated to 3.8 billion pounds from tobacco smuggling alone.'

[62] Customs and Excise Management Act 1979, s 49.

[63] Above s 141.

[64] Above s 152.

[65] *Lindsay* (n 61) [21].

[66] Above, where the circular letter of 13 July 2000 sent to various Customs Officers is quoted saying: 'One of the most direct ways to strike at the smugglers' activities is by seizing the vehicles they use to smuggle in their contraband. As the Paymaster General has said, we are determined to ensure that this sanction is as tough as it can be. The more effective this sanction is, the more we will hit the smugglers in the pocket and reduce the profitability of their illegal trade.'

[67] For example, where a motor vehicle was adapted for use by a disabled driver (see above).

[68] *Smith* (n 26).

and Excise[69] dealt with the forfeiture of a vehicle used by its owner for smuggling. In that sense, the victim's guilt was clear, unlike *AGOSI* or *Air Canada*. However, the Court of Appeal held that, in at least some cases, the decision to seize the goods had to include a consideration of the proportionality of forfeiture. Where goods are smuggled without an intention to sell at a profit, there must be some consideration of the individual's culpability, including such factors as 'the scale of importation, whether it is a "first offence", whether there was an attempt at concealment or dissimulation, the value of the vehicle and the degree of hardship that will be caused by forfeiture.'[70]

The belief that wrongdoers who act for profit may be subject to harsher treatment is consistent with the Strasbourg cases.[71] However, it is the converse of the situation in *Lindsay* that normally arises: that is, the Court accepts that it lies within a State's margin of appreciation to impose a strict law on those who operate for profit. In *Lindsay*, the fact that the victim was not operating for profit reduced the scope of judicial deference. In addition, it is significant that the property owner was guilty of smuggling: that is, even *AGOSI* suggests only that P1(1) operates to the benefit of a party innocent of crime.

Two days after it handed down its judgment in *Lindsay*, the Court of Appeal gave its decision in *International Transport Roth GmbH v Secretary of State for the Home Department*.[72] As in *Yildirim v Italy*, the smuggling of clandestine entrants was the issue. However, the Court of Appeal held, by a 2-1 majority, that the penalties imposed on carriers for bringing 'clandestine entrants' into the United Kingdom were incompatible with P1(1). Part II of the Immigration and Asylum Act 1999 imposed a fixed penalty of £2000 for each clandestine entrant on the owner, hirer and driver of the vehicle, unless they could show either that they were acting under duress, or that they had no actual knowledge of entrant and they had an 'effective system' for preventing the carriage of entrants which was operating properly on that occasion. In addition, the vehicle could be detained if there was a serious risk that the penalty would not be paid and no other security had been given. In that event, the owner or driver could apply to the court for release, which the court could order if (a) satisfactory security had been tendered; (b) there was no real risk of the penalty not being paid; or (c) there was a real doubt as to whether the penalty was payable and the applicant had a compelling need to have the transporter released.[73]

The first issue concerned the nature of the proceedings. Simon Brown and Jonathan Parker LLJ held that the penalties were criminal in nature, and hence the Article 6 guarantees relating to the right to a fair trial were applicable. Both

---

[69] *Lindsay* (n 61).

[70] Above [64] (followed in *R (on the application of Hoverspeed Ltd) v Customs and Excise Comrs* [2003] QB 1041 [187]).

[71] Chapter 7, 141–45.

[72] *International Transport* (n 1). (The panel in *International Transport* comprised Simon Brown LJ, Laws LJ and Jonathan Parker LJ; in *Lindsay*, it was Lord Phillips MR, Judge LJ and Carnwath J).

[73] As described by Simon Brown LJ, *International Transport*, above [7].

concluded that the scheme was disproportionate in relation to Article 6,[74] and from that concluded that the interference under P1(1) was necessarily disproportionate as well. Whether this follows so neatly is doubtful, but clearly it was assumed by both judges. Indeed, Simon Brown LJ stated that, under both Article 6 and P1(1), 'ultimately one single question arises for determination by the court: is the scheme not merely harsh but plainly unfair so that, however effectively that unfairness may assist in achieving the social goal, it simply cannot be permitted?'[75] This is correct, of course, in the sense that proportionality is relevant to both Article 6 and P1(1); however, it does not necessary follow that the same facts are relevant or have the same weight in the proportionality test under each right, or that the intensity of review is the same under each right. Indeed, both Simon Brown and Jonathan Parker LLJ assumed that the strict necessity principle applies to P1(1) although, as explained in chapter 5, it is doubtful that it does.[76] Moreover, both found that P1(1) was violated, in addition to Article 6. For Simon Brown LJ, it made little difference whether the liability was criminal or civil: if the liability was civil, the 'penalty far exceeds what any individual ought reasonably to be required to sacrifice in the interests of achieving improved immigration control';[77] but if criminal, the imposition of a substantial fixed penalty violates 'The hallowed principle that the punishment must fit the crime'.[78]

While *International Transport* and *Lindsay* represent the current view of the Court of Appeal, it is uncertain whether the House of Lords or European Court of Human Rights would reach similar conclusions. Indeed, the judgment in *Yildirim* seems directly contrary to the majority judgment in *International Transport*. As explained above, it could be argued that the confiscation in

---

[74] The difficulty in classifying proceedings under Article 6 arose in relation to the second and third elements of the criteria laid out in *Engel & Others v The Netherlands (No1)*, Series A No 22 (1979–80) 1 EHRR 647 [82]. (The criteria are: the classification of the offence under national law; the nature of the offence; and the degree of severity of the penalty that the person concerned risks incurring.) Simon Brown LJ, above [35] saw the scheme as criminal because 'the true nature of the scheme is dictated by the conduct which the legislation is seeking to deter, and that is both dishonesty and carelessness.' By contrast, Laws LJ, above [95], stated that 'it is entirely obvious that the Crown's concern in seeking this legislation from Parliament, and Parliament's concern in passing it, was to prevent clandestine illegal migrants from entering this country, pure and simple . . . .. The deterrence of dishonesty and carelessness is not at the heart of it at all.' Again, at [97] he stated that 'The statute is not interested in obloquy, shame or guilt. It is not interested in retributive justice. The scheme is put in place, and put in place only, as a means towards the fulfilment of the executive's particular responsibility to secure the state's borders by effective immigration control.' Jonathon Parker LJ concluded that the proceedings were criminal, due to the emphasis on dishonesty.

[75] Above [26].

[76] Chapter 5, 135–8; in *International Transport*, see Simon Brown LJ, above [52], Jonathan Parker LJ, above [193] and [181]. Strict necessity was not addressed as such in AGOSI (n 45), although Court did say that there was a wide margin of appreciation ([52]); see also *Air Canada* (n 28) [48].

[77] Simon Brown LJ, above [47].

[78] Above. While Jonathan Parker LJ seemed to put more emphasis on the criminal nature of the liability, his reasons for finding incompatibility with P1(1) were brief and it is not clear whether he would have come to a different conclusion on proportionality had the liability been civil.

Yildirim was preventive, rather than punitive. However, there were strong similarities with the UK scheme: in particular, property was seized immediately under both schemes, although subject to recovery by owners who could prove that they acted in 'good faith' (in Italy) or that they were not aware they were carrying a clandestine entrant and had adequate systems to prevent entry (in the United Kingdom). On this basis, there is little to separate the two systems, and Laws LJ's dissenting opinion in *International Transport* is much closer to the reasoning in *Yildirim*. He pointed out that the extent of deference depends on the specific context; in this case, there was a potential conflict between the executive's responsibility for the security of borders and the judiciary's responsibility for criminal justice. But since he concluded that the forfeiture was civil rather than criminal, and since the complaint concerned the severity of the penalty, it was appropriate to show greater deference to the legislature. That is, the penalty was civil in nature and had been set by Parliament, and the courts should be very reluctant to impose substantive limits on rules of civil liability. Moreover, P1(1) was not an unqualified right, unlike Article 6; indeed, the third sentence was plainly intended to reserve an extensive discretion to States to determine the severity, incidence and enforcement of penalties.

While this suggests that *International Transport* may be anomalous, or at least that the UK approach will involve a closer scrutiny of penalties than that in Strasbourg, the Third Section's judgment in *Azinas v Cyprus* shows that there is some support for the idea that the the punishment must fit the crime.[79] In this case, the applicant was convicted of stealing, breach of trust and abuse of authority relating to his conduct as a senior civil servant. He was sentenced to 18 months' imprisonment, but no fine was imposed and the Cypriot authorities did not bring civil proceedings to recover property from him. However, in separate disciplinary proceedings, the Public Service Commission decided that he was guilty of the most serious type of misconduct, from which it followed that he would be dismissed from his post and have his pension taken from him. He challenged the loss of his pension under P1(1), and the Court found in his favour, for two reasons. First, the disciplinary process was inflexible, as the loss of pension followed automatically from dismissal; secondly, the loss of the pension was too severe in any event. It seems that the Third Section felt that the applicant had suffered enough: to go beyond the imprisonment and dismissal was simply excessive.

The Third Section's judgment is not entirely clear, as it both accepted that disciplinary measures served the legitimate aim of 'protecting the public and safeguarding its trust in the integrity of the administration'[80] while also stating

---

[79] Appl No 56679/00, 20 June 2002 (Third Section), 28 May 2004 (Grand Chamber). The Grand Chamber declared the inadmissible for failure to exhaust domestic remedies. Eleven of the seventeen judges declined to say anything on the merits. Mr Wildhaber (joined by Mr Rozakis and Mrs Mularoni) would not have found a violation on the merits; Mr Costa and Mr Garlicki issued a joint dissenting opinion on the exhaustion of remedies, but agreed with Mr Wildhaber on the question of the fair balance; Mr Ress agreed with the initial decision of the Third Section.

[80] Above (Third Section) [44].

that 'the retrospective forfeiture of the individual's pension cannot be said to serve any commensurate purpose'.[81] This suggests that the forfeiture failed the rationality test, which would represent a marked change from its position in other cases. Indeed, it is difficult to see why the forfeiture would not, at the very least, enhance trust in the integrity of administration. It may be excessive, but it does not seem irrational. However, the Court also said that the withdrawal of the pension was particularly harsh because it deprived the applicant and his family 'of any means of subsistence',[82] which seems to shift the emphasis from rationality to proportionality. In any case, it seems that the Court is willing, in at least some cases, to impose substantive limits on the use of forfeiture as a penalty, even where the guilt of the individual is clear.

The case was referred to the Grand Chamber, which found for Cyprus, but only on the procedural basis that the applicant had failed to exhaust domestic remedies. Four of the fifteen judges expressed doubts over the majority judgment in the first hearing, but the remainder said nothing. The picture on the relationship between degree of guilt and the severity of penalties therefore remains confused. In Strasbourg, *AGOSI*, *Azinas* and *Yildirim* suggest that forfeiture cannot be used as a penalty unless the victim is responsible, in some way, for the conduct that justifies the forfeiture or penalty. In the United Kingdom, *International Transport* and *Lindsay* support this position. Against these cases, one could cite the majority in *Air Canada* and the dissent of Laws LJ's in *International Transport*.[83]

As a final word, it is worth noting that *Lindsay* and *International Transport* were part of a group of Court of Appeal cases decided in 2002 in which a fairly high level of scrutiny was applied to P1(1).[84] Subsequently, several of these cases were overturned by the House of Lords, but neither *Lindsay* nor *International Transport* were reconsidered. Nevertheless, the reasoning in the cases that did reach the House of Lords turns on the Court of Appeal's perspective on the impact on specific individuals of schemes of broad application. The broad issue is whether the proportionality test should concentrate on the impact in the specific case, or the general impact on the class of those affected. Put differently, may a scheme of general application may have harsh effects in a specific case? Plainly, there must be a point at which the impact on an individual is so great that the fairness of the scheme as a whole is called into question. Nevertheless, as explained elsewhere,[85] the European Court in *James* also said that a scheme

[81] Above.

[82] Above.

[83] In addition, although not directly on point, the judgments of the House of Lords in *Smith* (n 26), *R v Benjafield* [2003] 1 AC 1099 and the Privy Council in *HM Advocate v McIntosh (No 1)* [2003] 1 AC 1078 evince a marked lack of sympathy for those caught by such measures.

[84] In addition to *Lindsay* (n 61) and *International Transport* (n 1), see: *Aston Cantlow and Wilmcote with Billesley Parochial Church Council v Wallbank* [2002] Ch 51 reversed by [2004] 1 AC 546; *Wilson v First County Trust Ltd (No 2)* [2002] QB 74 reversed by [2004] 1 AC 816 (sub nom *Wilson v Secretary of State for Trade and Industry*); and *Marcic v Thames Water Utilities Ltd* [2002] QB 929, reversed by [2004] 2 AC 42.

[85] Chapter 5, 158–9.

may produce anomalies and windfalls (at the expense of the owner) without falling foul of P1(1). In relation to the forfeiture of property or imposition of fines, the *International Transport* and *Lindsay* judgments indicate that proportionality required some consideration of the individual's circumstances, in at least some cases. However, both courts appear to base this conclusion on the doctrine of strict necessity, as the possibility that allowing a discretion to modify a penalty to suit the specific circumstances of the case would not have frustrated the aim of the penalty. Whether this is appropriate under P1(1) is controversial. While the majority of European Court judgments suggest that strict necessity is not part of the P1(1) proportionality test, the *Azinas* reasoning runs to the contrary. In the United Kingdom, the House of Lords has shown greater deference to the legislature and executive in such questions. Indeed, in its judgment in *Wilson v FCT,* the Court of Appeal stated that the relevant legislation should have given the courts a discretion avoid hardship in specific cases.[86] On appeal, this point was rejected by the House of Lords.

It is noteworthy, therefore, that the Court of Appeal in both *International Transport* and *Lindsay* were particularly concerned with the lack of flexibility in forfeiture provisions. The issues in *Lindsay* and *International Transport* do not, of course, arise in the context of social justice (as in *James*) or consumer protection (as in *Wilson*), and it seems that the Court of Appeal was particularly concerned with forfeiture that is intended to have a punitive effect. Whether the House of Lords or European Court of Human Rights can be persuaded that it is appropriate to adopt a different approach, involving a closer level of scrutiny, remains to be seen.

CONFISCATION AND CIVIL RECOVERY UNDER THE PROCEEDS OF CRIME ACT 2002

In recent years, the UK Government has fixed upon the recovery of proceeds of crime as an important element in crime control. As it is clear that the Crown does not have a common law or equitable right to property representing the proceeds of crime,[87] or to the value of such property:[88] claims to proceeds or profits must be statutory. The development of statutory claims began with the Drug Trafficking Offences Act 1986, which provided for 'confiscation orders'. Similar provisions on confiscation were incorporated in the Criminal Justice Act 1988,

---

[86] *Wilson* (n 84). Similarly, in *Qazi v Harrow LBC* [2001] EWCA Civ 1834 (reversed by [2003] UKHL (2004) 43 1 AC 983) the Court of Appeal held that there should have been some discretion in the court or the council to ensure that an eviction was compatible with the tenant's Article 8 right to respect for the home.

[87] See *Webb v Chief Constable of Merseyside* [2000] 1 QB 427 where it was held that, in the absence of a criminal conviction, law enforcement agencies have no common law or equitable right to seize and retain the proceeds or profits of crime solely on the basis that they were derived from crime.

[88] See *R v Cuthbertson* [1981] AC 470, where the House of Lords quashed an order for the forfeiture of about £750,000, representing the proceeds of drug trafficking.

the Criminal Justice (International Co-operation) Act 1990, the Criminal Justice Act 1993, the Drug Trafficking Act 1994, the Proceeds of Crime Act 1995 and the Terrorism Act 2000. The most recent legislation is the Proceeds of Crime Act 2002, which consolidates and extends the statutory regime on confiscation following conviction. It also includes a new civil remedy of 'civil recovery,' which is available even where there has been an acquittal or no criminal proceedings are likely to be brought.

A confiscation order is intended to allow the State to claim the value of proceeds of crime, and hence it is not made against specific assets and has no immediate effect on the defendant's title to the assets. However, the enforcement of an order may result in the seizure of any or all of the assets in which the defendant has an interest, whether or not the assets were acquired legitimately. In addition, the calculation of the proceeds may work on the basis of statutory assumptions that may also operate very harshly, with the result that confiscation often not reparative nor even restitutionary, but punitive.[89] The provisions on 'criminal lifestyle' are particularly onerous: if the court finds that the defendant had a criminal lifestyle, it is assumed that *all* property obtained or held by the defendant in the six years preceding the commencement of proceedings were obtained by criminal conduct.[90] Whether the defendant had a criminal lifestyle is also determined by irrebuttable statutory presumptions, with the result that (for example) a defendant who has committed three unrelated offences over the preceding six years will be deemed to have had a criminal lifestyle and therefore subject to confiscation of all property acquired over that period, provided that the benefit is at least £5000.[91] The severity of confiscation is compounded by its cumulative effect, as illustrated by *R v Smith*,[92] which concerned a defendant found guilty of smuggling cigarettes into the United Kingdom without paying the excise duty. The duty remained payable, the cigarettes and the ship on which they were smuggled were forfeited, and a confiscation order was made for the amount of the duty on the basis that it could be regarded as a benefit from tax evasion.[93]

---

[89] See the example given in P Alldridge, *Money Laundering Law* (Hart Publishing, Oxford, 2003) 134–35, where a commercial contract was gained by bribery: the confiscation order would look to the total payment received, without deduction for expenses in performing the contract.

[90] Proceeds of Crime Act 2002, s 10.

[91] Above s 75(1), (2)(b), (3)(a) and (4).

[92] *Smith* (n 26). The confiscation order was made pursuant to the Criminal Justice Act 1988, Part VI, but the Proceeds of Crime Act 2002 is similar.

[93] The Human Rights Act 1998 was not discussed, but Lord Rodger's speech suggests that a human rights challenge on the grounds of proportionality would not have been successful: at [23], he stated that 'if in some circumstances it can operate in a penal or even a draconian manner, then that may not be out of place in a scheme for stripping criminals of the benefits of their crimes. That is a matter for the judgment of the legislature, which has adopted a similar approach in enacting legislation for the confiscation of the proceeds of drug trafficking.' (On the cumulative effect, *cf Allen v The United Kingdom*, Reports 2002–VIII 357 (2002) 35 EHRR CD289, where the European Court of Human Rights suggested that the effect of a tax liability could be discounted if the Revenue gives an undertaking before a court not to pursue it. In practice the Revenue would often lose very little, if anything, by giving such an undertaking, as forfeiture and confiscation together (even confiscation

The civil recovery procedure, in Part 5 of the 2002 Act, allows the Director of the new Assets Recovery Agency to 'recover, in civil proceedings before the High Court or Court of Session, property which is, or represents, property obtained through unlawful conduct'.[94] It is therefore proprietary, unlike the confiscation procedure, and there are provisions that allow recoverable property to be followed into the hands of third parties. Unlike confiscation, civil recovery may be used 'whether or not any proceedings have been brought for an offence in connection with the property.'[95] However, like confiscation, the defendant is not permitted to offset any expenses incurred in acquiring the assets.

Plainly, the Government has been attracted to the idea of using civil proceedings as a response to crime.[96] Despite the severity of these provisions, and the questionable use of statutory assumptions to establish prior criminality, the Privy Council, the House of Lords and the European Court of Human Rights have made it clear that confiscation orders do not involve the determination of a criminal charge for the purposes of Article 6(2).[97] The crucial point is that the orders can only be made where the defendant has already been convicted of a criminal offence. Whether civil recovery orders should be treated differently has not been considered in Strasbourg or by the appellate courts in the United Kingdom, but in *Re Assets Recovery Agency, Walsh & Proceeds of Crime Act 2002*, Coghlin J considered that the proceedings were not criminal because they could not culminate in a conviction. In his view, 'the essential focus of the statutory scheme is recovery of property and not the conviction and punishment of individuals for breaches of the criminal law.'[98]

Even if the courts could be persuaded that the Article 6 criminal guarantees should apply, the focus would be on the process by which confiscation and civil recovery orders are determined, rather than the severity of the measures.[99] Given the potential impact of these provisions, the question of severity is an important one. Whether a challenge under P1(1) would have a real chance of

---

alone) would often strip the individual of all his or her assets. In *Smith*, at [14], Lord Rodger noted that 'The respondent has never paid the duty on the cigarettes. He remains liable to pay it, however, even though he has been imprisoned for the fraudulent evasion of the duty and even if a confiscation order is made against him.')

[94] Section 240(1)(a) (all types of property); s 240(1)(b) contains a specific power in relation to cash. In Scotland, these powers are exercised by the Scottish Ministers (s 316).

[95] Section 240(2).

[96] Especially where the agency retains property or funds it seizes, as in the United States: see *Alldridge* (n 89) 223–24.

[97] *McIntosh* (n 83) (PC); *Benjafield* (n 83) (HL); and *Phillips v The United Kingdom*, Reports 2001–VII 29 [2001] Crim LR 817.

[98] [2004] NIQB 21 [19]. But see the Joint Committee on Human Rights, *Third Report* (HL Paper (2001) No 43, HC Paper (2001) No 405) [28]–[34]: civil recovery is a penalty because it is neither compensatory or restitutionary in the private law sense and given that the penalty is imposed on the basis of criminal conduct in absence of conviction, and the type and severity of the penalty, it is likely that the proceedings are criminal for the purpose of Article 6.

[99] Although the severity of the penalty would be relevant to determining the nature of the procedural safeguards required to satisfy Article 6.

success depends on the view taken of the purpose of confiscation and civil recovery.[100] If these provisions can be construed as entirely preventive or reparative, it is much more likely that they would survive scrutiny than if they were not. On the face of it, they are not: the decision to grant a confiscation or civil recovery order does not require proof of a connection with any future criminal activity (as in *Butler v The United Kingdom*).[101] In this sense, the seizure is not preventive. Neither is it reparative, as the orders do not require the identification of a specific loss (as in *Porter*).[102]

While the punitive nature of confiscation and civil recovery suggest that the proportionality analysis may work in favour of the respondent, it is worth noting that the European Court in *Raimondo* and related cases took a very broad view of crime prevention. Indeed, in *Raimondo*,[103] *Riela*[104] and *Arcuri*,[105] the preventive aspect was established entirely by evidence that property had been acquired with proceeds of crime. This is significant, because it seems that the Home Office may argue that confiscation and civil recovery orders for property have a similar general preventive effect. Under the Proceeds of Crime Act, the Director of the Assets Recovery Agency has the power to bring confiscation and civil recovery proceedings, and section 2(1) of the Act states that 'The Director must exercise his functions in the way which he considers is best calculated to contribute to the reduction of crime'.[106] Notes of Guidance issued by the Secretary of State operate on the assumption that both confiscation and civil recovery necessarily have this effect. Where a criminal conviction has been obtained, the Secretary of State considers that 'criminal confiscation of the proceeds of crime will best contribute to the reduction of crime'; however, where there is no criminal conviction and none is likely to be obtained, 'civil recovery is in general more likely to contribute to the reduction of crime than the taxation of such property.'[107] Moreover, early indications from the courts in civil recovery cases suggest that they do not question this assumption. Indeed, as put by Coghlin J in *Walsh*, 'The purpose of the legislation is essentially preventative in that it seeks to reduce crime by removing from circulation property which can be shown to have been obtained by unlawful conduct thereby diminishing the productive efficiency of such conduct and rendering less attractive the

---

[100] Or, if not a challenge, then at least an argument under ECHR Proceeds of Crime Act 2002, s 266(3)(b): 'The court may not make in a recovery order . . . (b) any provision which is incompatible with any of the Convention rights (within the meaning of the Human Rights Act 1998 (c 42)).'

[101] Above (n 10).

[102] Above (n 38).

[103] Above (n 4).

[104] Above (n 12).

[105] Above (n 16).

[106] Section 2(5) also states that the Director must have 'regard to any guidance given to him by the Secretary of State'; s 2(6) provides that this 'guidance must indicate that the reduction of crime is in general best secured by means of criminal investigations and criminal proceedings'.

[107] Home Office, Guidance by the Secretary of State to the Director of the Assets Recovery Agency on how she should exercise her functions so as best to contribute to the reduction of crime, 20 January 2003.

"untouchable" image of those who have resorted to it for the purpose of accumulating wealth and status.'[108] Arguably, this would be enough to satisfy the Strasbourg court that the purpose of a civil recovery order is essentially similar that of the orders in *Raimondo* and related cases.

There are, however, several points regarding the Proceeds of Crime Act 2002 that distinguish it from the legislation considered in *Raimondo*. Firstly, it is not limited to organised crime. In all of the cases from Italy, the European Court has emphasised the threat to the rule of law from organised crime. The Court has not offered a description of 'organised' crime, but it has associated it with both the 're-investment' of proceeds of crime and the corruption or intimidation of public officials. Either way, the nature of the problem (and hence the need for prevention) is not the same as it is with isolated criminal activity. As stated above, the Proceeds of Crime Act 2002 provisions do not require proof that a confiscation or civil recovery order is directed against a criminal organisation, or that proceeds are intended for use in subsequent criminal acts. It may have been the case that the Parliament had criminal organisations in mind as the primary target of confiscation and civil recovery,[109] but the statutory provisions have been drawn much more widely than necessary to hit that target.

In any case, the Government has not claimed that the Proceeds of Crime Act 2002 is entirely preventive. While section 2 of the 2002 Act states that the Director can only act with a view to reducing crime, the Home Office has said that Part 5 was intended 'to establish as a matter of civil law that there is no right to enjoy property that derives from criminal conduct.'[110] While it may be argued that the detail of the Part 5 reveals that it goes further than the recovery of proceeds, this raises a fundamental question: to what extent does P1(1) entrench general principles of civil obligations? Plainly, even in its own terms, a principle that there is no right to retain the proceeds of crime runs contrary to the principle of relativity of title,[111] but the real issue is whether P1(1) limits the modification of private law to this extent.

As discussed in chapter 8, the courts have not (yet) stated that P1(1) entrenches or excludes any specific forms of civil liability. However, as civil recovery is a form of liability that can only be owed to the State, it creates the risk of self-serving decisions on the part of law enforcement agencies. Currently, recovered assets are channelled through the Home Office, which distributes the bulk of the funds amongst law enforcement agencies engaged directly in asset

---

[108] *Walsh* (n 98) [19].

[109] Although seems to have been assumed in *Walsh*, above, when comparing the Proceeds of Crime Act 2002 with the legislation in *Raimondo* (n 4): 'It is clear that Parliament intended the civil recovery procedure implemented by Part 5 of the POCA to fulfil a similar role in the public interest in support of the struggle against organised crime, paramilitary and otherwise, which currently holds in thrall many sections of the community in this jurisdiction.'

[110] See the Memorandum of the Home Office written in response to the *Third Report* of the Joint Committee on Human Rights (n 98), in Joint Committee on Human Rights, *Eleventh Report*, HL Paper (2002) No 75, HC Paper (2002) No 475, Appendices to the Minutes of Evidence, [24].

[111] See *Webb v Chief Constable of Merseyside* (n 87).

recovery, with a substantial portion of the remaining assets going to crime prevention and education projects. Hence, there is a danger of self-interested action on the part of law enforcement agencies, although admittedly it is not as acute as it would be if the agency that recovered the assets could retain them. Nevertheless, the incentive to over-use these powers invites closer scrutiny on the part of the courts. In particular, there is good reason to adopt an approach to scrutiny as rigorous as that in the typical expropriation of property, where P1(1) normally requires market value compensation, and restricts the use of presumptions that may interfere with an accurate assessment of the value of property. Plainly, compensation is not the issue with respect to civil recovery, but there should be closer scrutiny to ensure that civil recovery become neither a route around ordinary criminal proceedings nor a means of enhancing public resources without adequate checks.

CONCLUSIONS

Human rights issues relating to forfeiture, confiscation and civil recovery seem to get caught between Article 6 and P1(1). As the Article 6 guarantees are comparatively strong, the courts are somewhat reluctant to apply them freely, at least where proceedings cannot lead to a criminal conviction. However, the civil process safeguards under Article 6 and P1(1) are comparatively weak, and so while they do apply to these cases, they do not offer much protection. Hence, it appears that State can easily justify the use of presumptions of fact and restrictions on the relevance of the guilt of the victim. In any case, neither Article 6 nor P1(1) offer a real opportunity to review the substantive aspects of these measures. It should not be impossible to do so: in particular, it should be possible to develop principles relating to each type of power over property as outlined in this chapter. For example, it has been argued that preventive measures can be applied where there is a real risk of harm, without proof of the property owner's involvement in the potential crime; that reparative measures that are limited to the recovery of damages for loss or restitution of ill-gotten gains can be justified, but closer scrutiny is needed where there is a risk that law enforcement agencies will use their powers for their own enrichment; and that punitive measures may be justified where there is some participation in the wrongful acts.

These issues need further examination from the courts, particularly in the light of the growing use of civil proceedings as a response to crime, but there is a further problem that the nature of the cases that come before the courts rarely provide clear instances of a power being exercised for only one of these purposes. This follows from the tendency in statutory drafting to set out the specific powers over property, and the persons who can exercise them, without stating whether the power should be used for a preventive, reparative or punitive purpose. Hence, a specific power may be exercised without its particular function being clear, or indeed whether it was intended to serve just one of the functions.

The rules regarding on the forfeiture of contraband and the vehicles carrying contraband are probably the most likely to create this confusion, as liability to forfeiture can be justified on the legal grounds that the goods were liable to forfeiture under the Customs and Excise Management Act 1979. As shown in *Air Canada*, there is no duty on Customs & Excise to explain whether the forfeiture was intended to be preventive, compensatory or punitive. The fact that the vehicle was carrying contraband is sufficient. Even with the new civil recovery remedy, it will not be clear whether the purpose of an order is preventive, reparative or punitive. The result of this combination of purposes is seen in the failure to develop a clear jurisprudence on any one of them.

10

The Purpose of Article 1 of the First Protocol

———⊱•⊰———

IN *MARCKX v BELGIUM*,[1] Sir Gerald Fitzmaurice said that 'the chief, if not the sole object of Article 1 of the Protocol (P1(1)) was to prevent the arbitrary seizures, confiscations, expropriations, extortions, or other capricious interferences with peaceful possession that many governments are—or frequently have been—all too prone to resort to.'[2] To construe it as a protection of all rights connected with property, such as those of inheritance or disposition, would 'inflate it altogether beyond its true proportions.'[3] But this was a dissenting opinion,[4] and P1(1) now deals with more than the oppressive acts of authoritarian governments. The Court has extended it to virtually any kind of State action that has a direct impact on property rights, and to many that have an indirect impact. Indeed, by the autonomous meaning doctrine, P1(1) may even apply to actions that have no effect on recognised property interests.

Sir Gerald Fitzmaurice's perception of the purpose of P1(1) was plainly not shared by the majority on the Court, although it is probably closer to the expectations of the lawyers, officials and delegates who participated in its formulation in 1950. This raises the central question of this chapter: what does the considerable body of case law tell us about the purpose of the right to property? Indeed, is there a single purpose that cuts across the different types of interference, or is it more accurate to say that it serves different purposes in different contexts?

The chapter begins by demonstrating that the primary purpose of P1(1) remains fundamentally conservative: it adds a further layer of protection to the support that private property already receives in national law, and as such it appears that stability of entitlement is the central aim of the Protocol. However, there are several secondary purposes that sometimes influence judgments that are worth considering. In particular, in some cases, the importance of property in supporting values of autonomy, dignity and identity are given more

---

[1] Series A No 31 (1979) 2 EHRR 330.
[2] Above [20].
[3] Above [17].
[4] Although note that similar comments from this opinion on Art 8 were cited, apparently with approval, by Lord Hope in *Qazi v Harrow LBC* [2004] 1 AC 983 [48].

prominence. In others, judicially-developed ideas of fairness are given more weight. Finally, the idea that P1(1) (and the Convention generally) has a role in determining the institutional structure of power is also considered.

THE PRIMARY PURPOSE: THE STABILITY OF
PRIVATE PROPERTY

In the post-war period, the founding members of the Council of Europe were committed to both the existing institutions of private property and the free market, and to the development of new institutions of social democracy. Most of those participating in the debates on the right to property saw these two goals as fundamentally opposed, and the nature of most claims under P1(1) tend to confirm this view. Ultimately, the right to property reflected (and still reflects) a conservative view of property, where broadening access to resources and guaranteeing social justice are seen as requiring some intervention in property rights that are already determined by other legal and political values. There was no sense that the institution of property itself might need re-examination in the postwar world. Social democracy plainly required change in the social and economic world, but that change would not be brought about by the courts. Indeed, the typical claim under P1(1) is one that invites the court to restrict the power of the State. This is certainly the pattern under P1(1): while the State does have positive obligations under P1(1), it is still unusual to find a claim that the State should have intervened in private relations or commercial life generally, and even more unusual to find that such a claim is upheld. Moreover, from the victim's perspective, the typical claim reflects a vision of private property as an unlimited set of rights, where positive law merely confirms the existence of a claim over material resources. Hence, it is only by rejecting the majority of claims that the courts confirm the initial expectation that P1(1) would allow social democracy to develop.

In fact, most claims are unsuccessful, and P1(1) has not presented a significant obstacle to social programmes. The European Court of Human Rights has refrained both from saying that social programmes of broad application violate P1(1), and from requiring States to take positive action to achieve social democracy. Similarly, in the short period that the Human Rights Act 1998 has been in force, the courts of the United Kingdom have taken a similar view. In *Wilson and others v Secretary of State for Trade and Industry*,[5] *Marcic v Thames Water Utilities Ltd*,[6] and *Aston Cantlow and Wilmcote with Billesley Parochial Church Council v Wallbank*,[7] the House of Lords overturned activist judgments of the Court of Appeal, thereby signalling that it would not use P1(1) to restrain or direct legislative programmes in any significant way.

---

[5] [2004] 1 AC 816.
[6] [2004] 2 AC 42.
[7] [2004] 1 AC 546.

We can therefore say that, as a starting point, P1(1) did not impose a radical agenda for action on the member States, and it does not do so now. As the Statute of Europe provides, the Convention reflects the 'common heritage' of the member States; it does not represent a rejection of that heritage. In that sense, the nomination of specific rights—such as P1(1)—did not break with tradition by compelling a re-distribution of property or a re-allocation of social obligations. In fact, much of the energy put into drafting P1(1) focused on the need to say nothing about these issues, in order to leave States with as much scope as possible to engage in economic restructuring (or not to engage in it) without the risk of a human rights review of their decisions. The European Court's jurisprudence reflects this objective, as it gives States a wide margin of appreciation when acting in furtherance of social justice, economic restructuring and regulating the use of property. Admittedly, concerns over subsistence have influenced the applicability test, particularly in relation to social welfare benefits, but ideas of social democracy carry little weight in terms of compelling or restraining State action that interferes with property. For example, the Court has rejected claims for social welfare where statutory law does not already provide it,[8] as well as claims that governments should be held to promises to safeguard savings against inflation.[9] Indeed, not even the European Social Charter has had a significant impact on the judicial development of P1(1).[10]

In this sense, P1(1) does not serve as an instrument of transformative policy. This is most evident in the Court's reluctance to look behind national rules of property law. While the autonomous meaning doctrine suggests that there is scope to question national rules, its real impact must be considered against the backdrop of Grand Chamber judgments such as *Malhous v The Czech Republic*,[11] *Polacek and Polackova v The Czech Republic*[12] and *Kopecký v Slovakia*.[13] There was no sense in these cases that the right to property required justice to be done to those dispossessed by authoritarian governments. Neither was there a sense that the Court was in a position to make difficult ethical judgments, even with the backing of the moral authority of an international convention on human rights. Hence, in cases such as *The Former King of Greece v Greece*[14] and *Jahn and others v Germany*,[15] it seems that property rights must be upheld, even where the manner in which the property was acquired raises serious questions regarding the legitimacy of acts under the former regimes.

---

[8]   Chapter 2, cases cited at n 136.
[9]   Chapter 2, cases cited nn 232 and 233.
[10]   ETS No 035 (entry into force: 26 February 1965); see especially Arts 12–14. The Social Charter was raised in *Zehnalova and Zehnal v The Czech Republic*, Reports 2002–V, regarding access by a disabled person to State buildings, but the application was declared inadmissible.
[11]   Reports 2000–XII 533.
[12]   Appl No 38645/97, 10 July 2002.
[13]   Appl No 44912/98, 28 September 2004; Chapter 2, 57–64.
[14]   Reports 2000–XII 119 (2001) 33 EHRR 21 (merits) (2003) 36 EHRR CD43 (just satisfaction).
[15]   Appl No 46720/99, 72203/01, 72552/01, 22 January 2004.

In these cases, the possibility that a different set of rules on the acquisition of property and wealth would do more to achieve the goals of social democracy was outweighed by the value of stability. While this may represent a faith that national rules of private law reflect human rights concerns, or the purpose of securing social democracy, it also allows the Court to avoid the controversies that would arise if they examined the legal basis for acquiring wealth. Indeed, it is noteworthy that the restitution cases are reasoned in a formal manner, where the results are made to appear to follow from the application of neutral principles of law of general application. Nevertheless, they do represent a preference for stability over justice (or other values) in the pursuit of social democracy. In this sense, the Court has made a conservative statement on property, whether it recognises it as such or not.

Although the value of stability underpins the P1(1) jurisprudence, it would be going too far to say that it dominates all judgments. In *Loizidou v Turkey*,[16] the long-lost property doctrine of *Malhous* and the other transitional justice cases carried little weight. It seems obvious that the continuing occupation of territory of one member State by another could not be ignored. Similarly, even in the *Former King of Greece*, the final award of damages demonstrated that property is not as inviolable as the judgment on the merits suggested.[17] There is also the general point that the meaning of P1(1) possessions has taken in the idea of 'legitimate expectations', with the result that some acts that would not be regarded as an interference with property are so regarded under the Convention.[18] But even so, the autonomous meaning doctrine is more often used to bring about stability where national law fails to do so, as in the cases on void 'contracts' and ultra vires representations of public authorities. As such, there is still an assumption that the right to property should guarantee a degree of stability and predictability in respect of the citizen's relationships with others and especially with their government in matters relating to the control of resources, even where that stability means that an unjust distribution of wealth cannot be altered by judicial action. Indeed, the right to property requires any attempt to redress an unjust distribution to be justified.

But while the emphasis of P1(1) is on the preservation of entitlements and national rules of property law under which entitlements arise and are protected, there may still be room for other objectives to emerge. As the Court has said, the Convention and its Protocols should be interpreted purposively, and in the light of changing circumstances. Plainly, the political and economic circumstances in Europe have changed dramatically over the last fifty years, and in that time, several other purposes to the right to property can be identified from the case law. Whether the impact of these has been marginal or significant is considered next.

---

[16] Reports 1996–VI 2216 (1997) 23 EHRR 5139.
[17] *Former King of Greece* (n 14); Chapter 6, 188–90.
[18] Chapter 2, 67–71.

POSSIBLE SECONDARY PURPOSES

Fairness

At its simplest, treating fairness as the purpose of a right to property would require some sharing of the burdens imposed by governmental action. While there may be specific circumstances where individuals may be expected to make sacrifices for others, it would be unfair to make one individual shoulder an excessive burden merely for the purpose of making the lives of others easier. Hence, the effect of the interference on the individual would be relevant in determining whether there has been a violation of P1(1).

Even if achieving fairness is one of the purposes of P1(1), it would only achieve it partially, as its restriction to property means that it does not have the potential to cover all harm or loss caused by State action.[19] Nevertheless, the rise of the fair balance test suggests that fairness is seen as one of the purposes of P1(1). However, the test has a narrow focus, as the assessment of the impact concentrates on the affected property to the exclusion of other factors. In the vast majority of cases, the relative impact on the victim's overall holdings or total wealth is ignored.[20] Similarly, the impact is rarely assessed in relation to the scheme as a whole: for example, in relation to planning laws, a property owner might gain as much as he or she will lose over the long run. In addition, there is an important set of cases where it seems that fairness not been addressed: those concerning individuals who are members of a class of persons affected by legislation of a broad impact. The test supposedly requires the courts to consider the interference from victim's perspective, as it involves an assessment of the severity of the impact. Often, States have been able to justify inflicting serious losses on isolated individuals by showing that the class of affected property owners are treated fairly. Just how far this goes cannot be predicted in advance: for example, in *James v United Kingdom*,[21] the European Court accepted that the compensation rules would produce windfalls for some tenants at the expense of their landlords; however, in *Pincová and Pinc v The Czech*

---

[19] For example, it has not been extended to cover exceptional damage caused by acts of public authorities, under the French idea of *égalité devant les charges publiques* or the German idea of *Sonderopfer*. See generally H Street, *Governmental Liability: A Comparative Study* (CUP, Cambridge, 1953) 78–79; and S Arrowsmith, *Civil Liability and Public Authorities* (Earlsgate Press, Winteringham, South Humberside, 1992) 240–50. For a Dutch example of the principle of *égalité devant les charges publiques* relating to planning law, see B Needham, 'The New Dutch Spatial Planning Act: Continuity and Change in the Way in which the Dutch Regulate the Practice of Spatial Planning' (Working Paper Series 2004/12, Research Group Governance and Places, University of Nijmegen, Netherlands, November 2004) 11.

[20] There are some isolated exceptions: see eg the Third Section in *Azinas v Cyprus*, Appl No 56679/00, 20 June 2002 (Third Section), 28 May 2004 (Grand Chamber); and *Jokela v Finland*, Reports 2002–IV, (2003) 37 EHRR 26.

[21] Series A No 98 (1986) 8 EHRR 123.

Republic,[22] the Court suggested that rules on restitution of land following the collapse of the Communist regime in the former Czechoslovakia could not proceed without considering the actual losses of specific landowners. Similarly, in *Marcic v Thames Water Utilities Ltd*[23] and *Wilson and others v Secretary of State for Trade and Industry*,[24] the House of Lords accepted that regulatory schemes might inflict particularly harsh losses on some individuals and give others windfalls, without infringing P1(1). However, Lord Nicholls suggested that, had the impact on individuals been more severe, he might have decided each case differently.[25] In any case, the fact that the fair balance is sometimes assessed by considering the impact on a class rather than the individual demonstrates that fairness to individuals is not the central concern. While it might be fair to say that those who are similarly affected by regulation cannot complain of their loss, that would not apply to those who are unusually affected. Indeed, *Pincová* demonstrates this.

Arguably, the differences in impact can be justified where the administrative cost of identifying every person who has suffered loss, and then accurately measuring and compensating for their loss, would produce a tax burden that might prove more oppressive than the regulation itself. In such cases, rational individuals would be willing to accept laws that leave some worse off than others, and in that sense, the laws remain fair.[26] For example, they might accept that there should be no right to be compensated for relatively minor losses caused by regulation. Similarly, they should also accept that a long-term scheme (such a planning law, or even the common law of nuisance) may cause a loss over the short term, but in many cases, those losses are likely to be counterbalanced by other gains over the longer term. To some extent, the case law recognises that these factors should affect the outcome in a specific case. For example, the European Court has said that the infliction of minor economic losses on individuals should not be treated as raising serious issues under P1(1).[27] Similarly, laws that regulate land use or the operation of markets generally do not require compensation to maintain the fair balance. However, the analysis does not identify the circumstances where unfairness may still arise. For instance, the likelihood of fair treatment over the long run would depend on a number of factors, such as the victim's capacity to protect its interests through the political process or by insuring privately or diversifying its assets.[28] While

---

[22] Appl No 36548/97, 5 November 2002.

[23] *Marcic* (n 6).

[24] *Wilson* (n 5).

[25] Above [80]; *Marcic* (n 23) [44]–[45].

[26] See FI Michelman, 'Property, Utility, and Fairness: Comments on the Ethical Foundations of "Just Compensation" Law' (1967) 80 *Harvard Law Review* 1165.

[27] Chapter 2, 82–83.

[28] See Michelman (n 26); W Fischel, *Regulatory Takings: Law, Economics and Politics* (Harvard University Press, Cambridge, MA, 1995); C Rose, 'Takings, Federalism and Norms' (1996) 105 *Yale Law Journal* 1121, L Blume and DL Rubinfeld, 'Compensation for Takings: An Economic Analysis' (1984) 72 *California Law Review* 569.

the Court has recognised that a capacity to plan should be taken into account, it has only done so in relation to commercial property. Even so, the case law does not make it clear whether the Court believes that commercial property is less deserving of protection than other property because it serves a different social function, or whether it believes that some commercial operators are able to plan for the risk.[29] More generally, in cases where the long-term or broader effects of an interference should raise doubts that the impact is as harsh as the victim asserts, the Court tends not to question the victim's assertion. Rather, they say that the public interest is particularly compelling, or that the situation falls within the State's wide margin of appreciation or legislature's area of discretion.[30]

In conclusion, the importance of the fair balance test suggests that achieving fairness is a concern of the courts, and it is not merely regarded as a means of achieving some other end. However, there is no clearly articulated conception of fairness in relation to property that applies to all cases, and in any case, the analysis of the impact of an interference is often either too broad or too narrow to be seen as seeking to further a goal of fairness. It may well be the case that such a conception does emerge in the future, or perhaps within the United Kingdom itself. However, it cannot be said that the jurisprudence has yet reached this point in either the Strasbourg or the United Kingdom.

Autonomy and dignity

In *Ghaidan v Godin-Mendoza*, Baroness Hale remarked that the 'essence' of the Convention is 'respect for human dignity and human freedom'.[31] What would this mean, and what has it meant, for the protection of property? Although property is often considered less important than other human rights, there are those who argue that it is central to all human rights. Indeed, the emphasis on dignity and freedom is compatible with Hegel's argument that property is essential to the development of the personality, where a person gains existence in the world by projects its will into material objects, including its body and mind.[32] By this means, a person's property constitutes it as a person in the material world, and identifies it to itself and to others. The institution of private property is therefore necessary to enable people to operate as autonomous and unique beings.[33]

---

[29] Chapter 5, 141–43.

[30] And similarly the Court tends not to question the State's assertion that the public interest is indeed as compelling as it says: Chapter 5, 132–35.

[31] [2004] 3 WLR 113 [132], referring to *Pretty v The United Kingdom* (2002) 35 EHRR 1 [65].

[32] G Hegel, TM Knox (tr), *Philosophy of Right* (Clarendon Press, Oxford, 1942) [1]–[70]; MJ Radin, 'Property and Personhood' (1982) 34 *Stanford Law Review* 957; and PG Stillman, 'Hegel's Analysis of *Property in the Philosophy of Right*' (1989) 10 *Cardozo Law Review* 1030.

[33] See Hegel, above [40]: 'it is only as owners that . . . two persons exist for each other'; Radin, above 977: the idea that the will is embodied in things suggests that the relationships that a person has with the things she regards as her own 'can be very close to a person's center and sanity.' See also

Moreover, according to some commentators, the human right to property should therefore incorporate freedom of contract, and it should protect any object or thing that may be bought or sold, including one's labour or one's body.[34] In general, the Court has rejected this argument. Freedom of contract is protected, but only as a right of property; labour itself is not property, and there are no cases on the body as property. Nevertheless, there are cases where the Court appears to recognise that the holding of specific property is connected with individual dignity or identity. One such case is *Chassagnou v France*,[35] where the European Court held that laws requiring certain landowners to allow hunting on their property violated P1(1), in part because the landowners in question were strongly opposed to hunting and sought to use their land as a wildlife preserve. Plainly, in this case, property fulfilled a function in realising personal beliefs and affirming identity, dignity and autonomy. Conversely, where property is held for a purely commercial purpose, the Court tends to favour the State when applying the fair balance test. As explained above, the reasons why commercial property deserves less protection are not entirely clear, but some judges may believe that the link with identity is weaker and therefore need for protection as a human rights is lessened.[36] However, *Chassagnou* is exceptional, and the commercial cases raise other questions regarding the link between private property and autonomy and dignity.

In addition, with all types of property, the link is weakened by the acceptance of the State's power to take property on payment of compensation. Property rules are liability rules as against the State, and hence it is difficult to argue that any specific object of private property has a direct relationship with the holder's autonomy or dignity, and even more difficult to argue that rights of private property must be upheld as a matter of human rights. In this context, it is worth noting that P1(1) applies to the imposition of a tax or other liability. Moreover, the European Court tends to find cases inadmissible where the applicant can shown no economic loss.[37] And, even in *Chassagnou*, the applicants' relief was only the payment of compensation; ultimately, the State could buy out their objections. As such, any connection with dignity and freedom is made with wealth alone, where the holding of property provides the doctrinal justification for judicial intervention, but the real objective is the protection of wealth and the power that goes with wealth. As far as this can be seen as a restriction on

---

JA Frowein, 'The Protection of Property' in R St J Macdonald, F Matscher and H Petzold, (eds), *The European System for the Protection of Human Rights* (M Nijhoff, Dordrecht, 1993) at 515: 'It is certainly correct to say that freedom as enshrined in the Convention cannot subsist without a meaningful protection of private property.'

[34] See T Daintith, 'The Constitutional Protection of Economic Rights' (2004) 2 *International Journal of Constitutional Law* 56 (especially 60–61) for a review of the differing positions.

[35] Reports 1999–III 21 (2000) 29 EHRR 615.

[36] Although conversely, in relation to goodwill, the Court seems to adopt a Lockean perspective: see *Van Marle v The Netherlands*, Series A No 101 (1986) 8 EHRR 483 and the discussion in Chapter 2, 76–77.

[37] Chapter 2, 82–83.

autonomy, it is only in the loose sense that the imposition of a liability reduces wealth and thereby reduces the choices that individuals have. The connection with identity or dignity is even weaker.

Nevertheless, even at this level, the Court has recognised that laws that leave an individual without a means of subsistence have a particularly harsh impact because they restrict the capacity for an autonomous life. Accordingly, such laws are subject to closer scrutiny.[38] In addition, the ideas of dignity, freedom and identity may be used to extend the scope of the right to property. This can be shown by considering cases on Article 14 of the German Basic Law. The Basic Law protects a number of fundamental rights, with the right to property appearing in Article 14.[39] Within the system of fundamental rights, the function of Article 14 'is to secure its holder a sphere of liberty in the economic field and thereby enable him to lead a self-governing life.' It relates to 'the realm of freedom within which persons engage in self-defining, responsible activity', and as such it is not 'primarily a material but rather a personal guarantee.'[40]

Several consequences follow from this. First, the scope of Article 14 is not determined purely by the civil law of property. Under Article 14, property is an 'autonomous legal institution, or, to use the standard alternative formulation, an objective constitutional value that the state is affirmatively obliged to preserve and foster.'[41] For example, rights to participate in social welfare schemes may be protected under Article 14, even if they would not qualify as property in the private law sense. Secondly, the extent of constitutional protection depends on the connection between the property in question and its role in securing personal liberty and autonomy, and its place within the broader social context. It follows that (for example) rights in the family home receive greater protection than commercial property.[42]

To return to P1(1), it could be argued that the development of the autonomous meaning doctrine reflects similar ideas of autonomy and dignity. Certainly, the cases specifically on social welfare are similar to the German

---

[38] See eg *Azinas* (n 20), and the social welfare cases (Chapter 2, 71–75); see also HG Schermers, 'The International Protection of the Right of Property' in F Matscher and H Petzold, (eds), *Protecting Human Rights: The European Dimension* (Carl Heymanns, Köln, 1988) 565, 572–75.

[39] Art 14 reads:

> (1) Property and the right of inheritance shall be guaranteed. Their substance and limits shall be determined by law. (2) Property entails obligations. Its use should also serve the public interest. (3) Expropriation shall only be permissible in the public interest. It may only be ordered by or pursuant to a law that determines the nature and extent of compensation. Compensation shall reflect a fair balance between the public interest and the interests of those affected. In case of dispute regarding the amount of compensation recourse may be had to the ordinary courts.

(Translation from Press and Information Office of the Federal Government, Foreign Affairs Division (1994), *Basic Law for the Federal Republic of Germany*.)

[40] *BverfGE* 24, 367; this translation is from DP Kommers, *The Constitutional Jurisprudence of the Federal Republic of Germany*, 1st edn (Duke University Press, Durham, NC, 1989) 257–58.

[41] Kommers, above 260.

[42] AJ van der Walt, *Constitutional Property Clauses: A Comparative Analysis* (Juta, Cape Town, 1999) 135–36.

cases. Similarly, the treatment of commercial property may also reflect the idea that it is important to consider the link between property, personal liberty and identity. However, these ideas are relatively undeveloped in the European Court's case law. For example, the jurisprudence on transitional justice demonstrates that the Court sees no compelling reason to ask whether those dispossessed by authoritarian governments now require some kind of restitutionary act to restore their dignity.[43] Furthermore, unlike the German courts, the European Court does not explicitly refer to ideas of autonomy or personal identity in property cases. While the ultimate effect may be one that protects these personal values, it is equally likely, if not more likely, that the primary effect is the protection of wealth as a means of moderating State activity.

Several points demonstrate this. To begin with, the relatively limited scope of the autonomous meaning doctrine under P1(1) means that the protection of autonomy and dignity is mediated through the private law rules on the acquisition and protection of property. While there is a superficial similarity with the German idea of an autonomous meaning for property, unlike the German courts, the European Court has not suggested that the doctrine is necessary in order to ensure that values of autonomy and dignity are upheld. In practical terms, the human right to property merely adds further support to the private law of property, without the identification of other interests that might require protection. In effect, the argument that the human right to property protects autonomy and dignity is conditional on proof that private law protects the same interests. However, private law does not always do so. National rules on private property often address concerns that have no necessary relationship with autonomy and dignity. For example, intellectual property rights are often justified in terms of their economic function, and yet the European Court has treated intellectual property as a P1(1) possession without any real analysis.[44] In a similar vein, Karl Llewellyn's famous criticism of the use of property concepts to determine the contractual rights under a contract for the sale of goods demonstrates that, even in the narrow context of a commercial sale, property serves different purposes in different contexts.[45] In addition, we can also refer to Bruce Ackerman's observation that there is a fundamental distinction between 'ordinary property' and 'scientific property'.[46] Ordinary property is based on social practices apparent to any interested observer, whereas scientific property is developed by legal specialists, and is not apparent to interested observers. Ackerman's analysis is not only significant for pointing out that property may be based on social practices, but also for noting that many forms of modern

---

[43] Although n that Schermers (n 38) 568 suggests that it is consistent with human rights principles that the right to property is lost after a period out of possession.

[44] See Chapter 2, 77–78.

[45] KN Llewellyn, 'Through Title to Contract and a Bit Beyond' (1938) 15 *New York University Law Quarterly Review* 157.

[46] B Ackerman, *Private Property and the Constitution* (Yale University Press, New Haven, 1977).

property have no clear basis in a social practice. Even where property has a basis in a social practice apparent to the ordinary observer, it does not necessarily follow that the social practice is itself based on ideas of autonomy and dignity. Under P1(1), both ordinary and legal property are protected, irrespective of their connection with autonomy and dignity.

More generally, the institution of private property may even allow individuals to be excluded from enjoying the most basic resources needed for autonomy and dignity. The emphasis in P1(1) on the conception of property as exclusion has the potential to deny the homeless and the poor from participation in social life, or indeed to any real measure of dignity. The Court has remained firm in its belief that the property enables exclusion, and that the provision of basic subsistence is an obligation of the State entirely separate from property.[47] Indeed, in *Larioshina v Russia*, the Court accepted that a State may have an obligation to provide some relief to victims of extreme poverty, but stated that this obligation would this would only raise an issue under Article 3 (relating to inhuman or degrading treatment).[48]

These observations can be supplemented by considering the role of P1(1) in relation to communal property. The function of property in constituting communities has been examined by many commentators.[49] But while the forms of group ownership recognised at national law are also recognised at international law, P1(1) does not go further in recognising the constitutive function of property in this respect.[50] This is not to say that the individual's interest in the community is not protected by the Convention, as the rights to association and freedom of religion play an obvious role in allowing individuals to participate in their community. To a limited extent, the access to a community is a factor to be taken into account the balancing the interests under other rights. For example, planning decisions concerning certain minority groups must take into account their way of life,[51] and the Court has recognised that denying access to quasi-public space may interfere with the Convention rights of association or freedom of expression.[52] In addition, legislation intended to protect a vulnerable community, as a community, would almost certainly be regarded as serving the public interest.[53] Hence, depending on the specific terms of the legislation, it should be possible to justify an interference with private property for this purpose.

---

[47] See Chapter 2, 71–75 (especially the cases cited at n 136) and Chapter 7, 218–23.

[48] Appl No 56869/00, 23 April 2002; see generally J Waldron, 'Homelessness and the Issue of Freedom' in J Waldron, *Liberal Rights: Collected Papers, 1981–1991* (CUP, Cambridge, 1993).

[49] Much of the academic writing concentrates on recovery of property by indigenous peoples, but see also WH Simon, 'Social-Republican Property' (1991) 38 *UCLA Law Review* 1335; and JW Singer, 'The Reliance Interest in Property' (1988) 40 *Stanford Law Review* 614.

[50] Chapter 2, 83–87.

[51] Eg *Chapman v The United Kingdom* (2001) 33 EHRR 18 [96]; *Connors v The United Kingdom*, Appl No 66746/01, 27 May 2004 [84]–[95]; *Wrexham County Borough Council v Berry* [2003] UKHL 26.

[52] *Appleby v The United Kingdom* (2003) 37 EHRR 38; see Chapter 7, 221–23.

[53] Cf *Beyeler v Italy*, Reports 2000–I 57 (2001) 33 EHRR 52, on the public interest in protecting cultural property.

However, it is doubtful that the right to property can be employed to require State action to protect property that has a communal aspect. Outside the recognised forms of communal ownership, there is unlikely to be any property interest that would be protected as a P1(1) possession. There is no positive right to communal property *qua* communal property, and an individual would need to hold some form of property right in order to establish a claim to communal property *qua* private (individual) property. While there have only been a few cases in which property has been related to the individual's identity as part of a community, it tends to be dismissed with little discussion. In *Gerasimova v Russia*,[54] the applicant complained that she was being forced to leave her flat and to move away from the community she had lived in for many years. While the Court acknowledged this complaint, it took the view that the State had discharged its responsibilities by providing her with alternative accommodation: nothing more was required. As an administrative example, it is interesting that the current plans of the Office of the Deputy Prime Minister for regenerating communities by destroying homes was originally believed to raise human rights concerns. However, as explained in chapter 7, the human rights concern was quietly dropped from later reports and plans, and in any case it had always been framed in terms of the adequacy of compensation rather than the need to preserve community life.

This brief analysis of the role of P1(1) in protecting individual dignity and freedom, and communal identity, demonstrates again that the purpose to right to property seems to go no further than the protection of existing entitlements. The formal existence of these interests under national law dominates the human rights analysis, with the result that questions regarding property, dignity, freedom and communal identity are addressed almost exclusively by national law. In the end, it seems that Baroness Hale's observation may be true of other Convention rights, but it cannot be said to be true of the right to property. To be sure, P1(1) does have this function in some circumstances, but there are too many circumstances where private property serves some other function to conclude that the protection of autonomy and dignity is anything more than a secondary purpose of the right to property. Indeed, it would be equally valid to conclude that P1(1) merely provides a legitimizing statement for all types of private property, irrespective of its function. In effect, treating property as a human right gives private property a moral legitimacy it might not otherwise have.

The rule of law and the risk of an abuse of power

Another view of the purpose of P1(1) concentrates on the context in which sovereign powers over property are exercised. This goes beyond the procedural matters covered by P1(1) and Article 6, as it says that the courts should be more

---

[54] Appl No 24077/02, 25 March 2004.

inclined to find an incompatibility with human rights if constitutional or administrative structures increase the risk of a human rights violation. In this way, the application of the right to property controls and reduces the risk of an abuse of the sovereign powers over property. The focus is on the structural context in which power is exercised, where specific cases only serve to indicate where the deeper problems lie.

To the extent that the Convention was intended to secure rule of law, it has a structural focus. There are two areas where the case law reflects this concern: the first arises in cases where there is a particular concern that decision-making does not seem to be subject to adequate control, and the second with the exercise of judicial deference itself. Each of these are considered below, but beyond these two areas, there is little sign that a structural analysis has played a significant role in the development of the law. This has happened partly because the European Court normally leaves it to the member States to determine how to adapt their legal systems and rules to ensure compatibility with Convention rights. When this is coupled with the limits on class actions, the scope for reviewing sovereign power on structural grounds is reduced. This is demonstrated by considering the American 'IOLTA' cases. These cases concerned the constitutionality of rules that require attorneys to pool certain client funds and deposit them in interest-bearing accounts, from which the interest is paid to public or charitable bodies. The central issue was whether there had been a 'taking of private property for public use' under the Fifth Amendment of the Constitution. If so, compensation would have been required. In *Phillips v Washington Legal Foundation*, by a 5-4 margin, the Supreme Court decided that a taking had occurred.[55] Then, in *Brown v Legal Foundation of Washington*, and by another 5-4 margin, it decided that IOLTA schemes did not violate the takings clause, because the amount of interest lost by a specific client would have been modest; moreover, these clients would not have earned interest under the client account system that applied before the IOLTA rules took effect.[56] Nevertheless, the margin was very narrow, and it is significant that the Supreme Court saw the cases as raising important constitutional issues concerning the exercise of sovereign powers over property, despite the relatively modest impact on specific individuals.

There is no corresponding case under P1(1), and it is doubtful that a similar case would be given careful consideration in any event. The Court has held that there is no breach of P1(1) involved in imposing obligations that involve the payment of modest fees or expenses. For example, in *Langborger v Sweden*, where the applicant objected to paying a compulsory fee to a tenants' union, the Court stated that 'the obligation to pay the small sums involved cannot be regarded as inconsistent with this Article (P1(1)).'[57] Similarly, in *Van der Mussele v*

---

[55] *Phillips v Washington Legal Foundation* 524 US 156 (1998).
[56] *Brown v Legal Foundation of Washington* 538 US 942 (2003).
[57] Series A No 155 (1990) 12 EHRR 416 [41].

Belgium,[58] pupil barristers were required to provide *pro bono* services which could involve personal expenditure. The Court held that there had been no violation of P1(1), on the basis that 'In many cases, a duty prescribed by law involves a certain outlay for the person bound to perform it. To regard the imposition of such a duty as constituting in itself an interference with possessions for the purposes of Article 1 of Protocol No 1 (P1(1)) would be giving the Article a far-reaching interpretation going beyond its object and purpose.'[59] In neither case is it clear whether the Court felt that the absence of a direct tax or other levy in favour of the State meant that there was no interference with the applicant's possessions, or whether there was an interference but it was not disproportionate. However, it is clear that the small scale of the interferences meant that there was no serious issue to consider. Unlike the Supreme Court in the IOLTA cases, the Court does not believe that the exercise of sovereign powers over property necessarily raises important issues for the courts.

Although the IOLTA cases were raised as class actions, structural issues are not confined to such cases. As discussed in chapter 7, Joseph Sax has argued that the Fifth Amendment should be read as requiring compensation in cases of the typical expropriation, but not for most regulatory interferences, because there the risk of an abuse of power is greater in cases of expropriation.[60] For Sax, the key consideration is whether the State agencies exercise sovereign powers to acquire resources for their own account. If so, they have a direct financial interest in reducing the amount of compensation to a minimum. Hence, requiring full market compensation reduces the incentive to abuse the power to acquire property by coercion. However, where State agencies merely resolve competing private claims to resources, the direct financial interest is not present and the risk of abuse is far less. Consequently, procedural safeguards are normally sufficient.

The European Court does not normally frame human rights issues in terms of the constitutional or administrative structures in which they operate. Moreover, although the principles on compensation are broadly consistent with Sax's proposals, they did not develop against the background of a theory on the structural context of power. In general terms, this approach reflects the Court's view that it should concentrate on specific facts of a dispute, rather than the theoretical possibility of an interference. Structural issues are only likely to be considered after repeated interferences of the same type, and then by reference to the Committee of Ministers for further action.

Plainly, an international tribunal may have reservations about making decisions that appear to require changes in the administrative structure in which sovereign power is exercised. The European Court may feel that a scheme such as IOLTA may involve an abuse of power, but that these would be constitutional

---

[58] Series A No 70 (1984) 6 EHRR 163.
[59] Above [49].
[60] J Sax, 'Takings and the Police Power' (1964) 74 *Yale Law Journal* 36.

issues rather than human rights issues. However, this raises interesting questions for the courts of the United Kingdom in cases under the Human Rights Act 1998. The national courts have a constitutional function not given to international tribunals, and as such should be more willing to consider structural aspects of decision-making. There was a sign of this in the Court of Appeal's judgment in *Wilson*,[61] where the Court of Appeal was concerned that the absolute prohibition on enforcement under the Consumer Credit Act 1974 excluded the traditional jurisdiction of the courts.[62] In particular, the courts were not able to perform their function of doing justice in the specific case. On appeal, however, the House of Lords gave this argument little weight.[63] Similarly, one might say that, in *Rowland v Environment Agency*,[64] the Court of Appeal recognised that the ultra vires rule operated as a kind of disincentive for governance that would respect human rights. However, the Court of Appeal merely applied the Strasbourg cases, and as such it is not an example of British courts taking a different view of the purpose of P1(1). It appears, at the moment, that the British courts have gone no further than the European Court in examining the relationship between the structures of power and the effects of those structures on human rights.

Constitutional and administrative structure

In some areas, the European Court exercises a closer supervisory role over decision-making that appears not to be subject to satisfactory controls. While unusual for it to find that the legality condition has not been satisfied, there are many cases where the manner in which power was exercised has led it to conclude that the fair balance was upset. In such cases, both the impact and the process by which the impact was produced are significant. In this sense, the Court's concern is with the structure in which power is exercised. For example, in the Third Section's judgment in *Hatton v United Kingdom*,[65] the Court held that the process of reaching a decision on noise quotas at Heathrow Airport had been flawed, and hence the United Kingdom had not justified its decision. This was overturned by the Grand Chamber,[66] but only after a close examination of the decision-making process.

A similar concern with structure arises in a series of cases from eastern Europe on the supervisory jurisdiction of superior courts and public officials over decisions of lower courts. These cases raise issues under both Article 6 and P1(1), because otherwise final judgments can be overturned without direct

---

[61] *Wilson v First County Trust Ltd (No 2)* [2002] QB 74.
[62] See also *Smokovitis v Greece*, Appl No 46356/99, 11 April 2002 on the power of the legislature to 'interpret' ministerial statements.
[63] *Wilson* (n 24).
[64] [2004] 3 WLR 249.
[65] (2002) 34 EHRR 1.
[66] (2003) 37 EHRR 28.

action by either party. It does not appear that the Court believes that such powers can never be exercised legitimately: in that sense, it is not purely a concern with the finality of judgments, but with the apparently uncontrolled way in which these powers have been exercised in some jurisdictions. As such, the potential for abuse is as important as the impact in the specific case.[67]

In addition, the Court's judgments may have an effect on administrative or constitutional structures. For example, the ultra vires cases in Strasbourg led the Court of Appeal to restrict the scope of the doctrine in *Rowland v Environment Agency*.[68] However, in these cases, the impact on administrative or constitutional structures arose because the European Court ignored these issues, and not because it gave them particular attention. Similarly, while *Hatton* and the supervisory jurisdiction cases show that the Court is occasionally sensitive to structural aspects, its concern seems to vary, depending on the nature of the case. For example, chapter 9 demonstrates that the courts in Strasbourg and the United Kingdom have taken a very deferential view of the proliferation of confiscatory powers. The interpretations of P1(1) and Article 6 leave individuals with little protection from State measures intended to respond to wrongdoing that has not been the subject of a criminal conviction. The possibility that powers may be abused, particularly when the law enforcement agencies that exercise these powers may benefit directly from them, has been given little weight in the cases.

Judicial deference

Judgments on the right to property are often characterised by a high degree of deference to determinations of other decision-makers. This is usually justified on the basis that the court is no more competent than the other decision-maker to determine the specific issue in question. Hence, deference only reflects a view of institutional competence in property matters rather than a view on the purpose of the right to property. As such, a judicial exercise of discretion does not represent a view that the right to property is not engaged; instead, it is more of an invitation to the national authorities to evaluate their actions against human rights standards. (Or, in the case of national courts, the invitation is to the administrative and legislative branches.) In effect, other decision-makers are given scope to develop their own interpretations of the right to property, within the broad outlines of the judicial interpretation.

In practice, however, it is doubtful that lawmakers see judicial deference in this way. It appears that States regard a judgment that the decision to implement specific rules falls within their margin of appreciation as a sign that no human rights issues arise. It is not a sign that there are issues to be considered, although only at the national level or by other organs of government. Similarly, within the

---

[67] See eg *Allard v Sweden* (2004) 39 EHRR 14.
[68] See also *Dangeville SA v France*, Reports 2002–III 71 (2004) 38 EHRR 32.

United Kingdom, there is little evidence that the judicial invocation of the area of discretion has led the executive or legislature to engage in this kind of interpretation. As explained in chapter 1, they assume that their responsibility is solely to act within the judicially-determined limits of the right to property, and not to give it further content. The area of discretion, like the margin of appreciation, provides a 'safe area', in which there is no need to consider human rights. In that sense, the interpretation of human rights standards remains external to the legislative and executive process, unlike the development of the fundamental law that provided a kind of unwritten bill of rights in the common law constitution.

If it is the case that deference is not taken as an invitation to develop legislative or executive principles of interpretation, what does it represent? Arguably, it is merely a prudential response that seeks to protect the judicial power by avoiding politically controversial decisions. Alternatively, it may represent a principle of the right to property; in effect, it limits the right to property to the acts described by Sir Gerald Fitzmaurice in *Marckx*, with some modest extensions. Indeed, there may be little to separate these two points. It is politically astute not to take an activist view on the right to property, because it is generally seen as less important than other rights. By limiting their intervention in property matters, the courts protect their power to safeguard other rights of greater importance. It may also identify those aspects of the right to property that deserve special attention. Indeed, the Italian eviction cases provide a striking example of the way in which deference can highlight specific issues.[69] The Court began by saying that the rules on evictions fell within Italy's margin of appreciation. However, as cases continued to come before the Court, it became apparent that Italy may have taken this to mean that it need do nothing to address the issue. The Court then began to say that the specific facts of some cases disclosed a violation of P1(1). Again, the cases continued to flood the Court. Finally, the Court adopted a general rule that a delay of more than four years from judgment to possession would violate P1(1). The essential facts were the same in these cases, but the margin of appreciation progressively narrowed as it became apparent that the real issues concerned the rule of law, rather than landlord-tenant relations.

Hence, the narrowing of the margin of appreciation occurs where the issues are regarded as central to the purpose of the right to property, and not necessarily where the courts feel that they are better placed to determine all the relevant facts or to balance all the relevant interests. The margin is narrowest in the types of cases that Sir Gerald Fitzmaurice identified as central to the right to property,[70] and where there are concerns over the maintenance of the rule of law (as the Italian eviction cases demonstrate). The margin is widest where the political opposition is likely to be greatest: that is, in cases involving regulatory

---

[69] See the cases cited Chapter 5, n 176.
[70] See eg *Akdivar v Turkey*, Reports 1996–IV 1192 (1997) 23 EHRR 143.

schemes of broad impact, where the breadth of the impact is an essential aspect of the policy itself. By contrast, the margin falls between these extremes where the interference could be seen as an isolated event, or where the rules in question are not an essential part of a scheme to which the government may have a strong political commitment. Hence, it often appears that it is not the degree of impact on the individual that is important, but the risk of controversy that drives decisions. There are, of course, many exceptions to these observations, but they represent the general pattern.

Accordingly, the exercise of deference does cast some light on the judicial perception of the right to property. Sir Gerald Fitzmaurice's concern with 'capricious interferences' is still central to the case law, although now it is reflected in the doctrine as a matter of judicial deference on property matters rather than the applicability of the right to property. It contradicts the goal of stability because it makes it conditional on the political context. That is, the stability and predictability of the citizen's relations with State agencies seems to depend on the investment of political capital by those agencies in the programme that led to the interference. Arguably, it is still consistent with the broader purpose of Convention and P1(1), in the sense that it ensures that human rights do not thwart the development of social democracy. In addition, it reflects the point that the legal content of P1(1) was determined with a retrospective perspective, without consideration of how that the content might support positive action rather than obstruct it.

CONCLUDING COMMENTS

The Convention and Protocol had both the retrospective function of reviving and reinforcing the traditional values of the constitutional law of the member States, and the prospective function of allowing States to improve the lives of their citizens by regulating economic life. As the content of the right to property was derived primarily (if not exclusively) from customary international law and the constitutional traditions of European States, it reflected the retrospective function. Consequently, discussions on proposals for a right to property reflected concerns with the prospective aspect, and it was assumed that this would be achieved by drafting the right so that it preserved State power. That is, there was no attempt to draft a right to property that might, by itself, provide an impetus for the development of social democracy. Hence, the discussions and the final text reflect a negative view of what a right to property should not do, rather than the opposite.

The purpose of the right to property is therefore a conservative, stabilising one, where it provides a further layer of support for entitlements already existing under national law. At a minimum, it reflects Sir Gerald Fitzmaurice's belief that the Convention and Protocol were only intended to protect against authoritarian oppression, while also acting as a check on all State action intended to modify existing entitlements. Yet, even as the right to property was being debated in the early meetings of the Council of Europe, there were other voices. The right to property was a natural right, necessary for the development of the individual; or, property had a social function, and that function should be reflected in all property laws, whether private, administrative or international in nature.[71] While it is safe to say that these views did not dominate the discussion, it is impossible to say that they were not influential in ensuring that a Protocol was finally agreed. Moreover, it is also apparent that these beliefs are held by some judges on the European Court of Human Rights, and from time to time they are reflected in the judgments. Nevertheless, they often arise in the same way that these views arose during the early debates on the right to property: in an unco-ordinated fashion, without a consensus on their role in practical decision-making, and more as a reflection of personal belief that as an institutional position.

[71] Chapter 1, 20.

Bibliography

MT ACEVEDO, 'The Intersection of Human Rights and Environmental Protection in the European Court of Human Rights' (2000) 8 *New York University Environmental Law Journal* 437.

B ACKERMAN, *Private Property and the Constitution* (Yale University Press, New Haven, 1977).

GH ALDRICH, 'What Constitutes a Compensable Taking of Property? The Decisions of the Iran–United States Claim Tribunal' (1994) 88 *American Journal of International Law* 585.

P ALLDRIDGE, *Money Laundering Law* (Hart Publishing, Oxford, 2003).

T ALLEN, *The Right to Property in Commonwealth Constitutions* (CUP, Cambridge, 2000).

ANON, 'The Burmah Oil Affair' (1966) 79 *Harvard Law Review* 614.

MR ANTINORI, 'Does Lochner Live in Luxembourg?: An Analysis of the Property Rights Jurisprudence of the European Court of Justice' (1995) 18 *Fordham International Law Journal* 1778.

S ARROWSMITH, *Civil Liability and Public Authorities* (Earlsgate Press, Winteringham, South Humberside, 1992).

N BAMFORTH, 'The True "Horizontal Effect" of the Human Rights Act 1998' (2001) 117 *Law Quarterly Review* 34.

P BENSON, 'Equality of Opportunity and Private Law' in D Friedmann and D Barak-Erez, (eds), *Human Rights in Private Law* (Hart Publishing, Oxford, 2001).

W BLACKSTONE, *Commentaries on the Laws of England I* (Clarendon Press, Oxford, 1765; reprint: Dawsons of Pall Mall, London, 1966).

AM BICKEL, *The Least Dangerous Branch: The Supreme Court at the Bar of Politics* (Bobbs-Merrill, Indianapolis, 1962).

D BEYLEVELD and S PATTINSON, 'Horizontal Applicability and Horizontal Effect' (2002) 118 *Law Quarterly Review* 623.

L BLUME and DL RUBINFELD, 'Compensation for Takings: An Economic Analysis' (1984) 72 *California Law Review* 569.

S BRIGHT, 'Liability for the Bad Behaviour of Others' (2001) 21 *Oxford Journal of Legal Studies* 311.

—— 'Ending Tenancies by Notice to Quit: The Human Rights Challenge' (2004) 120 *Law Quarterly Review* 398.

R BROWNSWORD, 'Freedom of Contract, Human Rights and Human Dignity' in D Friedmann and D Barak-Erez, (eds), *Human Rights in Private Law* (Hart Publishing, Oxford, 2001).

M BRUNETTI, 'The Iran–United States Claims Tribunal, NAFTA Chapter 11, and the Doctrine of Indirect Expropriation' (2001) 2 *Chicago Journal of International Law* 203.

R BUXTON, 'The Human Rights Act and Private Law' (2000) 116 *Law Quarterly Review* 48.

AC CAIRNS, 'The Judicial Committee and Its Critics' (1971) 4 *Canadian Journal of Political Science* 301.

Committee on Transport, Local Government and the Regions, *6th Report* (HC Paper (2002) No 240–I).

Compulsory Purchase Policy Review Advisory Group, *Fundamental Review into the Laws and Procedures relating to Compulsory Purchase and Compensation* (Transport and Regions Department of the Environment, London, 2000).

Council of Europe, *Collected edition of the 'Travaux Préparatoires' of the European Convention on Human Rights: Recueil des Travaux Préparatoires de la Convention Européenne des Droits de l'Homme* (M Nijhoff, The Hague 1975–85).

WR CORNISH and G DE N CLARK, *Law and Society in England, 1750–1950* (Sweet & Maxwell, London, 1992).

S COYLE and K MORROW, *The Philosophical Foundations of Environmental Law: Property, Rights and Nature* (Hart Publishing, Oxford, 2004).

P CRAIG, *Administrative Law*, 4th edn (Sweet & Maxwell, London, 1999).

—— 'The Courts, the Human Rights Act and Judicial Review' (2001) 117 *Law Quarterly Review* 589.

T DAINTITH, 'The Constitutional Protection of Economic Rights' (2004) 2 *International Journal of Constitutional Law* 56.

Department of Transport, Local Government and the Regions, *Planning: Delivering Fundamental Change* (Office of the Deputy Prime Minister, 2001) <http://www.odpm.gov.uk/stellent/groups/odpm_planning/documents/p/odpm_plan_605841.pdf>.

Department of Transport, Local Government and the Regions, *Compulsory Purchase and Compensation: the Government's Proposals for Change* (Office of the Deputy Prime Minister, December 2001) <http://www.odpm.gov.uk/stellent/groups/odpm_planning/documents/p/odpm_plan_605835.hcsp>.

R DESGAGNE, 'Integrating Environmental Values into the European Convention on Human Rights' (1995) 89 *American Journal of International Law* 263.

S DJAJIC, 'The Right to Property and the *Vasilescu v Romania* Case' (2000) 27 *Syracuse Journal of International Law and Commerce* 363.

R DOLZER, 'Indirect Expropriations: New Developments?' (2002) 11 *New York University Environmental Law Journal* 64.

E DREWNIAK, 'Comment: The Bosphorus Case: The Balancing of Property Rights in the European Community and the Public Interest in Ending the War in Bosnia' (1997) 20 *Fordham International Law Journal* 1007.

D ELVIN and J MAURICI, 'The Alconbury Litigation: Principle and Pragmatism' [2001] *Journal of Planning & Environment Law* 883.

RA EPSTEIN, *Takings: Private Property and the Power of Eminent Domain* (Harvard University Press, Cambridge, MA, 1985).

HR FABRI, 'The Approach Taken by the European Court of Human Rights to the Assessment of Compensation for "Regulatory Expropriations" of the Property of Foreign Investors' (2002) 11 *New York University Environmental Law Journal* 148.

D FARRIER and P MCAUSLAN 'Compensation, Participation and the Compulsory Acquisition of "Homes"' in JF Garner, (ed), *Compensation for Compulsory Purchase: A Comparative Study* (The United Kingdom National Committee of Comparative Law, London, 1975).

MG FAURE, 'Environmental Regulation' in B Bouckaert and G De Geest (eds), *Encylopedia of Law and Economics*, ch 2300 (online at <http://encyclo.findlaw.com/> and <http://allserv.rug.ac.be/~gdegeest/>).

D FELDMAN, 'Parliamentary Scrutiny of Legislation and Human Rights' [2002] *Public Law* 323.

—— 'Proportionality and the Human Rights Act 1998' in E Ellis, (ed), *The Principle of Proportionality in the Laws of Europe* (Hart Publishing, Oxford, 1999).

—— 'Human Dignity as a Legal Value: Part I' [1999] *Public Law* 682.

W FISCHEL, *Regulatory Takings: Law, Economics and Politics* (Harvard University Press, Cambridge, MA, 1995).

—— 'Voting, Risk Aversion, and the NIMBY Syndrome: A Comment on Robert Nelson's "Privatizing the Neighbourhood"' [1999] 7 *George Mason Law Review* 881.

—— 'Zoning and Land Use Regulation' in B Bouckaert and G De Geest (eds), *Encylopedia of Law and Economics*, ch 2200 (online at <http://encyclo.findlaw.com/> and <http://allserv.rug.ac.be/~gdegeest/>).

JA FROWEIN, 'The Protection of Property' in R St J Macdonald, F Matscher and H Petzold, (eds), *The European System for the Protection of Human Rights* (M Nijhoff, Dordrecht, 1993).

R GIBBARD, 'The Crichel Down Rules: Conduct or Misconduct in the Disposal of Public Lands' in Elizabeth Cooke, (ed), *Modern Studies in Property Law, Vol 2* (Hart Publishing, Oxford, 2003).

Gerald Eve Chartered Surveyors and the University of Reading, *The Operation of the Crichel Down Rules* (Office of the Deputy Prime Minister, London, 2000).

JW GOUGH, *Fundamental Law in English Constitutional History* (Clarendon Press, Oxford, 1955).

M GRANT, 'Human Rights and Due Process in Planning' [2000] *Journal of Planning & Environment Law* 1215.

K GRAY, 'Property in Thin Air' (1991) 50 *Cambridge Law Journal* 252.

—— 'Equitable Property' (1994) 47 *Current Legal Problems* 157.

—— and SF GRAY, 'Civil Rights, Civil Wrongs and Quasi-Public Space' (1999) 1 *European Human Rights Law Review* 46.

—— —— 'Private Property and Public Propriety' in J McLean, (ed), *Property and the Constitution* (Hart Publishing, Oxford, 1999).

A GREAR, 'A Tale of the Land, the Insider, the Outsider and Human Rights (an Exploration of some Problems and Possibilities in the Relationship between the English Common Law Property Concept, Human Rights Law, and Discourses of Exclusion and Inclusion)' (2003) 23 *Legal Studies* 33.

MA HELDEWEG, RJGH SEERDEN and KR DEKETELAERE, 'Public Environmental Law in Europe: a Comparative Search for a *ius commune*' [2004] *European Environmental Law Review* 78.

G HEGEL, TM KNOX, (tr), *Philosophy of Right* (Clarendon Press, Oxford, 1942).

Home Office, 'Memorandum', in Joint Committee on Human Rights, *11th Report*, HL Paper (2002) No 75, HC Paper (2002) No 475, Appendices to the Minutes of Evidence.

Home Office, *Guidance by the Secretary of State to the Director of the Assets Recovery Agency on How She should Exercise her Functions so as Best to Contribute to the Reduction of Crime*, 20 January 2003.

D HOWARTH, 'Nuisance and the House of Lords' (2004) 16 *Journal of Environmental Law* 233.

W HOWARTH, 'Environmental Human Rights and Democracy' (2002) 14 *Journal of Environmental Law* 353.

J HOWELL, 'Land and Human Rights' [1999] *Conv* 287.

M HUNT, 'The "Horizontal Effect" of the Human Rights Act' [1998] *Public Law* 423.

WI JENNINGS, 'Constitutional Interpretation: The Experience of Canada' (1937) 51 *Harvard Law Review* 1.

Joint Committee on Human Rights, *3rd Report* (HL Paper (2001) No 43, HC Paper (2001) No 405).

G KODILINYE, 'The Statutory Authority Defence in Nuisance Actions' (1990) 19 *Anglo-American Law Review* 72.

DP KOMMERS, *The Constitutional Jurisprudence of the Federal Republic of Germany*, 1st edn (Duke University Press, Durham, NC, 1989).

RW KOSTAL, *Law and English Railway Capitalism, 1825–1875* (OUP, Oxford, 1994).

C KRAUSE and G ALFREDSSON, 'Article 17' in G Alredsson and A Eide, (eds), *The Universal Declaration of Human Rights: A Common Standard of Achievement* (M Nijhoff, The Hague, 1999).

Law Commission of England and Wales, *Towards a Compulsory Purchase Code: (1) Compensation* (Law Com Consultation Paper No 165, 2002).

Law Commission of England and Wales, *Towards a Compulsory Purchase Code: (1) Compensation* (Law Com No 286, 2003).

A LESTER 'UK Acceptance of the Strasbourg Jurisdiction: What Really Went on in Whitehall in 1965' [1998] *Public Law* 237.

—— D PANNICK, 'The Impact of the Human Rights Act on Private Law: The Knight's Move' (2000) 116 *Law Quarterly Review* 380.

KN LLEWELLYN, 'Through Title to Contract and a Bit Beyond' (1938) 15 *New York University Law Quarterly Review* 157.

I LOVELAND, 'The Impact of the Human Rights Act on Security of Tenure in Public Housing' [2004] *Public Law* 594.

—— 'Making It Up as They Go Along? The Court of Appeal on Same Sex Spouses and Succession Rights to Tenancies' [2003] *Public Law* 222.

P MACKLEM, 'Rybná 9, Praha 1: Restitution and Memory in International Human Rights Law' (Working Paper No 11, 2004, Center for Human Rights and Global Justice Working, Faculty of Law, New York University and Public Law Research Paper No 04–12, University of Toronto, 1 November 2004).

FA MANN, 'Outlines of a History of Expropriation' (1959) 75 *Law Quarterly Review* 188.

PJ MARSHALL, 'Parliament and Property Rights in the Late Eighteenth-Century British Empire' in J Brewer and S Staves, (eds), *Early Modern Conceptions of Property* (Routledge, London, 1995).

E MCWHINNEY, *Judicial Review in the English-Speaking World*, 2nd edn (University of Toronto Press, Toronto, 1960).

J MAURICI, "Gypsy Planning Challenges in the High Court" [2004] *Journal of Planning Law* 1654

M MENDELSON, 'The United Kingdom Nationalization Cases and the European Convention on Human Rights' (1986) 57 *British Yearbook of International Law* 33.

TJ MICELI and K SEGERSON, 'Takings' in B Bouckaert and G De Geest (eds), *Encylopedia of Law and Economics* (online at <http://encyclo.findlaw.com/> and <http://allserv.rug.ac.be/ ~gdegeest/>).

FI MICHELMAN, 'Property, Utility, and Fairness: Comments on the Ethical Foundations of "Just Compensation" Law' (1967) 80 *Harvard Law Review* 1165.

T MILLINGTON and MS WILLIAMS, *The Proceeds of Crime: Law and Practice of Restraint, Confiscation and Forfeiture* (OUP, Oxford, 2003).

H MOUNTFIELD, 'The Concept of an Unlawful Interference with Fundamental Rights' in J Jowell and J Cooper, (eds), *Understanding Human Rights Principles* (Hart Publishing, Oxford, 2001).

PT MUCHLINSKI, 'Holding Multinationals to Account: Recent Developments in English Litigation and the Company Law Review' (2002) 23 *Company Lawyer* 168.

B NEEDHAM, 'The New Dutch Spatial Planning Act: Continuity and Change in the Way in which the Dutch Regulate the Practice of Spatial Planning' (Working Paper Series 2004/12, Research Group Governance and Places, University of Nijmegen, Netherlands, November 2004).

D NICOL, 'The Human Rights Act and the Politicians' (2004) 24 *Legal Studies* 451.

—— 'Are Convention Rights a No-Go Zone for Parliament?' [2002] *Public Law* 438.

—— 'Remedial and Substantive Horizontality: the Common Law and *Douglas v Hello! Ltd*' [2002] *Public Law* 232.

Nolan Committee on Standards in Public Life, *3rd Report of the Nolan Committee on Standards in Public Life: Standards of Conduct in Local Government in England, Scotland and Wales* (1997) (Cm 3702–1).

Lord Normand, 'The Judicial Committee of the Privy Council—Retrospect and Prospect' [1950] 3 *Current Legal Problems* 1.

Office of the Deputy Prime Minister, *Compulsory Purchase and the Crichel Down Rules*, ODPM Circular 06/2004.

D OLIVER, 'The Human Rights Act and Public Law/Private Law Divides' [2000] *European Human Rights Law Review* 343.

A O'NEILL, 'The Protection of Fundamental Rights in Scotland as a General Principle of Community Law—the Case of *Booker Aquaculture*' (2000) 1 *European Human Rights Law Review* 18.

BH OXMAN and B RUDOLF, '*Beyeler v Italy*' (2000) 94 *American Journal of International Law* 736.

W PEUKERT, 'Protection of Ownership under Article of the First Protocol to the European Convention on Human Rights' (1981) 2 *Human Rights Law Journal* 37.

G PHILLIPSON, 'The Human Rights Act, "Horizontal Effect" and the Common Law: a Bang or a Whimper?' (1999) 62 *Modern Law Review* 824.

M POUSTIE, 'The Rule of Law or the Rule of Lawyers? Alconbury, Article 6(1) and the Role of Courts in Administrative Decision-Making' (2001) 6 *European Human Rights Law Review* 657.

Press and Information Office of the Federal Government, Foreign Affairs Division (1994), *Basic Law for the Federal Republic of Germany*.

MJ RADIN, 'Property and Personhood' (1982) 34 *Stanford Law Review* 957.

—— 'The Liberal Conception of Property: Cross Currents in the Jurisprudence of Takings' (1988) 88 *Columbia Law Review* 1667.

M REDMAN, 'Compulsory Purchase, Compensation and Human Rights' [1999] *Journal of Planning & Environment Law* 315.

A REICHMAN, 'Property Rights, Public Policy and the Limits of the Legal Power to Discriminate' in D Friedmann and D Barak-Erez, (eds), *Human Rights in Private Law* (Hart Publishing, Oxford, 2001).

C ROSE, 'Takings, Federalism and Norms' (1996) 105 *Yale Law Journal* 1121.

J ROWAN–ROBINSON 'Utility Wayleaves: Time for Reform' [2001] *Journal of Planning & Environment Law* 1247.

GA RUBIN, *Private Property, Government Requisition and the Constitution, 1914–1927* (Hambledon Press, London, 1994).

P SALES and B HOOPER, 'Proportionality and the Form of Law' (2003) 119 *Law Quarterly Review* 426.

RA SALGADO, 'Protection of Nationals' Rights to Property under the European Convention on Human Rights: *Lithgow v United Kingdom*' (1987) 27 *Virginia Journal of International Law* 865.

J SAX, 'Takings and the Police Power' (1964) 74 *Yale Law Journal* 36.

HG SCHERMERS, 'The International Protection of the Right of Property' in F Matscher and H Petzold, (eds), *Protecting Human Rights: The European Dimension* (Carl Heymanns, Köln, 1988).

E SCHWELB, 'The Protection of the Right to Property of Nationals under the First Protocol to the European Convention on Human Rights' (1964) 13 *American Journal of Comparative Law* 518.

JM SELLERS, 'Litigation as a Local Political Resource: Courts in Controversies over Land Use in France, Germany, and the United States' (1995) 29 *Law and Society Review* 475.

WH SIMON, 'Social–Republican Property' (1991) 38 *UCLA Law Review* 1335.

AWB SIMPSON, *Human Rights and the End of Empire: Britain and the Genesis of the European Convention* (OUP, Oxford, 2001).

JW SINGER, 'The Reliance Interest in Property' (1988) 40 *Stanford Law Review* 614.

WB STOEBUCK, 'A General Theory of Eminent Domain' (1972) 47 *Washington Law Review* 553.

M STALLWORTHY, 'Environmental Liability and the Impact of Statutory Authority' (2003) 15 *Journal of Environmental Law* 3.

PG STILLMAN, 'Hegel's Analysis of Property in the *Philosophy of Right*' (1989) 10 *Cardozo Law Review* 1030.

H STREET, *Governmental Liability: A Comparative Study* (CUP, Cambridge, 1953).

M TAGGART, 'Expropriation, Public Purpose and the Constitution' in C Forsyth and I Hare, (eds), *The Golden Metwand and the Crooked Cord: Essays on Public Law in Honour of Sir William Wade QC* (Clarendon Press, Oxford, 1998).

P THOMAS, 'The Planning and Compulsory Purchase Act 2004: The Final Cut' [2004] *Journal of Planning & Environment Law* 1348

LH TRIBE, *American Constitutional Law*, 2nd edn (Foundation Press, Mineola, NY, 1988).

—— *American Constitutional Law*, 3rd edn (Foundation Press, New York, 2000).

United Kingdom, *Report of the Royal Commission on Churches (Scotland)* (Cd 2494, 1905).

United Kingdom, *Report of the Crowther Committee* (Cmnd 4596, 1971).

United Kingdom, *Reform of the Law on Consumer Credit* (Cmnd 5427, 1973).

AJ VAN DER WALT, *Constitutional Property Clauses: a Comparative Analysis* (Juta, Cape Town, 1999).

HWR WADE, 'Horizons of Horizontality' (2000) 116 *Law Quarterly Review* 217.

J WALDRON, 'Homelessness and the Issue of Freedom' in J Waldron, *Liberal Rights: Collected Papers, 1981–1991* (CUP, Cambridge, 1993).

H WECHSLER, 'Toward Neutral Principles of Constitutional Law' (1959) 73 *Harvard Law Review* 1.

LE WEINRIB and EJ WEINRIB, 'Constitutional Values and Private Law in Canada' in D Friedmann and D Barak-Erez, (eds), *Human Rights in Private Law* (Hart Publishing, Oxford, 2002).

Index